Ex Libris

J.E. JENNINGS
2006

BRITISH
FLYING
BOATS

PETER LONDON

SUTTON PUBLISHING

Sutton Publishing Limited
Phoenix Mill · Thrupp · Stroud
Gloucestershire · GL5 2BU

First published 2003

Title page photograph: The first Supermarine Scarab, M-NSAA, undergoes trials at Worthy Down, near Winchester, Hampshire. The code indicates M-Spain, N-Naval, S-Ship, A-Amphibian and A for the first example (the last bearing M-NSAL). Flight tests took place over the summer of 1924 and beside the Spanish buyer were observers representing the Greek government, though no orders were placed by that country. *(Fawley Historians)*

British Library Cataloguing in Publication Data
A catalogue record for this book is available from the British Library.

ISBN 0-7509-2695-3

Typeset in 10.5/13.5 Photina.
Typesetting and origination by Sutton Publishing Limited.
Printed and bound in England by J.H. Haynes & Co. Ltd, Sparkford.

Saunders-Roe's dainty Cutty Sark monoplane first flew in July 1929 and was one of three related designs by the Cowes-based company. Here, Genet Major-powered VR-HAY, bound for Hong Kong; in the background, the Cutty Sark prototype. *(Author's Collection)*

Contents

ACKNOWLEDGEMENTS

This book looks at the evolution, commercial development and military career of the British flying-boat from its inception prior to the First World War until its demise during the 1950s. Ask someone to name a flying-boat and the response will probably be 'Sunderland' – but there were many, many other types too. A one-volume account of such a wide subject is necessarily a summary, but I hope I have been able to strike a balance between the lesser-known designs, the brave attempts and failures, and the household names.

It would not be possible to write a book like this without the considerable assistance received from individuals 'who were there', who have generously volunteered their recollections and data, and from the small band of kind enthusiasts across Britain who enjoy researching the history of aviation. The staffs of museums, archives and libraries have also been unfailingly helpful, despite often being hard-pressed for resources. I am therefore very pleased to acknowledge with gratitude the support provided by the following people and institutions during the compilation of this history:

Aeronautical Quality Assurance Directorate, Air-Britain, the late L.S. Ash, Chris Ashworth, Colin Bacchus, Bernard Baily, Simon Barr, Peter Barron, Group Captain David Bevan-John, BAE SYSTEMS, British Hovercraft Corporation, Brough Heritage Group, the late Jack Bruce, Canadian Forces Photographic Unit, Eric Cheer, Civil Aviation Authority Library, John Dell, Neville Doyle, Tony Dunn, John Evans, Fawley Historians (Dave Etheridge, Colin van Geffen, Clare Murley), Fleet Air Arm Museum (Jerry Shore), FR Aviation Ltd, Wing Commander Vince Furlong, GKN Aerospace Services (David Cheek), Peter H.T. Green, Val Hall, Jim Halley MBE, J.C. Hamon, Harold Hanna, Captain Vic Hodgkinson, Squadron Leader Bill Holloway, John Hurst, the Imperial War Museum, *Irish Times*, Philip Jarrett, Gordon Kinsey, Keith Lee, Stuart Leslie, Juliet Luffman, Alec Lumsden, Malcolm McCarthy, Charles McKenzie, the late Ken Meckcoms, Ministry of Defence Air Historical Branch, W.F. Murray, Newsquest Ltd, The Nottage Institute, Public Archives of Canada, Public Record Office, RAF Museum, Royal Air Force Association, Barry Saxton, Short Brothers plc, C.A. Sims, R. Stride, Ray Sturtivant, Sutton Publishing (Anne Bennett, Simon Fletcher, Michelle Tilling and Bow Watkinson), John Thompson, Warrior (Aero-Marine) Ltd (James Labouchere), Bob Wealthy, Carl Whiteley, and Windermere Nautical Trust (Diane Matthews).

Particular thanks are warmly extended to Bryan Ribbans, webmaster of www.seawings.co.uk, for his support in terms of material freely shared, and for his ideas and enthusiasm that helped broaden my approach to the subject.

All reasonable measures have been taken to identify correctly the sources of the photographs that appear in this book. However, because of the passage of time, as well as the uncertain origins of some of the photographs, it may be that in a few instances use has accidentally been made without correct acknowledgement of the originator. Please accept my apologies if your name has not been justly included. Should such a situation arise, and the publisher notified accordingly, I would be pleased to make a suitable amendment for inclusion in any future editions of this book.

This book is dedicated to my dear friend Brian (Woody) Woodsford.

1 BEGINNINGS

The origins of the British flying-boat, that is to say a water-based aircraft employing a hull rather than a fuselage and floats, can be traced back to within a few years of the dawn of flight. The opening decade of the twentieth century was a period of enormous aeronautical experiment that witnessed many aircraft of wildly varying competence, including numbers of freakish efforts. During that time, despite scant encouragement from official bodies, a core of determined British designers and aspiring aviators pressed ahead with considerable fortitude in their belief that heavier-than-air, powered, sustained and controlled flight would soon be achieved in this country. Their perseverance paid off and by the turn of the decade and just beyond, the leading British pioneers had attained a measure of success – with landplanes. Thoughts quickly turned to the possibility of marine aircraft; initially it was believed by some that flying from water might be safer than from land. However, as the inevitable crashes started to occur it became clear aquatic impact could often be as painful as hitting terra firma.

Marine aviation presented new problems – as if there weren't already sufficient to face with land-based types at that time. As well as (to say the least) immature design and construction principles, and temperamental, low-powered engines, the earliest 'web-footed' aviators were obliged to contend with an environment where river (or, for the more adventurous, sea) could warp, soak, corrode, pound, be ingested by or otherwise interfere with their frail aeroplanes. The hydrodynamic properties of the first marine aircraft were understandably questionable, while their frictional resistance on the water was far greater than that of a landplane on grass. In addition, in the air both the weight and drag of maritime adaptations, be they floats or hull plus stabilising floats, were considerably greater than those of a land undercarriage. These factors placed additional strains on the feeble engines of the day.

Despite such obstacles, however, the first waterborne aeroplanes quickly followed their landplane counterparts. Among the pioneer community some had backgrounds or contacts in boat-building, which was useful in the construction of the emerging marine types. Initially floatplanes were constructed rather than flying-boats; it was expeditious to attach floats to an existing fuselage using an arrangement of struts. However, a body of opinion soon emerged that concluded a hull would be more substantial, seaworthy and efficient. During the Edwardian period the evolution of fast motor-boat technology had yielded wooden hulls of lightweight but resilient construction. These were stepped across the underside to break the natural suction effect of the water as speed was gained and thus release

the craft into a surface-skimming or hydroplaning state employing the forward hull lower surface or planing bottom. As that technology was embraced by some of the early aviators, and as boat-builders and naval architects started to become involved, the concept of a flying-boat emerged in which a hull was used as a fuselage and to provide buoyancy.

The first serious attempt to build a flying-boat in Britain resulted in the Humphreys Biplane, also known as the *Wivenhoe Flyer*. It was designed by Jack Humphreys, a dentist by profession, and constructed near Wivenhoe on the River Colne in Essex with the assistance of nearby Forrestt's boatyard, and the building programme commenced in October 1908. A 45ft-span sesquiplane biplane, the aircraft employed a small single-seat hull and curved wings incorporating triangular ailerons. It was powered by a single 35hp JAP V8 air-cooled engine driving two counter-rotating propellers through a system of shafts, gears and centrifugal clutches and fed by a simple gravity fuel tank. Lateral stability on the water was provided by downward-inclined wing-tips each embodying an air-box. An accident during the first launch on 3 April 1909 caused the machine to turn turtle and sink in a cross-wind; subsequently recovered, in the following month it succeeded in skimming at speeds of around 12 knots. Unfortunately, the air-boxes created considerable drag in the water and the *Flyer* never lived up to its name.

Following growing pressure on the government from the early aviators, the press and the general public over the lack of central support for aviation in Britain, on 13 April 1912 the Royal Flying Corps was constituted. This comprised a Military Wing controlled by the War Office and a Naval Wing run by the Admiralty's new Air Department, headed by the aerophile First Lord Winston Churchill. The Naval Wing

The Humphreys Biplane and workforce on the River Colne during the spring of 1909. The small hull has a pointed prow while the lower wing-tip air-boxes are visible. The pusher JAP engine is situated at the mid-point in the pronounced wing gap, driving two paddle-like pro-pellers and fed from the small gravity tank above. At least two versions of the wing boxes were tested, the version shown and a slimmer type; variations of propellers were also fitted. The outer wing sections have a feather-like appear-ance. *(The Nottage Institute)*

began to acquire a mixed bag of aircraft including seaplanes; as yet there were no indigenous flying-boats to be had.

However, in the autumn of that year there appeared a small unequal-span biplane flying-boat bearing some similarity to the contemporary French Donnet-Levêque. Designed by T.O.M. (later Sir Thomas) Sopwith, its tandem two-seat hull was built at Cowes on the Isle of Wight by prominent boat-builders S.E. Saunders Ltd. Sam Saunders and Sopwith had met during the latter's holidays at Streatley-on-Thames, where Saunders had owned other premises. Sopwith had a passion for the sea and raced competition motor-boats, including the very successful *Maple Leaf IV* produced by Saunders. The hull of his new aircraft was skinned using Saunders' proprietary method of wood lamination known as Consuta, whereby plywood was sewn with copper wire around its edges and across the surface to prevent separation. At least one step was employed, with a flat planing bottom tapering aft to a point. The aircraft was powered by a high-mounted Gnôme tractor engine, probably of 70hp, but it seems to have been a disappointment for Sopwith did not pursue it. Instead he sought Saunders' expertise in high-speed hydrodynamic design, and Britain's first successful flying-boat began to take shape at the end of 1912. Though it was Sopwith's brain-child it incorporated a Saunders single-step, two-seat side-by-side, Consuta-covered hydroplane hull, 21ft long and weighing only 180lb, designed by Sydney Porter. The hull employed a curved, vee-profile planing bottom, whereas Sopwith's first hull had been without either characteristic. A 41ft-span biplane flight structure utilising wing-warping for lateral control, a bow elevator and a single fin and rudder were supplied by Sopwith. The aircraft was named *Bat Boat* after Rudyard Kipling's fictional flying-machine and was powered by a 90hp Austro-Daimler engine arranged as a pusher, this configuration shielding the propeller from spray. Its flight surfaces were built at Kingston during late 1912 and the hull freighted from Cowes for assembly.

The first *Bat Boat* takes shape at Sopwith's premises in a disused roller-skating rink at Kingston, on the cusp of 1912 and 1913. Its bow-mounted elevator can be seen, and while the empen-nage is yet to be added the Daimler engine is in place. During February 1913 the aircraft was exhibited at the Olympia Aero Show. *(J.M. Bruce/G.S. Leslie Collection)*

The second *Bat Boat* at Netley, 16 August 1913. Allocated the serial 38, this version of the aircraft never wore that number but the airframe later received a modified tail unit and served as 38 at various stations until November 1914. While flying from Calshot it was used by Lieutenant Spenser D.A. Gray, Hawker's observer during the Singer competition and the station's flight commander. *(J.M. Bruce/G.S. Leslie Collection)*

The third *Bat Boat* in Singer competition configuration with a Green engine and amphibious undercarriage. In February 1914 this example was purchased by the Admiralty and serialled 118 it became generally based at Calshot, being used in bomb-dropping experiments and surviving until March 1915 when it was dismantled. *(Fawley Historians)*

The first version of the Radley-England Waterplane. The hulls featured flat bottoms, a sharp bow profile and a long triple-engine installation driving a large-diameter four-bladed pusher propeller, above which was mounted the fuel tank. A prominent elevator was employed, while the hulls were mounted on extensions to the inboard interplane struts; the struts connecting the prows with the forward interplane struts seem to have been added after initial trials. *(Bob Wealthy)*

In March trials were made by Sopwith from Cowes but the aircraft was severely damaged following a brief hop. A second example was assembled by the Hamble River, Luke & Company while a third probably embodied parts of the first but adopted a revised tail-boom layout, tailplane and twin rudders; neither used the previous bow elevator. On 8 July, fitted with a simple undercarriage, modified empennage and a 100hp Green engine, the third *Bat Boat* won the Mortimer Singer prize for all-British amphibious aircraft – capable of landing on land or water. Six out-and-back flights were made from Hamble, touching down on the Solent at a buoy 5 miles distant, all within five hours, the pilot being Harry Hawker. Winnings of £500 were secured and subsequently the Austro-Daimler was reinstated.

Meanwhile the Admiralty had established Naval Air Stations at Eastchurch (Naval Wing HQ) in November 1912, at Grain, at the mouth of the River Medway, for experimental purposes during the following month, at Calshot on the Solent for training and trials on 22 March 1913 and at Great Yarmouth in Norfolk on 15 April. Felixstowe in Suffolk was commissioned on 5 August. The second *Bat Boat* was delivered to the Admiralty during June 1913, allocated the serial 38. Via Calshot, it travelled to Brighton in August but sank at its moorings on the 23rd of that month. Repaired and with a further revised tail layout featuring a single fin and rudder, 38 passed to Grain, then Felixstowe and Great Yarmouth. Finally it went to Scapa Flow, Orkney, a further station commissioned in August 1914, where it was destroyed in a gale on 21 November.

The year 1913 also witnessed the appearance of the Radley-England Waterplane, a twin-hulled six-seater biplane with a wingspan of 45ft 4in. The Waterplane was powered by three 50hp Gnôme rotary engines mounted one behind the other between the wings, driving a common crankshaft leading to a single four-bladed pusher propeller. The machine was a collaboration between James Radley and E.C. Gordon England and was built at Portholme, Huntingdon; it flew from Shoreham, Sussex, in April. During that summer the Waterplane operated from a base for

The reworked Radley-England Waterplane employed clinker-built hulls of deeper profile than their forebears while the engine installation was revised to a more conventional single configuration. The vertical tail surfaces were similar to those employed by the first model. The aircraft is seen at Shoreham. *(Philip Jarrett)*

marine aircraft at the eastern end of Brighton beach (established by father and son inventors Magnus and Herman Volk), until it sank there after hitting a floating object. The aircraft was salved and some parts possibly used in a second version employing a single 150hp Sunbeam engine and two new clinker-built two-seat hulls built by the South Coast Yacht Agency. This was entered in the 1913 Daily Mail Seaplane Circuit of Britain contest but last-minute engine problems signalled its withdrawal and it was eventually abandoned.

At Cowes, Saunders had commenced work on a flying-boat designed by the Australian Arthur Wigram of Wigram Flying Boats Ltd. The aircraft was a tandem two-seat biplane employing a pusher 100hp Green engine. Its tail surfaces were mounted high away from the water on a boom arrangement projecting from the single-step hull. The Wigram machine was also entered for the 1913 Circuit of Britain race but its construction was abandoned, probably as a result of lack of funds.

Also in 1913, the pilot E.W. Copeland Perry and designer F. P. H. (Percy) Beadle of the Perry, Beadle Company at Twickenham produced their Perry Beadle B.3 flying-boat, a 35ft-span tractor biplane in which the hull-mounted 60hp ENV F Type engine drove two propellers, positioned mid-gap, via chains and sprockets. Saunders built the Consuta-covered tandem two-seat wooden hull. For lateral stability on the water the aircraft relied on its lower wing, also Consuta-skinned, which sat on the surface when at rest while the (air) rudder was partly immersed. The aircraft visited the March 1914 Olympia Aero Show and was subsequently tested at Cowes with a 90hp Curtiss OX engine. It moved to the Eastbourne Aviation Company and then to the Lakes Flying Company at Lake Windermere for trials lasting until June 1915. Unfortunately the lower wing created great resistance on the water and it proved impossible to take off, while the novel drive train was found impractical; the airframe was subsequently dismantled.

During October 1913 the wealthy English aviation enthusiast Captain Ernest Bass (of the Bass brewing concern) flew an American Curtiss Model F flying-boat from the Volks' base; it was an advanced design employing a stepped hull though it was

The Perry Beadle B.3 being launched for trials on Lake Windermere. The chain-drive linking the hull-mounted engine with the two propellers is in evidence, while the radiator is located just under the upper wing centre-section. The lower wing is positioned relatively low on the hull, a product of the absence of wing-floats to ensure lateral stability. The slipway is steep and while helpers cling on to the empennage the lower hull undergoes inspection.
(J.M. Bruce/G.S. Leslie Collection)

The Perry Beadle B.3 on Windermere during 1915. The forward hull profile, just visible, is deep and uncompromising with no attempt at sweep. The passenger sat ahead of the would-be pilot, and inset ailerons were employed on the upper surfaces only. The aircraft was sold to the Lakes Flying Company when Perry, Beadle closed down, but it never flew under either owner. *(J.M. Bruce/G.S. Leslie Collection)*

criticised as frail and suffering from poor control. The Bognor-based fledgling aviation company White & Thompson maintained Bass's aircraft at their Middleton works in Sussex, becoming the exclusive agent for the Curtiss Company in Britain and the Dominions. The firm also briefly acquired the services of Lieutenant John Cyril Porte as test pilot. In 1911, aged just 27, Porte had been invalided out of the Navy with pulmonary tuberculosis, but had acquired his aviator's certificate in France. He flew White & Thompson's first (more-or-less) indigenous waterborne type in March 1914, a design stemming from Bass's Model F – as modified by Porte, Bass and the American pilot Earl Cooper – so with strong Curtiss ancestry, though incorporating revised flight surfaces. Elaborately named the White & Thompson Bass-Curtiss Airboat, it employed a 100hp Anzani. Porte left the company in April 1914 to join Glenn Curtiss in the United States, to collaborate on a planned trans-atlantic flying-boat, the Curtiss Model H Boat *America*. His place was taken by E.C. Gordon England, a former partner in the Waterplane and by then a freelance pilot.

Colourful Noel Pemberton Billing's PB.1 (later renumbered PB.7) flying-boat emerged during 1914, constructed by his boat-building company at Woolston on Southampton Water during his entry into aviation. A single-seat 30ft-span biplane powered by a 50hp Gnôme, the PB.1 featured a single-step hull designed by Linton Chorley Hope, a marine architect who went on to influence flying-boat hydrodynamics deeply for many years. Ailerons were fitted to the wings and a conventional tail layout adopted. Shown at the 1914 Olympia event, the aircraft failed to fly during trials on Southampton Water that spring owing to its low-powered engine, high water drag and high thrust line, despite being reworked to feature twin chain-driven propellers, in which form it became the PB.9. The PB.2 monoplane project (later redesignated the PB.11) employed a generally similar hull

Noel Pemberton Billing's PB.1 (later the PB.7) being launched from his premises at Woolston, Southampton, during the spring of 1914, in its original configuration. The pilot sits aft of the wings while the engine nacelle is acutely tilted. The propeller has yet to be fitted. At the nose is a grapnel controlled from the cockpit. *(Author's Collection)*

The modified PB.7 (by then known as the PB.9) under test with the engine mounted between the wings just above the hull, and the cockpit moved forward as a counterbalance. Two propellers driven by chains were positioned mid-gap. The aircraft was tested by Howard Pixton during May 1914 but unfortunately neither version achieved flight and the PB.9 was scrapped later that year. *(Author's Collection)*

layout to the PB.7 though it was a two-seater, while the PB.3 was an enlarged PB.2 with two 90hp Austro-Daimler engines; neither saw the light of day. The later PB.7 (itself subsequently renumbered PB.19) flying-boat took partial shape but was not completed; the forward hull of this design consisted of a cabin motor-boat that could be slipped from the flight surfaces when at rest and used independently.

Meanwhile an improved and enlarged *Bat Boat* known as the Type 2 had appeared, powered by a 200hp Canton-Unné pusher and with a span of 54ft. It employed a deeper hull but retained side-by-side seating, with no fin and a single oval rudder. The Type 2 was manufactured at Kingston. The first was ordered by the German Navy and was displayed at the 1914 Olympia Aero Show. Tests at Woolston followed during May before the aircraft joined the German Naval Air Arm serialled 44, based at Kiel-Holtenau for training duties, reflecting the surprisingly normal trading relations between the two countries even while international political tensions escalated. The second example was ordered by the Admiralty and was flying by April 1914, probably from Calshot, fitted with wireless telegraphy equipment and serialled 127. It passed to the Greek Naval Air Corps in July. The final Type 2, equipped with a 225hp Sunbeam Mohawk, was ordered in March 1914 for entry as no. 3 in that year's Daily Mail Seaplane Circuit of Britain race, to be piloted by Howard Pixton. However, the contest was cancelled in August after the outbreak of war and the aircraft impressed for naval service serialled 879. Its life thereafter featured several periods of unserviceability before it was finally deleted in April 1915.

A further flying-boat emerged during August 1914, conceived by Messrs J.J. Talbot and W.B. Quick and built at Fambridge in Essex. A biplane, its upper and lower wings of parallel chord were joined by curved tips. Biplane elevators were

PEMBERTON-BILLING, Ltd.

IN FLIGHT

ILLUSTRATIONS DEMONSTRATING THE LATEST TYPE OF

"SUPERMARINE"

(FLYING LIFEBOAT)

Telephone : No. 38, Southampton.   *Telegrams : "Supermarine."*

BUILT UNDER PEMBERTON-BILLING'S PATENTS AT HIS SOUTHAMPTON WORKS

AFTER ALIGHTING— THE WINGS DETACHED

SOUTHAMPTON, ENGLAND

The Pemberton Billing PB.7 (later the PB.19) was advertised as a flying lifeboat. Of two ordered by the German Navy, the first was almost complete by July 1914 but work ended with the outbreak of war. *(Author's Collection)*

The first *Bat Boat* Type 2, on display at the March 1914 Olympia Aero Show. Larger than its forebears, though of similar form, the aircraft adopted a sturdier Sopwith-built hull, featuring a step vented through the use of brass panels attached to the sides. This example was ordered by the German Naval Air Arm. (*J.M. Bruce/G.S. Leslie Collection*)

The Talbot-Quick Waterplane on its launching chassis by the banks of the River Crouch during August 1914. Its pusher engine and four-bladed propeller can be seen, while the simple hull is separated from the flight surfaces by an array of struts. The centre of gravity was obviously high, and small wing-floats were subsequently added in an attempt to provide lateral stability on the water – though the machine later capsized and was abandoned. (*J.M. Bruce/G.S. Leslie Collection*)

The White & Thompson No. 1 Seaplane at Middleton wearing its Circuit of Britain Race number on the rudder. The smaller inscription on the rudder makes reference to a Curtiss patent. Though the aircraft was impressed as 883 at the onset of war, it was retained by the company for trials purposes. *(J.M. Bruce/G.S. Leslie Collection)*

White & Thompson's No. 2 Seaplane seen at Middleton, with Norman Thompson standing by the hull. The large four-bladed pusher propeller is much in evidence while the upper wing trailing-edge cutaway allowing its clearance is also displayed. Supplementary fin area is supplied at the centre of the upper wing. Following its impressment as 882, the aircraft gained a great reputation for reliability while flying from Grain and Felixstowe. *(J.M. Bruce/G.S. Leslie Collection)*

positioned at the nose and the tailplane to the rear. It was powered by a water-cooled pusher engine positioned mid-gap, and the flight structure was strut-mounted to a boat-shaped hull while the pilot sat at the wing leading-edge. Despite a number of attempts, the Talbot-Quick Waterplane succeeded only in capsizing; it never flew.

During that year Ernest Bass and Compton C. Paterson joined forces on the Bass-Paterson flying-boat, a two-seat side-by-side biplane with sharply swept wings and a Consuta-covered Saunders hull. Designed by Paterson, the aircraft employed a hull-mounted 100hp Green pusher driving the propeller by chain. The wings were bolted to the 13ft 9in hull in much the same arrangement as the *Bat Boats'* while the tailplane, fin and rudder were positioned on struts reminiscent of Sopwith's aircraft – in fact the Bass-Paterson was sometimes referred to as a *Bat Boat*. Unfortunately it caught fire during tests at Cowes early in 1915 and was burned out.

White & Thompson, meanwhile, had opened a flying-boat training school at Middleton, and the intended 1914 Daily Mail race had spurred on the company's managing director Norman Thompson to produce two entrants. A twin-engined machine had already been started; soon a single-engined design was commenced. The twin, the White & Thompson No. 1 Seaplane, was a two-seat side-by-side dual-control biplane flying-boat powered by two 90hp Austin-built Curtiss OX engines driving pusher propellers. Its hull was built by Williams & Co. of Littlehampton, an old-established yacht and motor-boat builder eventually subsumed by White & Thompson. Again derived from Curtiss technology, the No. 1 Seaplane was to have been race no. 9 but during trials by Gordon England it refused to leave the water. On 10 August 1914, however, Percy Beadle joined the company and the modifications he introduced during the autumn seem to have been successful. The No. 1 was impressed for use by the Navy as 883.

The single-engined White & Thompson machine was the No. 2 Seaplane, once more drawn from Curtiss origins, and given race no. 6. Saunders produced the Consuta-skinned hull, which featured a single planing step and side-by-side accommodation. The aircraft was powered by a 120hp Beardmore Austro-Daimler water-cooled engine driving a four-bladed pusher propeller. Its hull arrived at Middleton during early July 1914 while the wings were taken from the Bass-Curtiss Airboat. The first flight was made on 1 August by Flight Lieutenant E.R. Whitehouse. The No. 2 was also impressed, becoming 882 and travelling first to Calshot, then to Grain for training and patrol duties before expiring at Felixstowe, being wrecked on 8 June 1915.

On 1 July 1914 the Naval Wing of the Royal Flying Corps became the Royal Naval Air Service (RNAS), attaining true independence. Seventeen days later a formation of aircraft from the RNAS took part in the Royal Review of the Fleet at Spithead, including *Bat Boat* 118. On 4 August Britain declared war on Germany.

2 THE FIRST WORLD WAR

Building a Force

Following the outbreak of war, plans were made to arm the *Bat Boat* with a machine-gun and a modest 150lb bomb-load but were not taken up. However, in October 1914 White & Thompson received orders from the Admiralty for eight of their No. 3 Boats, derived from the No. 2 Boat. Confusingly, these aircraft were also known as the NT.2 and, with an improved hull, the NT.2A. Generally similar to the No. 2, the No. 3 was powered by a 120hp Beardmore Austro-Daimler pusher with the exception of the final example which had a 150hp Hispano-Suiza. The major airframe difference was the use of two fins fitted one above each pair of inboard inter-plane struts on the No. 3 design, rather than the single central wing fin of the No. 2. The No. 3 Boats, serialled 1195–1200 and 3807–3808 (the two NT.2As), were delivered to the RNAS between February and October 1915. They operated mostly from Calshot, Dover, Fort George (Inverness-shire) and Dundee, performing training flights, watching over cross-Channel surface vessels and also carrying out anti-submarine patrols against Germany's U-boats, though their bomb-load was only 150lb; anti-Zeppelin patrols were also occasionally undertaken. 1199 was interned by the Dutch government in February 1915 having force-landed on the Wester Scheldt; subsequently purchased, it received the identity G1 and was on charge to the Dutch Navy until at least the end of 1917, thus becoming the longest surviving No. 3 Boat.

Over the early summer of 1915 Norman Thompson and Percy Beadle conceived a larger twin-engined flying boat, the NT.4. Six (8338–8343) were ordered in July and a further four (9061–9064) in December. The NT.4 employed a four-bay 77ft 10in unequal span pusher biplane configuration, with a single-step hull featuring a glazed cockpit housing the crew of two in a blunt nose. Apart from 8338 which initially was powered by 100hp Greens, the type employed two uncowled Hispano-Suiza engines in either 150hp or 200hp form. Armament usually consisted of a .303in Lewis gun mounted on the cockpit roof and a bomb-load of up to 460lb. At the time of its procurement the NT.4 was intended to be used for long-range anti-submarine patrol work.

No. 8338 commenced trials at Bognor during October 1915 but the type took a very long time to enter service; it was January 1917 before 8339 was delivered while 9064 followed during June. The delays were caused by changes in the choice of engine, and to both hull and flight structures in order to improve hydro- and aerodynamic performance – during trials the aircraft had been found to be severely

The penultimate Norman Thompson No. 3 Boat (or the first NT.2A), serialled 3807, seen at Calshot. This example was wrecked by the commanding officer of Calshot while attempting to pursue Zeppelin L31 during the night of 25/26 September 1916 after its engine failed. The No. 3's sole offensive weapon was a single cockpit-mounted .303in Lewis machine-gun. A simple beaching trolley supports the aircraft. The large fin and slim rear hull area were typical of several Norman Thompson types. 3807's roots in the No. 2 Seaplane are very clear. *(Author's Collection)*

Norman Thompson NT.4 8343 at Killingholme float-plane and flying-boat base. Its cockpit glazing is limited and must have afforded a rather poor view. The aircraft sits on a two-wheel main beaching chassis, its pusher configuration necessitating a trailing-edge cutout in the upper wing to accommodate the propellers. It was delivered to Killingholme in March 1917. *(J.M. Bruce/G.S. Leslie Collection)*

NT.4A N2142 being manhandled on the slipway. This aircraft flew from Calshot training school, being delivered during September 1917, but was not of great longevity – it was deleted in the following March. As well as teams of men to manoeuvre the aircraft on land at that time, lorries, tractors and even traction engines were pressed into service. *(J.M. Bruce/G.S. Leslie Collection)*

tail-heavy on the water and in the air. Meanwhile in September 1915 the White & Thompson Company had become the Norman Thompson Flight Company Limited.

The improved NT.4A included a modified hull with increased cockpit glazing, larger engine radiators and an improved fuel system; twenty (N2140–N2159) were ordered in May 1917. That programme too was lengthy, partly because in early 1918 the Admiralty suspended work, having reconsidered the types it required for long-distance anti-submarine operations. Norman Thompson was eventually allowed to complete N2140–N2155 as the timber had already been cut and fittings fabricated for those examples, deliveries being made between November 1917 and the following May.

However, the Admiralty settled on Curtiss H.12 and Porte/Felixstowe flying-boats for its long-range duties; a contract for an additional twenty NT.4As (N2740–N2759) was suspended in February 1918 and cancelled during June. Norman Thompson became obliged to look elsewhere for work, while the NT.4s and NT.4As were employed mostly for training, making 20-minute hops generally from Calshot, Killingholme (Lincolnshire) and occasionally at Cattewater (Plymouth), though 8339 and 8340 carried out anti-submarine patrols over the North Sea from Dundee. The prototype, 8338, was fitted experimentally with a two-pounder recoilless Davis gun installed above the cabin though that arrangement never entered service.

-o0o-

John Porte returned to Britain at the outbreak of war. Despite his ill health he joined the RNAS and was given command of RNAS Felixstowe in September 1914. Drawing on his experience he put forward a proposal to Captain Murray Sueter, the Air Department's director, for the purchase of Curtiss aircraft for the

RNAS. By the following March Porte had on strength six Curtiss flying-boats as well as White & Thompson's No. 2 Boat 882. Of the Americans, two were H.1s and four H.4s, both developed from the *America*; they were large twin-engined aircraft with single-step hulls. The H.4 was ordered in quantity for the RNAS but was found to suffer from a weak hull of mediocre hydrodynamic properties, and from unreliable Curtiss engines of insufficient power. Porte and his team,

NT.4A nose area. Streamlining was not at the top of the list of improvements, but at least the glazing is increased compared with the NT.4. The hydrodynamic portion of the hull is broad with a shallow V-bottom while the exposed engines, their attendant radiators and pusher propellers are positioned as far as possible from the threat of damage by spray. *(Ray Sturtivant)*

including J.D. Rennie, the chief technical officer at Felixstowe, therefore spent considerable time during 1915 and 1916 in detailed experiments with the Curtiss flying-boats. Particular attention was given to variations of hull design in an effort to improve seaworthiness and durability. The work was strictly empirical: steps were added and removed, and relocated fore and aft, the beam was amended, dead rise varied to assess shock-absorption and spray characteristics, and wing float profiles and attitudes altered.

These labours led to the Felixstowe series of flying-boats, beginning with the singular but important F.1. A new hull to Porte's design, 36ft in length, single-stepped and known as the Porte I, was fitted to the flight structure of H.4 3580. The addition of a second (and later a third) step and an increase to the vee-shape of the planing bottom gave remarkably improved hydrodynamic performance with dry bows on take-off combined with reasonably shock-less landings. The F.1 retained the serial 3580 despite its extensive modifications and survived at Felixstowe's Seaplane School until January 1919.

Alongside his early experimental work, Porte designed and built a huge flying-boat which was promptly dubbed the 'Baby'. The prototype, 9800, was powered by three 250hp Rolls-Royce engines arranged as two tractors and a central pusher, and had a wingspan of 124ft, a single-step plywood-covered hull of 56ft 10in, and an enclosed cockpit; provision was made for five crew. Empty weight was well over 18,000lb. 9800 first flew on 20 November 1915 but was found to wallow in a following sea; a 3ft extension to the bows improved water-handling

The sole Felixstowe F.1, 3580. Porte's I hull was fitted to the H.4's flight surfaces, a straightforward cross-braced wooden box-girder structure on to which the planing bottom was grafted, while two 150hp Hispano-Suizas replaced the original 100hp Anzanis. The open cockpit provided better visibility than the enclosed type employed by the H.4, made possible by the cleaner hydrodynamic performance around the bow area. The F.1 was a breakthrough and marked the beginning of the Felixstowe series. *(Author's Collection)*

considerably. The aircraft was none the less under-powered, attaining a maximum speed of only 78mph.

Ten production machines (9801–9810) were constructed by May, Harden & May of Hythe, on Southampton Water, the majority powered by the Rolls-Royce Eagle VII (325hp) or VIII (360hp) though some employed a central 260hp Green, and all were somewhat sprightlier than the prototype. Ten hulls (9811–9820) were also built. Deliveries took place between May 1916 and March 1917, and anti-submarine patrols were flown mostly from Felixstowe and Killingholme. On 1 October 1917 9810 was engaged by two enemy seaplanes and a landplane near the Dutch-maintained North Hinder Light Vessel situated 55 miles from Felixstowe and equidistant from the Hook of Holland. With two damaged engines the aircraft was forced to alight, its wireless/telegraphy (W/T) operator wounded. On the water, despite being machine-gunned by the Germans, repairs were effected and the aircraft was taxied slowly to Sizewell Gap, north of Orfordness, eventually being towed to Felixstowe by trawler. Meanwhile the prototype was used in two experimental episodes, the first involving additional armament when it was fitted with a six-pounder Davis recoilless gun, presumably as an anti-submarine measure – though the gun is thought not to have been fired. The aircraft was also flown with two torpedoes, one under each lower wing. The second experiment involved the mounting of a single-seat fighter, Bristol Scout C3028, above the upper wing. The composite successfully took off on 17 May 1916 and the Scout was released without incident at 1,000ft over Harwich, but the feat does not seem to have been

The Porte 'Baby' prototype, 9800, on the hard standing at Felixstowe during the spring of 1916. Bristol Scout C3028 is mounted above its upper wing as the pick-a-back experiment unfolds. In the background the camouflaged Felixstowe sheds and the power station can be seen. The 'Baby' sits in a launching cradle that runs down the slipway and into the water. *(J.M. Bruce/ G.S. Leslie Collection)*

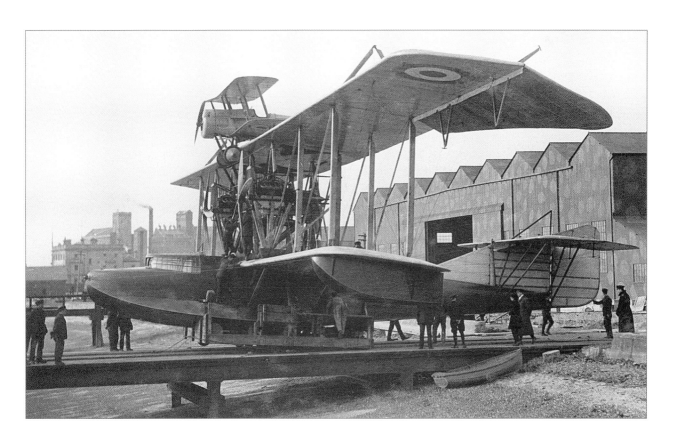

AD Flying Boat prototype 1412 on its beaching chassis. This aircraft was unique among the AD machines in featuring a partly enclosed cockpit. The early examples suffered with mediocre performance on the water, but this was improved with the help of the National Physical Laboratory and its Walter Froude model testing tank. Perhaps 1412 is factory-fresh here, for it is not wearing its serial number. *(J.M. Bruce/G.S. Leslie Collection)*

repeated. 'Baby' production remained at ten as Porte's continuing experiments yielded improved performance from subsequent designs.

In mid-1916 the AD Flying Boat appeared from the Admiralty's Air Department, the product of a team established to develop and procure aircraft of its own. The department's Harris Booth took overall programme responsibility while hull design proceeded under Lieutenant Linton Hope, the marine architect who had previously worked on Pemberton Billing's PB.1. The resultant aircraft was a tandem two-seat single-engined pusher biplane with a 50ft 4in span, intended for patrol and reconnaissance duties. Power was usually provided by a 200hp Hispano-Suiza. The hull was a two-step wooden monocoque structure of circular wooden formers spaced by stringers and planked diagonally with moulded sheets of laminated mahogany strips in two criss-crossing layers. This arrangement was intended to provide flexibility, and resilience in the face of shocks from heavy landings and rough seas. The construction of the first prototype was by May, Harden & May, with further examples by the reconstituted Pemberton Billing company known as the Supermarine Aviation Works Ltd, headed by Hubert Scott-Paine after the departure of Noel Pemberton Billing – a change effected during September 1916. The prototype AD Flying Boats (1412 and 1413) differed slightly, the former employing a semi-enclosed cockpit and – for a time – a 150hp Sunbeam engine, while the latter was Hispano-powered and featured an open cockpit and a slightly deeper radiator.

Unfortunately a serious fore-and-aft oscillation of the hull against the water during take-off, which came to be known as porpoising, together with severe yawing owing to the small fin and rudder, and excessive weight were all revealed during trials. However, following the relocation of the main step, redesign of the aft step and amendments to the fin and rudder, performance was deemed acceptable and the AD Flying Boat

Production AD Flying Boat N1522 was powered by a 200hp Hispano-Suiza engine. By September 1917 it was operating from Calshot School, as seen here, but served for only four months, being withdrawn in January 1918. *(Author's Collection)*

Transportation, First World War-style! AD Flying Boat N1523 aboard a Royal Navy tender. Presumably the wings and propeller are following on, for they are not in evidence here. N1523 joined the Type Test Flight at Grain during March 1918 for experimental purposes, but was deleted in the following December. *(J.M. Bruce/G.S. Leslie Collection)*

The prototype Norman Thompson NT.5 N1040, with the original flat-topped rear hull; subsequent examples adopted a triangular section hull aft of the wings, with the apex uppermost. N1040 was completed in January 1917 and travelled to Calshot during the following month, which is possibly where this photograph was taken. The dainty aircraft served until October of that year when it was struck off. *(J.M. Bruce/G.S. Leslie Collection)*

Ouch! An NT.5 has taken a tumble while an FBA Model B rests at the shoreline together with an NT.2B. A party attempts to right the crumpled aircraft while several two-wheeled beaching trolleys are in evidence. To the right a solitary figure has been marked on the print with an arrow – was he the culprit? *(J.M. Bruce/G.S. Leslie Collection)*

entered production. Both the Sunbeam Arab and Wolseley Python engines were installed experimentally but the Python at least was not a success. Supermarine-built examples were N1290 (possibly), N1520–N1529, N1710–N1719 and N2450–N2455. N1520 was accepted at Grain in September 1917 and deliveries were complete by April 1918, the programme again a victim of engine shortages and changes. Some machines flew from Calshot and Grain but many went straight into store; numbers eventually coalesced into the post-war Supermarine Channel.

Norman Thompson's NT.5 appeared in early 1917. This was a modified Franco-British Aviation (FBA) Model B, a small, two-seat side-by-side biplane flying-boat powered by a 100hp Gnôme Monosoupape pusher, designed by Louis Schreck in 1915 and built in France for the French Navy. Forty examples were ordered for training purposes by the RNAS. However, the Model B hull was found insufficiently durable, and in July 1916 Norman Thompson were engaged to supply strengthened hulls. The wing form and tailplane were also revised; altogether the modifications were so extensive that the company applied its own nomenclature. Twenty NT.5s (N1040–N1059) were supplied together with new hulls for four additional 'boats and ten spare hulls. Deliveries were made between February and May 1917, the aircraft flying mostly from Calshot but also from Killingholme.

In addition Hampshire's Gosport Aviation Company built sixty FBA Model B flying-boats (N2680–N2739) under licence delivered between November 1917 and September 1918, the majority to 209 Training Depot Station at Lee-on-Solent. Gosport had been formed as the aviation subsidiary of Camper & Nicholson, the yacht designers and builders, and was headed by Charles Nicholson and Sir Charles Allom.

The year 1917 also saw the emergence of Percy Beadle's NT.2B trainer. Norman Thompson planned to build on the No. 3 Boats with a two-seat flying-boat to

N26, the sole Norman Thompson NT.2A, was built as a private venture prototype for the NT.2B and was purchased by the Admiralty for £1,000 plus the price of the hull. At Calshot it was used for training, being deleted during March 1918. *(Ray Sturtivant)*

Norman Thompson NT.2B N2575 gets aloft. The design's derivation from the No. 3 Boat is obvious. N2575 was powered by a 200hp Hispano-Suiza and arrived for service at Calshot's 210 Training Depot Station in May 1918, but during the following month it moved to Lee-on-Solent, from where it operated until January 1919. *(Author's Collection)*

replace the NT.5 in RNAS service. An order had been placed for ten NT.2Bs (N1180–N1189) in November 1916; in parallel, an experimental private venture 'boat was built, apparently (and confusingly) known as an NT.2A in a second use of that nomenclature. This version was certainly derived from the No. 3 Boat, and was of open-cockpit configuration. Serialled N26, the sole example was powered by a 140hp Hispano-Suiza. The aircraft was completed during January 1917 and delivered to Calshot for trials in the following April.

The production aircraft, the NT.2B, was a 48ft 5in span sesquiplane biplane powered by a variety of single pusher engines in the 150–200 hp class, and with the distinctively large fin of previous Norman Thompson types. The 27ft 4½in hull was of single-step configuration with side-by-side enclosed seating and generous cockpit glazing. Subsequent orders followed but a disappointment for Norman Thompson was the cancellation of their January 1917 contract for three School Biplane Flying Boats, N107, N108 and N109. These aircraft had also been intended as trainers and would have employed two 200hp Hispano-Suiza 8Bs or Sunbeam Arabs, but the order was terminated in April 1917. None the less the situation appeared to have a silver lining, for the Admiralty had decided to standardise flying-boat training on the NT.2B.

F-Boats

The first Curtiss H.8 ordered for the RNAS, 8650, is reported to have arrived at Felixstowe during March 1916. Unfortunately trials revealed that its two 160hp Curtiss engines did not provide sufficient power for take-off when fully laden at 7,800lb, while the hull structure was considered weak, troubles echoing those with the H.1 and H.4. 8650 was therefore fitted with two 250hp Rolls-Royce engines and take-off under fully-laden weight was duly accomplished, though hydrodynamic performance deteriorated. Porte elected to produce an entirely new hull similar to that of the Felixstowe F.1; this resulted in the sole Felixstowe F.2, which employed the flight surfaces of 8650 and retained that serial.

The new hull, known as the Porte II, was 42ft in length with a pronounced vee-bottom and two steps, one beneath the rear spar and the other 7ft aft. It was designed and constructed over the spring and early summer of 1916, and fitted probably during the first half of July. A cross-braced box girder arrangement was adopted, with the steps attached to the hull (in contrast to the Curtiss boat-built approach), and a semi-enclosed cockpit was provided. The F.2 was tested later that month; major improvements were noted to seaworthiness and, as with the F.1, landings were found comparatively shock-free. The hull was stronger than that of the H.8 without any weight penalty, while buoyancy was increased. These improvements were achieved despite John Porte having no formal training in engineering or boat-building, and employing a scratch team of draughtsmen, boat-builders and carpenters at Felixstowe. Porte was a great organiser and had considerable insight into the design and construction work necessary; he was also a very experienced pilot with first-hand knowledge of operating and maintaining the flying-boats he built. 8650 patrolled the North Sea from the end of July, but on 30 September it put down and was lost near the Sunk Light Vessel east of the River Naze.

The F.2 led to a production version, the F.2A, and thence to the F.2C, F.3, F.4 and F.5, all designed by Porte. Collectively they were known as the F-Boat series, and the F.2A, F.3 and F.5 were manufactured in considerable numbers. The production programmes for these large aircraft (the span of the F.2A was over 95ft) were complex. Porte's little band had no manufacturing facilities so subcontractors produced the F.2A: the Aircraft Manufacturing Company at Hendon, S.E. Saunders, May, Harden & May, and also Curtiss (their examples being referred to as the H.16), together with the US Naval Aircraft Factory at League Island, Philadelphia. The beauty of Porte's uncomplicated hull design was that if necessary it could be constructed by companies with no previous boat-building experience. Six firms built F.2A hulls: Aldous & Co. (10 hulls ordered), Dixon Brothers & Hutchinson (5), Summers & Payne (13), Saunders (67), Camper & Nicholson (6) and Norman Thompson/Williams & Co. (4). At least fifteen hulls were used to upgrade H.12s, these examples becoming known as H.12 Converts. The first delivery took place during mid-November 1917 when the Saunders-built F.2A N4280 arrived at Felixstowe's Seaplane School; by March 1918 161 were on order. By the end of the war the RAF had on strength 53 F.2As and 69 H.16s.

The F.2A was powered by two 360hp Rolls-Royce Eagle VIII engines, a far cry from the total 320 hp of the Curtiss H.8. Its defensive armament was exceedingly heavy by the standards of the day and consisted typically of one or sometimes twin Lewis guns mounted on a bow Scarff ring, one on a dorsal Scarff ring, one in each of two waist positions, and optionally one mounted on the port side of the cockpit canopy; as many as nine such guns were sometimes carried. Offensive weaponry comprised two 230lb bombs on racks below the lower wings. Loaded weight was almost 11,000lb, and maximum speed just over 95mph. The cockpit layout was at

F.2A N4287, showing the enclosed cockpit layout and early aileron configuration. This aircraft was delivered to Killingholme on 20 March 1918. It was flown mainly by American personnel and bombed no fewer than three suspected U-boats, on 26 June, 28 June and 13 July. It was transferred to the United States NAS on 20 July but deleted from the station's strength on 5 September. The serial number is painted in unusually large characters. N4287's beaching chassis is typical of the type used by the F.2A, with a main axle supplemented by smaller wheels fore and aft. *(J.M. Bruce/G.S. Leslie Collection)*

F.2As under construction at the East Cowes site of S.E. Saunders during the summer of 1918. In the foreground is N4453, an enigmatic aircraft for which no delivery record has survived. It is of the later, open-cockpit variety. In the background is N4454. As well as several early experimental Porte hulls, Saunders built F-Boats N4280–N4309, N4080–4099 and N4430–4479, many of which were delivered after the war had ended, some as F.5s. *(Author's Collection)*

On the water, F.2A N4441 taxying with a relaxed-looking crew. Another Saunders-built example, this aircraft was delivered just after the Armistice, arriving for service at Felixstowe. It employs the later, constant-chord horn-balanced ailerons and the open cockpit arrangement. The considerable span is emphasised, while the aft hull layout ensures the tail is kept well away from the water. The personnel move lithely about the airframe. *(Author's Collection)*

A group of aviators gather at the bows of a moored late model F.2A. The marked width of the hydrodynamic portion of the hull is shown, while the bow Scarff ring has been removed. The aircrew are wearing padded flying suits and helmets while to the right stands a corporal sporting a set of headphones but no flying clothing. *(Author's Collection)*

F.2As were used for a number of experimental purposes: here, a hydrophone is being tested, its operator wearing clumpish headphones. No fewer than eleven different types of directional and non-directional acoustic hydrophone were developed by the British during the First World War and the equipment was very much to the forefront of the technology of the day. *(J.M. Bruce/G.S. Leslie Collection)*

The cockpit of F.2A N4510 was enclosed and fitted with two large control wheels, but there were very few instruments to distract the pilot from his labours! N4510 was delivered from May, Harden & May to Grain via Calshot on 25 January 1918 and by March was operating from Felixstowe. On 8 April it was obliged to make a forced landing following an engine failure, and sank in heavy seas while in tow. *(J.M. Bruce/G.S. Leslie Collection)*

first partly enclosed and featured dual-control, a great asset as the typical endurance of the F.2A was six hours. This could be extended to around 9½ hours using additional fuel in cans, though shortcomings lay in the long-run fuel pipes and problematic wind-driven fuel pumps. None the less the type established itself as a first-class flying and fighting machine. Modifications included the substitution of the cabin top and semi-enclosed cockpit by an open arrangement, incorporated in aircraft manufactured from around September 1918, which improved visibility and increased speed slightly. Constant-chord, horn-balanced ailerons were fitted on the later examples, relieving some of the physical effort in piloting the aircraft. At least two F.2As were equipped with two upper-wing gunnery positions each mounting a twin Lewis installation but whether either saw active service in such configuration is unknown. Deliveries eventually amounted to 173 F.2As and 75 H.16s.

The two F.2Cs, N64 and N65, featured a modified Porte hull of deeper profile but lighter construction than previously, with revised steps, open cockpits and amendments to the bow gun position. Employing Rolls-Royce Eagle VIIIs, N64 was test-flown at Felixstowe during February 1917, N65 following three months later powered by 322hp Eagle VIs. Also in May, bomb-racks were fitted and the rudder controls revised. With the F.2A on order the F.2C did not enter production, but both examples were used operationally over the summer of 1917.

The Felixstowe F.3 was similar to, though slightly larger than, the F.2A and despite being built in greater numbers was inferior in some ways, being slower and less manoeuvrable, though it could carry a heavier bomb-load and had a greater range. The hull was somewhat prone to leaking, the result of an alteration in the construction method around the planing bottom that turned out to be a backward step (so to speak). Armament remained heavy with typically four or five Lewis guns and provision for the carriage of four 230lb bombs. The prototype F.3 was in fact

Felixstowe flying-boat N64 reveals its great wingspan and beaching chassis. Though it started life as the open-cockpit F.2C, this aircraft was subsequently adapted to form the prototype F.3, as seen here, with an enclosed cockpit. Auxiliary vertical areas are employed between the interplane struts just outboard of the engines. In the background are what appear to be two Curtiss H.12s. *(Philip Jarrett)*

Felixstowe F.3 hull under construction at the premises of Boulton & Paul, November 1917. The Porte method of construction was a basic box-section structure to which longerons and spacers were added and a separate planing bottom later attached, featuring prominent flares. *(J.M. Bruce/G.S. Leslie Collection)*

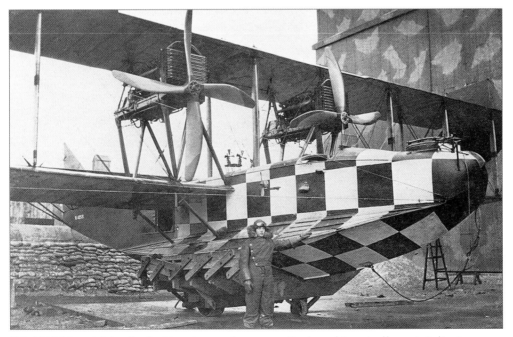

F.3 N4258 exhibits its bold colour scheme on its beaching trolley at Felixstowe, a camouflaged hangar forming the backdrop. N4258, manufactured by Dick, Kerr & Co. at Preston, was delivered to the Marine Aeroplane Depot at South Shields during July 1918, moving to Felixstowe in September. *(J.M. Bruce/G.S. Leslie Collection)*

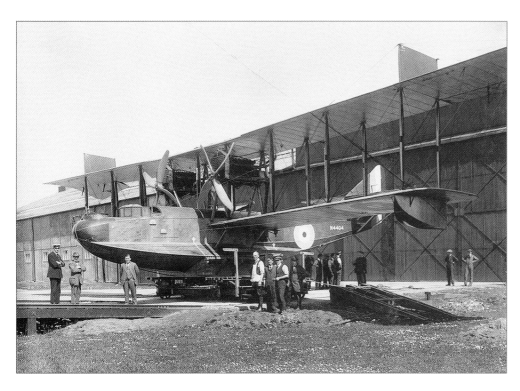

F.3 N4404 at the Brough premises of the Phoenix Dynamo Co. Ltd. This aircraft was delivered to MAD Brough in April 1918 and arrived at Houton Bay on 19 May. Sadly just four days later it was wrecked when the hull hit an unseen object during take-off, and it was struck off in June.
(J.M. Bruce/G.S. Leslie Collection)

the reworked F.2C N64 returned from its brief operational career. Following its conversion during October 1917, N64 first flew in revised form later that month from Felixstowe, employing 320hp Sunbeam Cossacks though production F.3s were again powered by Rolls-Royce Eagle VIIIs. The aircraft later rejoined Felixstowe's War Flight, surviving until the following April when it was deemed worn out. By March 1918 263 F.3s were on order though only one was operational. Production was undertaken by Short Brothers at Rochester, Dick, Kerr & Co. at Preston and Lytham St Annes, and the Phoenix Dynamo Manufacturing Co. at Bradford. As with the F.2A, output was delayed by engine shortages but by the Armistice 96 F.3s were in service with the RAF. The selection of the F.3 meant that a rival proposal from Handley Page at Cricklewood, the T/400 biplane flying-boat, was not pursued though two experimental serials (N62 and N63) were allocated.

To meet the need for anti-submarine patrols in the Mediterranean it was decided to manufacture a batch of F.3s on Malta. These aircraft were built by the Dockyard Constructional Unit using local labour, which included experienced carpenters among the men and female fabric workers. The first Maltese F.3, N4310, was test-flown in March 1918 while further examples N4311–N4321 and at least nineteen within the range N4360–N4397 were completed up to the Armistice. The F.3 was used experimentally to test servo-operated controls and also a form of automatic landing device.

The final operational F-Boat was the F.5. The prototype, N90, was tested at Felixstowe during November 1917. The F.5 too was powered by the Eagle VII and VIII and featured a deeper hull than the F.3, but it retained two steps and an open side-by-side cockpit; defensive positions were as for the F.3 and provision

was made for four Lewis guns (at least), while a load of four 230lb bombs was carried. Though the flight surfaces of N90 were initially derived from those of the earlier F-Boats the ailerons of the production F.5 were constant-chord and horn-balanced from the outset, extending beyond the wing tips, while a different wing section was employed.

With the F.3 in production, the Ministry of Munitions decided to avoid additional sets of jigs, tools and templates where possible and the F.5 was manufactured using numbers of F.3 parts and components, so the later machine became something of a hybrid. The F.5 hull employed a wooden skin overall, whereas the decks and aft flanks of previous Porte hulls had been fabric-covered. Empty weight grew from 7,958lb (F.3) to 9,100lb (F.5) and the F.5 was a little slower than its predecessor. Water and air qualities were found very satisfactory. However, the final F-Boat appeared too late to see war service. British manufacturers of the F.5 were the Gosport Aviation Company, the Aircraft Manufacturing Company, May, Harden & May, the Phoenix Dynamo Manufacturing Company, S.E. Saunders and Short Brothers. As Gosport's aviation work grew, additional premises were acquired at Driver's Yard near Northam Bridge, Southampton; the completed F.5 hulls were floated to the new site where the flight structures were added and the aircraft flown from Southampton Water. In addition, Boulton & Paul built a total of seventy F.3 and F.5 hulls. Prior to the Armistice the F.5 went into production overseas, being built by Canadian Aeroplanes Ltd of Toronto and the United States Naval Aircraft Factory.

N90, the prototype Felixstowe F.5, at Grain during 1918. Built at Felixstowe, the aircraft participated in hydrophone trials during May 1918 and after the war travelled abroad, visiting Copenhagen and Helsingfors during July 1919 before returning to Kent. It subsequently crashed at Calshot and was written off. *(Author's Collection)*

Operations

The progress of Norman Thompson's NT.2B was delayed by changes in its powerplant. Initially the Beardmore Austro-Daimler was adopted in 120hp and 160hp forms, but the Admiralty subsequently decreed the 150hp Hispano-Suiza be used. The final six of the original batch (N1184–N1189) were so equipped, being delivered by October 1917. Deliveries of the second batch commenced in December 1917 and while the first two or three aircraft employed the 150hp Hispano, in a further amendment 200hp Hispanos were assigned for the balance. Other contracts were placed with S.E. Saunders for 24 NT.2Bs (N2500–N2523) and with Supermarine for 75 examples. The increased torque of the Hispano necessitated installing the engine on starboard-slewed mountings, but in any case at that time those engines were urgently required for fighter aircraft, so another replacement became necessary.

The 200hp Sunbeam Arab was selected and NT.2B production was halted in June 1918 for six weeks for engine mounting modifications. Unfortunately the Arab proved problematic as a pusher, the original propeller was found unsuitable and another slewed installation became necessary. As the programme dragged on, the Admiralty attempted to cancel Supermarine's contract but production of the airframes was too far advanced. However, of the 295 NT.2Bs ordered in total, it appears that only 156 were built – and of those, few entered service before the war ended. Most went into store minus engines.

The delays seriously affected elementary flying-boat pilot training; shortages of pilots became acute as the F-Boats went operational and more crews were needed. Those NT.2Bs that served during the war flew mostly from Calshot and Lee-on-Solent. Calshot's first arrivals were N1180 and N1181 in June 1917, while Lee took delivery of N1187 and N1189 during the following October. N2260–N2265 all flew from Lee from November 1918, by which time it was known as 209 Training Depot Station, but all had left by January 1919 as had a number of other examples – a brief tenure indeed.

Meanwhile the F.2A fought a short but distinguished campaign against Germany's submarines, airships and fighter floatplanes. Hunting the U-boats was much the most urgent task, for their potential to influence the course of the war by depriving Britain of her essential maritime trade became profound. In February 1917 Germany declared a second phase of unrestricted submarine warfare against all merchant vessels found in the waters surrounding Britain and Ireland. The shipping and crew losses, particularly during the spring of 1917, were appalling and quite un-sustainable. During 1917 some 3,730,000 tons of British merchant shipping was sunk by U-boat actions and in the first half of 1918 the figure was 1,784,000 tons.

A truly enormous effort had to be made by Britain to oppose the submarines, in terms of manpower, equipment, technical development and the evolution of tactics. Naval patrols, mines and Q-ships proved the most effective weapons while the convoy system afforded some protection, but aircraft (and also airships) played a part. The large flying-boat was better suited to lengthy maritime missions far from the coast than the floatplane, which tended to be somewhat slower, so more at risk from enemy aircraft, and often had less endurance. A typical bomb-load of the floatplane, for example the Short 184, was a maximum of 520lb, which compared well with the F.2A's 460lb (though unfavourably with the F.3), but in terms of machine-guns with which to strafe surface enemies and defend itself the Felixstowe series was remarkably well-equipped. Moreover, should an engine failure occur, the flying-boat stood a somewhat better chance than the floatplane of alighting safely and, once repairs were effected, of taking off again – though it has to be said that even flying-boats of substantial appearance have never been really at home on the open sea.

An operational stricture of the U-boats was their limited battery-powered underwater endurance which obliged them to surface frequently in order to recharge, and their commanders therefore often chose to run at surface level if possible. However, the increasing aerial force around the British coastline and beyond discouraged the submarines from rising in areas where aircraft were known to patrol, which in turn hampered their ability to move and helped to erode their effectiveness. The key to the U-boat campaign, perhaps easier to see in hindsight, was to ensure an uninterrupted flow of merchant shipping to and from Britain; sinking the submarines was not an absolute necessity as long as they were prevented from attacking the vital supply lanes. Though only one U-boat (UB32) was sunk solely by aerial attack during the First World War, it was in contributing to the overall deterrent that the F-Boats were successful, their considerable endurance coming into its own.

The first F.2As entered service at Great Yarmouth during February 1918. The type also flew from Calshot, Dundee, Felixstowe, Houton Bay (Orkney), Killingholme and Westgate/St Mildred's Bay (Kent) – bases from which they were most likely to find enemy submarines. Aircraft from Felixstowe and Great Yarmouth in particular patrolled an area christened the Spider Web. An octagon 60 nautical miles across and covering 4,000 square miles, its centre was at the North Hinder Light Vessel – well under an hour's flying time from the East Anglian stations. The area was traversed by most U-boats as they travelled from their ports into the North Sea or the English Channel.

At surface cruising speed it took the submarines typically around 10 hours to cross the Spider Web. Their detection was aided by wireless fixes from stations along the British coast, which were used to guide the flying-boats. The Spider Web patrols had commenced in April 1917 and during the first year twenty-three suspected U-boats were attacked, mostly by H.12s, though when the F.2As arrived they quickly joined the fray. Between May and November 1918 Felixstowe and Curtiss aircraft between them made twenty-eight suspected sightings of German submarines, attacking eighteen; F.2A N4287, based at Killingholme, made three such attacks between 26 June and 13 July.

The F.2As also fought the German Brandenburg floatplane fighters stationed at Borkum, Norderney and Zeebrugge. On 4 June 1918 the greatest battle of the war between waterborne aircraft took place when four F.2As and an H.12 Convert from Felixstowe and Great Yarmouth went searching for the enemy seaplanes. One F.2A was lost owing to a broken petrol feed pipe, its crew being interned in Holland, while the H.12 set off in pursuit of some German aircraft that had attacked the struggling F-Boat after it had force-landed. The three remaining F.2As encountered fourteen enemy floatplanes near the islands of Terschelling and Ameland. At least three Brandenburgs were shot down while two F-Boats experienced trouble, one with petrol starvation, the other with a defective engine, but all three returned to Felixstowe after a patrol lasting 6 hours. Following that engagement the F.2As were painted in flamboyant colour schemes to make them more visible on the sea if forced down. Those from Great Yarmouth were painted to individual taste in checks, stripes and zig-zag patterns, while the Felixstowe examples were somewhat more standardised on variations of stripes and squares.

To increase the radius of action, a scheme was devised by John Porte whereby F.2As were towed toward the continental coastline on lighters drawn by destroyers. Patrols at extended distances thus became possible, particularly over the Heligoland Bight where the German Navy was active. On 19 March 1918 the first towed mission set off for the enemy coast, taking H.12 8677 and F.2As N4282 and N4513. Two German seaplanes attacked the party and one was shot down by N4282; a safe return was made by the British force, and similar operations were subsequently carried out.

Patrols were also carried out against Zeppelins. Zeppelin stations were located at Tondern, Nordholz, Wittmundshaven and Ahlhorn along the north German coast. A remarkable encounter took place on 10 May 1918 when Killingholme-based F.2A N4291 attacked Zeppelin L56 over Heligoland, climbing to 8,000ft and shooting at it from below; some time after the engagement the airship ignited in a mass of flame.

The F.3s generally flew on anti-submarine patrols rather than pursuing an air-to-air fighting role, as they were somewhat slower and less manoeuvrable than the F.2As; they usually operated in areas of limited or no enemy air activity. Numbers were based at Cattewater, Houton Bay and Tresco though some did fly from Felixstowe. Those built on Malta naturally served in the Mediterranean, and one accompanied the Allied fleet in the attack on the Albanian port of Durazzo on 2 October 1918.

The two F.2Cs patrolled from Felixstowe and Grain over the summer of 1917. On 24 July N65 assisted with the suspected sinking of the small mine-laying U-boat UC-1, 6 miles south-south-west of the North Hinder Light Vessel, dropping two bombs; on that occasion John Porte was aboard. However, it later emerged UC-1 had already been sunk on 19 July, probably by a mine, and N65's claim had to be set aside; the aircraft was finally damaged beyond repair at Grain during the following March. N64 was used for hydrophone trials in January 1918 and was struck off charge as worn out in the following May.

Further Developments

The War Office's Royal Aircraft Factory at Farnborough built only one flying-boat type. This was the CE.1 (or Coastal Experimental 1), a response to the unleashing of the second phase of unrestricted submarine warfare by Germany. At that time the Porte/Felixstowe aircraft had not yet entered service and the need for maritime patrol flying-boats was very grave. Despite its association with the Royal Flying Corp's landplane force, the Royal Aircraft Factory sought to alleviate the flying-boat

shortage and the CE.1 was the result. Work under W.S. (later Sir William) Farren commenced in June 1917 and after a rapid programme the first of two prototypes (N97 and N98) travelled to Hamble for tests. N97 made its first flight in January 1918, piloted by Farren himself.

The CE.1 was a tandem two-seat 46ft-span biplane of similar general layout to the pre-war *Bat Boats*, though of course very much more substantial, and was powered by a 230hp RAF.3a pusher engine driving a four-bladed propeller. The hull was a planked, single-step arrangement, the aft portion featuring a concave underside, with a stern-mounted water rudder. The cockpits were extensively glazed, the pilot occupying the rear position, and three gun mountings were installed, one at the bow and two between the cockpits, one on either side. The folding wings were bolted to the hull and equipped with bomb-racks. The single fin and rudder were supported on booms, and were symmetrical about the tailplane.

Following the early flights of N97 modifications were made to the control surfaces, engine installation and radiator shutters. Official trials with the first example began at Grain during April 1918 and in the following month the aircraft was used to verify in full-scale the results of experiments into porpoising carried out by the National Physical Laboratory using model hulls. However, the performance of the CE.1 was assessed as inferior to the F-Boats then coming into service (though better than the Short 184 floatplanes used widely by the RNAS at the time) and so only the prototypes were built.

The second RAF Coastal Experimental 1, N98, employed a 260hp Sunbeam Maori and was fitted with Wireless/ Telegraphy equipment. It arrived at Grain for appraisal during April 1918 and travelled to Westgate in the following January; via a short sojourn at Yarmouth, by June it had joined 219 Squadron at Westgate. The aircraft sits on a double-wheeled chassis and shows its unusual tapering rear hydrodynamic portion. *(Fleet Air Arm Museum)*

Concurrently with the CE.1 programme, Norman Thompson, Supermarine, J. Samuel White of Cowes and Blackburn at Leeds were all involved with prototype *Baby* single-seat flying-boat scouts. These were a response to the Admiralty Department's Specification N.1(b) issued by the Air Board in April 1917, which called for a small tractor or pusher floatplane or flying-boat to act as an escort to the RNAS patrol flying-boats. Top speed required was 85 knots, with a ceiling of at least 10,000ft and endurance of 3 hours, all in laden condition. Armament was to be a single Lewis gun, but with provision for a further such weapon above the top plane. Folding wings for shipboard storage were also specified. The requirement was intended to yield a replacement for Sopwith's earlier *Baby* seaplane.

Supermarine's response was a pusher biplane of 30ft 6in span with forward-folding wings, designed by F.J. Hargreaves. The aircraft employed a two-step Linton Hope hull form with an open cockpit, derived from the AD Flying Boat, together with a small fin mounting an inverted camber tailplane at its top, well clear of interference from the water. It was powered by a 200hp Hispano-Suiza. The first Supermarine N1.B, N59, was flown in February 1918 by Flight Lieutenant Goodwin before undergoing trials at Grain during April. Performance was found to be a very fast 116 mph at sea level and later, with a 200 hp Sunbeam Arab, the service ceiling was determined as 10,700ft. The original protruding prow was subsequently modified to a smoother profile. A second example, N60, travelled to Grain in the form of spares while a third, N61, was not completed.

Curiously, in view of the requirement for a single-seater, Norman Thompson's offering to N.1(b) was a tandem two-seater. Again the aircraft was a biplane pusher, with an equal span of 34ft 3in, the folding wing employing four ailerons. A single-stepped hull was adopted, derived from that of the NT.2B, though it featured open cockpits, while the tail layout departed from previous designs with a slimmer fin

Supermarine N.1B N59 at Grain, where it arrived for performance trials in April 1918. It later travelled to Felixstowe for further appraisal. N59 was initially flown without the small fin above the tailplane. The object that looks like a large water rudder is actually the port wing float. (*J.M. Bruce/G.S. Leslie Collection*)

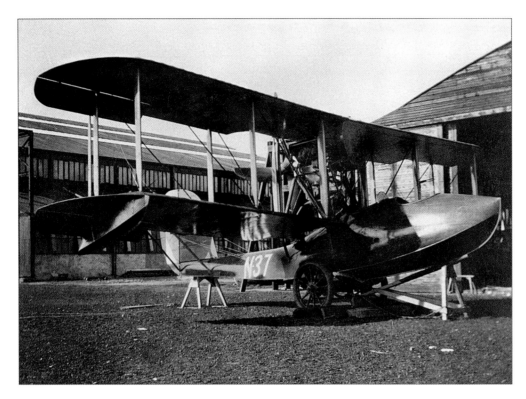

Norman Thompson's TNT N.1B N37 at the company's Middleton premises. The fin is a departure from previous Norman Thompson types and the hull has a prominent flare to the chine. The tandem windscreens are apparent while again a pusher arrangement is adopted, giving the engine and propeller protection from spray. The aircraft was damaged in a crash-landing in January 1918 while based at Grain but was not struck off until the following June. *(J.M. Bruce/G.S. Leslie Collection)*

Blackburn's N.1B was not completed, but the contemporary model reveals a graceful biplane pusher with a slim two-step hull. Unlike the Supermarine offering, the Blackburn tail unit was of biplane configuration; Harris Booth had joined Blackburn from the Admiralty's Air Department and perhaps this was a reflection of his previous approach with the AD Flying Boat. *(BAE SYSTEMS)*

(viewed from the side) than hitherto. The aircraft was initially powered by a 150hp Hispano-Suiza, later replaced by the 200hp version. A single prototype, N37, was ordered in April 1917 and became known as the TNT – the Tandem Norman Thompson. It was first flown during October by the American freelance test-pilot Clifford Prodger and the company's assessment of its performance was very favourable. N37 travelled to Grain for trials in December but was damaged in a crash-landing during January 1918; once repaired, it resumed tests. Unfortunately the evaluators did not share Norman Thompson's uncritical view of the TNT; although the makers had alleged a top speed of 108mph that claim could not be proved at Grain, and the aircraft also took a long time to unstick. N37 remained the sole example of the TNT and on 31 December 1917 Percy Beadle left Norman Thompson for the Gosport Aviation Company.

J. Samuel White's Wight Triplane flying-boat came from a prominent and long-established ship-building company that also designed and manufactured aircraft; their usual waterborne types were floatplanes, though flying-boats had been contemplated as paper projects. In December 1916 White's had received an order for one small experimental triplane single-seat fighter flying-boat serialled N14, to the Admiralty's early Type 4 requirement, and the company felt that this machine could also answer the demands of Specification N.1(b). Powered by a tractor 130hp Clerget rotary engine, the Triplane was of similar general configuration to its rivals, apart from its wing form. An attempt at flight was made in June 1917 but the machine failed to leave the water; later that month it did become airborne but its hull design drew criticism. Modifications to the hull bottom were carried out and further trials took place in September. However, the test-pilot (possibly Marcus Manton) concluded that the Triplane was dangerous to fly and the contract was terminated. White's parallel Wight Biplane flying-boat project to Specification N.1(b) withered at the same time and was never built, though the serial N15 was possibly allocated.

The Blackburn Aeroplane & Motor Company Ltd had been registered in June 1914 and produced both landplanes and waterborne aircraft, including the large GP Seaplane and its land-based equivalent, the Kangaroo torpedo-carrying anti-submarine type. The company had also built the Sopwith *Baby* under licence. Blackburn's response to N.1(b) was a beautifully streamlined biplane of 34ft 10in span, intended to employ a 200hp Hispano-Suiza pusher tucked under the upper centre-section, and with a Linton Hope-type two-step hull. Again the wings were designed to fold, while jettisonable wheels were considered to permit take-offs from land. A Lewis gun was intended to be mounted on the fore-decking ahead of the pilot. Construction of the first prototype, N56, was slow, and by November 1918 it was still only partly completed; when the war ended the *Baby* programme came to a halt. The hull of N56 was stored while two further examples, N57 and N58, at sub-assembly stage, were disposed of.

-oOo-

Norman Thompson experienced further frustration with their N.2C design to the Admiralty Department's Specification N.2(c) issued in April 1917 for a medium-

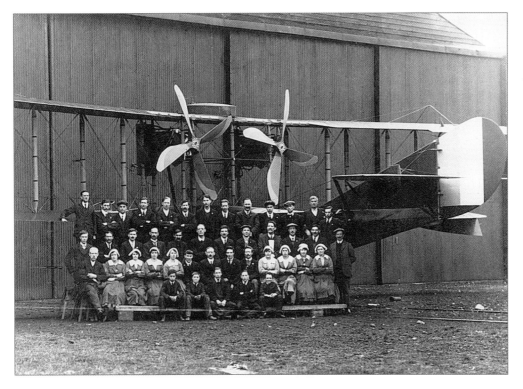

The sole Norman Thompson N.2C at the Middleton site, with members of the workforce doing their best to disguise its appearance. Following the broadening of the rear step after its initial trials, handling was somewhat improved though porpoising and tail-heaviness were still marked. N82 was allotted to Grain in October 1918 but in the following month trials were cancelled and the aircraft was deleted at the end of the year.
(J.M. Bruce/G.S. Leslie Collection)

sized twin-engined flying-boat. Regarded by the company as a replacement for the NT.4 and NT.4A, the N.2C employed the wings of the earlier aircraft, combined with a revised rudder featuring a shorter stern-post than the previous types. It was somewhat lighter than the NT.4, while the two-step hull was designed along the comparatively simple lines of the Porte/Felixstowe cross-braced box-girder arrangement. The specification called for the use of two 200hp Hispano engines, but the company felt this would be inadequate, proposing instead a tri-motor layout. The Admiralty rejected that idea and eventually two pusher 200hp Sunbeam Arabs were adopted, driving four-bladed propellers. A contract for two prototypes (N82 and N83) was placed with Norman Thompson during November 1917, the month in which the first F.2A was delivered.

N82 commenced trials on 1 August 1918 but the water suction around the aft portion of its hull was so great that the aircraft rose to a stalling attitude before wholly leaving the surface. The rear step was deepened in an effort to improve matters, but it was noted that the weight was 600lb in excess of the design estimates. On 16 October the N.2C was tested again but was found to suffer from marked porpoising at speed, as well as being tail-heavy in flight. The Armistice ended official interest in the type and the second example was never completed.

John Porte's last and most ambitious design to see the light of day was the Felixstowe F.4 Fury triplane flying-boat powered by five 325hp Rolls-Royce Eagle VIIs (later Eagle VIIIs). The 123ft-span Fury was the largest British aeroplane of its day and quickly acquired the nickname 'Super Baby'. The hull employed two steps while a simple four-longeron cross-braced box-girder structure was again adopted, planked diagonally with two layers of cedar over an inner longitudinal skin. The keelson and floors were built-up lattice-girder structures and the bottom was covered by three layers of cedar and mahogany to a thickness of half an inch. To avoid the splitting that had occurred at the hull joints in some earlier F-Boats, the planking was steamed and bent around the chines, obviating the need for any jointing at those points. Accommodation consisted of a side-by-side cockpit, a bow position, and a dorsal position, for the flight engineer; defensive armament was intended to be at least four machine-guns while a substantial bomb-load was also envisaged.

The wing form of the F.4 consisted of upper and central wings of equal span with balanced ailerons, and a lower wing shorter by one bay. The central wing mounted the five engines arranged as two tractors, and three pushers two of which were positioned in the slipstream of the tractors, while a long trailing-edge cut-out accommodated the four-bladed pusher propellers. The tail arrangement was novel too, a large raked central fin mounting a biplane tailplane and incorporating three rudders, a pair between the tailplanes and a third smaller example above them at the top of the fin. All control surfaces were fitted with small motors acting as servos as it was considered that their operation might be physically beyond the pilot in some circumstances, but the aircraft proved remarkably light to handle and the motors were removed.

Serialled N123, the Fury's first flight took place from Felixstowe on Armistice Day with John Porte at the controls. Though all-up weight was 24,000lb, at an

The Felixstowe F.4 Fury, the so-called 'Super Baby', dwarfs its admirers at Felixstowe. The original tail configuration is in situ, with the small central fin visible at the top of the rudder. The aircraft later acquired a camouflage scheme, subsequently replaced with a white hull finish. In the background are two F-Boats and in the foreground the wreckage of a third. A large model of the F.4 survives in the Southampton Hall of Aviation, fitted with the later tail. *(Fleet Air Arm Museum)*

overload of 28,000lb, both air and water characteristics remained very favourable. The aircraft was later flown at 33,000lb, and subsequently with twenty-four passengers, fuel for seven hours and ballast of 5,000lb – no mean feat! The hull bottom received some modifications and a third step was added temporarily. The tail was also revised, permanently, to a more conventional layout of three fins and rudders with a biplane tailplane. The F.4 was spruced up when its sober hull was painted white. Though the design received no production order, N123 continued test-flying; plans were started to fly the aircraft across the Atlantic during June 1919 but funding failed to materialise. Joining 4 Communications Squadron at Felixstowe, on 11 August the Fury crashed during take-off with loss of life at the start of an intended flight to Africa.

Though several other British flying-boat types were commenced before the end of the First World War, only the Phoenix P.5 Cork appeared prior to the Armistice. With the success of the Linton Hope hull employed by the AD Flying Boat, in terms of both construction and eventually water performance, the Admiralty pressed ahead with the design of a twin-engined machine roughly the size of an F-Boat, the stimulus for which was the Air Board's issue of Specification N.3(b) in April 1917. Two hulls designed by Linton Hope were manufactured by May, Harden & May – the Hope-type hull required a labour force experienced in boat-building. The completed hulls were passed to the Phoenix Dynamo Manufacturing Co. for the attachment of flight surfaces and engines under a contract placed with that company in November 1917. The serials N86 and N87 were allocated to the prototypes.

By the time the hulls were under way, Phoenix had gained experience of aircraft manufacture through production of F.3s and F.5s, among other types. In November 1917 the company formed its own design team. The hulls supplied to Phoenix were not identical. The first was referred to as the P.5, featuring a planing surface extending aft to the rear step, and the second as the P.5A, with a shorter planing bottom not extending past the main step but including a second step attached directly to the hull. Phoenix adopted the designation, applying P.5 to N86 and P.5A to N87, but in the event the P.5 hull was used in the construction of N87 and the P.5A in that of N86.

Accommodation within the hull consisted of a bow position intended to house a Scarff-mounted Lewis gun, tandem open cockpits featuring dual-control and a flight engineer's position under the wings; aft of the wings were two apertures for waist weapons. Flight structure and engine installation design was by William Oke Manning, lately of the Air Department. The wings were of unequal span, the upper with marked dihedral and fitted with ailerons, the lower bereft of either, its main spar passing through the top of the hull. Wing-tip floats were fitted which were identical to those of the F.3. The engines, cowled 360hp Eagle VIIIs, were mounted between the wings, fed from three prominent gravity tanks positioned below the upper wing centre-section. The tail unit consisted of a single large fin and rudder with a high-mounted tailplane.

N86 was completed in July 1918, Clifford Prodger making the maiden flight on 4 August from No. 2 Marine Acceptance Depot at Brough on the River Humber,

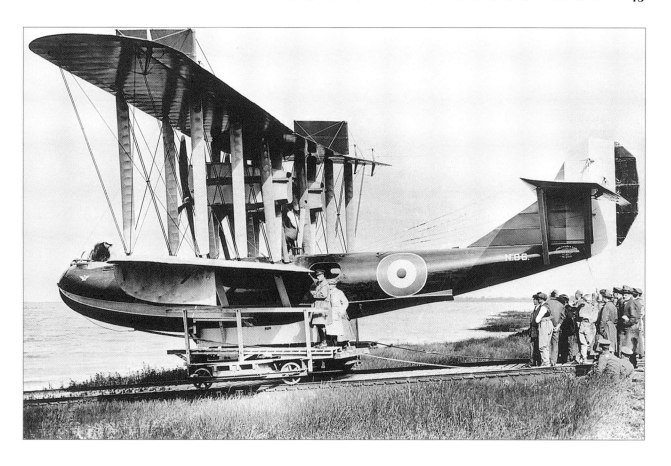

which prior to being commandeered had been used by Blackburn and by the Phoenix-built F.3s and F.5s. By that time the aircraft was known as the Cork I. Testing at Grain later that month revealed a better performance than the F.3's, with generally good airborne and hydrodynamic properties. However, the load water line was high which led to the wings of the second example being mounted just above the hull. Additionally, the rudder of N86 was enlarged.

In a comparison between N86 and the prototype F.5, N90, it was found that the Cork was superior in terms of speed, climb and range, and could carry a heavier load. The construction of the Cork II, N87, was delayed by modifications to the P.5 hull but the aircraft eventually flew on 28 March 1919. Despite the very promising performance, again the Armistice put paid to any prospect of production. In 1919 the Phoenix aviation department was shut, by which time a civil ten-passenger version of the Cork, the P.8, existed in plan form and Manning was contemplating an extraordinarily large 100,000lb civil flying-boat project named the Eclectic which was never built. Shortly after receiving 450hp Napier Lion engines and becoming the Cork III, during September 1922 N87 was wrecked in a gale at Newhaven following a forced landing. N86 continued tests at Grain and Felixstowe until mid-1924.

Phoenix P.5 Cork I N86 on the Brough slipway during the summer of 1918. Following eventful company trials during which it was holed on rocks but successfully recovered, and given an enlarged rudder, N86 passed to the Marine Aircraft Experimental Station at Grain on 24 August. Superior in a number of ways to the F-Boats then in service, N86 was considered a little nose-heavy and still somewhat under-ruddered, but water performance was praised. *(J.M. Bruce/ G.S. Leslie Collection)*

3 THE 1920s

Hard Times

When the war ended, many military aircraft production contracts were abruptly cancelled or much reduced and industry rapidly cut back its aviation interests, while the Royal Air Force suddenly found itself with thousands of unwanted aeroplanes. Attempts were made to sell the surplus and some types joined foreign air forces but few had appeal in the new civil market, which in any case was negligible at first. For some manufacturers circumstances were too much to bear; by 1924 Airco, Alliance, BAT, Nieuport, Martinsyde, Sage and Sopwith had either closed down or been absorbed or restructured, along with Norman Thompson from the flying-boat community, which was taken over by Handley Page during 1919, and Phoenix, which subsequently re-emerged as a component of English Electric.

Of the surplus flying-boats only a handful went into civilian use. The NT.2B was offered by Handley Page's Aircraft Disposal Company for £1,100 complete with Wolseley Viper engine, but only G-EAQO became British-registered (eventually travelling to Peru), though others went to Canada, Estonia, Japan and Norway. NT.4A N2155 briefly became G-EAOY but the registration was cancelled in October 1920. Various Felixstowe aircraft assumed civil identities; two H.16s and nine F.3s travelled to Canada as part of the Imperial Gift to that Dominion, while a tenth F.3 became G-CYEP. In April 1920 one example passed to Portugal as C-PAON. Others

F.2A N4567 travelled to Chile after the First World War, assuming the identity *Guardiamarina Zanartu* after a Chilean midshipman who died on 3 March 1921 while attempting to save a friend from a burning DH9 that crashed at El Bosque Military Air School at Santiago. It was the first flying-boat to be seen in South America. (*Bryan Ribbans*)

joined the British register as G-EAQT and G-EBDQ, the former fitted out as a luxury air yacht and travelling to Botany Bay, but subsequently ignored and scrapped. A single F.2A (ex-N4567) was shipped to Chile.

In November 1919 Percy Beadle left the Gosport Aviation Company for S.E. Saunders. His place was briefly taken by Lieutenant-Colonel John Porte, who teamed up with his old associate Herman Volk, by then general manager of Gosport. F.5 N4634, civilianised by Gosport and allocated construction number G.6/100, was

John Porte's Gosport G.9 featured in the firm's literature but never saw the light of day. The company was referred to in this advertisement as the Gosport Aircraft and Engineering Co., a change from its earlier title. The aircraft was designed to be powered by four 450hp Napier Lion engines in tractor/pusher pairs. *(Fawley Historians)*

A late production Felixstowe F.5, N4836, on the hardstanding. This aircraft was built by Short Brothers and first flew from Rochester on 20 January 1920. It served with the Air Pilotage Flight at Calshot between December 1922 and at least October 1923 before eventually being struck off. *(Author's Collection)*

The sixth F.5 of fifteen built by Shorts for the Japanese Navy, seen on Rochester's slipway on 10 May 1920. These aircraft marked the onset of the purchase of various British flying-boats by the Japanese, both civil and military. The final three F.5s for Japan employed Napier Lion engines and one was fitted with a 1-pounder shell-firing anti-shipping gun. *(Short Brothers via Bryan Ribbans)*

registered to the company as Gosport Flying-Boat G-EAIK in August 1919. It was flown by Lieutenant-Colonel R. Hope-Vere at the Amsterdam Air Traffic Exhibition, while an FBA was displayed on Gosport's stand there, but G-EAIK reverted to its previous identity in August 1920. Meanwhile Porte drafted several large flying-boats, the biggest of which was the Gosport G.9, a 29,000 lb triplane derived from the Fury. The aircraft was intended to carry mail and freight, as well as twelve passengers, but it was never built; in October 1919 its designer died aged just 35. Despite his worsening health John Porte had exerted a profound influence on the development and operation of the military flying-boat. In September 1921 Britain's reduced RAF flying-boat force was standardised on two of his aircraft, the F.2A and the F.5, while the F.3 was declared obsolete. The American-built 400hp Liberty-powered F.5L became the United States Navy's standard flying-boat during the early 1920s. The Japanese Navy purchased fifteen F.5s manufactured by Short Brothers, deliveries commencing in August 1921, and the Aichi Tokei Denki Co. of Nagoya built more than fifty under licence in a factory planned by Shorts, the aircraft remaining in service until 1929.

It was a time of high unemployment, economic depression and industrial unrest, creating a difficult balance in the aviation industry (and elsewhere) between preserving the core labour forces, staying at the forefront of technology, finding the funds with which to do so, and exercising careful commercial judgement, all in the face of a government whose support was patchy to say the least. During 1921 a Committee on National Expenditure chaired by Sir Eric Geddes was formed to make recommendations on future public spending reductions, which included allocations to the Services. Despite the grim situation, however, several new flying-boat types were built during the immediate post-war years in an effort to capture the surviving markets.

Late in 1919 an amphibian flying-boat emerged from the aviation department of Vickers Ltd, then led by Rex Pierson. Vickers' first hulled type, it was the first British aircraft designed from the outset as an amphibian, and it was intended for operation particularly in remote and undeveloped areas. Built at Weybridge, named the Viking I and registered G-EAOV, it first flew from Brooklands in November 1919. The Viking I was a two-bay 37ft span pusher biplane powered by a 275hp Rolls-Royce Falcon III. Its enclosed cockpit featured dual-control and cabin seating was for four. The hull skinning was of Consuta – Vickers had acquired a controlling financial interest in Saunders during 1918. A biplane tailplane with twin fins and rudders was adopted. Unfortunately the hull was found to be prone to hydrodynamic instability and porpoising. On 18 December 1919 G-EAOV crashed in fog near Rouen en route to the Paris Air Show; its pilot (and Vickers' chief test pilot) Sir John Alcock of transatlantic fame was killed.

The Mk II Viking also appeared in 1919 and embodied several changes. It was equipped with the more powerful Rolls-Royce Eagle VIII, its hull profile was revised along the bows and planing bottom, and a water rudder was installed. The wheel track was widened, wing area increased and a third fin and rudder added. Registered G-EASC, the Viking II first flew at Cowes in June 1920 in the hands of Vickers test-pilot Captain Stan Cockerell. It visited that year's Olympia Aero Show and in August went to the Antwerp Seaplane Trials, which it won.

Vickers Viking I G-EAOV shows its lines. The single-step hull featured a narrow beam and almost vertical slab sides, intended to simplify production, but in the event only one example was built. The narrow track undercarriage retracted forwards to mid-hull height. *(J.M. Bruce/G.S. Leslie Collection)*

The sole Sea Lion I G-EALP at rest in Bournemouth Bay at the time of the 1919 Schneider Trophy Race in September. The aircraft wears race no. 5. Derived from the Supermarine N.1B, the maximum speed of the Sea Lion was 147mph compared with the *Baby*'s 116mph. *(Author's Collection)*

During 1919 Supermarine produced their Sea Lion I, developed by F.J. Hargreaves from the N.1B *Baby* and possibly using the hull of the unfinished N61. The Sea Lion was of similar configuration but was powered by the 450hp Napier Lion IA, from which it partly took its name and which had one of the best power/weight ratios of any aero engine at that time. It was a 35ft unequal span single-seat pusher biplane, and the fin and rudder resembled those of the N.1B but were larger.

The Sea Lion I, registered G-EALP, entered the first post-war international Schneider Trophy race for flying-boats and seaplanes, an event of great prestige that as it developed did an enormous amount to stimulate the development of both airframes and engines. That said, the 1919 race held at Bournemouth was memorable mainly for its bungled organisation and the poor weather. Fog and administrative misunderstandings delayed the start, which was attended by aircraft from Britain, France and Italy. Squadron Leader Basil Hobbs in G-EALP managed to take off safely despite some nearby rowing boats, but the limited visibility caused him such concern that he temporarily alighted offshore rather than risk flying blind into the nearby cliffs. While taking off once more though, the Sea Lion hit a floating obstacle that holed its hull and on landing by the Boscombe Pier course marker boat it quickly filled with water. Hobbs was safely picked up but the aircraft sank partially. It was salved and later returned to Woolston but never flew again, and the race itself was declared void.

At that time too, Supermarine resuscitated the AD Flying Boat, having purchased stored examples from the Admiralty in early 1919. Passenger seating for three or four was added, as well as a water rudder. The reworked aircraft employed the 160hp Beardmore and was named the Channel; all-up weight was 3,400lb. The first to appear was G-EAED (ex-N1529), whose Certificate of Airworthiness (C of A) was

Supermarine Channel N1711 became G-EAEK. N1711 was from the original batch of ten AD Flying Boats bought by Supermarine after the war, and flew until February 1921 when it was scrapped. The hull roundel has been painted out as the aircraft, seen at Woolston, undergoes transformation to a civil type. It bears the name *Sheldrake* on the bow, a title shared with a later Supermarine design. *(Author's Collection)*

issued on 23 July 1919. As well as providing joyrides, a passenger service was commenced between Bournemouth and Southampton. The company also applied to operate a cross-Channel service from Bournemouth to Cherbourg, Le Havre and St Malo; in the meantime, during August a service began between Southampton and the Isle of Wight, all routes operating as the weather allowed. The French route ended in October owing to lack of public support, but in May 1920 Supermarine sold three Channels to Det Norske Luftfartreideri (DNL) A/S of Christiania (now Oslo). These were G-EAEH, G-EAEI and G-EAEL, which assumed Norwegian identities N9, N10 and N11 and arrived during August for the new Bergen-Haugesund-Stavanger mail-carrying route. During mid-1920 the company supplied four Channels (F-38, F-40, F-42 and F-44) to the Norwegian government, after a competition in which Vickers' Viking proposal was seen off; F-40 remained in service until March 1928. A further success that year was the departure of three Channels (G-EAGE, G-EAEJ and G-EAEF) to Bermuda to provide an inter-island service, flying for the Bermuda & West Atlantic Aviation Company on charter and pleasure flights. Fitted with a bow camera port, two more Channels were used to survey the Orinoco Delta in Venezuela.

Still pursuing military developments, Supermarine produced a single-seat fighter flying-boat, the Sea King I, the design of which commenced in October 1919. The aircraft first flew early in the following year, attaining a maximum speed of 110 mph. The Sea King was also derived from the N.1B, a 35ft 6in span biplane again employing Linton Hope hull principles and powered by a 160hp Beardmore pusher. It was exhibited at Olympia, where no sales were made, but the aircraft was retained as an engine test-bed, being fitted with a 240hp Siddeley Puma which yielded a maximum speed of 121mph. A Napier Lion-powered amphibious version was also contemplated, for which a top speed of 141mph was estimated.

The autumn of 1920 witnessed one of the few incentives provided by the government to British civil aviation at that time, in the form of an Air Ministry Civil Aeroplane Competition offering prizes totalling £64,000. The commercial passenger waterborne class was entered by Fairey, Vickers, Saunders and Supermarine. The competition took place at Felixstowe and Martlesham Heath over September and October 1920. Of the marine entrants the Fairey was a floatplane while the Vickers and Supermarine offerings were derivations from existing flying-boats. The Saunders contender, however, was new. Vickers' entrant was the Viking III, G-EAUK, which incorporated further changes from earlier Marks; its powerplant was the 450hp Napier Lion, while the nose was lengthened, the water rudder amended, the wing area again increased and a small central fin added to counter the increased torque.

Supermarine's contender was the Commercial Amphibian G-EAVE, the first aircraft for which 26-year-old Reginald Joseph Mitchell had overall design authority. Mitchell had joined the company in 1917 as personal assistant to Hubert Scott-Paine; following the departure of F.J. Hargreaves in 1919 he was appointed chief designer. Though derived from the AD Flying Boat, the Commercial was much heavier at 5,700lb all-up. The aircraft was designed and built hurriedly for the competition. The hull form was once more based around the Linton Hope pattern with two steps grafted to the underside, and a distinctive boat-like prow was adopted. The open cockpit was positioned close to the wing and passenger accommodation for two (the

Supermarine's partially assembled Sea King I taking part in the parade during the 1920 Woolston Hospital Carnival. It was also exhibited at that year's Olympia Aero Show, where it was the only single-seat flying-boat fighter on display. The forward hull form is reminiscent of the profile adopted by the final Channel. *(Author's Collection)*

The Sea King I at Olympia during July 1920. The overall appearance of the aircraft was much akin to the earlier N.1B. To the right is a Channel, while the Supermarine hoarding is visible to the left. Despite its intended military role the Sea King is seen here unarmed. *(Author's Collection)*

Vickers Viking III on the Thames riverbank, wearing its naval testing serial N147 as well as its civil registration G-EAUK; its name is painted on the bows. The main undercarriage retraction mechanism is displayed, as is the slim hull form again adopted by Vickers without flare at the chine. The photograph was taken at the time of the trials between London and Paris to determine the feasibility of a passenger service. *(Author's Collection)*

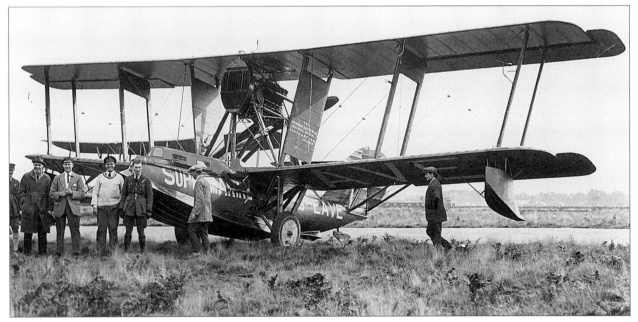

Supermarine's Commercial Amphibian G-EAVE showing off its boat-like bow profile and amphibious capability. The forward hull area was given over to a small passenger cabin, while the cockpit was situated further aft; the pilot's headrest is just visible. The combined water-rudder and tail skid can also be seen. *(Author's Collection)*

minimum number permitted under the competition) was in the enclosed and glazed forward portion. Power came from a 350hp Eagle VIII pusher mounted between the unequal span, folding biplane wings. The undercarriage consisted of a steel strut, manually operated main arrangement mounted below the inner inter-plane struts under the lower wing centre-section, and a combined water rudder-cum-tail skid. Overall span was 50ft and the maximum speed just over 90mph.

With its wartime experience of flying-boat construction, Saunders viewed the competition as a good starting point for its own waterborne aircraft. Designed by Percy Beadle assisted by chief draughtsman H.W. Gravenell, also an ex-Norman Thompson employee, and A.W. Prickett, together with hull designer Sydney Porter, the company's Kittiwake was of innovative and complex construction. Its hull was a two-step Consuta-covered structure with a shallow vee-bottom into which the main, narrow track undercarriage members retracted, and equipped with a water rudder/tail wheel at the stern post. Surmounting the hull was the cockpit, fully enclosed and with partial dual-control, while above that was the enclosed cabin, seating seven. The high aspect-ratio Consuta-covered wings of just over 68ft-span incorporated inter-plane ailerons and an unusual camber-changing mechanism in the leading and trailing-edges intended to offset high loadings. The lower wing was attached to the bottom of the middle hull tier and braced to the lower hull with two pairs of struts, while the upper wing was secured to the passenger cabin and blended with its upper surface. The tail unit too was novel: an adjustable incidence tailplane with divided elevators, three fins and a central rudder. Power came from two 200hp ABC Wasp II engines mounted on the inner (metal) inter-plane struts. Unfortunately its new features delayed the appearance of the Kittiwake.

The Viking III narrowly won the competition together with a prize of £10,000, while the £4,000 second prize was doubled and awarded to the Commercial Amphibian, the Ministry applauding its good performance despite employing a lower-powered engine than its rival. The Fairey III floatplane (G-EALQ) took the £2,000 third prize. The competition was notable for the good humour among its participants, and the manufacturers were allowed to use their own pilots during the tests. Unfortunately during October the Commercial Amphibian crashed; regarded as a stepping stone, it was not rebuilt.

The Kittiwake finally made its first flight on 19 September from Cowes, piloted by Norman Macmillan and registered G-EAUD. Unfortunately, shortly after take-off the leading-edge camber mechanism collapsed almost entirely and the aircraft stalled; on landing it hit a rock and was holed, sinking partially. Following repairs further flights were attempted but the aircraft refused to leave the water. It was found that the port engine was a subcontracted production example delivering only around 150hp, while the starboard engine was of pre-production build, virtually hand-made and giving the promised power. Additional problems were also identified; the ailerons were ineffective at small angles while the undercarriage was found to fail under static load. Six months passed while modifications to G-EAUD were completed. In March 1921 the Kittiwake flew again, this time piloted by F. Warren Merriam, and it performed desultory trials until the summer when it crashed and was extensively damaged in the hands of an Air Ministry pilot. No orders were received

and during July 1921 the Kittiwake was scrapped. The aircraft had cost around £10,000 to build. In March Vickers had disposed of their interest in Saunders and later that year Cowes' aviation department closed; Beadle left the company.

Supermarine sold further Channels during that year. G-NZAI travelled to the New Zealand Flying School, operating between Auckland and Onerahi. In July it became the first aircraft to visit Fiji and survived until around 1926, its hull subsequently being employed as a boat. Three Channel IIs passed to the Japanese Navy; the later mark was powered by the 240hp Siddeley Puma while wing-floats and hull lines were slightly revised. Another, numbered 46, was purchased by the Royal Swedish Navy to evaluate the flying-boat type for naval use. The final Channel II passed to the Chilean Naval Air Service in 1922, a three-seater intended for armed reconnaissance missions.

By December 1921 Supermarine had completed their Sea King II flying-boat fighter. The Sea King II employed a 300hp Hispano-Suiza and was derived from the Sea King I; again a two-bay pusher configuration was adopted, with a single-seat two-step Linton Hope hull. The tail was more conventional than that of the original Sea King, having a prominent fin and rudder together with a lowered tailplane. An amphibian undercarriage was fitted similar to that of the Commercial Amphibian, together with a water rudder/tail skid. Its first flight took place early in 1922 and the Sea King II was found to be unusually manoeuvrable, inherently stable and free from porpoising.

Following their success in the Ministry's competition, during February 1921 Vickers began trials with Viking III G-EAUK to evaluate the possibility of a passenger service connecting London and Paris using the Thames and the Seine. The journey took around 2½ hours, which was considered reasonable. G-EAUK subsequently passed to the Royal Navy for deck-handling trials on HMS *Argus*, serialled N147. The trials passed favourably and the company commenced a further version, the Viking IV. This

Saunders Kittiwake G-EAUD gets off from the Medina on its first flight, which ended inauspiciously following a collapse of the wing camber-changing gear. The three-tier hull arrangement gave the aircraft a most unusual appearance. Its gravity tanks protrude prominently above the upper wing surface while the interplane ailerons lent a further novel dimension. The Kittiwake never found a buyer and G-EAUD remained the sole example. *(Author's Collection)*

One Channel II was purchased by the Swedish Navy; seen here at Woolston, it was subsequently coded 46. Its modified bow area bears a Scarff-mounted machine-gun. Sadly this aircraft was lost in a fatal accident soon after delivery. *(Author's Collection)*

Supermarine's final Channel was supplied to the Chilean Naval Air Service and was later allotted the identity 8. The forward portion of the hull was substantially revised from previous layouts. Again the aircraft was equipped with a bow-mounted machine-gun; it bears Chilean national markings. *(Author's Collection)*

Vickers' Viking IV F-ADBL was delivered to the French Navy in September 1921. Adopting a commercial configuration despite the identity of its buyer, it was, however, readily adaptable for military duties. F-ADBL was the first Viking IV manufactured; it was referred to as the Type 54 and featured an enclosed cockpit although some Viking IVs employed the open variety. *(Author's Collection)*

Viking V N157 seen in a Middle Eastern setting. The aircraft arrived at Hinaidi for testing during June 1923. Following rather brief trials it was cannibalised at Hinaidi to repair the first Viking V, N156, probably around October of that year. *(J.M. Bruce/G.S. Leslie Collection)*

incorporated further refinements: the nose area was made more blunt, the beam increased and the main step moved slightly aft, while the 450hp Lion was retained. The cockpit was generally fully enclosed. Wheel brakes were installed and the span increased to 50ft on most examples; loaded weight rose from 4,545lb to 5,790lb. The Viking IV proved a popular aircraft and twenty-six examples were sold around the world – a counterpoint to the widespread austerity within the industry at that time and a useful diversification from Vickers' land-based aircraft.

The first purchaser was the French Navy, to which one example was delivered in September 1921 as F-ADBL. The Japanese Navy acquired two in May 1921, these operating from the carrier *Hosho*, while a further ten (V201–10) were delivered in early 1922 for service with the Dutch East Indies forces in the Java area. The Russian Trade Delegation purchased one for use around Leningrad while a 360hp Eagle IX-powered version joined Laurentide Air Services of Canada in May 1922 but was considered underpowered. Another, open-cockpit version G-EBED, was initially retained as a demonstrator but was later sold for charter work, subsequently finding employment as an air taxi at a St Moritz sports centre, where it would land on soft snow as a flying-boat and take-off from a hard surface as an amphibian!

During 1922 Vickers prepared a tailored version of the Mk IV. The aircraft, G-EBBZ, was intended for use in a round-the-world flight by Sir Ross Smith, who had previously commanded the famous Australian Vickers Vimy flight. G-EBBZ featured open cockpits and provision for the stowage of stores rather than passenger accommodation. However, on 13 April the aircraft crashed shortly after leaving Vickers' Weybridge site on a test-flight; tragically Smith and his mechanic were killed.

That spring too, two Vikings (N156 and N157) joined the RAF for use in Iraq, to assess the suitability of the amphibian type in such areas. These aircraft were known as Viking Vs though essentially they were Mk IVs around which had been written Air Ministry Specification 2/22, whence the procurement stemmed. It was found that hull clearance on the uneven desert ground was sometimes insufficient, while the makeshift surfaces also gave the undercarriages a stern test. The need was also confirmed for aircraft of metal structure in such climates, to avoid loss of rigging truth inherent in wooden aircraft under such conditions.

During 1923 further orders were received for the Viking IV. The United States Navy bought one as a fleet spotter and the River Plate Aviation Company of Argentina acquired two Eagle-powered commercial variants for a Buenos Aires–Montevideo service. The Argentine Navy received four and the Canadian Air Force two (to which skis were fitted during the winters). The Canadian Vickers subsidiary of the main company subsequently built six examples at Montreal – the first native aircraft constructed for use by the Canadian Air Force.

Schneider Races

Meanwhile, the Schneider Trophy competitions had continued. The 1920 race held at Venice was taken by the Italians in a contest uncluttered by entrants from any other country; the venue for the 1921 race was also Venice, which Italy claimed again under similar circumstances. For the August 1922 race at Naples, however, a French team also entered with two aircraft, and a British team with just one,

Supermarine's Sea Lion II. The other competitors received financial assistance from their governments, but David Lloyd George's administration did not support the race and the Sea Lion was funded privately by Hubert Scott-Paine and Commander James Bird, a co-director at Supermarine, assisted by the loan of a 450hp Lion II engine from Napier's. The French challenge withdrew at the last minute so the Italian and British teams were left to fight it out.

In fact Mitchell's new Sea Lion had started life as the Sea King II, which had not sold since its appearance the previous year. The revised aircraft had its undercarriage removed and the powerplant shrouded within a streamlined fairing, while the wings were narrowed in chord. Registered G-EBAH, it made a few brief test-flights before hurriedly departing for Naples on board the SS *Philomel*, the date of the event having been brought forward at short notice by the Italians.

The race was held on 12 August. The Macchi and Savoia aircraft got away quickly, while the Sea Lion II, piloted by Supermarine test pilot Henri Baird, was a slower starter. However, Baird was able to coax his aircraft to around 160mph, faster than it had ever travelled previously, and managed to pass the Italians by climbing over them and then diving away, thereby attaining a speed of some 200mph. With the Italians unable to catch him, Baird passed the finishing line with another 200mph dive. His average speed around the course had been 145.7mph,

Supermarine's Sea Lion II had been reworked from the Sea King II fighter that had remained at Woolston since the end of 1921. As G-EBAH it formed Henri Baird's winning mount in the August 1922 Schneider Trophy race. The fin and rudder profile was much enlarged from that of the Sea King I, to counter the torque of the more powerful engine. *(Author's Collection)*

and in January 1923 the Fédération Aéronautique Internationale (FAI), the regulator of international aeronautical sport, awarded the Sea Lion II the first World Record in the marine aircraft class, for duration (1hr 34min 51.6sec), the longest distance accomplished (230 miles), the fastest time to cover 100km (28min 41.4sec at 130mph) and the fastest time to cover 200km (57min 37.4sec at 129.4mph). The achievement was even more impressive given the absence of government support and on returning to Southampton the Supermarine team was fêted by the public. The Sea Lion II then passed to the Air Ministry as N170, travelling to Felixstowe for high-speed research.

The 1923 Schneider event came to Cowes and was run from S.E. Saunders' premises over 27–8 September. Entries were received from the United States, France and Britain. The British government again refused to support its national team financially, while the American administration funded its challenge to the tune of around two million dollars. Initially there were three British contenders, but the Sopwith-Hawker G-EAKI force-landed near Weybridge prior to the competition. This left entries from Supermarine and from Blackburn.

Blackburn had announced its intention to enter in March. As a starting point the company dusted off the hull of the N.1B N56 which had lain in store at Brough since late 1918. To this was added a single-bay narrow-gap sesquiplane wing form, mounted to the hull top and strut-braced to its sides. A single, braced tailplane was adopted together with a prominent single fin and rudder. A smoothly cowled 450hp Napier Lion was positioned on top of the upper centre-section,

The Sea Lion III as N170 under the ownership of the Air Ministry. It survived until July 1924, when it was lost at Felixstowe in a fatal accident while in the hands of a pilot unused to its waterborne characteristics; taking off, it bounced, stalled and dived into the sea. *(Author's Collection)*

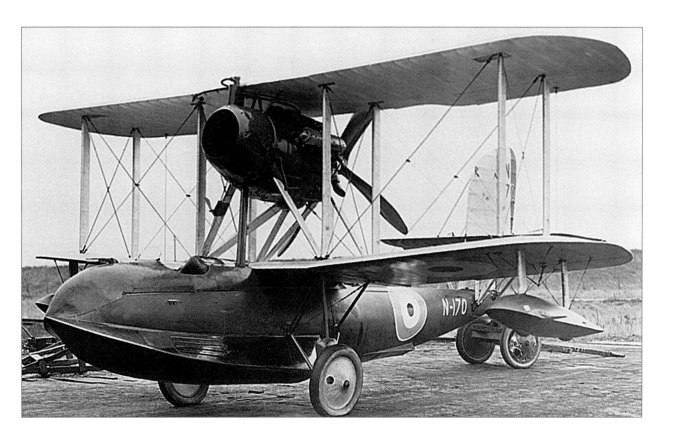

driving a tractor propeller (although the original N.1B had been planned as a pusher). The graceful result was named the Pellet, assuming the identity G-EBHF in July 1923. A launch followed early in September but unfortunately the aircraft was caught by the tide and turned turtle, throwing its would-be test pilot R.W. Kenworthy into the water.

Frantic work ensued to dry and repair the airframe, strip and rebuild the engine, and fit larger wing-floats in time for the competition; subsequently G-EBHF travelled to Hamble by train and was assembled at the Fairey works. His spirits at least undampened, Kenworthy made a first test-flight on 26 September but found the Pellet very nose-heavy in the air; meanwhile the engine over-heated owing to insufficient radiator area and a forced landing was made off Calshot. Modifications to the cooling system were effected overnight and the propeller was changed from the wooden original to a metal type. Next morning, with only minutes to spare before the start of the competition, the Pellet was re-launched and Kenworthy attempted a take-off, but the aircraft began to porpoise severely and then left the water in a semi-stalled state; the starboard wing dropped and struck the water, and the Pellet turned over and sank – fortunately the pilot escaped and was rescued. The aircraft was also recovered but no attempt was made to rebuild it.

British representation was therefore confined to Supermarine's entrant. The company had no new aircraft with which to enter but Sea Lion II N170 was

The sole Blackburn Pellet G-EBHF of course bore a strong resemblance to the earlier unfinished N.1B though with a fundamental difference: it was of tractor layout. It is seen on the Brough slipway shortly before its first launch in September 1923. The aircraft has its Schneider race no. 6 applied to the hull and rudder. (*Author's Collection*)

retrieved from the Ministry, redesigned still further under Mitchell and re-engined with a 525hp Series III Lion pusher in a slippery cowling, yet again thanks to a loan from Napier. The hull bottom profile was revised to reduce resistance, the hull lengthened slightly and the rudder again enlarged though the fin was reduced. Span and wing area were also reduced while all-up weight rose by some 400lb. In this form the aircraft became known as the Sea Lion III. Though its mannerisms on the water necessitated almost jumping aloft at full power following a very short take-off run, the aircraft performed well in the air, achieving around 160mph during trials; before the competition it reverted to its civil identity G-EBAH.

By the day of the race only four contenders survived of the eleven entered: two Curtiss CR-3 biplane floatplanes from the United States Navy, a French CAMS 38 biplane pusher flying-boat and the Sea Lion III, piloted by Henri Baird. The CR-3s started first, followed by Baird and then the French entry though the latter retired after one lap with engine trouble. Despite attaining some 170mph, sadly Baird could not catch either American aircraft and the race was won by Lieutenant D. Rittenhouse at an average speed of 177.38mph, a new world record. None the less, Supermarine had put up a formidable effort against a team that had received such generous financial support. A further Supermarine racing flying-boat design, the Sea

The Sea Lion III was painted with an image of its namesake prior to the 1923 Schneider Race. The device needed some concentration before the representation of the animal became clear to the author! Standing in the cockpit is Henri Baird. Race no. 7 is visible, though the reinstated civil registration, G-EBAH, is mostly out of shot. *(Author's Collection)*

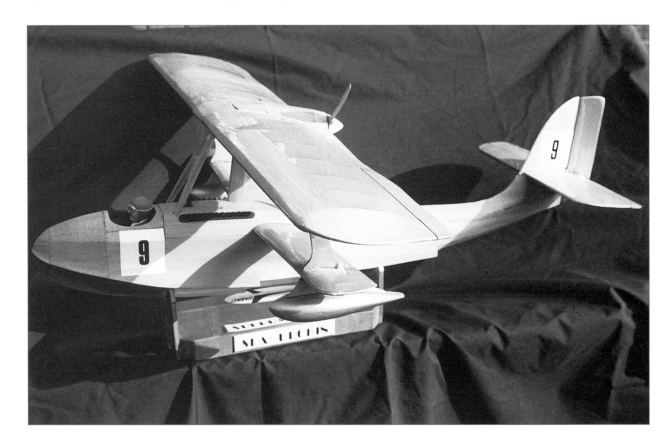

Urchin, powered by a hull-mounted Rolls-Royce Condor, remained confined to paper; subsequent Schneider Trophy races were dominated by floatplanes. Meanwhile the Sea Lion III returned to the Air Ministry, reverting to N170 and flying from Felixstowe.

Large 'Boats, Small Orders

Despite widespread cancellation of aircraft production contracts following the Armistice, some government-funded development work continued. Two new large flying-boats with wartime origins emerged during the early 1920s. The first was the 112ft-span Vickers-Saunders BS.1 Valentia, a response to Admiralty Specification N.3(b) dated April 1917 (later Air Ministry Specification XXX) which sought a long-range twin-engined reconnaissance flying-boat. Three examples were ordered in May 1918, serialled N124, N125 and N126. The aircraft was a cooperative effort between Vickers and Saunders, reflecting their financial association at that time, and the project was led by Rex Pierson. The flight structures were designed and built at Vickers' Barrow-in-Furness site. The all-wooden hull was designed by Saunders and constructed at Cowes; it was a two-step, slab-sided arrangement reminiscent of the Viking layout, which abandoned the flared profiles of the Porte and Linton Hope-style hulls. Just aft of the bow mooring aperture was the dual-control side-by-side cockpit, with a dorsal gunner's position aft of the mainplanes.

The build programme was something of a walk in the park. The first Valentia, N124, finally flew from Cowes on 5 March 1921 in the hands of Stan Cockerell.

Supermarine's Sea Urchin was never built, partly owing to design difficulties with the drive train from the hull-mounted engine to the wing-mounted propeller, but a faithful flying model was constructed by Mr John Thompson, a former Vickers-Armstrong Ltd employee. An electric DD Speed 400 6V motor powers the aircraft, which has a 30in wingspan and an all-up weight of 26oz. The race no. 9 is fictional, for the Sea Urchin was never entered in a race. *(Colin van Geffen)*

Sadly it crashed at Newhaven during its delivery flight to Grain but completed the journey for trials in April. However, upon alighting on 14 June the prow collapsed; the aircraft was dismantled. The second example, N125, force-landed in the sea off Bexhill on 15 March 1922 while on delivery to Grain. N126 did not fly until March 1923 and arrived at Grain for appraisal during the following month; it lacked the aileron and elevator extensions previously employed. Maximum speed was found to be an impressive 105mph. N126 was later used for trials with a Coventry Ordnance Works (COW) gun installation, finally being struck off charge in November 1924. A civil seventeen-passenger version remained a study only.

The other large military flying-boat with wartime origins came from Short Brothers of Rochester and emerged in the spring of 1921. Shorts had moved to the Medway during 1913 and had designed and built many floatplanes, but did not produce flying-boats until the later stages of the war. Horace, the eldest brother, was a dominating personality who showed no interest in flying-boats despite the progress made by Linton Hope and John Porte – but Porte's well-known dislike of the floatplane breed may have influenced Horace Short's own views. The youngest brother, Oswald, was regarded by Horace as insufficiently experienced to be allowed freedom in aeroplane design, though he had made a big contribution to the firm and had (on paper) contemplated large waterborne aircraft schemes of his

Vickers-Saunders BS.1 Valentia N124 at rest in the mouth of the Medina off Cowes. Larger and much heavier than the Felixstowe F.5, the Valentia employed two 650hp Rolls-Royce Condor IA engines set between the wings; weight loaded was 21,300lb. The tail configuration consisted of three rudders and a single central fin, with twin tailplanes. This example was launched on 2 March 1921. *(British Hovercraft Corporation)*

own. When Horace died in April 1917 Oswald took control at Rochester and the company began the manufacture of F.3 and F.5 flying-boats as part of the Ministry of Munitions' accelerated wartime production programmes.

In 1918 that experience led Oswald to tender for the supply of a twin-engined long-range patrol flying-boat, like the Valentia a response to Specification N.3(b). The design took the form of a large 113ft 6in biplane, like the Valentia powered by two Condor IA engines and with an all-up weight of 18,000lb. The hull form, derived from Shorts' experience with the Porte flying-boats, comprised a ply skin over a braced spruce frame. The planing bottom was given a concave flare at each side of the keel, intended to minimise sideways wash and so reduce overspray of the propellers and wing-floats. An open side-by-side cockpit was provided, together with a bow aperture with provision for mounting a 37mm quick-firing anti-submarine gun, and a dorsal gunner's position aft. The tail unit was an equal-span biplane configuration with a large fin and three balanced rudders. A contract for three examples (N120, N121 and N122), named the N.3 Cromarty, was issued just after the Armistice and construction commenced in February 1919.

In the post-war climate only the first aircraft, N120, was completed. It was eventually launched at Rochester during March 1921 and made its first flight on 11 April in the hands of Short's test pilot John Lankester Parker. Testing at Felixstowe began on 21 October, the aircraft first undergoing a period of mooring-out to establish its soakage weight. After initial flight appraisal the tailplane stiffeners were

On the hump . . . Short's Cromarty N120 at speed under test on the Medway. Though a fair bow wave is created, the flight surfaces are well away from the water. Over the the summer of 1921, prior to its appraisal at Felixstowe, modifications were made at Grain to the wingtip floats while the hull received reinforcement, the tail unit bracing was improved and the propellers given metal sleeves.
(Short Brothers)

modified. Climbing trials led to the replacement of the original propellers by those from the damaged Vickers Valentia N124 and later the engines were uprated to improve performance; maximum speed became 95mph.

The Cromarty passed to the RAF's Flying-Boat Development Flight in July 1922, joining F.5 N4038, the Napier Lion-powered F.5 N4839 and the Phoenix Cork III N87. On 4 August the Flight left Grain for the Isles of Scilly, its purpose to gain experience of operating in remote areas without the usual supporting facilities. That said, several vessels also made the journey: parent ship HMS *Ark Royal*, the destroyer HMS *Tintagel* and a floating dock towed by the tug HMS *St Martin*. The Cromarty was temporarily delayed at the last moment while an engine change was effected, but joined the other aircraft at Spithead where refuelling experiments were carried out. Via Portland and Plymouth the Flight arrived at the Isles of Scilly on 21 August, anchoring in the exposed St Mary's Roads. In poor weather and a frequent swell, much data was acquired in operating, maintaining and refuelling the aircraft away from their usual bases, while the value of the floating dock was acknowledged during periods when conditions were suitable for its use. Unfortunately, though, the flying-boats became saturated and corroded, and the unit retreated back to Portland – less one of their number. The Cromarty had taxied on to a shallow reef which holed its hull and it had to be beached at St Mary's. It was found beyond economic repair and was broken up in situ. Plans to construct a civil Cromarty were not pursued.

Two flying-boats from the Fairey company at Hayes, Middlesex, stemmed from the Air Board's wartime Specification N.4 (later RAF Specification XXXIII), though

On the rocks . . . the Cromarty came to grief at St Mary's, principal of the Isles of Scilly, while participating in trials to assess the possibilities of operating remotely without purpose-built facilities. It was later beached facing the sea while the damage was inspected, but was subsequently broken up on the shoreline, useful remains being recovered by HMS *Ark Royal. (Fleet Air Arm Museum)*

contracts were placed after the Armistice in the spring of 1919. N.4 sought a very large four-engined open-sea reconnaissance and fleet cooperation flying-boat, again employing the Condor engine. Fairey had much experience of waterborne aircraft through their Campania, Hamble Baby and III Series floatplanes, but had not previously built a flying-boat. None the less, as the other, more established flying-boat manufacturers were fully engaged in production (though that was very soon to change), the N.4 contracts went to Fairey. In fact, many of the major elements of the aircraft were subcontracted because of shortage of space.

Both aircraft employed Linton Hope-type wooden two-step hulls, the patents to which the company had acquired; Hope had joined Fairey during 1919 though he died during the following year. Construction of the hull for the first aircraft, named Atalanta and serialled N118, was subcontracted to the Gosport Aviation Company, for whom it was designed by Charles Nicholson. Widely spaced flexible web frames were adopted, and light longitudinals used rather than the heavier longitudinals of the earlier Felixstowe flying-boats. It was intended the flight structure be added by the Phoenix Dynamo Manufacturing Co. During 1919 N118's hull travelled by road to Phoenix, where it was stored. The hull of the second Atalanta, N119, was built by May, Harden & May but the aircraft was assembled by Dick, Kerr & Co. at Lytham St Annes. The hull of a variant named the Titania (N129) was constructed by William Fife & Sons on the Clyde but Fairey built the flight structure at Hayes; the two parts finally met at Fairey's Hamble site near Southampton. N129's hull subsequently travelled to Hayes for modifications and then returned to Hamble. The movements of the vast assemblies caused headaches in terms of transport and route planning that must have been reminiscent of some of the F-Boat production programmes.

At the time the Fairey aircraft were the largest flying-boats in the world; with a span of almost 140ft, employing four Condors in tractor and pusher pairs driving four-bladed propellers, the Atalanta weighed in at 30,500lb. An open two-seat side-by-side cockpit was adopted, along with a bow mooring position able to mount a defensive machine-gun, while two apertures were provided for beam guns. Flight surfaces took the form of unequal span biplane mainplanes and a biplane tail unit with three fins and rudders, while offensive weaponry comprised a 1,000lb bomb-load. The Titania incorporated some improvements and was slightly heavier: Condor IIIs were employed (the Atalanta was powered by Condor Is) while Fairey trailing-edge camber-changing flaps were installed on upper and lower mainplanes.

N119 travelled from Lytham to the Marine Aircraft Experimental Unit (MAEU) at Grain by road during January 1921 and was assessed there by Dick, Kerr personnel before trials began on 22 July 1922. Engine runs were performed in November and December, and preliminary taxying runs commenced on 28 May 1923 before a first flight was finally made on 4 July. The MAEU moved to Felixstowe in March 1924 and on 1 April became the Marine Aircraft Experimental Establishment (MAEE); the aircraft also travelled to East Anglia, remaining until 1925 at least. Meanwhile N129 had been transported to Grain in April 1923, being assembled there by staff from Phoenix but thereafter lying fallow. Titania moved to Felixstowe in June 1924 before eventually flying for the first time on 24 July 1925 and remained there until it was

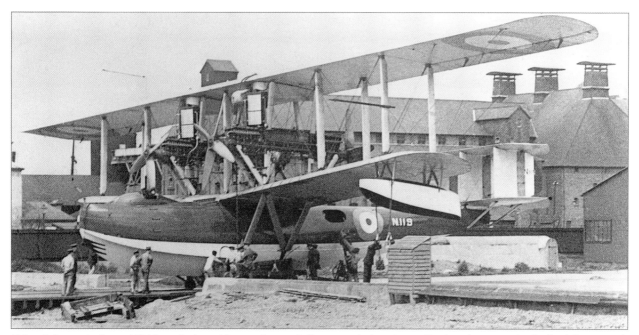

Fairey's huge Atalanta N119 on its beaching trolley at Felixstowe during 1924. During that year the hull of the aircraft was damaged, but was subsequently repaired and later modified. N119 stayed with MAEE until at least 1925. The people in the photo give a good idea of the size of the Atalanta – compare it with the photo of Felixstowe F.2A N4441 on p.27. *(J.M. Bruce/G.S. Leslie Collection)*

The Titania, Fairey's variant of the Atalanta, also seen at Felixstowe. In the background is the power station building. A very close relation, N129 was no more successful than N119 in securing a production order and though Fairey looked at the possibility of a civil version nothing emerged in the form of hardware. *(Bryan Ribbans)*

scrapped in around 1928. N118, the first Atalanta, was never completed; its hull was subjected to flotation tests at Grain before it too was scrapped.

In the meantime during 1920 Vickers had drafted a design for a huge all-metal biplane flying-boat known as the Vigilant, to be powered by no fewer than eight coupled Condor IAs. The Vigilant was seen as either a transatlantic civil or a military project and was conceived jointly at the company's Weybridge and Barrow sites. Its wingspan was 220ft, weight around 110,000lb and maximum range 2,000 miles, completely eclipsing the Fairey flying-boats and bigger even than the Eclectic. A contract was awarded for two examples (N131 and N132) but was later cancelled.

Supermarine Amphibians

The N.3 and N.4 Specifications had yielded large, expensive aircraft that were terminally vulnerable in the post-war environment. At Supermarine, however, two much smaller types appeared at around the same time, the second of which attained successful sales. These were the Seal and Seagull reconnaissance and fleet-spotting deck-landing amphibians.

Following its evaluation of the Commercial Amphibian (which may also have borne the name Seal I), the Air Ministry ordered a single Seal II (N146). Designed by Mitchell, the Seal II incorporated the improvements proposed following the assessment of the earlier type. A two-bay 46ft equal span biplane with rearward folding wings, the aircraft employed a tractor 450hp Napier Lion IB; previous Supermarine designs had been pushers. Its wooden hull followed Linton Hope lines, with an oval section and two steps. Accommodation comprised a single-seat open cockpit placed well forward and armed with a single machine-gun, together with a

Supermarine Seal II N146 sporting its modified, balanced rudder, at the bottom of the Woolston slipway, its amphibian undercarriage well clear of the water. This aircraft led to the Seagull series of aircraft that helped sustain Supermarine through a generally lean time for the British aviation industry, and the type was exported to Australia and Japan. *(Author's Collection)*

Seagull I serving with the Japanese Navy, seen at the Tokyo naval base during 1923. *(Author's Collection)*

similarly equipped dorsal position, while the W/T operator sat just aft of the wings. An amphibian undercarriage and a water rudder-cum-tail skid were installed.

N146 first flew in May 1921 and was tested at Grain during June, following which its fin and rudder were revised to prevent yaw. Another example passed to the Japanese Navy, while N146 was further modified under Air Ministry Specification 7/20, being renamed the Seagull I in July 1921. This involved the installation of a 480hp Napier Lion II and redesign of the radiator, as well as modifications to the ailerons and wing-floats. Two Seagull IIs (N158 and N159) with an amended fuel tank layout were ordered by the Ministry in February 1922, while another travelled to Japan.

In May 1923 five Seagull IIs (N9562–N9566) built to Specification 21/21 formed 440 (Fleet Reconnaissance) Flight, Fleet Air Arm. During February of that year five further examples were ordered (N9603–N9607) and in June thirteen more (N9642–N9654) to Specification 13/23, six of which were allocated to the carrier HMS *Eagle*. However, the main duty of the Seagull became coastal reconnaissance as the Fleet Air Arm's preference moved towards aircraft capable of operating as either landplanes or floatplanes, such as Fairey's outstanding IIID. Two Seagulls entered the 1924 King's Cup Air Race as nos 1 and 2, but one, piloted by Henri Baird, lost its propeller which sliced through the petrol tank, necessitating a very hurried landing near Newcastle; the other finished last.

During 1926 several Seagull IIIs were acquired by the Royal Australian Air Force (RAAF) and were based at Point Cook, Victoria, forming 101 Fleet Co-operation Flight. Though it is thought that only six examples were built, seven serials were allotted. The Australian Seagulls were almost identical to the Mk II apart from modifications to the cooling system, though they were a little slower. Initially employed on photographic reconnaissance, particularly over Papua, Queensland and the Great Barrier Reef, in February 1929 the aircraft embarked

Seagull II N158, one of two pre-production examples. Armament has yet to be fitted. Following maker's trials in April 1922, N158 was used for deck-landing trials with HMS *Argus* and was assessed at RAE Farnborough. It later entered comparative trials with a Fairey IIID at Martlesham Heath and Grain. In an eventful life thereafter, it crashed in March 1923 and though rebuilt was subsequently wrecked in a gale; repaired once more, it returned to Martlesham for further testing. *(Author's Collection)*

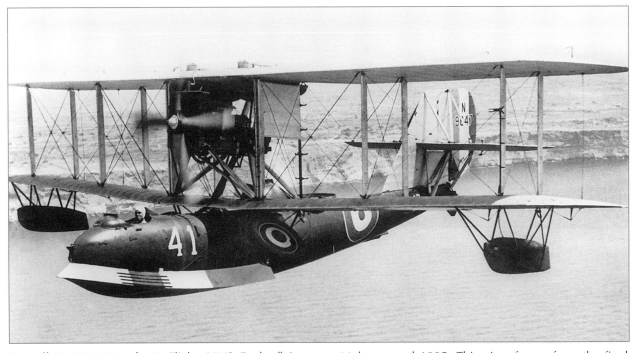

Seagull II N9647/41 of 440 Flight, HMS *Eagle*, flying near Malta around 1925. This aircraft was from the final production batch. It served out its days at the School of Naval Co-operation at Lee-on-Solent between July 1925 and May 1926. The Supermarine lineage is particularly noticeable around the bow. *(Author's Collection)*

in Australia's first indigenous seaplane carrier, HMAS *Albatross*. Four years later they transferred to the heavy cruisers *Australia* and *Canberra*. The Seagull apparently had a tendency to porpoise and was uncomfortable in open sea conditions, but its length of service with the Australians makes light of these alleged shortcomings.

Three examples received civil identities, G-AAIZ (ex-N9605, the sole Seagull IV), G-EBXH (ex-N9653) and G-EBXI (ex-N9654). N9605 was tested with experimental twin fins and rudders together with Handley Page slots, while N9644 employed a Bristol Jupiter IX radial pusher for trials at Felixstowe. In the summer of 1929, G-AAIZ flew as a six-seater with the short-lived Tours and Travel Association on a Woolston–Channel Islands service.

While the Seal/Seagull programme was running, Supermarine had also been busy in the commercial sector, producing the Sea Eagle amphibian, again developed from the Commercial Amphibian and intended for service between Southampton and the Channel Islands. During June 1922 the Air Ministry had approved a Southampton–Cherbourg–Le Havre route, which subsequently embraced the Channel Islands, in the name of the British Marine Air Navigation Company registered in March 1923. The Ministry subsidised the enterprise and paid for three Sea Eagles, G-EBFK, G-EBGR and G-EBGS; Hubert Scott-Paine assumed a

Royal Australian Air Force Seagull III A9-3 demonstrates the method by which the aircraft could be hoisted aboard ship. The engine is still running, while a crewman sits in the dorsal position which features its own windshield. *(Fleet Air Arm Museum)*

directorship while Supermarine and the Asiatic Petroleum Company (Shell-Mex) became the major industrial shareholders.

The Sea Eagle took the characteristic Supermarine form, a 46ft-span pusher biplane powered by a 360hp Rolls-Royce Eagle IX with a two-step hull providing enclosed accommodation for six in the bow, aft of which was an open cockpit adjacent to the centre-section. G-EBFK took part in that year's King's Cup piloted by Henri Baird. Regular services between Southampton (Woolston) and Guernsey began on 25 September 1923 though the French connection was never implemented. This was the first scheduled British flying-boat service, the pilots Baird and Bailey from Supermarine and all three Sea Eagles participating.

On 31 March 1924, following the recommendations of the Hambling Committee and endorsement by the Cabinet, Imperial Airways was formed as Britain's national airline from an amalgamation of the British Marine Air Navigation Company, Handley Page Transport, Instone Air Line and the Daimler Airway. Hubert Scott-Paine became a director of Imperial. The Sea Eagles continued the service under their new owner from 1 May though G-EBFK crashed on the 21st of that month. Further services were run during 1926 but G-EBGS was lost in January 1927 after being rammed by a ship in St Peter Port. G-EBGR soldiered on until 1928 when it was withdrawn and thereafter the route was

Sea Eagle G-EBFK, the first example, on the slipway at Woolston. It first flew during June 1923 and received its Certificate of Airworthiness on 11 July; the aircraft was fulsomely praised in terms of both air and water performance. *(Author's Collection)*

served by Short's Calcutta G-EBVG, the service finally ending on 28 February 1929. However, the hull of G-EBGR was retained.

In February 1924 the Spanish Royal Naval Air Service ordered twelve Scarab single-engined amphibians from Supermarine, based on the Sea Eagle, for reconnaissance and bombing duties. The Scarab's two-step hull featured an open single-seat cockpit behind which was a gunner's position mounting a single Lewis gun, and aft of that the W/T operator. Again a biplane pusher configuration was adopted, the wing form of equal 46ft span and aft-folding. The powerplant chosen was again the Eagle IX. Twelve 50lb bombs were carried in a revolving chamber within the hull, released through an aperture in the hull bottom which was closed when on the water; four underwing 100lb bombs were also carried. An undercarriage similar to that of the Seagull was fitted. The aircraft were built during 1924, receiving Spanish identities M-NSAA to M-NSAL, and the first example flew during May. A maximum speed of 93mph was achieved, while the estimated range was 250 miles.

A brand-new Spanish 10,000-ton seaplane tender arrived at Woolston during the summer of 1924 to collect the new flying-boats, though one had apparently crashed during trials and was not delivered. Unfortunately it was found that the Scarabs were just too large to fit the dimensions of the tender's lift, so they could not be lowered into her hold. Instead, they were lashed to the deck with wings folded, and covered with tarpaulins while all concerned hoped for the best.

The second of the three Sea Eagles, G-EBGR, at rest at Woolston. The cabin hatch is open and also visible are the ladders to assist entry and exit to the cabin and cockpit. The pilot is positioned aft of and above the cabin as with the Commercial Amphibian. The hull of G-EBGR survived long after the aircraft was withdrawn from service. *(Author's Collection)*

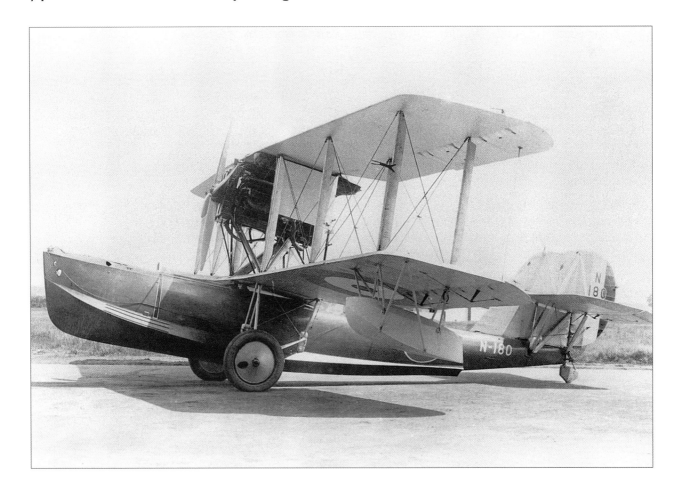

However, the vessel encountered a gale in the Bay of Biscay and seven machines were damaged. On arrival in Spain, the intact examples were shipped on almost immediately to Morocco to assist the Spanish Foreign Legion in their campaign against Abd-el Krim's Riff insurgents.

The enigmatic Supermarine Sheldrake amphibian, N180, was similar to the Scarab – indeed it may have been seen by the company as a Scarab prototype. The Sheldrake employed a tractor 450hp Napier Lion V rather than the pusher Eagle IX, and only one was ordered, by the Air Ministry, in December 1923. Again the span was 46ft and a crew of three accommodated, while offensive capability remained a 1,000lb bomb load. N180 was delivered to MAEE Felixstowe in January 1925, equipped (it is thought) with a form of Seagull hull. However, a modified hull was fitted in June, similar to that of the Scarab but with a Vickers machine-gun position aft of the wings and provision for a Lewis gun in the nose. With its larger engine the Sheldrake was faster than the Scarab, attaining a maximum speed of 103mph, while its empty weight was 350lb greater. It was noted at MAEE by May 1927 and later that month made its only known public appearance at the Hampshire Air Pageant fly-past at Hamble, wearing temporary identity 17. It was seen once more at MAEE in January 1928.

The year 1924 witnessed the appearance of two further Supermarine flying-boats, both from Mitchell, in response to two Ministry contracts for single examples. The

The sole Supermarine Sheldrake showed a marked resemblance to the Scarab. Only one example was built as Supermarine began to concentrate on a twin-engined flying-boat programme that would eventually yield the very successful Southampton. *(Author's Collection)*

first had been placed in 1921, as the Ministry contemplated a replacement for the Felixstowe F.5, and was to Specification 14/21. This resulted in the Scylla, initially planned as a torpedo-carrying triplane powered by three 550hp Condor engines and armed with defensive Scarff rings in bow and dorsal positions; the pilots were accommodated in a raised open cockpit amidships. However, the aircraft was eventually built as a monoplane employing two Eagle IXs; serialled N174 it arrived at Felixstowe during early 1924 and was used for taxying trials only. Its hull form featured a deep bow profile with two steps and accommodation for five, while the tail configuration was biplane with twin fins and rudders.

The second aircraft was the Swan amphibian, a civil type originally drawn up to meet a possible requirement by Instone Air Line. The Ministry found Supermarine's work of interest and a single Swan was ordered to Specification 21/22 as N175. The original design was a twelve-passenger type with a two-step hull featuring a prominent raised prow and cabin accommodation in the forward part. As with the Scylla, the open twin cockpit was located in an elevated central section. Of equal 68ft 8in span, the wings folded forward to minimise storage space. In fact the aircraft was completed as a military reconnaissance amphibian, again using Eagle IXs though it received no armament, and its first flight was on 25 March 1924, piloted by Henri Baird.

Before long Napier Lion IIBs were fitted and the undercarriage removed, which improved performance, while the wing-folding mechanism was discarded; the aircraft then became known as the Swan Mk II. On 27 June 1924 N175 was inspected at Woolston by HRH Edward Prince of Wales; in August it travelled to Felixstowe for trials that proved very successful. Over the first half of

Supermarine hulls seen at the company's premises. From left to right: Sea Lion II G-EBAH wearing the 1922 Schneider competition race number; Seagull II, either N158 or N159; and very unfinished Scylla N174. The photograph was taken prior to September 1923. *(Author's Collection)*

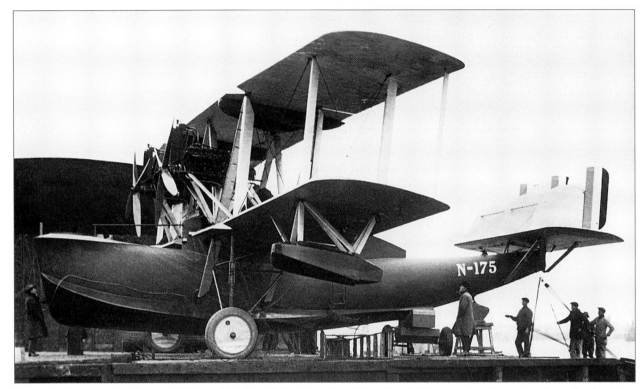

The sole Supermarine Swan, N175, on Woolston's hardstanding. The wing-folding mechanism is in place, the leading-edge incisions permitting forward movement of the outer wings. The aircraft is in military configuration, but as G-EBJY it later served with Imperial Airways fitted with wicker passenger seating and cabin windows. *(Author's Collection)*

On 27 June 1924 His Royal Highness Edward, Prince of Wales, visited Woolston and was shown the Swan. On the prince's left are Squadron Commander James Bird, managing director, and then Reginald Mitchell, chief designer. The prince also saw the Seagulls under construction at Woolston at that time. *(Fawley Historians)*

1924, meanwhile, Mitchell had redesigned the Swan to include a nose-mounted machine-gun, two gun positions on the upper wing, and underwing bombs. Later he streamlined the raised cockpit area and the high bows, before moving the cockpit forward.

Following its return from MAEE, the Swan was modified to a ten-passenger civil configuration, becoming G-EBJY and first flying in its new form on 9 June 1926; again the pilot was Baird, accompanied by a full complement in the cabin. G-EBJY was loaned to Imperial Airways during the 1927 season, operating on the Channel Island service; it also journeyed to Deauville, Le Touquet and Cherbourg before being scrapped in the autumn. The major importance of the Swan was that its very favourable appraisal at MAEE led to the issue of Specification R.18/24 to Supermarine.

Vickers Types

At Vickers the Vulture and Vanellus had appeared, the final variants of the Viking and also known as the Viking Mks VI and VII. The Vulture retained a similar hull layout to its predecessors but employed a redesigned, non-folding wing with a thicker section, stronger spars and a single bay. Two Vultures were built as a private venture. G-EBGO (also known as the Vulture Mk I), powered by a 450hp Napier Lion pusher, was registered in June 1923. The second, G-EBHO (Vulture

Vickers' Viking VI G-EBHO, also known as the Vulture II, shows off its amphibious qualities. This aircraft had an eventful life and eventually fell foul of extremes of climate during its attempted round-the-world flight. *(Author's Collection)*

Mk II) was registered in August and initially employed an Eagle IX while the fin above its upper tailplane was temporarily deleted.

Both aircraft took part in a pioneering round-the-world attempt, leaving Calshot on 25 March 1924. G-EBHO, converted to Vulture I standard, was the main aircraft used, while G-EBGO was shipped to Tokyo as a spare. The flight was made by Squadron Leader A.S.C. MacLaren, Flying Officer W.N. Plenderleith and Sergeant R. Andrews, and the planned route was via the Aegean to the Persian Gulf, on to India, Burma, Singapore and Tokyo, across the Bering Sea, over Alaska, Canada and across the North Atlantic, returning to Britain. However, by Burma two engine changes had been necessary and at Akyab Island the aircraft was obliged to stand out in a monsoon for two days. Unfortunately the heat of India followed by the sogginess of Burma took its toll; G-EBHO crashed while attempting to leave Akyab on 24 May, so the reserve aircraft was shipped in and the attempt continued. Once more the weather struck, however, this time over the Bering Sea in the form of fog, and G-EBGO crashed near Nikolski off the Siberian coast on 2 August, so the endeavour ended after some 13,000 miles of flight.

Vickers' disappointment was perhaps tempered by an order from the Ministry for a development of the Vulture named the Vanellus. A single aircraft, N169, was constructed to Specification 46/22, featuring a monoplane tail that improved the

The replacement Vickers round-the-world aircraft, Vulture I G-EBGO, is assembled at Akyab following its shipment from Japan after the demise of G-EBHO. Conditions seem rather basic but at least the airmen appear cheerful! *(Fleet Air Arm Museum)*

dorsal gunner's field of fire, while the other defensive position was placed aft of the cockpit. Wing-folding was reinstated, and full span ailerons were fitted on all four wings; overall span was 46ft, while power again came from a 450hp Napier Lion pusher. N169 was delivered to the Royal Aircraft Establishment (RAE) at Farnborough during March 1925 and later carried out comparative trials with a Seagull aboard the carrier HMS *Argus*, but no further orders were placed. At that time too, Vickers' aviation interests were turning toward other types of aircraft, notably large transports and bombers, and the Vanellus was the company's final amphibian.

The First Metal Hulls

A problem that affected all wooden flying-boat hulls and floats if moored out for any length of time was water soakage. This could inflict a severe weight penalty – half a ton might be added to a large hull – and encouraged the wood to split, leak and rot. The development of the metal hull during the mid-1920s was a fundamental step forward in flying-boat technology.

On 20 August 1920 Short Brothers had flown their Silver Streak all-metal landplane employing a duralumin primary structure, an experiment born from a wartime shortage of wood suitable for aircraft manufacture; the type was later purchased and evaluated by the Air Ministry. After extensive structural and corrosion testing, by the end of the following year the Ministry began tentatively to embrace the principle of metal construction. Oswald Short was keen to build a metal-hulled flying-boat and visited the United States Navy during 1923 in an attempt to sell the idea of a Cromarty fitted with an all-metal hull, but to no avail. However, in early 1924 Shorts received a request from the wealthy Australian Lebbaeus Hordern, who had previously purchased F.3 G-EAQT, for a miniature flying-boat for cruising and fishing around Botany Bay. In this way the metal-hulled Short S.1 Stellite (later renamed the Cockle) came about – the smallest flying-boat in the world at the time. Shorts' team for the project included Oscar Gnosspelius and Arthur Gouge in the Experimental Department, and C.P.T. Lipscomb, an expert in working with duralumin through previous involvement with the airships R37 and R38. Lipscomb had joined Shorts in 1914 and would eventually become chief designer.

The new aircraft was launched in April 1924 and was found to be virtually leak-proof. A single-seat monoplane, its high-mounted 36ft wing was of metal with a fabric covering, and the tail was of conventional arrangement. The Cockle was initially powered by two 32hp Bristol Cherubs but their vibration was found excessive so they were replaced by two Blackburne V twins governed to a mere 16hp each, on which the aircraft could just about take off. The hull was duralumin throughout, a monocoque structure utilising two steps and a flared vee-bottom. Registered G-EBKA, the Cockle was first coaxed into the air on 7 November 1924 from Rochester in the hands of John Parker. Although it was underpowered and achieved only 68mph with the Blackburns, the metal hull stood up very well against corrosion and the rigours of operation. Re-engined once more with (modified) Cherubs, a maximum speed of 73mph was achieved. In fact the Cockle never travelled to Australia but was assessed by the Ministry at Felixstowe during July 1925 serialled N193, being withdrawn from use in 1929.

While work on the Cockle was proceeding the Ministry placed two contracts, one with Shorts for a single metal-hulled flying-boat, the other with Saunders for a wooden-hulled variety. Both were considered experimental and each embodied a Felixstowe F.5 flight structure. Saunders' offering assumed the serial N178, while that from Shorts was N177. The Saunders hull was of patented hollow-bottomed ventilated layout, a slab-sided Consuta-covered arrangement, while the Shorts hull was of duralumin throughout. Such was the Ministry's concern over the metal hull that Shorts were obliged to provide an indemnity accepting the loss of 100 per cent of their contract price (£10,000) should it not prove completely watertight.

Francis Webber designed the Shorts hull, a two-step monocoque structure derived from the metal Cromarty project. The fore-body was integral with the upper part of the hull and, as with the Cockle, the steps were separately built on to the shell, which assisted drainage and ventilation of the 'interior' surface. Double curvature was avoided wherever possible to minimise panel beating and work-hardening of the metal which could lead to fatigue. Below the waterline the hull was coated with Rylard white seaplane enamel; the remainder received Rylard clear varnish. A side-by-side cockpit was provided, with two gunners' apertures, one in the bows, the other aft of the mainplanes. Power was provided by two Eagle VIIIs.

Shorts' S.2 N177 first flew from Rochester on 5 January 1925 piloted by John Parker, and passed to the MAEE on 14 March, where it remained until at least February 1926. After a year it was closely inspected, having undergone a bruising

Short Cockle G-EBKA on the Medway. The figure in the cockpit emphasises the miniature dimensions of the aircraft, while its engines and propellers are truly tiny. Before the Cockle would fly, the wing incidence had to be increased. The aircraft is seen with its original fin and rudder, both of which were subsequently enlarged to mitigate swing in the event of an engine failure. *(Short Brothers)*

F.5 N178 featured a Saunders-designed and built hollow-bottomed ventilated hull. Unfortunately the on-water control was inferior to that of the standard F.5 with a tendency to turn out of the wind before hump speed was reached. In the air the aircraft handled similarly to the F.5 despite the increased keel area forward. The programme was not a success and by May 1925 N178 had been scrapped. *(British Hovercraft Corporation)*

Short S.2 N177, the so-called Tin Five, on the Rochester slipway. This aircraft represented the start of a number of very successful Short designs. The photograph was taken prior to launching on 31 December 1924. Following its rigorous testing at Felixstowe N177 passed into the hands of Blackburn where it ended its days. *(Short Brothers)*

set of trials; it had also been moored out for long periods. Very little corrosion was found and the hull structure had comfortably endured the robust treatment, while water performance was improved on that of the standard F.5. The only disadvantage that emerged with metal hulls was a tendency toward encrustation with barnacles and other marine life (more markedly in tropical operations) but this could be minimised by regular cleaning. The Ministry's reservations over the metal hull finally evaporated, and Shorts were requested to tender for an improved version of the Cromarty. Saunders' offering, tested in 1924, was found difficult to take off, suffered from soakage and was not pursued. Though wooden-hulled flying-boats appeared after the S.2, from the mid-1920s their days were numbered.

English Electric Flying-Boats

Two new types that emerged at around the same time as the Short S.2 came from the English Electric Company Ltd, formed in December 1918 principally from the amalgamation of the Phoenix Dynamo Company, the Coventry Ordnance Works and Dick, Kerr & Company. In the uncertain post-war world these concerns recognised the economic and technical benefits (or even necessity) of joining together. W.O. Manning, formerly of Phoenix, became chief designer; he was joined briefly by Henry Knowler, who had previously worked at Vickers under Rex Pierson, and an aviation department was re-established at the former Dick, Kerr site at Preston. Dick, Kerr's site at Lytham on the River Ribble was also retained.

The first flying-boat from the new company was the P.5 Kingston, designed by Manning – Knowler had left to join S.E. Saunders during the summer of 1923. A response to the Ministry's requirement for a coastal patrol and anti-submarine flying-boat with the F.5 long in the tooth, the Kingston was similar to the Cork, a twin 450hp Napier Lion-powered 85ft-span biplane employing a two-step Linton Hope wooden hull, though with a revised continuous rear planing surface to improve

The prototype English Electric Kingston hull under construction at the former Dick, Kerr factory. The Linton Hope structure is about to be covered by diagonal planking. Compare the complexity of this form of construction with John Porte's F.3 on p. 30. (*J.M. Bruce/G.S. Leslie Collection*)

English Electric Kingston N168 at Lytham in May 1924 just prior to its first flight. Shortly after this photograph was taken, the aircraft sank by the bow on the Ribble. The three crew escaped unhurt, while the Kingston drifted downstream before being taken under tow by the Preston Corporation tug *Aid*. Refloated, the aircraft was again damaged; inspection of the hull concluded that it had struck flotsam, a most unlucky start to the programme. *(J.M. Bruce/G.S. Leslie Collection)*

water performance. Accommodation consisted of a bow position, tandem open cockpits featuring dual-control, and a flight engineer's area below the wings. Lewis gun positions were located one in the aft of each engine nacelle and one in the bow. The floats were redesigned from those of the Cork while the tailplane was somewhat larger than hitherto. The order for a prototype Kingston, N168, was placed during 1923 against Specification 23/23. Construction was carried out at Preston and assembly at Lytham.

N168 was launched from the Lytham slipway for its first test-flight on 22 May 1924. Unfortunately, it hit a floating obstacle during take-off in the hands of Major H.G. Brackley, then Air Superintendent of Imperial Airways; it sank partially but was recovered. The accident did not affect the Ministry's order for four Kingston Is (N9709–N9712), the hulls of which were manufactured at Lytham and the flight structures at Preston. The first example travelled to MAEE during November 1924 where it received a favourable trials report in terms of air handling though its water performance was criticised; severe bouncing was experienced on both take-off and landing. On 25 May 1925 the engines of N9709 were pulled from their mountings during a take-off at Felixstowe and the upper wing failed while the hull cracked in two places; again the occupants survived. The three subsequent Kingston Is appeared between November 1924 and February 1925.

By March 1925 the Kingston II had emerged, its serial N9712 being a duplication of the final Mk I. Possibly the Mk II utilised the flight surfaces of the earlier aircraft for these were identical to previous Kingstons. However, the Kingston II employed a metal hull, designed around the expedient of taking many of the wooden parts of

The metal-hulled Kingston Mk II N9712. The unusual engine nacelle gunners' gondolas were retained. The metal hull profile was somewhat different from its predecessors, being deeper with a raised prow, and featured an inbuilt planing bottom with a hard chine rather than a 'fuselage' to which the hydrodynamic portions were added. *(Author's Collection)*

the previous layout and metalising them using duralumin and stainless steel. The planing bottom was integral with the main hull and fluted to encourage cleaner running, while the sides from the chine to the decking minimised double curvature. Arriving for trials at Felixstowe during December, it was found that N9712 did not meet the standards set by the Kingston I, particularly in terms of climbing, while on the water a porpoising tendency was identified and the aircraft behaved sluggishly. The hull was considered overweight. N9712 remained at MAEE for experimental flying until at least October 1927. Its hull was subsequently subjected to strength tests, probably to destruction.

The final Kingston, Mk III N9713, reverted to a wooden hull and appeared early in 1926. Its flight structure remained generally as for previous Kingstons but the hull was new, with a deep fore-body, sharp but slim vee-bottom and high stern, constructed along similar lines to the hull of the Gosport Aviation-built Atalanta. Two gunners' nacelles were proposed for the upper wing, each for two crew and two Lewis guns, but they were not fitted; such arrangements had previously been found very uncomfortable. N9713 arrived at Felixstowe in March 1926, where the hull proved clean-running with no porpoising and the aircraft speedy with a good rate of climb. Concurrently, however, Supermarine were manufacturing their very successful Southampton maritime patrol flying-boat, of similar (though slightly smaller) configuration. In March 1926 English Electric announced the closure of its aircraft interest. By the mid-1920s a significant proportion of the British aviation industry was in questionable financial shape with a low volume of orders spread thinly across the manufacturers; the Ministry went as far as suggesting that some firms, including English Electric, should leave the aircraft business altogether.

The company's experience with its M.3 Ayr flying-boat probably influenced the move from aviation. Again designed by Manning, assisted in part by Knowler, the type was intended as a fleet gunnery and spotter aircraft with a crew of four and all-up weight of just under 7,000lb. The Ministry became interested and the Ayr was built to Specification 12/21. It was a rakish swept-wing large-gap sesquiplane, and lateral stability on the water was provided by the lower wings rather than the usual wing-floats. The 46ft-span upper wing was negatively staggered and mounted the uncowled powerplant, a 450hp Napier Lion IIB, while the lower employed extreme dihedral. Ailerons were (necessarily) fitted to the upper wing only, while the lower wing was divided into watertight compartments, the inter-plane struts taking a bold N-form. The single tailplane was mounted high on the prominent fin and rudder assembly.

Accommodation within the wooden two-step hull consisted of a bow gunnery-cum-mooring position, an observer's position with a camera-gun in an aperture just aft, a single-seat cockpit amidships, a W/T post within the hull, and a dorsal gunnery ring. Hydrodynamic tests of the novel layout were carried out in model form at the National Physical Laboratory and the results appeared promising. Construction of two prototypes, N148 and N149, began during 1923 but was leisurely and took second place to work on the Kingston; only N148 was ever completed. It was finally launched at Lytham on 10 March 1925. An attempt was made at a flight-test by Marcus Manton, then English Electric's test-pilot, but the aircraft refused to take off. Gentle taxying proved problematic as the Ayr rocked from one lower wing to the other, while at speed the water thrown up from the bow submerged those wings and caused the aircraft to start to dive under. Further efforts were made with the ballast altered and Scarff rings removed but the Ayr never left the water.

A fine study of the sole English Electric Ayr N148, of unusual but graceful appearance. An unhappy project, however, the aircraft failed to fly. It was transported to RAE Farnborough during 1926 for structural tests and its hull was subsequently abandoned on the Basingstoke Canal, along with that of Kingston I N9712. *(J.M. Bruce/G.S. Leslie Collection)*

Woolston's Breakthrough

By mid-1924 the Ministry had at last contracted for a replacement for its faithful but aged Felixstowe F.5s. This was Mitchell's Supermarine Southampton, which set a new standard in waterborne aircraft of the day. The Southampton stemmed from the Swan, MAEE trials of which had been so favourable that in August 1924 the Ministry ordered six wooden-hulled Southampton Is (N9896–N9901) off the drawing-board, to Specification R.18/24. A further example (N218), with a metal hull, was procured for experimental use. A second order for twelve further Southampton Is (S1036–S1045 and S1058–S1059) was placed in July 1925 against Specification 11/25, and these appeared during 1926.

The first Southampton, N9896, first flew on 10 March 1925 from Woolston piloted by Henri Baird, before quickly passing to Felixstowe where very successful trials were performed – for example the aircraft could maintain height on one engine, quite a feat at that time. The Southampton I was powered by two Napier Lion V engines mounted on pylons between its two-bay 75ft-span biplane mainplanes. Ailerons were fitted to all four wings and the wing structure was high-mounted using spar bracing tubes to take the main loads from the lower centre-section to reinforced hull frames, rather than the usual practice of building the wing roots into the hull. The Southampton's hull comprised an inner 'fuselage' to which were attached the planing bottom and two steps, the area between the two being divided into watertight compartments. The bow mooring position was equipped with a Scarff-mounted Lewis gun; aft were twin open tandem cockpits, and below the wing centre-section, were engineering and navigation areas. Two offset dorsal defensive machine-gun positions were also provided. The tail configuration of the Southampton was similar in general arrangement to that of the Swan.

The prototype Southampton, wooden-hulled N9896, seen under construction at Woolston. The inner hull was unobstructed and allowed the crew members to move freely about the aircraft. The control wheels are in place, as well as the Scarff rings, while the centre-section of the lower wing is taking shape. The hull has yet to receive its high gloss finish. In the background is Seagull II N9565. *(Author's Collection)*

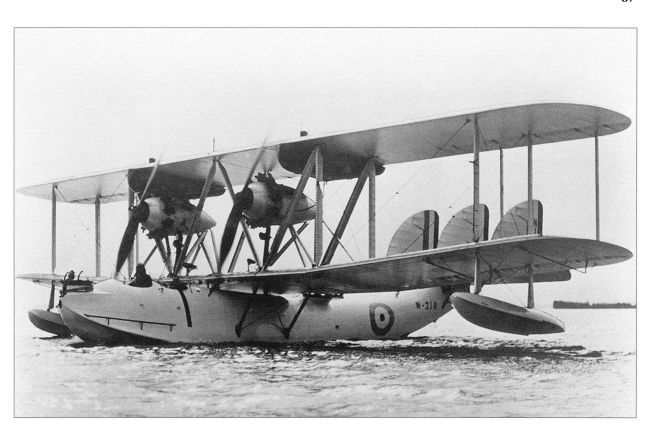

Over the summer of 1925 the new type entered service with 480 (Coastal Reconnaissance) Flight at nearby Calshot. That year Supermarine expanded, acquiring some of the ex-Admiralty sheds at Hythe formerly occupied by May, Harden & May for erection of the aircraft. During the autumn four Southamptons exercised around the British and Irish shorelines, trouble-free episodes confirming that operations could be safely carried out in isolated coastal waters. In July 1926 S1038 and S1039 flew the flag overseas, commanded by Squadron Leader G.E. Livock and travelling from Plymouth to Egypt via Bordeaux, Marseilles, Naples, Malta, Benghazi and Sollum to Aboukir, before returning via Athens and Corfu, a distance of almost 7,000 miles. That summer and autumn four examples from 480 (CR) Flight toured the east and south-east coastal towns of England, creating great public interest.

Meanwhile the experimental Southampton N218 had flown. The advantages of its metal hull became obvious; 900lb less in weight (500lb in structure weight and 400lb in water soakage), and in trials an increase in range to 540 miles or more depending on the loading. The metal hull retained the grace of its predecessor but was single-skinned rather than employing a 'double-bottom', providing greater roominess and storage area. N218 was initially powered by two 500hp Napier VA engines, which became the standard powerplant for the metal-hulled production Southampton, the Mk II. Over time nearly all the Southampton Is returned to Woolston where they received metal hulls and were redesignated Mk IIs. The metal-hulled aircraft weighed in at 15,200lb loaded and top speed was 95mph at sea level; endurance was over 6 hours.

N218, the first experimental Southampton. Following its evaluation as the basis of the Southampton II, N218 received Jupiter IXs instead of its original Lion VAs, later replaced by Jupiter XFBMs, while Handley Page slots were also fitted, though these were not added to other examples. N218 also employed four-bladed propellers for a time. *(Author's Collection)*

A Southampton I in the rain at Calshot. In the background is the famous landmark of Henry VIII's Calshot Castle. Most of the wooden-hulled Southamptons were retrospectively given metal hulls and were redesignated Mk IIs. The beaching gear attaches directly to the aircraft rather than forming a cradle in which it sits. The anti-fouling treatment beneath the hull waterline is noticeable. *(Author's Collection)*

Refuelling metal-hulled Southampton II S1300 at the water's edge. The aircraft flies a flag from an interplane strut. S1300 was one of a batch of five aircraft ordered in 1928. The metal hull retained the favourable hydrodynamic properties of its wooden forebear and featured very clean lines, while many of the light alloy parts were anodised to protect against corrosion. *(Author's Collection)*

During October 1927 a further and ground-breaking long-range flight, this time to the Orient and beyond, was commenced by four Mk II aircraft of the RAF's Far East Flight. The principal objects were to open the air route to Australia and the east, and identify suitable landing sites. Weaponry was removed and fuel capacity increased. The journey included a circumnavigation of Australia, the crews again acquiring much experience of unsupported operations. It was felt the geographical information collected would prove valuable in developing future operations, both military and commercial. The expedition was led by Group Captain H.M. Cave-Brown-Cave and was extended to take in Hong Kong, Indo-China and Burma, a spare aircraft being used for the Hong Kong visit on Air Ministry orders. The tour proceeded at an average ground speed of around 80mph and covered some 27,000 miles over fourteen months. Only minor modifications were needed, including the installation of Leitner-Watts metal propellers and increased radiator surfaces; again the Southampton emerged with flying colours, being found durable and reliable. The Far East Flight ended its marathon at Seletar in Singapore on 11 December 1928, and reformed as 205 Squadron, the first RAF unit in the region and commanded by Squadron Leader Livock.

During September 1930 a 2,900-mile trip to the Baltic was made by 201 Squadron, formed out of 480 (CR) Flight, employing Southampton IIs S1228, S1229, S1234 and S1058. Esbjerg, Copenhagen, Stockholm, Helsinki, Tallinn, Riga, Memel, Gothenburg and Oslo were visited, and demonstrations made before various government and air force representatives as well as the public. Again the tour passed without incident. Southamptons eventually served with 201 Squadron (Calshot), 203 (Iraq), 204 (Mount Batten), 205 (Singapore) and 210 (Felixstowe and Pembroke Dock).

Southampton S1152 at Singapore, one of the aircraft comprising the RAF's Far East Flight. An awning has been erected to provide protection from the sun; the port engine also appears to be covered. S1152 was one of five aircraft used during the remarkable trip to the East – the others were S1149, S1150, S1151 (seen in the background) and a spare, S1127. Not surprisingly S1152 shows signs of wear, while the starboard engine and both propellers have been removed. *(Fleet Air Arm Museum)*

Of the three experimental Southamptons following N218, N251 became the Saunders A.14, while N252 was not a typical Southampton at all, being a three-engined sesquiplane. N253 initially employed steam-cooled Rolls-Royce Kestrel IIMS engines and led to the Southampton IV, the prototype of the Scapa. The wings of N253 were metalised, with light alloy spars and ribs, while the struts were of steel with light alloy fairings. Meanwhile, N218 flew with a variety of engines during its life, including the 450hp Bristol Jupiter IX and later the 570hp Jupiter XFBM (the Pegasus prototype), while Handley-Page leading-edge slots were also tested though with no improvement in performance. Various production aircraft were also used from time to time to conduct tests and evaluate new ideas. N9896 was fitted with integral wing fuel tanks in combination with hull-mounted tanks, in place of the original externally mounted wing tanks, but the modification was not taken further. The same aircraft tested defensive gondolas positioned above the upper wing centre-section and mounting fore-and-aft Scarff rings but control problems were experienced and once more the idea was not pursued. Southampton N9900 was used for torpedo-carrying and dropping trials while S1059 was fitted with an enclosed cockpit canopy, subsequently adopted by those aircraft operating with 203 Squadron in Iraq.

Following its successful exposure overseas, and as its reputation grew for ruggedness and reliability, the Southampton secured export orders. Eight (or possibly nine) examples passed to the Argentine Navy, five with wooden hulls, the remainder featuring the metal variety, all powered by 450hp French Lorraine 12E engines. These were apparently coded HB-1 to HB-8 though three are known to have carried

Southampton N253, with an all-metal airframe, had arrived at Felixstowe by June 1931. It was tested for over a year and re-engined with Kestrel IVs, becoming K2888. It remained in use until at least April 1934. *(Author's Collection)*

Southamptons were exported to Argentina; here metal-hulled HB-6 gets off on a proving flight from Woolston sporting Argentine national markings. *(Author's Collection)*

Royal Australian Air Force wooden-hulled Southampton A11-2 was used for parachuting; the jumping-off platforms and their temporary occupants are seen. Both Australian examples are thought to have been ex-RAF. A11-2 was flown by the RAAF No. 1 Training School. *(Vic Hodgkinson)*

identities P-156, P-157 and P-158, while oddly HB-1 and HB-2 seem to have been the final aircraft delivered. The Royal Australian Air Force acquired two Southampton Is while a Mk II passed to Japan, operating from the Oppama Naval Air Depot and later Yokosuka before arrival at the Kure Arsenal. It was subsequently modified into an 18-seater airliner and flew from Kyushu with Japan Air Transport becoming J-BAID. In 1933 Turkey purchased six, powered by Hispano-Suiza 12 Nbr engines. S1235 was used briefly by Imperial Airways as a cargo and mail carrier, operating as G-AASH between Alexandria and Salonika from November 1929 to January 1930. The Southampton programme ran until 1934. It was a terrific success for Supermarine, and the type stayed in service with the RAF until the mid-1930s.

From the Southampton emerged the three-engined Nanok (Polar Bear). This aircraft resulted from an enquiry by the Danish Navy for a torpedo-carrying flying-boat, and an order was placed for one example in June 1926. Powered by three 430hp Armstrong Siddeley Jaguar IV engines and employing a hull similar to the Southampton's, the Nanok first flew from Woolston on 21 June 1927 wearing Danish markings and serialled 99, capable of carrying two torpedoes stored one beneath each lower wing. Unfortunately it was found nose-heavy and slightly down on the specified top speed, and the Danes terminated the contract. However, it was subsequently purchased by the Hon. A.E. Guinness, of the brewing family, acquiring the registration G-AAAB in September 1928 and being re-named the Solent. It was civilianised and fitted out as a luxury air yacht with provision for up to twelve passengers, while 400hp Jaguar IVAs were installed. Until mid-1931 the Solent flew between Hythe, on Southampton Water, Dùn Laoghaire in County Dublin, and Lough Corrib in County Galway – the Guinness family owned nearby Ashford Castle in Mayo – but it was scrapped three years later.

Work on the Southampton and other projects, notably the Schneider floatplane racers, caused Supermarine's Seamew amphibian to make slow progress. Designed

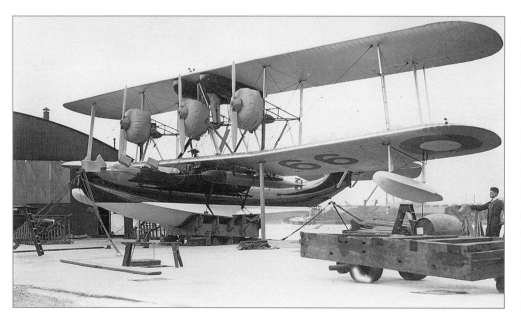

The sole Nanok nears completion on the Woolston hardstanding. Its three engines wear protective covers, while the nacelles are yet to be installed. The aircraft displays Danish national markings and bears the identity 99. Below the lower wing is a dummy torpedo, used for assessing the performance of the aircraft with such a weapon in place. *(Author's Collection)*

My goodness! Rejected by the Danes, the Nanok became Solent G-AAAB. Under Guinness ownership the aircraft flew widely in the Irish Free State, and is seen here in Dublin harbour. The defensive apertures are still in place. The Solent was withdrawn from use in July 1931. *(Irish Times)*

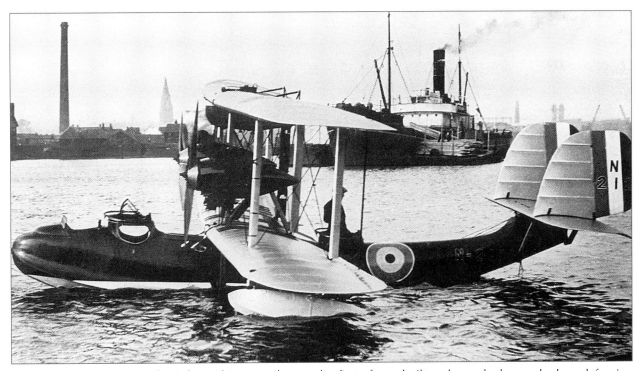

Seamew N212 at rest on the Itchen. This example was the first of two built and reveals the perched-up defensive position aft of the cockpit, though no armament is fitted. The general form is reminiscent of the Southampton though the Seamew was much smaller at a weight of 5,800lb. The aircraft arrived at Felixstowe for assessment in June 1928 and returned in September 1929, suffering a mainplane fitting failure before crashing while taxiing on the Felixstowe slipway. In the background a timber ship unloads into barges. *(Author's Collection)*

to Specification 29/24, two (N212 and N213) were ordered during 1925 but only in the spring of 1926 did detailed work commence, and that was interrupted as other activities took precedence. The first example finally flew on 9 January 1928 piloted by Henri Baird. The Seamew, a 46ft-span biplane amphibian, was powered by two 230hp Armstrong Siddeley Lynx IV radials and employed a crew of three: pilot, navigator and gunner; its wooden hull was again similar in form to that of the early Southampton. The wings were designed to fold for ship-board operation and were of composite metal and wooden construction, while twin fins and rudders were adopted.

MAEE trials with N212 over the summer of 1928 unfortunately revealed a nose-heaviness, and a spray pattern even on calm water that damaged the propellers. The company later discovered that the aircraft had been built using a faulty form of stainless steel in the fittings. N213 was fitted with smaller-diameter, four-bladed propellers in an attempt to solve the problem of spray but this resulted in a loss of climbing performance. With an outmoded wooden hull and defective fittings, it was always in the Southampton's shadow and a decision was made to scrap the Seamew programme. N212 contributed to the decision on 12 April 1930 by crashing while taxiing on the Felixstowe slipway.

Interlude – Beardmore

The engineering and ship-building firm William Beardmore & Co. Ltd of Dalmuir, Dumbartonshire, had entered aviation shortly before the First World War and during hostilities built large numbers of aircraft under licence as well as designs of its own. The company had also planned to enter its WB.IX flying-boat, G-EAQI, in the Air

A contemporary impression of the Beardmore WB.IX reveals radical thinking. The passengers were carried in the forward portion of the hull, while the pilot was positioned aft. An empennage configuration reminiscent of the *Bat Boat* and the CE.1 was adopted. Amphibian undercarriage was featured in combination with a combined tailskid-cum-water rudder. *(Philip Jarrett)*

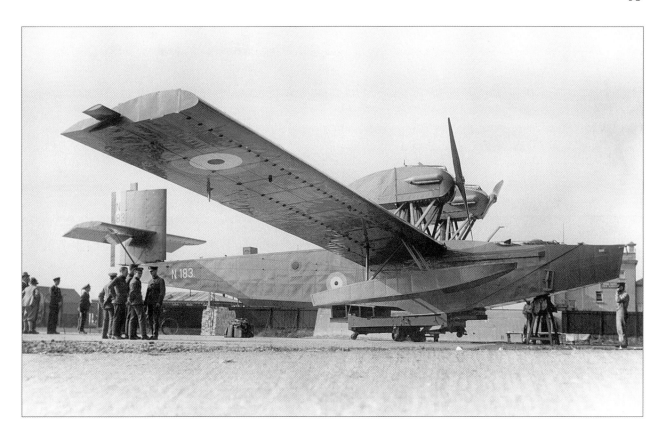

Ministry's 1920 civil aircraft competition. A radical six-passenger biplane featuring four hull-mounted 230hp Galloway Adriatic engines driving two wing-mounted propellers, the WB.IX hull form was based round a braced duralumin longitudinal system, the main portion being of roughly circular section, while the keel and chines were of rock elm and the planing bottom skinned with mahogany. However, the aircraft was scrapped prior to completion.

In 1924 Beardmore concluded a manufacturing licence with Rohrbach Metallflugzeugbau of Berlin. The constructional concepts for large metal aircraft developed by Dr Adolf Rohrbach had caught the eye of the Ministry, which with the Short S.2 programme well under way decided to take investigations further by comparing a large monoplane metal-hulled flying-boat with the wooden biplane types then in service. Specification 20/24 was written to define the new requirement and in November 1924 Beardmore received a contract for two all-metal 94ft-span Rohrbach Ro IV flying-boats known as the BeRo.2 Inverness, serialled N183 and N184. To hasten the programme and also circumvent the post-war treaty forbidding aircraft manufacture in Germany, the first example was constructed in Berlin but assembled at Rohrbach's Metal Aeroplane A/S premises in Copenhagen; N184 was Beardmore-built.

The Inverness was no oil painting. An ugly, high aspect-ratio cantilever monoplane, the cumbersome rectangular wings of N183 were thick-sectioned and set at a large angle of dihedral. Balanced ailerons were employed and the wings also contained the fuel tanks, while the wing-floats were positioned rather near to

Designed by Germans, assembled by Danes, badged by North Britons: Beardmore BeRo.2 Inverness N183 reveals great ugliness. Its wing-floats seem excessively long and the slab-sided hull appears primitive. The testing programme was very disappointing and the Beardmore-built example N184 fared scarcely any better. *(Philip Jarrett)*

the hull. Two 450hp Napier Lion V engines drove two-bladed propellers and were mounted close together on pylons above the wing centre-section to clear spray, together with a clumpish radiator assembly. A square fin and rudder and square tailplane were adopted, the tailplane being mid-mounted on the fin. The hull was a two-step, slab-sided arrangement featuring a boat-like prow. Accommodation for the crew of four consisted of a nose position, side-by-side cockpit and a dorsal post. The metal used in the construction and skinning was generally duralumin, with some steel fittings.

N183 visited MAEE Felixstowe for trials between September 1925 and April 1926, during when it was piloted by Herr Landmann. Unfortunately many deficiencies were identified both in design and construction, including dirty hydrodynamic performance with a tendency to porpoise, poor performance and instability in the air, tail vibration, poor aileron control, a poor and over-complex fuel system, weakness of the main step and poor detail design. Modifications were proposed but eventually the aircraft was destroyed in May 1927 during strength tests. The Beardmore-built example, N184, incorporated changes to the fuel and cooling systems and to the rudder but did not fly until 30 November 1928. Despite the revisions, in April 1929 MAEE terminated the programme because both flight and water characteristics remained unacceptable and N184 was scrapped.

Saunders Disappointment

Following the failure of the Kittiwake it was 1923 before an aircraft design department was re-established at Cowes. Bernard Thomson arrived from Hawker as chief designer; his deputy was Henry Knowler and the two men were joined by David Nicholson. At that time too the Vickers interest was bought out. Two new flying-boats were commenced, the A.3 Valkyrie under Knowler assisted by Thomson and the A.4 Medina by Thomson helped by Captain F. Shepherd as hull designer, in parallel attempts to break into the military and civil markets respectively. The Valkyrie was conceived as a general duty type and work began against Specification 14/24, though the aircraft was eventually built to Specification 22/24. The A.3 was one of a number of different flying-boats ordered as singletons or in very low volume by the Air Ministry during the mid- and late 1920s to help determine the optimum between durability, reliability, maintainability, load-carrying and performance.

A 97ft equal span biplane, the Valkyrie was powered by three 675hp Rolls-Royce Condor IIIA engines. Its two-step wooden Consuta-covered hull was a monocoque arrangement in part embodying the Linton Hope principle, which Knowler had worked with on the Phoenix Cork, but without the bulkheads previously used as these had concentrated the inevitable seeped water loads. Though the majority of the hull was an elastic structure, the central section was rigid and mounted a fore-and-aft pylon to which the lower wing was attached. Accommodation consisted of a bow gunnery and mooring position, dual-control tandem open cockpits behind which were the radio and navigation posts, and two staggered dorsal defensive positions. A braced monoplane tailplane was employed, with a single fin and a large rudder sporting a hefty servo-rudder. Armament consisted of three Scarff-mounted Lewis machine-guns and a bomb-load of up to 1,100lb. The aircraft,

serialled N186, first flew in the spring of 1926 in the hands of test pilot Frank T. Courtney before travelling to Felixstowe for evaluation during January 1927.

Sadly the assessment was unfavourable. Water handling was poor at slow speeds because no water rudder had been fitted and the (air) rudder did not become effective until the central engine was running at a fairly high speed, while a dirty take-off and mild porpoising were encountered. In flight, tail-flutter and a marked tendency to fly port wing low were experienced while aileron control was heavy and the aircraft tended to roll to port; the fuel system was also criticised. However, the Valkyrie remained controllable with one engine stopped in flight, while top speed and endurance were found useful. The aircraft returned to Cowes for aileron and rigging alterations.

Meanwhile the sole A.4 Medina, G-EBMG, had appeared. The aircraft was built for the Air Ministry via the Air Council's Research and Development Department to Specification 31/24, with possible use by Imperial Airways in mind. Specification 31/24 specified Armstrong Siddeley Lynx engines of around 240hp but these were not sufficiently powerful for the Medina, which weighed in at 11,560lb – by comparison, Supermarine's twin Lynx-powered Seamew tipped the scales at a mere 5,800lb. Instead, two 450hp Bristol Jupiter VIs were selected, mounted under the upper centre-section. An unusual inverted sesquiplane biplane, the Medina employed Warren girder bracing rather than conventional inter-plane struts. Both upper and lower wings carried ailerons and were of deep high-lift RAF 33 section. A triangular tailplane was mounted high on the fin, while a large rectangular rudder was employed. The hull was a two-step arrangement with flat tumble-home sides, covered with Consuta. Seating for seven was provided in an enclosed cabin while the cockpit was of open side-by-side configuration; only the port position had controls. Nearly all the movable surfaces were actuated through rotating shafts or push-pull rods.

The handsome Saunders A.3 Valkyrie N186 on the Cowes slipway, early 1927. Appearances were deceptive; despite its impressive lines the aircraft failed to meet a number of minimum require-ments laid down by Specification 22/24. Though the bomb-rack mountings are in place the racks themselves have yet to be fitted, while the underwing serial marking is still to be applied.
(Saunders-Roe)

The Medina was also a disappointment. After a first flight during November 1926 in the hands of Captain F.J. Bailey, during trials carried out at the end of that year dirty water performance was discovered at low speed while at higher speeds porpoising occurred. Hull leaks and splitting of the Consuta covering were also noted. The aircraft was allocated the serial N214 for service trials but no orders were placed and it was finally scrapped at Cowes during 1929. Meanwhile Thomson had left Saunders in July 1926, before the aircraft had been completed, and Knowler had become chief designer.

Progress: Shorts and Blackburn

Shorts' S.2 led to an order against Specification 13/24 during early 1925 for a prototype metal-hulled S.5 Singapore I; designs proffered by Fairey and Saunders, also to 13/24, were not taken up. Despite the S.2's success, frustration must have been felt at Rochester; Supermarine had already received a contract for six metal hulls to fit retrospectively to their wooden Southamptons, while a single such hull had been ordered for English Electric's Kingston II. Design of the Singapore's hull had commenced under Francis Webber in the spring of 1924 and over that summer he and Arthur Gouge conducted many trials with models using the National Physical Laboratory test-tank and later Shorts' own new tank, but their approaches were at variance. Webber resigned after Gouge was able to show that a reduction in beam, and substitution of the original planing bottom flutes with a flared bottom, would lead to cleaner running and could virtually eliminate porpoising. Gouge was promoted to chief designer.

The resulting aircraft was a graceful 93ft-span sesquiplane powered by two Condor IIIs and employing Frise ailerons on the fabric-covered upper wings only, the main structure and the wingtip floats being of duralumin. The hull form featured two steps, with pronounced sweeps fore and aft, and a deep keel combined with Gouge's slim beam. Accommodation consisted of a bow position armed with a

Saunders A.4 Medina G-EBMG at rest off Cowes, August 1927. The fin and rudder are of unusual profile while the inverted sesquiplane layout, Warren interplane girder structure and thick wing section are all prominent. The object that at first glance appears to be some form of prow-mounted lamp is in fact a Saunders-built prefabricated summer-house on the far bank! (H. Hanna)

Scarff-mounted Lewis gun, an open side-by-side cockpit and, aft of the wings, two gunners' positions with further Lewis guns. The interior contained a W/T station, as well as cooking facilities and bunks affording crew comfort during independent operation over substantial periods. A tall single main fin and rudder were adopted together with two auxiliary fins and rudders mounted on the tailplane to assist straight flight in the event of an engine failure, the structure again of duralumin with fabric covering. Serialled N179, the Singapore I first flew on 17 August 1926 piloted by John Parker and passed to Felixstowe during November; subsequently its auxiliary fins and rudders were removed and a large servo aerofoil was added to the main rudder, while 675hp Condor IIIAs were fitted along with four-bladed propellers. The planing bottom was reinforced.

By the mid-1920s Blackburn had acquired a fine reputation for the design and manufacture of naval landplanes and floatplanes. Convinced too of a profitable future for the flying-boat, the company had appointed Major J.D. Rennie as hull and float designer late in 1923. Rennie had previously been John Porte's chief technical officer at Felixstowe, and latterly had been employed by the Air Ministry. At Blackburn he worked with Major F.A. Bumpus, Blackburn's chief designer; drawing on the company's experience with the large Cubaroo biplane, the two set about the Iris flying-boat, another substantial aircraft with a span of 95ft 6in. Designed to Specification 14/24 (against which the Valkyrie had also been commenced), the RB.1 (Reconnaissance Boat 1) Iris Mk I was a three-bay equal span reconnaissance biplane with ailerons on all four wings, employing three Condor IIIs driving four-

Singapore I N179 in original configuration with small auxiliary fins and rudders, subsequently discarded, and Condor IIIs driving two-bladed propellers. The fore-body was later revised. The faired steel-tube interplane struts mounted monocoque engine nacelles that allowed the engines to be worked on or removed easily. The photograph was taken at Felixstowe in November 1926. *(Author's Collection)*

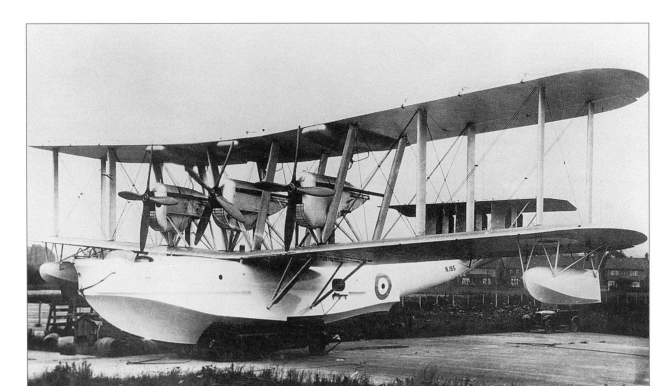

bladed propellers, mounted as self-contained units with their own oil tanks and starting equipment. A prominent biplane tail assembly was adopted, the upper of greater span and the lower used as a trimmer, together with three fins and rudders. The flight surfaces were of composite metal and wooden construction.

The wooden two-step hull, skinned with plywood, featured a pronounced vee-bottom and was equipped with a bow defensive position mounting a Lewis gun, a side-by-side open cockpit with dual controls, aft of which was a similar aperture but without controls, and a dorsal Lewis gun position. Two further guns could be mounted outside the hull by the aft portholes, while a 1,040lb bomb-load was provided. The usual crew complement was five, and four bunks were provided together with a galley. The new aircraft took two years to emerge and, serialled N185, was launched from Blackburn's Brough site on to the River Humber on 19 June 1926; assessment at Felixstowe lasted until August.

By that time Rennie was designing a duralumin hull for the Iris, the planing bottom integral with the hull, utilising two steps and a deep flared fore-body to minimise spray and provide a clean take-off. On its return from Felixstowe in March 1927 N185 was fitted with the metal hull together with replacement engines, Condor IIIAs, and improved metal wingtip floats. The central rudder was moved and converted to act as a servo unit while a tail gunner's position was introduced. The aircraft was redesignated RB.1A Iris II and launched in its new form on 2 August, travelling to Felixstowe for reappraisal.

On 12 August the Iris II joined up with three rival flying-boats, the wooden Valkyrie N186, the all-metal Singapore I N179 and Southampton N218, for a 3,000-mile tour

Blackburn's Iris I N185, showing its all-white wooden hull. Mounted above each engine under the upper wing was a 302-gallon fuel tank, just visible here. With military equipment removed the aircraft could have carried three crew and eighteen passengers; a proposal for a commercial version of the Iris was sent to a Mr Barker in New York during December 1926 but nothing came of it. *(Author's Collection)*

of Scandinavia departing from Felixstowe and commanded by Squadron Leader C.L. Scott. As well as flag-waving, the expedition was intended to evaluate and compare the aircraft under operational conditions. The Iris transported Sir Samuel Hoare, then Air Minister, as far as the Air Traffic Exhibition at Copenhagen. Stops were made at Esbjerg, Oslo, Copenhagen, Gdynia, Danzig, Helsinki and Stockholm before a return to Felixstowe on 11 September. The Southampton developed an engine fault at Danzig while the Valkyrie experienced a similar problem, being towed into Königsberg. The metal-hulled aircraft completed the 5,000-mile journey without incident despite some heavy seas, but during the tour the Valkyrie's hull soaked up a substantial amount of water – a trait not previously revealed as the aircraft had not spent long periods afloat. Although further tests were made by MAEE following the cruise and a metal hull was considered for N186, that programme came to an end.

The Ministry was impressed by the performance of the Iris II during the tour and issued Specification R.31/27 for a developed version, the long-range capability of which would complement the shorter-range Southamptons. Contracts for three Iris IIIs (N238, S1263 and S1264) were signed in February and March 1928. On 29 September the Iris II departed on another cruise, again flown by Squadron Leader Scott, this time to study its behaviour in the tropics, visiting Marseilles, Naples, Athens, Aboukir, Alexandretta, Baghdad, Basra, Jask and Karachi on the outbound journey, and returning to Calshot via Basra, Hinaidi, Habbaniyah, Alexandretta, Aboukir, Benghazi, Malta, Naples, Marseilles and Hourtin. Some 11,360 miles were covered in a flying time of 125hr 5min, at an average speed of 92mph. The only troubles concerned the starboard engine which had to be replaced at Jask, and choked filters necessitating a 10-mile taxi into Hinaidi. Further testing at Felixstowe followed before the aircraft was struck off.

N185 later received a metal hull, becoming the Iris II, and is seen here off Felixstowe. New low-drag nacelles with chin radiators have been installed. The wing-floats were also revised and their mountings simplified. In the background are the dock buildings. *(Gordon Kinsey)*

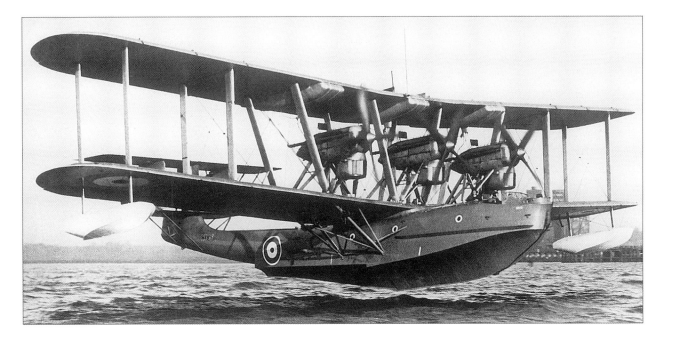

N238, the pre-production Iris III, seen at Brough along with some technology from a previous age. Traction engines were sometimes used to manoeuvre the larger flying-boats on land, where they could be very cumbersome. N238 was first flown on 21 November 1929 by N.H. Woodhead and travelled to Felixstowe later that month. Its crash at Batten Bay in Plymouth Sound on 4 February 1931 resulted in nine fatalities. *(Blackburn via Bryan Ribbans)*

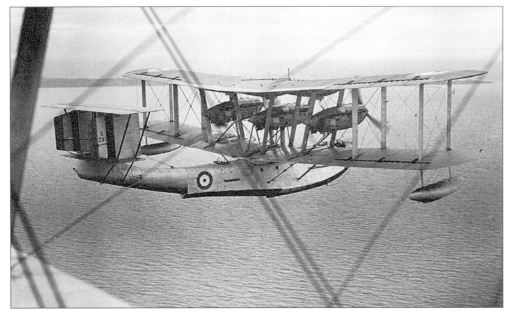

S1263, the first production Iris III, viewed from an accompanying aircraft. This example was lost on 12 January 1933 in an accident at Plymouth Sound when it collided with a naval pinnace while landing, by which time it had been converted to Iris V configuration. *(Bryan Ribbans)*

More Shorts' Developments

The Singapore I performed well during the Scandinavian tour but Shorts did not receive a production order. However, the aircraft went on to great things, being loaned to Sir Alan Cobham. Cobham initially planned to fly round the world but, having determined that the worst headwinds he might experience could cause the range of the Singapore to fall below the minimum required, he settled for a survey of Africa on behalf of Imperial Airways. That company had no funds to sponsor the enterprise, but finances were acquired from private individuals and industry. Minus military equipment and registered G-EBUP, the aircraft left Rochester on 17 November 1927, commencing an epic tour that went smoothly until arrival at Malta's RAF Kalafrana station, where a heavy swell damaged the wing-floats. The Singapore was quickly beached but sustained a further battering in the process. Following repairs, on 21 January 1928 Cobham set off for Benghazi and thence Tobruk, along the Nile to Mongalla (southern Sudan) and on to Entebbe and Mwanza on Lake Victoria. Via a survey diversion to Khartoum and back, Lake Tanganyika and Lake Nyasa were visited and the aircraft arrived at Durban on 8 March where it came out of the water for inspection and maintenance. Calls followed to Cape Town (30 March), Libreville (Gabon) – where G-EBUP touched bottom – and Lagos. An engine change was made at Fresco Bay and the Singapore carried on to Freetown (Sierra Leone), Porte Etienne (Mauritania), Grand Canary, Casablanca and Gibraltar. Via Barcelona and Bordeaux, Plymouth was made on

Singapore I N179 in its later form, employing Rolls-Royce Buzzards, Handley-Page slots and with the auxiliary fins and rudders removed. The forward hull profile has also been reworked. Prior to its conversion the aircraft had served with Alan Cobham as G-EBUP. It was exhibited at the July 1929 Olympia Show and made its first flight in its new build state during the following October. *(Author's Collection)*

31 May. A tour of British coastal resorts and ports followed before the Singapore finally returned to Rochester on 4 June 1928. A distance of over 23,000 miles had been flown during a flying time of 330 hours, and more than fifty possible flying-boat bases within Africa and around its coast had been surveyed.

The Singapore, re-serialled N179, returned to the Ministry, in whose hands its punishing regime continued. It was fitted with 825hp Rolls-Royce H.10 engines (later known as Buzzards) and, on the upper wing, Handley Page automatic slots. The hull fore-body was lengthened and the planing bottom amended to simulate that of the emerging Calcutta flying-boat. The revised aircraft was re-launched on 2 October 1928 and later travelled to Felixstowe where it ended its eventful life.

Arthur Gouge's S.8 Calcutta followed the Singapore. In 1926 the Air Council had agreed to add two three-engined flying-boats to Imperial Airways' fleet, a configuration preferred at that time not least for safety reasons. Shorts proposed a design generally similar to the Singapore I and received an order from the Director of Civil Aviation for two Calcuttas, G-EBVG and G-EBVH, to Specification 14/26. Avro also tendered with their Types 606 and 607 but were not selected. The Calcutta

The first Short Calcutta, G-EBVG. Above the upper wing are emergency radio masts. This aircraft served as a crew trainer during 1936 but returned to Imperial in September of that year; it was capsized by a storm at Mirabella, Crete, on 28 December. *(Author's Collection)*

Calcutta G-EBVH makes a pass for the camera. The second example first flew on 3 May 1928 and served on Imperial Airways' routes as *City of Athens* until it joined Air Pilots' Training Ltd at Hamble in June 1937, being dismantled for spares later that year. *(Short Brothers via Bryan Ribbans)*

followed the broad layout of the Singapore I but employed three 540hp Bristol Jupiter XIF engines and a deeper, wider metal hull. An open cockpit featuring full dual-control was employed, aft of which was a radio cabin and then comfortable seating for fifteen passengers; behind this again were the galley and toilet facilities. The first Calcutta, G-EBVG, was launched from Rochester on 13 February 1928 and John Parker flew it briefly the following day. A full Certificate of Airworthiness was granted for G-EBVG on 27 July and on 1 August Parker landed it on the Thames between the Vauxhall and Lambeth bridges, mooring off the Albert Embankment for three days during which period the aircraft was inspected by MPs.

Following several charter flights, both Calcuttas operated between Southampton and Guernsey. In February 1929 Imperial Airways took over full ownership of them from the Air Council. A third example, G-AADN, appeared in April 1929 and all three began a Genoa–Alexandria route via Ostia, Naples, Corfu, Athens, Suda Bay (Mirabella) and Tobruk, named *City of Alexandria* (G-EBVG), *City of Athens* (G-EBVH) and *City of Rome* (G-AADN), this forming part of Imperials' Croydon–India service. A fourth aircraft, G-AASJ *City of Khartoum*, was ordered, and another for the French government, F-AJDB, which flew on 1 September 1929. Subsequently a naval Calcutta (S.762) was supplied to the French Navy, designated S.8/2; Shorts agreed a manufacturing licence with Breguet for further examples.

On 26 October 1929 G-AADN was lost after leaving Ostia in a gale when the port engine developed a fault, necessitating a forced landing off Spezia. Though taken in tow by a local tug, the lines parted and the aircraft turned turtle; the three crew and four passengers perished. A fifth example was ordered for Imperial, G-AATZ *City of Salonika*, employing Bristol Jupiter XFBM engines, and first flew on

28 May 1930. During 1931 the Calcuttas were joined in the Mediterranean by the later Short Kent flying-boats with greater range, and passed to the Khartoum–Kisumu (Kenya) section of the Cairo–Cape route. They also continued along part of the Indian route from time to time, between Castelrosso and Haifa. Though G-AASJ was lost in an accident at Alexandria on 31 December 1935 the Calcutta service ran until 1936, and the type was subsequently used for crew training at Hamble; G-EBVG continued to serve, re-engined with Armstrong Siddeley Tiger VIs, while G-AATZ survived until 1939.

Large Military Types

At Blackburn the Iris III had emerged. The prototype, N238, flew for the first time on 21 November 1929 in the hands of 'on-loan' Boulton & Paul test pilot Squadron Leader C.A. Rea, accompanied by Major Rennie. The three examples, N238, S1263 and S1264, joined 209 Squadron at Mount Batten (formerly Cattewater) and were similar to the Mark II but employed a duralumin flight structure, while power came from three 675hp Condor IIIBs. The wingtip floats were redesigned, overload fuel tanks positioned under the wing roots and additional port holes provided. Testing of N238 at MAEE on the cusp of 1929 and 1930 revealed improved take-off, climb and two-engined performance compared with the Iris II; S1263 first flew on 5 February. During their time in service the Iris IIIs were the largest aircraft operated by the RAF and performed many long-distance overseas flights. In June 1930 S1263 and S1264 left Mount Batten for Reykjavik, and though S1263 became stranded with water in the fuel the second aircraft arrived in 11 hours flying time with a refuelling stop at Thorshaven – the return journey was the first non-stop flight between Iceland and Britain. On 25 August S1264 flew non-stop from Mount Batten to the Portuguese naval seaplane base at Bom Succeso near Lisbon, the first flying-boat to cross the Bay of Biscay, continuing on to Gibraltar before returning home.

The French civil Calcutta, F-AJDB. The flare at the chine is visible while the underside of the hull has received a coat of anti-corrosion paint. Powered by three Gnôme-Rhône Jupiter 9Akx engines, the aircraft arrived at St Raphael for service on 10 September 1929. It was later adapted for optional use by the French Navy.
(Short Brothers via Bryan Ribbans)

S.E. Saunders also sought to develop a metal hull but by the late 1920s the company was far from affluent. However, in the spring of 1928 Southampton N251 was loaned by the Air Ministry for the installation of a prototype. Knowler's hull was a duralumin structure with Alclad plating, a new corrosion-resistant alloy of duralumin sheet coated on each side with pure aluminium. Straight line frames were employed while longitudinal corrugations in the hull planking replaced the conventional riveted stringer, so simplifying construction. Double-curvature was minimal, especially around the vee-bottom. The crew dispositions were as for the Southampton layout though it is thought armament was not fitted. The Southampton flight surfaces and engines were retained and the aircraft became known as the Saunders A.14. Re-assembly of N251 was performed at Felixstowe. Initial testing in the spring of 1930 augured well, for behaviour was favourable on the water and in the air. By the summer the Saunders A.7 three-engined metal-hulled flying-boat was about to start trials and Knowler's 'corrugated' hull form became the standard approach at Cowes until the mid-1930s. Unfortunately in mid-July the A.14 hull revealed signs of distortion and buckling; local internal reinforcing became necessary.

Meanwhile by 1927 the Ministry was searching for an eventual replacement for the Southampton, but employing three engines to improve performance and safety. Three specifications were issued in pursuance of the requirement: R.4/27, R.5/27 and R.6/27. Industry responded with proposals by Blackburn (the Sydney to R.5/27), Saunders (the A.7 to R.4/27), Short Brothers (a Calcutta development to R.5/27) and Supermarine (the Air Yacht, probably to R.4/27, and the Southampton X to R.6/27). The Ministry procured prototypes from each company except Shorts.

Saunders A.14 N251 shows its slab-sided hull incorporating longitudinal corrugations rather than stringers. For aircraft where great speed was not essential the additional drag imposed by the corrugations was not significant. The lines of the planing bottom avoided a curved profile, instead employing a horizontal area immediately inboard of the chines, to which a narrowed straight-line vee-bottom was joined. These principles continued in use by Saunders-Roe until the completion of London production. *(Alec Lumsden)*

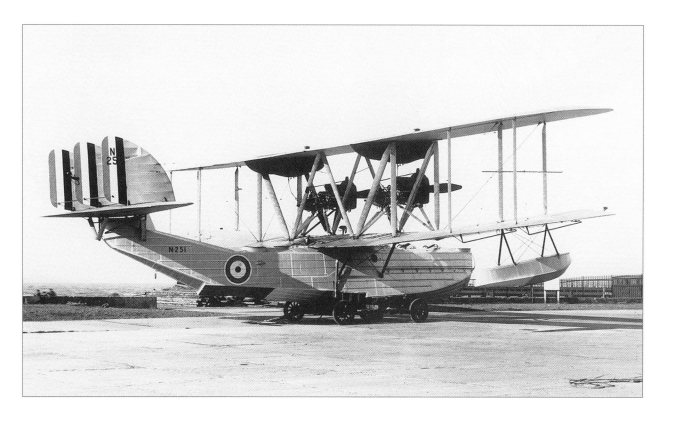

The single Southampton X was very different from previous aircraft of that name and was ordered in June 1928. Its stainless steel hull remained a Supermarine project but its sesquiplane wings were completed by Vickers at Weybridge, reflecting the Vickers (Aviation) Ltd merger embracing the Woolston company which took place that year. For their Mk X, Supermarine employed a corrugated form of hull structure reminiscent of the approach taken by S.E. Saunders at that time, again intended to keep weight down and simplify construction. A side-by-side cockpit layout was employed while Scarff rings equipped bow and dorsal positions and provision was made for a bomb-load of 1,000lb.

Trials with the Mk X, by then serialled N252, commenced in March 1930 in the hands of Supermarine test pilot Captain J.F. (Mutt) Summers. In August the aircraft travelled to Felixstowe for further assessment, but was found seriously overweight compared with design estimates: 13,427lb empty compared with the intended 10,090 lb. The effect on top speed and climbing ability was markedly adverse, even with changes of engines from 430hp Armstrong Siddeley Jaguar IVs to 525hp Armstrong Siddeley Panther IIAs and later 570hp Bristol Jupiter XFBMs. Attempts were made to lighten the airframe but without success and the design was dropped.

A contract for one Saunders A.7 Severn was placed in April 1928. After a long gestation Knowler's new aircraft appeared at Felixstowe for trials during July 1930 serialled N240. It was an 88ft-span sesquiplane powered by three 490hp Bristol Jupiter XIFP engines and employing a two-step hull similar to that of the A.14, with

Southampton X N252. Unfortunately the aircraft came out well over its predicted all-up weight: 23,000lb against 17,580lb. This naturally had a serious effect on performance, which changes to more powerful engines and a weight reduction exercise were unable to mitigate. Specified service ceiling was 11,800ft, but the greatest altitude achieved during Felixstowe trials was 6,400ft. With these fundamental problems, the programme was not pursued. *(Author's Collection)*

external longitudinal corrugations and minimal double curvature. Accommodation consisted of a bow position, open side-by-side cockpits with dual-control, a navigation and wireless room with sleeping area and galley extending under the wings, a dorsal defensive post and a tail-gunner's position, while the crew complement was five. The flight structures were of metal with fabric covering, the tail employing twin fins and rudders. Armament contemplated was three defensive machine-guns and a bomb-load of up to 1,840 lb.

In terms of water and air characteristics MAEE found much to praise, though trials confirmed the A.7 was under-elevatored and heavy on the rudders, so larger elevators and prominent servo-rudders on outriggers were installed. Unfortunately the Severn suffered from unduly light construction that led to a succession of structural failures, particularly of the hull. Though these were mostly minor the aircraft could not have withstood the rigours of service life in such form. The A.7 returned to Cowes for modifications and reinforcing but never entered production, N240 remaining the sole example. Following its trials, which included a Middle East cruise during the summer of 1931, in February 1932 the aircraft passed to 209 Squadron for maritime patrol duties as an interim measure while that unit was building up strength, but it was lost in the Channel on 13 July. The serial N245 was allocated to a paper twenty-one passenger civil variant of the Severn.

It is thought that Supermarine's Air Yacht also had its roots in Specification R.4/27. Planned as a three-engined reconnaissance biplane, an alternative monoplane layout was also contemplated and eventually adopted, while provision was made for a civil variant. The Air Yacht was the first multi-engined monoplane built by Supermarine, its parasol 92ft mainplane mounting three

Saunders A.7 Severn N240 seen during tests in the Solent. The aircraft travelled to the Middle East during the summer of 1931, being trialled extensively while based at Aboukir, and performance was considered acceptable. Unfortunately, though, the aircraft suffered from frailty, particularly of the hull, the engine mountings and many of the minor fittings. (Saro via W.F. Murray)

G-AASE

Supermarine's singular Air Yacht G-AASE *Flying Oma* was intended for use by the Hon. A.E. Guinness, as seen here. It was eventually sold to American Mrs June Jewell James, who named it *Windward III* and adorned it with a swastika for good luck, which worked in an oblique sort of way: the aircraft crashed but those aboard were saved! With its sponsons and parasol wing layout the Air Yacht was a considerable departure for Supermarine and the company did not produce any similar types subsequently. *(Fawley Historians)*

490hp Armstrong Siddeley Jaguar VI radials; wing structure was duralumin and the covering fabric. Unusually for a British manufacturer, lateral stability on the water was by means of sponsons, reminiscent of the Air Yacht's Dornier contemporaries. The wing was attached to the sponsons by sharply sloping V-struts and to the hull centre-section with two sets of N-struts, later supplemented by two further struts between wing and sponsons.

The metal two-step hull accommodated an open two-seat side-by-side cockpit and a generous cabin area, while triple fins and rudders were employed over a monoplane tailplane. In the event only the civil version was built, the sole example intended for the Hon. A.E. Guinness. The Air Yacht first flew in February 1930 piloted by Henri Baird, and was slowly fitted out with luxurious accommodation and facilities including a lounge complete with settees, as well as beds, a toilet and bath, a pantry and full electric lighting. The aircraft acquired its Certificate of Airworthiness on 22 December 1931, becoming G-AASE and christened *Flying Oma*. However, Guinness purchased a Saunders-Roe Cloud and the unwanted Air Yacht was stored at Hythe while an alternative buyer was sought.

4 THE 1930s

Saunders-Roe

In July 1929 S.E. Saunders Ltd was renamed Saunders-Roe Ltd, usually abbreviated to Saro. The company's board included newly knighted Sir Alliott Verdon Roe and businessman John Lord as joint managing directors. Roe had sold his interest in Avro to Sir John Siddeley of Armstrong-Whitworth Aircraft Ltd in 1928; he was fascinated by waterborne aircraft and wished eventually to develop very large flying-boats. The new concern quickly launched three similar private venture amphibious monoplane programmes, aimed at both civil and military markets, and all designed by Henry Knowler. The first was the A.17 Cutty Sark, commenced during March 1929, the prototype of which employed a hull using conventional frame and stringer construction.

The Cutty Sark was of modest size; span was 45ft, length 34ft 4 in, height 11ft 2 in and wing area 320sq ft. Accommodation was provided for two crew and two passengers, the cockpit was fully enclosed and dual-control standard. The wing was a thick-sectioned wooden Avro-Fokker watertight cantilever design of sufficient buoyancy to support the entire aircraft in the event of a flood, and was brought to Saro by Roe and Harry Broadsmith. The tail unit was of typical monoplane configuration, a welded steel, fabric-covered structure.

With one exception the A.17 was powered by two engines, mounted high over the wing on pylons and toed out slightly. The first example, G-AAIP, initially employed two 105hp Cirrus Hermes Is. G-AAIP first flew on 4 July 1929 from Cowes, piloted by Flying Officer Edward Chilton, before travelling to MAEE for its Certificate of Airworthiness trials in August which proved satisfactory. In May 1930 it passed to Messrs S. Kirston and R. Mace for a commercial service between Woolston and St Helier harbour, being named *Silver Bat* during that period. Re-engined with two 120hp de Havilland Gipsy IIs, G-AAIP departed on a 3,000-mile European sales tour on 26 March 1931 piloted by Stuart Scott, returning to Lympne on St George's Day. During January 1932 the aircraft passed to Captain Campbell Shaw and Flight Lieutenant Tommy Rose for use on their Isle of Man Air Service between Douglas harbour and Liverpool. G-AAIP was scrapped during 1935, by which time eleven further Cutty Sarks had appeared, incorporating the 'corrugated' metal hull form; powered by a variety of different engines, most were configured as amphibians from new.

The second and third examples were constructed during early 1930. The second initially wore Saro B conditions identity L1 but joined the Matthews Aviation Company in Hobart, Tasmania, as VH-UNV before being written off in April 1938.

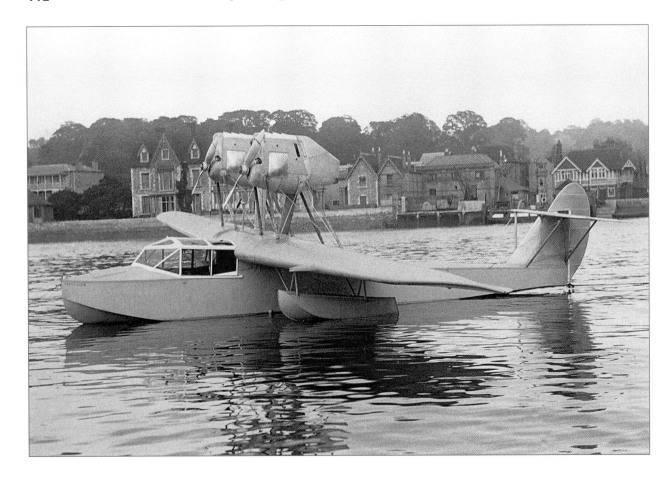

The third, like the second Gipsy II-powered but minus undercarriage, wore B mark L3 and travelled to New Zealand for use by the Governor-General where it retained that identity. The fourth, G-AAVX, went to the Royal Singapore Flying Club in December 1930, becoming VR-SAA during October 1934. A.17/5 G-ABBC was launched at Cowes during July 1930, and served businessman Francis Francis before passing to British Amphibious Air Lines Ltd in March 1932, operating from Squires Gate to Douglas and also from Blackpool seafront. During November 1930 the sixth example emerged serialled S1575, passing to the Seaplane Training Flight at Calshot before travelling to the MAEE for trials as a potential service trainer. Unfortunately the assessors were somewhat critical; S1575 crashed at Cowes in January 1934 while still wearing its military markings, and the type was not adopted by the RAF.

The seventh and eighth Cutty Sarks travelled to Hong Kong. The seventh became VR-HAY and was used by the Far East Aviation Company. The eighth, allotted L5, was fitted with a bow machine-gun and racks for small bombs but returned to Cowes after its intended sale to the Kwangsi Air Force was cancelled. Eventually, in February 1937, it joined Air Service Training Ltd (AST) at Hamble, becoming G-AETI. G-ACDP and G-ACDR had also been purchased by AST, arriving during April 1933. The AST Cutty Sarks were powered by two 140hp Armstrong Siddeley Genet Major Is, and G-AETI lasted until 1940. The eleventh and final examples journeyed abroad, meanwhile. G-ABVF was a pure flying-boat registered in March 1932 and powered by a single

Saunders-Roe's Cutty Sark prototype G-AAIP initially adopted small-diameter four-bladed propellers but these were soon dispensed with. At this early stage of its life the aircraft was still a pure flying-boat. The Cutty Sark was exhibited at Olympia in July 1929 before being purchased by Norman Holden and flying from Selsey Bill. The aircraft is seen here at Cowes, its name painted on the bows.
(C.A. Sims)

Armstrong Siddeley 240hp Lynx IVC radial; during May of that year it was purchased by the Japanese round-the-world pilot Yoshihara for a flight from San Francisco to Japan, but was crashed by him in Alaska. The final Cutty Sark, Genet-powered G-ADAF, travelled to San Domingo where by February 1935 it was flying for R.H. Kulka Ltd.

The A.19 Cloud was the largest of Saro's three cousins. The layout was similar to the Cutty Sark's but it had a span of 64ft and length of over 47ft, and again employed the 'corrugated' hull arrangement. Accommodation was for two crew and six to eight passengers and once more various engines were adopted. The first example, powered by two 300hp Wright Whirlwind J-6s, was flown from Cowes by Captain Stuart Scott on 15 July 1930 as L4. It received its Certificate of Airworthiness at the end of that month as G-ABCJ, and subsequently served in Canada as CF-ARB before returning to the makers in January 1934. Re-engined with 340hp Napier Rapier IVs, it resumed the identity G-ABCJ and was retained by Saro for tests before being loaned to Jersey Airways in August 1935. It was finally withdrawn from use in December 1936.

The second Cloud, G-ABHG, was ordered by the Hon. A.E. Guinness in mid-1930 and first flew on 18 February 1931 powered by three Lynx IVCs rather than a

The second A.17, VH-UNV, was the first of the Cutty Sarks to employ the 'corrugated' hull form. On the rudder it wears a Matthews Aviation badge. It was destroyed in an accident at Pinkenba on 5 April 1938. *(Author's Collection)*

twin configuration. However, before the aircraft had received its Certificate and was finally delivered, two 425hp Pratt & Whitney Wasps had been installed. Despite that, it retained much originality, being fitted with a large auxiliary aerofoil above the engines to supplement lift and assist flow over the tail, together with twin fins and three rudders. Named *Flying Amo*, it became based at Eastleigh. It was of great longevity, passing to Imperial Airways at Hythe for basic marine instruction, and later being used by BOAC at Poole for crew training before being withdrawn in June 1941.

G-ABXW *Cloud of Iona*, again equipped with Whirlwind J-6s, was launched in July 1932. Via British Flying Boats Ltd it passed to Guernsey Airways in September 1934 but crashed in bad weather off Jersey on 31 July 1936 with the loss of ten lives. The final civil-registered Cloud was G-ACGO, which flew in July 1933 powered by 340 hp Armstrong Siddeley Serval IIIs. Piloted by Stuart Scott, G-ACGO made an extensive European sales tour before joining the Bata shoe company in July 1934 as OK-BAK, re-engined with 300hp Walter Pollux radials. In 1936 it passed to Ceskoslovenské Státní Aerolini (CSA). During the German occupation of Czechoslovakia it was stored; after the war its wing could not be located but the hull was converted into the motor-launch *Delfin* (Prague Licence no. PO2-21), which was based on the Vltava until the mid-1960s.

The eighth Cutty Sark assumed Saro B conditions identity L5, just visible behind the wing-float. Armed for use by the Kwangsi Air Force, the aircraft sports a bow-mounted machine-gun and underwing bomb-racks. After the sale had fallen through, L5 became G-AETI, receiving Genet Major radials, and later joined Air Service Training at Hamble. *(British Hovercraft Corporation)*

Saro Cloud G-ABHG at rest off the Saunders-Roe premises at Cowes. It had previously employed three Lynx IVC radial engines but these were replaced, as seen here, by two 425hp Wasps. The tail arrangement was also unique by the time of this photograph, though the aircraft had started life with a standard Cloud configuration. Finally, the auxiliary wing lends a further novel dimension. The name *Flying Amo* is applied at the bows. *(British Hovercraft Corporation)*

Cloud OK-BAK was ex-G-ACGO. This example was powered by Walter Pollux radials for its sale to Bata; the rocker boxes protrude through the Townend rings. The aircraft is fitted with deflectors aft of the engine struts, to improve elevator control through rectifying a partial stall at the central region of the wing. The photograph was taken in the Solent just before delivery took place. *(British Hovercraft Corporation)*

In the meantime the Air Ministry had considered the Cloud as a navigational trainer; a further A.19 (K2681) was ordered, actually the third built. Launched at Cowes on 20 July 1931, it appeared at that year's Hendon SBAC Show coded 12. This version accommodated either six pupils plus wireless, signalling and electrical apparatus, or four pupils plus similar equipment together with increased fuel tankage for endurance of up to 5½ hours. The dual-control cockpit was utilised for flying training, and the military variant could also be fitted with gun rings in both bow and aft compartments, together with four 50lb bombs on underwing racks.

Trials led to several modifications including enlarged elevators, revisions to the horn balances, modified Townend rings, stiffening of the engine mountings, strengthening of the fin and tailplane, and reinforcement of the hull bottom and floats. Between 1932 and 1934 the Ministry ordered sixteen Clouds in three batches: K2894–K2898, K3722–K3729 and K4300–K4302. The RAF production version, known as the A.29, employed Armstrong Siddeley Serval Is and IIIs. The aircraft entered service with B Flight of the Seaplane Training Squadron at Calshot in August 1933, and was also flown by 48 Squadron (part of the School of Air Navigation, which absorbed B Flight in January 1936), the School of Air Pilotage and 9 Elementary and Reserve FTS, retiring in mid-1939. The Cloud in particular was a success for Saunders-Roe and helped provide a stable platform for more ambitious projects during the later 1930s.

'Military Cloud' prototype at MAEE during December 1931, employing exposed Double Mongoose engines. The aircraft bore the code 12 at first but was later allocated the serial K2681. Rigorous trials led to a number of modifications before the type entered production. *(Author's Collection)*

The A.21 Windhover completed Saro's trio of related amphibians and flying-boats, being mid-way in size and weight between the Cutty Sark and the Cloud. Possibly the added complexity of its third engine deterred buyers, but in any event only two examples appeared. The first was first flown from Cowes on 16 October 1930 by Stuart Scott, initially in flying-boat form. Powered by three 120hp Gipsy II engines and registered ZK-ABW, the aircraft travelled to MAEE on 22 October for trials. Though some frailty was detected in the hull plating around the step and local reinforcing had to be carried out, the assessment was generally favourable. The take-off was clean and free of porpoising, while the flying qualities were good with light, well-harmonised controls. ZK-ABW was intended for Dominion Airways in New Zealand but instead travelled as an amphibian to Matthews Aviation, becoming VH-UPB and flying with Cutty Sark VH-UNV. It operated between Melbourne, King Island and Launceston from January 1933 to February 1934. In mid-May 1936 it was destroyed in an accident off King Island.

The second Windhover, an amphibian from new, acquired its Certificate of Airworthiness in July 1931 as G-ABJP. Rather sluggish control was experienced near the stall and, because of the handling anomaly between engines-on and -off, a small winglet similar to that of Cloud G-ABHG was added, an arrangement also

A.29 Cloud K3722. Townend rings are fitted, and the aircraft has lost its engine strut fairings as part of a programme intended to improve elevator control. Practice bombs are mounted underwing. K3722 was severely damaged at Andover during February 1934 when it blew backwards into a hangar door during freak winds while with the School of Air Pilotage. Repaired, it served with 9 Elementary and Reserve FTS before being struck off in November 1938. *(Author's Collection)*

adopted by the first example. That month, G-ABJP was sold to Francis Francis and based at Heston, but Gibraltar Airways purchased it for a Tangier service that ran between 23 September and 3 January 1932, during which period it was named *General Godley*. It lay fallow for several months afterwards but by July had been acquired by the Hon. Mrs Victor Bruce who christened it *City of Portsmouth*, intending to use it to secure the world flight-refuelled endurance record.

For the attempt the aircraft's fuel capacity was greatly increased; 75- and 84-gallon tanks were added in the fuselage and a 75-gallon tank in the mainplane. Hand- and wind-driven fuel pumps were installed, together with emergency fuel jettison valves, while the undercarriage was removed to save weight. Mrs Bruce began her first attempt from Clarence Pier, Southsea, but after two hours was obliged to alight for adjustments. A second flight ended after 15 hours 40 minutes when fog prevented the refuelling aircraft, converted Bristol Fighter G-ABXA, from finding Mrs Bruce. However, the third attempt, made over 9–11 August 1932, lasted 54 hours 13 minutes, during which the Windhover was successfully refuelled over Sussex. Unfortunately, high oil temperature resulted in another abandonment and

Saro Windhover A.21/1 as VH-UPB, seen with Matthews Aviation Ltd. Like Cloud G-ABHG, by then it employed an auxiliary wing to improve elevator performance, although it had acquired its Certificate of Airworthiness as a pure monoplane. VH-UPB had started life as a flying-boat. The other Windhover, G-ABJP, had been built as an amphibian and was also later fitted with a second wing. *(Author's Collection)*

Mrs Bruce did not capture the world record; her time would have been a British record had the aircraft carried a sealed barograph but sadly, as part of the quest to save weight, none had been fitted. G-ABJP passed to Jersey Airways in May 1935, by which time its tankage had reverted to standard and the undercarriage had been reinstated. It was finally withdrawn in 1938.

Parnall's Tiny Moment

While the Saro amphibians were emerging, Harold Bolas, chief designer with the Bristol-based concern of George Parnall & Company, was contemplating a diminutive experimental flying-boat named the P.1 Prawn. Parnall had no history of designing flying-boats but had previously produced a number of successful aircraft, among them floatplanes. None the less, the firm secured a contract for one Prawn from the Air Ministry to Specification 21/24, which was entitled 'Single-Seater Boat Seaplane for Storage in Restricted Space', possibly with use by submarines in mind. Apart from being an exercise in miniaturisation, the aircraft was intended to investigate the effects and problems of mounting its single engine in the nose, or prow, rather than in any more usual location (for flying-boats) further away from the water. Serialled S1576, it was a single-seat 28ft-span parasol monoplane powered by a single 65hp Ricardo-Burt engine, its two-step hull of duralumin with stainless steel fittings and the wings fabric-covered. The tail consisted of a conventional single fin and rudder combined with a single tailplane. Shorts had a hand in the construction of the hull and possibly the wing-floats, but sources vary as to the extent of their involvement.

Parnall's diminutive Prawn; its size can be gauged from the cockpit headrest. The powerplant is in the raised position and the miniature propeller is notable. The engine was similar to the type considered for use as an auxiliary motor in the *R.101* airship. In the distance is Blackburn's Sydney, which would probably put the date of the photograph at 1931 or 1932. The Prawn languished at Felixstowe until 1934 when it was scrapped. *(Author's Collection)*

The novelty of the Prawn, apart from its size (it was even smaller than Shorts' Cockle), lay in its engine installation, which was able to elevate by up to 22 degrees to ensure clearance of the propeller from the water as the aircraft changed its attitude during take-off. A four-bladed propeller of the smallest possible diameter was fitted, also for that reason. When lowered, the engine nacelle lay flush with the lower bow area of the hull, the propeller boss forming the prow; forward vision was much improved in the latter position. The Prawn took six years to materialise from the issue of the specification, possibly because the idea of a submarine carrying an aeroplane had palled, but it travelled to Felixstowe during 1930 by when H.V. Clarke had become Parnall's chief designer. It seems the aircraft may never have flown; its engine overheated during taxying trials and whether it was rebuilt is not known. The programme was taken no further and Parnall turned instead to a large land-based military general-purpose biplane.

Biplanes and Monoplanes

Blackburn's Iris IIIs S1263 *Leda* and S1264 spent the spring and summer of 1931 serving with 209 Squadron generally in the Mediterranean and Near East, but sadly the prototype, N238, had crashed in Plymouth Sound on 4 February that year after a poor approach. A replacement was ordered, serialled S1593 and named *Zephyrus*, which first flew on 25 June after a speedy twenty-week build programme. S1593

In marked contrast to the Prawn was Iris S1593, viewed at Brough, which started life as the final Mk III production aircraft and was later modified to Iris V standard. *Zephyrus* travelled to Malta during June 1933 and following its conversion to a test-bed for the Napier Culverin was based at Felixstowe from September 1937 until it was struck off in April 1938, though during that period it amassed only 15 hours 35 minutes flying time. *(Author's Collection)*

adopted a revised prow profile and an aperture forward of the bow gun ring to accommodate a 30mm COW quick-firing cannon.

To improve performance and engine reliability, eroded as weight had grown in terms of fuel and equipment carried, Blackburn suggested S1593 be re-equipped with 825hp Rolls-Royce Buzzard IIMS engines driving larger propellers and mounted in more streamlined nacelles. In late 1931 the Ministry agreed to the modification of all three Iris IIIs and on 5 March 1932 S1263 flew with Buzzards as the Iris V, piloted by A.M. Blake. Trials at Felixstowe were satisfactory and the aircraft was also evaluated on East Loch Tarbert before joining 209 Squadron. S1593 returned to Blackburn's premises during December 1932 and flew as an Iris V on 31 March 1933, retaining the COW gun installation. Meanwhile, S1264 sank at its moorings off Felixstowe in a gale on 3 January 1933, though it was recovered and taken to Brough for repair and conversion. S1593 went on to test the 720hp Napier Culverin I engine, a licence-built Junkers Jumo IVC diesel, first flying in that configuration on 9 June 1937 in the hands of A.M. Blake and carrying out extensive ground running as well as flight tests.

The remaining Iris was the Mk IV, the origins of which had emerged as early as 1926 when the company had drawn up a version employing three 700hp Armstrong Siddeley Leopard engines, with an estimated reduction in weight of 2,100lb counterpointed by increased speed and range. Eventually Iris II N185 received three 800hp Leopards, the centre unit arranged as a pusher, first flying in

The Iris IV was a late-life conversion of N185 employing three Armstrong Siddeley Leopard engines arranged as two tractors and a pusher. The pusher configuration was adopted to aid investigations into cooling of pusher radials and to examine the relative efficiency of tractor and pusher propellers. The aircraft is seen here at Brough. Blackburn contemplated a civil passenger-carrying version of the Iris during 1931 but those plans were not taken up. *(Author's Collection)*

its new form on 6 May 1931, again piloted by Blake. During trials at Felixstowe, this aircraft flew at an all-up weight of 35,000lb, becoming the heaviest Iris.

By the time the Iris IV was flying, Brough was engrossed with the RB.2 Sydney, a fundamental departure from its previous flying-boats. J.D. Rennie's response to Specification R.5/27 sought to exploit the success of the Iris II metal hull but married to a monoplane wing so as to achieve a sizeable decrease in weight and drag. A contract for one Sydney was placed in February 1928. Blackburn decided to build a civil variant at the same time, powered by three 515hp Bristol Jupiter IX engines and named the CB.2 (Commercial Boat) Nile. The Nile was intended to carry three crew and fourteen passengers together with baggage and mail. It would serve on the Alexandria to Cape Town route of Cobham-Blackburn Air Lines Ltd, formed in April 1928, in which Alan Cobham Aviation Ltd held an interest. The Nile's hull was exhibited at the July 1929 Olympia Aero Show and was almost complete by February 1930, when the British government decided Imperial Airways would assume responsibility for all Empire air routes. Cobham-Blackburn's aspirations were dashed; work on the Nile stopped later in February and its hull was subsequently used for tests into stressed skin strength.

The cockpit of the Iris, showing the two large control wheels and the flight instruments. The engineering panels are aft, out of shot. *(Blackburn via Bryan Ribbans)*

The Sydney programme continued, however. Though its two-step hull was somewhat similar to that of the Iris it was more spacious as the sides were perpendicular rather than sloping in toward the decking. With a crew of five, accommodation consisted of a bow mooring position with a Lewis gun and a side-by-side dual-control enclosed cockpit, behind which were engineering and navigation posts. Aft of these were dorsal and tail gun positions. The main step featured a simple vent intended to help break water suction on take-off.

The 100ft span deep-section wing was mounted on a tubular steel faired pylon and braced by long struts to the hull chine. Frise ailerons equipped the tapering outer sections while the centre section bore the wing-float struts. The three 525hp Rolls-Royce F.XIIMS engines were located along the wing leading-edge, their nacelles fitted with radiator shutters, while the main 560-gallon fuel tank was situated in the pylon. Both wing and tailplane were of all-metal construction and fabric-covered. Racks beneath the wings could carry either two 550lb or four 250lb bombs, or two torpedoes. The all-up weight of the Sydney was 23,350lb. The aircraft, serialled N241 and painted silver, first flew on 18 July 1930 from Brough in the hands of C.A. Rea.

After tests delayed by a seized centre engine the aircraft travelled to Felixstowe on 9 December painted battleship grey overall. At MAEE modifications were made to the tail (by inserting struts between the rudder posts), as well as to the wing and its bracing. The pylon was found to adversely affect elevator control (the elevator

The sole Blackburn Sydney, N241, undergoing engine trials at Brough on 18 July 1930, prior to its first flight. Its hull is in an all-silver scheme. The tail unit is devoid of fins, the central rudder acting merely as a trimmer and the outer pair sporting trailing-edge servo tabs. Armament is not fitted. *(Author's Collection)*

chord was subsequently increased by 20 per cent), while the vented step was found to provide only negligible improvement over the conventional form. Sadly, repeated unserviceability dogged the Sydney during its first stay with the testing authorities, which lasted until January 1932; after a second visit it was struck off with no production ensuing.

-o0o-

Supermarine's fortunes in the early 1930s included a major disappointment concerning their Type 179 Giant commercial flying-boat, a fall-out from their rejected submission to R.6/28 that gave rise to Shorts' Sarafand. A civil version of Woolston's offering, to Specification 20/28, it was a seven-crew, forty passenger high-wing 160ft-span all-metal monoplane powered by six pylon-mounted tractor-pusher paired engines. This matured into a version employing six Rolls-Royce Buzzard MS engines arranged as two pairs of tractor-pushers and two outboard tractor singletons. All-up weight ranged between 65,000–74,000lb but was later indicated as 72,500lb. The aircraft was intended for use particularly in the Mediterranean.

In early drafts part of the passenger accommodation was in the thick-section wing leading-edge, but this was later altered to a more conventional arrangement within a luxurious hull. Maximum speed was calculated at 145mph, range at 1,300 miles and (final) loaded weight 75,090lb. A contract was awarded for one example,

On 28 November 1930 N241 is launched for the first time in its new scheme of battleship grey. Its centre engine is stopped; the nacelles and chin radiators resembled those of the Iris II. The forward hydro-dynamic portion of the hull is also similar to the Iris. The pylon mounting the wing is displayed; the oil coolers can just be made out in the side area. The wing struts around the floats were later modified. *(BAE SYSTEMS)*

Supermarine's Type 179 Giant was never completed. An impression of the aircraft is here grafted to a view of Woolston. Although the design was considered for use in the Mediterranean, it bears the name *Santa Fe*, lending a transatlantic feel. *(Supermarine via Fawley Historians)*

G-ABLE, in April 1931. Construction of the hull was well under way when during the following year the Air Ministry cancelled the project as an economy measure.

By way of no real compensation at all, in October 1932 the Air Yacht found a buyer. Following its sojourn at Hythe it was purchased by Mrs June Jewell James, a wealthy American who intended to use it for Mediterranean cruises. Re-engined with three 525hp Armstrong Siddeley Panther IIA engines and re-named *Windward III*, the Air Yacht commenced a tour carrying Mrs James and her guests, with Henri Baird as first pilot. Cherbourg, St Nazaire and later Naples were reached, the journey in part made during poor weather, but at Naples Baird had to seek medical attention. The Air Yacht was then flown by Tommy Rose but on 25 January 1933 the aircraft stalled and fell into the sea off Capri. The party were rescued by local fishermen and the damaged aircraft was beached, but it seems the only parts brought back to England were the engines.

Rochester Takes the Lead

Following assessment of the responses to its 1927 specifications for a Southampton replacement, the Ministry had ordered prototypes from each competitor except Short Brothers. Rochester complained; acknowledging the company's track record of successful flying-boats, the Ministry issued Specification R.32/27 to Shorts and by 1930 the Singapore II had emerged. Arthur Gouge's design featured a hull similar to that of the Singapore I but with a more prominent keel and a deeper fore-body. A side-by-side open cockpit was provided, just aft of which were the radio and navigation positions, with rest bunks, ice box, cooker and work bench installed to support long-range operations. A crew of six was envisaged. Armament consisted of a Lewis gun at the mooring position and two more amidships. Wingspan was

Short Singapore II N246 off Calshot, with Southampton S1124 in the background. The aircraft sports its triple fin-and-rudder configuration; later the cockpit was enclosed. On the dorsal decking is a long-range fuel tank. The bulged lower wing roots accommodated cantilever extensions from the hull main-frames that replaced the chine struts of the Singapore I (among other Short flying-boats), and also contained the main fuel tanks. The radiator arrangements were modified several times. *(Bryan Ribbans)*

90ft but compared with the Singapore I the area was greater, as the lower wing of the Mk II was increased in span; the maximum all-up weight of the Singapore I had been 20,000lb but the Mk II weighed in at 31,500lb. The tail layout consisted of a large single fin and rudder sporting a large Flettner servo, together with a mid-mounted tailplane. The Singapore II was initially powered by four 480hp Rolls-Royce pre-production F.XII engines mounted in cowled pusher-and-tractor pairs and supported by struts reduced in numbers compared with the Singapore I, which lowered drag. The struts used on the Singapore I to connect the lower wings with the hull chines were replaced by a flared lower wing root incorporating cantilever extensions from the hull main-frames.

The new type, serialled N246, was launched from Rochester's no. 3 shop on 27 March 1930 and flew later that day in the hands of John Parker. On 9 May it travelled to Felixstowe. Its single rudder was found inadequate and was later replaced with a triple fin and rudder arrangement. At that time too the tailplane was modified and a tail gunner's position added, while the upper ailerons were reduced but lower wing ailerons added. Rolls-Royce Kestrels were installed and the reworked aircraft was flown by Parker on 17 February 1931. In company with the Saro A.7, and with a dorsal overload fuel tank added, the Singapore II left for Aden on 15 August for tropical trials, which proved successful. On its return to Britain a modified planing bottom and wing-floats were installed together with a new radiator layout; Shorts continued to refine the cooling system and the planing bottom, and the aircraft also acquired an enclosed cockpit. N246 then formed the basis for the production version, the Singapore III, being finally used at Felixstowe for drop tests from various heights from the 50-ton crane there.

In parallel with the Singapore II, Shorts had produced the S.8/8 Rangoon which first flew in the same year. In their response to Specification R.5/27 Shorts had sought to exploit the Calcutta with a hull based around that of the Singapore but somewhat larger. Though the Ministry had declined Shorts' proposal, that work formed the basis for an offer to the French Navy while a Calcutta development was also tendered to the Japanese Navy. By the time design was under way on the French version, the Ministry had issued Specification R.18/29 for a large flying-boat to re-equip 203 Squadron in Iraq. The combination of very high temperatures and humidity had damaged the squadron's earlier Fairey IIID floatplanes and wooden-hulled Southamptons, and though metal-hulled Southamptons had been introduced their flight structures were wooden and their hulls were not sufficiently ventilated for comfortable tropical use.

Three Rangoons (S1433, S1434 and S1435) were ordered by the Ministry to R.18/29, a similar design to the French Naval Calcutta; both variants were fitted with enlarged fuel tanks between the outboard engine nacelles instead of above them as in the British Calcuttas. However, the Rangoon featured enclosed cockpits equipped with sun blinds, as well as a fresh-water tank and an ice box, bunks and a work bench. Built alongside the final civil Calcutta, construction was all-metal except for the fabric covering of the wings and tail unit. The Rangoons were powered by three 525hp Bristol Jupiter XIF engines and carried a crew of five. Armament consisted of a Lewis gun in the bow position and two amidships, and a bomb-load of 1,000lb.

The first example, S1433, was flown at Rochester on 24 September 1930 by John Parker; the second and third followed in December. Via crew training at Felixstowe the aircraft flew in formation to Basra, arriving in February 1931. The duties of 203 Squadron consisted mainly of patrols along the coastline of the Trucial States and helping with the suppression of smuggling along the trade routes in that part of the world. Their Rangoons proved trouble-free even in the acute climate and were

Shorts' first Rangoon, S1433. This aircraft was allocated to 203 Squadron in January 1931, arriving at Basra for service during April. In late 1933 it was modified by Shorts to Specification R.19/31 to receive a stainless steel planing bottom, returning to 203 Squadron in March 1934. From August 1938 it served with 210 Squadron based at Pembroke Dock. *(R. Stride)*

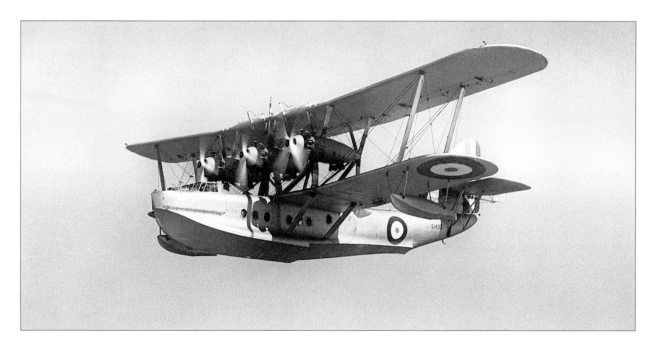

popular with their crews; two more (K2134 and K2809) were ordered in 1931 to Specification R.19/31D. Both featured stainless steel planing bottoms. K2134 first flew on 9 March 1932 and K2809 on 1 November. Meanwhile, the sole French Naval Calcutta had been launched in June 1931 and was flown by John Parker on 9 July before departing for Le Havre on 30 August. Four similar aircraft, referred to as Rangoons but employing Gnôme-Rhône K.9 engines, were manufactured under licence by Breguet. The Breguet Br 521-01 Bizerte flown by the French Navy adopted Shorts' hull principles, as did the civilian Br 530 Saïgon intended for operation by Air Union.

The association between Shorts and Japan, begun through the manufacture of F.5s by Aichi under Rochester's guidance, was renewed in the late 1920s. By 1928 Kawanishi Kokuki Kabushiki Kaisha had been established at Kobe and the following year Yoshio Hashiguchi, Kawanishi's chief engineer, travelled to England. At that time the Japanese Navy sought a fast, long-range patrol flying-boat; Shorts demonstrated the Singapore I and the Calcutta to Hashiguchi who preferred the Calcutta but not with Jupiter engines, Japanese rights to which were held by local rivals Nakajima; however, he had experience of the Eagles powering the F.5s. Rolls-Royce offered 820hp Buzzards which were confirmed as acceptable.

The resultant aircraft, the S.15 K.F.1, took a form generally similar to the Rangoon but substantially bigger, with a span of 101ft 10in and an all-up weight of 39,000lb. Its metal wing main structure comprised duralumin box spars and tubular lattice

The final Rangoon, moored off Calshot. K3678 also employed a stainless steel planing bottom and first flew on 7 September 1934, being delivered to Felixstowe two days later. It arrived with 203 Squadron in June 1934 and later served with 210 Squadron at Gibraltar, but was subsequently damaged in a gale at Malta.
(Dave Etheridge)

ribs, while the three Buzzards were disposed in mid-gap monocoque nacelles; above each was a vertical radiator. A separate centre-section was not employed. Both upper and lower wings utilised Frise ailerons while the mid-portion of the upper and the roots of the lower were bulged to accommodate the fuel tanks, which provided capacity for the specified range of 2,000 miles. The tail unit consisted of a single main fin and balanced rudder, with a mid-mounted variable incidence tailplane carrying small supplementary fins and rudders used to counteract yaw in the event of an engine failure. The hull was flared along its chine and, like the Singapore II and the later Rangoons, employed a stainless steel planing bottom. Two separate open side-by-side cockpits were provided and further accommodation consisted of engineering and wireless positions, a ward-room, galley and accommodation for eight suitable for long-range operations. Defensive posts were provided in bow and tail positions, together with two amidships, all armed with Scarff-mounted Lewis guns.

On 10 October 1930 the K.F.1 flew for the first time, sporting Shorts' B Conditions identity M-2 and Japanese Hinomaru markings; the pilot was John Parker, who found all was well. Following company trials, M-2 travelled to Felixstowe for evaluation; it was issued with a Certificate of Airworthiness (a rarity for a large military flying-boat!) in favour of Kawanishi on 2 December and was then shipped to Japan. A team from Shorts including C.P.T. Lipscomb travelled east to re-erect it at Naruo, and Parker followed to carry out the first flights. The aircraft was launched at the end of March 1931 and Parker piloted M-2 for the first time in Japan on 8 April; six days later he flew the aircraft at its maximum weight and the

Shorts' S.15 K.F.1 M-2 arrived at Felixstowe for assessment on 22 October 1930. Its relationship to the Rangoon is clear, though the latter was powered by Jupiters. The Kawanishi-built examples featured enclosed cockpits. *(Philip Jarrett)*

design was accepted for production under licence. Shorts personnel stayed in Japan for over a year in an advisory capacity. Kawanishi built four K.F.1s, designated the Navy Type 90-2 (later H3K2), and the first flew during March 1932. The second emerged in November, and the third and fourth the following year. The licence-built examples were used for reconnaissance and training until 1936, during which period one was lost in a fatal accident during night flying training, caused by an altimeter lag error.

Built in the same no 3. shop as the K.F.1 was the S.14, later named the Sarafand. With work under way on the Singapore II, Oswald Short had turned to the idea of building a very large military flying-boat of great range, having in mind trans-atlantic capability and flights with the minimum of staging between the far-flung parts of the British Empire. The company submitted preliminary drawings to the Ministry's Directorate of Technical Development while Oswald Short also sought out the Chief of the Air Staff, Sir Hugh Trenchard. Short persuaded Trenchard to fund the project despite the latter's lack of enthusiasm over large aircraft in general and his personal belief that flying-boats were not really essential for the RAF. Specification R.6/28 was prepared around Oswald Short's plans and issued in late 1928; a contract was placed for one example of the new flying-boat. Supermarine's rival Type 179 design was declined at that time.

Construction of the S.14, serialled S1589, began in the summer of 1931, following detailed wind-tunnel tests at the RAE. A year later the hull had been completed while the lower wing and the engine installations were in place. However, no. 3 shop was not large enough to allow the attachment of the upper

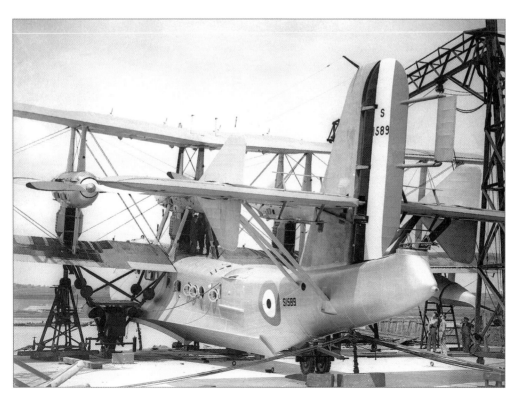

The huge upper wings of the Short Sarafand were erected during June 1932 at a former barge-yard a little way down the Medway from Short Brothers' no. 3 shop, where the previous phases of con-struction had been carried out. Scaffold lifts were used to raise the wings into place and final assembly was carried out in the open. The aircraft was launched in completed state on 30 June.
(Short Brothers via Bryan Ribbans)

wing, so on 15 June 1932 the aircraft was moved outside wearing a jury-rig across its lower wing and nacelles, and also minus the lower wing-tips. It was floated down the Medway to a new slipway where it was hauled ashore for final assembly. On the evening of 30 June the S.14 was first flown by John Parker with Oswald Short as second pilot. Parker found the controls light and responsive; few modifications were needed before the second flight on 3 July.

The Sarafand had its roots in the Singapore II but was very much bigger at a mighty 70,000lb all-up weight, and with a span of 120ft. Again the two-step hull employed a stainless steel planing bottom, with a swept-up prow and prominently flared chines tapering to slimmer middle and upper sections. A series of watertight bulkheads was placed beneath the hull floor while most of the floor panels were detachable to allow inspection of the bilges. Several watertight shutters were also provided to close off sections of the hull above the water line if necessary. A crew of ten was planned. In the bow was positioned the usual mooring-cum-defensive post; instead of a Lewis gun it could if required be equipped with a 1½-pounder cannon. Aft was an enclosed side-by-side dual-control cockpit that included an autopilot.

The facilities within the huge hull were very comprehensive. A passageway connected the cockpit with the ward-room, which was equipped with a chart board and table as well as the engineer's control panels. Aft again, below the centre-section, was a cabin containing a folding table and four bunks, intended for senior officers or passengers, then a galley and a crew cabin, again with four bunks. Two further bunks, a stretcher, work bench and a toolkit were stowed just ahead of the staggered dorsal defensive positions, and that area included a detachable cover on the decking through which a complete spare engine could be loaded; two spare propellers were also carried. Aft of the dorsal gunners' positions were a toilet and a further stowage area, while a catwalk led to the tail gunner's post. A telephone intercom system linked the crew stations while a heated cupboard was provided for drying wet clothes. Initially the radio post was sited near the dorsal gunners, but it was later relocated to the ward-room.

Because of the great span and considerable end loads, the wing spars were of stainless steel rather than duralumin. Of equal span, the wings featured detachable tips; the upper was bulged at the centre and the lower at the roots to accommodate the fuel tanks which between them held 3,382 gallons. The three monocoque engine nacelles accommodated six 825hp Rolls-Royce Buzzard II engines in tractor and pusher pairs, supported by a system of vertical girders, splayed struts to the wing roots and intermediate horizontal struts. The wing-floats featured stainless steel bottoms and were fitted with sacrificial zinc anode plates to minimise corrosion. The tail unit consisted of a huge single fin and rudder, together with a servo rudder, and a mid-mounted tailplane bearing auxiliary fins fitted to counteract yaw in the event of an engine failure, in much the same way as the K.F.1.

On 10 July 1932 Parker flew S1589 at Kingsnorth before several hundred members of the Press and public. His display lasted forty minutes and was most impressive, the Sarafand performing with massive daintiness on the water and in

11 July 1932: with the gentlemen of the Press observing from the MV *Essex Queen* off Kingsnorth, John Parker demonstrates the Sarafand, reaching speeds of around 150mph at a weight of 55,000lb. Parker had flown the aircraft on only four previous occasions; his display lasted forty minutes and was considered a masterpiece of exhibition flying. A chase-plane is visible on the left. *(Short Brothers via Bryan Ribbans)*

the air – at the time it was the second largest aircraft in the world. Oswald Short and Arthur Gouge could be proud of their giant. On 2 August S1589 passed to MAEE for trials which lasted until June 1933 when it returned to Rochester for overhaul. A further period at MAEE followed, with a new Alclad planing bottom. In June 1935 the Sarafand led a formation of varied flying-boats at the RAF's Hendon display and after further tests, particularly into ground effect, it was scrapped during the following year. Consideration was given to ordering additional examples for use as mobile headquarters in the Far East but the idea was not taken up. From its first flight the Sarafand had proved trouble-free, providing Shorts with the experience, confidence and much technical data to press ahead with further large and complex projects.

-oOo-

Though Rochester was deeply involved with military flying-boats the company did not neglect the commercial market, supplying a new type to Imperial Airways. In October 1929 the Italian authorities had barred Imperial from using several vital seaports including Genoa and Tobruk (in Italian colonial territory), which had affected part of the Cairo route. Imperial considered Mersa Matruh in Egypt as a stopping point but the harbour there was not always safe. Concluding that the Mirabella–Alexandria stage of the route must therefore be flown non-stop, the airline approached Shorts with a requirement for three new commercial flying-boats. These should be four-engined, with maximum passenger space and mail-carrying capacity (air mail was an extremely good revenue earner), comfortable and seaworthy, and incur minimum operational and maintenance costs – quite a wish-list! Arthur Gouge responded with the S.17 Kent, the three examples of which were G-ABFA *Scipio*, G-ABFB *Sylvanus* and G-ABFC *Satyrus*; manufacture began during October 1930 and *Scipio* first flew on 24 February 1931 in the hands of John Parker.

The Kent stemmed from the Calcutta, particularly around the flight surfaces. The wings were similar but larger at 113ft span, and were equipped with four Frise ailerons, while the wing-floats were mounted in the same way as on the earlier aircraft. Four 555hp Bristol Jupiter XFBM engines driving four-bladed propellers were disposed equidistantly at the mid-gap, mounted on single pairs of vertical struts and employing horizontal spacers after the Short fashion. Three fuel tanks were situated in the centre of the upper wing, while the fin and rudder were reminiscent of the Calcutta. Equipped with a stainless steel planing bottom and chine plating below the water line, a two-step hull configuration was employed. Beyond the bow mooring hatch was the dual-control side-by-side enclosed cockpit, then the radio and navigation positions; aft again were the main passenger cabin and a mail compartment. The cabin was spacious, 14ft long and with 6ft 6in headroom, and was well appointed for fifteen passengers, with tables positioned between the seats and a wide central gangway. Large square windows were

Short S.17 Kent G-ABFB *Sylvanus* at speed on the Medway on the day of its launch, 31 March 1931, piloted by Major Herbert Brackley. This example was delivered to Hythe for Imperial Airways on 26 May. The Prince of Wales joined Brackley that day for a flight in G-ABFB over the Canadian Pacific liner *Empress of Britain*, making her maiden voyage. *(Short Brothers)*

provided for good visibility. Aft were the steward's position, a galley and a lavatory. Care was taken to sound-proof the cabin as much as possible while the engine exhausts were fitted with full collector rings and long tail pipes in a further effort to reduce noise.

Parker left for Japan soon after *Scipio*'s first flight and further trials were carried out by Imperial Airways' Major Herbert Brackley, who coincidentally had previously helped train Japanese F.5 pilots at the Aichi factory. Brackley's first flight took place on 12 March at a weight of 28,000lb; next day he flew the Kent at a fully laden 32,000lb. On 25 March *Scipio* travelled to Felixstowe for Certificate of Airworthiness trials. *Satyrus* flew on 2 May and the following day *Scipio* left Hythe on its maiden commercial flight. Over the next few weeks Brackley concentrated on the introduction into service of the second and third flying-boats, and on checking out pilots; he received warm personal thanks from Oswald Short for his work on the acceptance programme.

Once the Italians had raised the bar on their ports, on 16 May *Satyrus* commenced Kent operations from Genoa on Imperial Airways' Mediterranean route. Unfortunately *Scipio* soon lost a wing-tip in heavy seas while *Sylvanus* collided with a Dornier Wal flying-boat in Genoa harbour, damaging two engines. The workload was therefore placed with the Calcuttas while repairs were effected, though the older flying-boats could not fly non-stop between Mirabella and Alexandria. The Kents were back in service by August, however, and the following October began operations from Brindisi.

From then on, Imperial's Indian and African routes were separated at Athens, a section of the Indian service operated by Kents via Castelrosso to Haifa, the African

Kent G-ABFB shows its hull profile for the camera. *Sylvanus* flew with Imperial until November 1935, but during that month was set on fire and burned out at Brindisi by an Italian arsonist. The type stayed in service until *Satyrus* was scrapped at Hythe during June 1938. *(Short Brothers via Bryan Ribbans)*

continuing to connect Mirabella with Alexandria. The Kents also flew an air mail route from Alexandria via Haifa to Cyprus between April and October 1932. Each aircraft travelled over 4,000 miles every week on these services and maintenance schedules were reduced, but no losses were incurred for mechanical or structural reasons. However, *Scipio* sank after a heavy landing at Mirabella on 22 August 1936. The final example, *Satyrus*, carried out three significant survey flights beginning with part of a proposed route to the Cape, flying to Lindi in Tanganyika, during April 1937. The second such expedition was made during June and July, and examined the Australian route, via Rangoon and Victoria Point, as far as Singapore. The final survey was made to Singapore via Bangkok during October and November 1937, and after a long life *Satyrus* was scrapped at Hythe in June 1938.

Meanwhile 203 Squadron's Rangoons had also conducted long-distance flights. During October 1933 a 4,000-mile return journey was made between Basra and Aden to survey the Arabian coastline in support of a future Imperial Airways route. In September and October 1934 three Rangoons under Group Captain R.E. Saul travelled from Basra to Melbourne to visit the centenary celebrations of the State of Victoria, a round trip of some 19,000 miles accomplished without incident despite severe monsoon conditions encountered in Malaya. A final example, K3678, arrived for service with the Squadron but in September 1935 203 began to re-equip and the type subsequently joined 210 Squadron at Pembroke Dock. During the Abyssinian crisis in September 1935 210 Squadron moved to Gibraltar but returned to Britain at the end of the year, retiring their Rangoons. S1433 travelled to Rochester where all military equipment was removed. Granted a Certificate of Airworthiness as G-AEIM on 26 September 1936, the aircraft became based at Hamble as an Imperial Airways crew trainer; it was scrapped there two years later.

Blackburn: Largest Biplane Flying-Boat

While Shorts had pursued their series of successful designs, the other flying-boat manufacturers had also been busy. Blackburn's R.B.3A Perth appeared in 1933. It was the largest biplane flying-boat employed by the RAF, with a maximum all-up weight of 38,000lb, and was the ultimate Iris development – in fact Iris V S1593 was modified to Perth standard as a prototype initially known as the Iris VI. Again designed by J.D. Rennie, the Perth was acquired to replace 209 Squadron's Iris Vs, against Specification 20/32. It was of all-metal construction with fabric-covered wings of 97ft span. Like the Iris V it was powered by three 825hp Rolls-Royce Buzzard IIMS engines. Each of these was contained in a duralumin nacelle of improved streamlining, the centre engine being mounted on struts above the hull, the two outboard engines on inter-plane struts. The nacelles also mounted the radiators, oil tanks and compressed air starter, while the three fuel tanks were located in the centre of the upper mainplane. A biplane tailplane was again adopted, together with three fins and rudders.

The Perth's two-step Alclad-covered hull was more spacious than that of the Iris because the new aircraft was beamier, a product of its increased weight and the need for greater buoyancy. Designed for a crew of five, the internal layout was reminiscent of the Iris though the side-by-side cockpit was enclosed. Aft were the

136   B r i t i s h   F l y i n g   B o a t s

navigator's position, wardrooms for officers and men (between which was the engineer's station), and aft again a toilet together with storage for marine equipment, spares and tools. Defensive armament consisted of a tail position and two dorsal posts, all Lewis-armed, and a bow position that instead of the Lewis could be equipped with a 37mm recoilless quick-firing COW gun for anti-submarine use. The Perth could also carry four 500lb or eight 250lb bombs.

The first example, K3580, flew on 11 October 1933 and travelled to Felixstowe, remaining there for six months. The first Perth to enter service, therefore, was K3581, launched and test-flown on 5 January 1934 before passing to 209 Squadron at Mount Batten. The third example, K3582, joined its sister in February, while K3580 arrived in May, by when a fourth, K4011, had flown. The first three aircraft set off on a survey for a North Atlantic air route on 12 September and visited the Faroes, via Oban, on 14 September, but the mission was abandoned because of dangerous Arctic ice floes.

The Perths' usual patrol area was over the Irish Sea and they sometimes used an advance base at Stranraer, their maximum range being 1,500 miles, but in October and November 1934 they were grounded while their tail units were inspected. In December all tail assemblies were removed and in March 1935 travelled to Brough for modification. As an interim measure over the summer 209 Squadron re-

Perth K3581 seen at Plymouth. This aircraft served with 209 Squadron but was twice withdrawn for modifications to the tail, before being struck off charge in May 1936. It was subsequently used for tests on hull treatment. *(Author's Collection)*

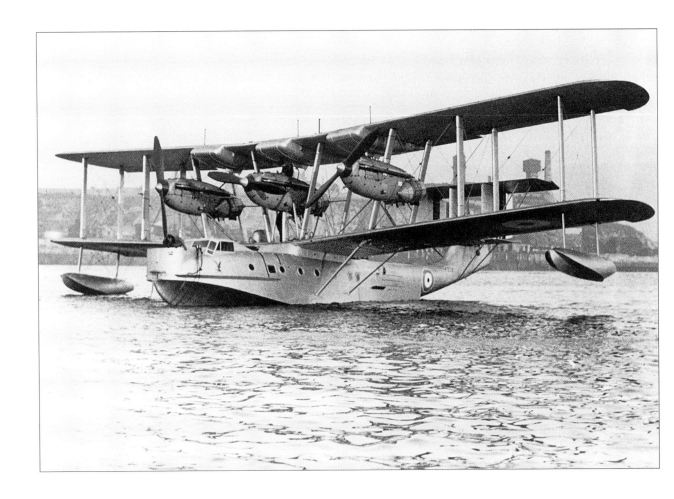

equipped with three prototype flying-boats (Saro London K3560, Short R.24/31 monoplane K3574 and Supermarine Scapa S1648) but the Perths returned in the autumn. K3580 was declared beyond economic repair in October 1935 after losing a float in heavy seas off Stornaway, Lewis, while K3581 ended its days at MAEE undergoing hull treatment tests and K3582 was deleted in January 1936. K4011, only nominally on charge to 209 Squadron, was retained by MAEE for experimental use.

South Coast Successes

At Supermarine two new designs had appeared during the early 1930s, the first intended as a successor to the Southampton. Mitchell had commenced a project initially known as the Southampton IV but which became the Scapa, using technology stemming from the Schneider race programme, the latest developments from Rolls-Royce and the resources of the wider Vickers company. The prototype was proffered in place of the final production Southampton II and at the same price, and the Ministry agreed to Supermarine's proposition. Building on the Southampton, the hull of the new type was broadly similar though cleaner and with an enclosed side-by-side cockpit. Construction of the hull was all-metal, light alloy with stainless steel fittings; flight surfaces too were of metal construction, and fabric-covered. The 75ft-span wing was more streamlined than previously, with some struttery replaced by wire bracing and the engines mounted in clean nacelles; drag was further reduced by dispensing with the engine pylons of the Southampton. Experimental Southampton N253 had employed Rolls-Royce Kestrels, improving

Perth K4011 throws up a bow wave while taxying at speed, but the cockpit and flight structures remain clear of spray. Though a 209 Squadron badge was carried at times, the aircraft never served with that unit, being employed mostly by MAEE. It was finally struck off during February 1938. *(Jim Halley)*

performance over the Lion-powered Southamptons; Mitchell adopted the 525hp Kestrel IIIMS for the Scapa.

The prototype, S1648, was built to Specification R.20/31D and first flew on 8 July 1932 in the hands of Mutt Summers. Following extensive company trials it travelled to MAEE on 29 October. The aircraft underwent rigorous testing including a ten-hour flight over the North Sea and a trip to Malta on acceptance trials in May 1933, where it joined 202 Squadron at Kalafrana and made a journey to Gibraltar before cruising on to Sollum, Aboukir, Lake Timsah and Port Sudan during June. The trials were successful and the Ministry ordered ten Scapas (K4191–K4200) to Specification 19/33D.

From May 1935 202 Squadron received its first examples and took them on a number of cruises after the fashion of the age, notably to the Aegean and later to Nigeria via Algiers, Gibraltar, Gambia, Gold Coast (now Ghana) and Lagos, a total of around 9,000 miles. During 1937 patrols were carried out to help protect neutral shipping against possible fall-out from the Spanish Civil War. By then 204 Squadron had also received the Scapa, re-equipping at Mount Batten during the summer of 1935 and travelling to Egypt during the Italian–Abyssinian conflict before returning to Britain. At Calshot, C Flight of the Seaplane Training Squadron, later 240 Squadron, also employed the type, of which four more were built; it remained in service until 1939.

Prototype Supermarine Scapa S1648 seen at Calshot during its early evaluation. This aircraft was used for tropical trials in the Sudan, and subsequently served at various times with 209, 202 and 204 Squadrons. Behind the aircraft are numbers of beaching chassis units. (*Author's Collection*)

Scapa K4200 being launched at Woolston. The resemblance of the fin and rudder profile and the rear hull area to that of the earlier Southampton is marked. K4200 first flew on 30 October 1935 and was delivered to 204 Squadron later that day. It joined 202 Squadron in November but in October 1937 hit a swell in Kalafrana harbour while taking off, and broke in two. *(Author's Collection)*

Scapa K4198 of 204 Squadron being fitted with modified wings at Kalafrana during 1936. The propellers have been removed and the aircraft jacked up, its beaching chassis unused. K4198 joined 240 Squadron in 1937 and survived until it was struck off in August 1940. *(Author's Collection)*

The second Supermarine design to emerge during 1933 was the Seagull V. The Royal Australian Air Force had issued a demanding requirement to the British aviation industry for a single-engined amphibian capable of being launched from a ship-board catapult, for reconnaissance, survey and communications duties. Operation from open seas in waves of up to 6 feet was required, and post-flight recovery was to be by ship's crane. A number of studies followed from Supermarine and Mitchell adopted the flat-sided hard chine hull layout reminiscent of Vickers' Viking series, a form found to cut through small waves rather than riding over them. The Air Ministry did not support the project at first and the private venture programme ran slowly in the face of other pressing activities, though Supermarine kept the Australians advised of developments.

By February 1933 the prototype's hull was complete at Hythe. Its monocoque layout was of light alloy with minimal double curvature and featured a single step, influenced by a design draftsman who had joined the company from Canadian Vickers. An enclosed cockpit, with provision for dual-control, and a cabin aft provided accommodation for the three crew – pilot, observer and wireless telegraphist. Two defensive positions were situated in the bow and amidships, the former also used for mooring, and both were equipped with a single machine-gun. A modest bomb-load could also be carried.

The 46ft-span wings were designed to fold in order to minimise storage space at sea. The main wing spars were of stainless steel though with the exception of the metal ailerons the remaining mainplane structure was of wood. Handley Page-Lachmann slats were fitted, and the wings contained the fuel tanks in their upper sections. The empennage was also mostly of wood and fabric apart from the fin, which was integral with the hull, and the tailplane spar. The 625hp Bristol Pegasus IIM2 engine was positioned mid-gap and arranged as a pusher. The propeller was rather near the tail but the threat of yaw induced by the unequal force of the corkscrew effect from the slipstream on the fin was contained by offsetting the engine nacelle 3 degrees to starboard. The Seagull V employed a fully retractable main undercarriage recessing completely into the lower wings and a metal tail wheel combined with a water rudder.

The main slinging point for attaching the aircraft to the ship's crane was located in the upper wing centre-section, access to which was by means of folding pegs on the outboard nacelle struts. The hooking-on gear was kept in a centre-section compartment. On alighting, the aircraft would come alongside the host vessel and a crewman would climb up to the centre-section, secure himself using an eye-bolt in the leading-edge and pass the hook from the crane through the slinging-point. The aircraft would then be hoisted aboard its vessel – an operation that was reasonably straightforward in calm waters but could be extremely tricky in rougher seas.

The prototype Seagull V was first flown by Mutt Summers on 21 June 1933 from Southampton Water. With the aircraft wearing the identity N-1, Summers performed an aerobatic display at the Hendon SBAC Show on 26 June which included a loop – a manoeuvre not usually associated with a biplane flying-boat, and carried out without prior consultation with Mitchell. The Seagull V then passed to Felixstowe but as N-2, to avoid confusion with a Southampton also allocated N-1.

Water trials found the aircraft unstuck fairly quickly and was generally clean-running. Ground handling, explored at Martlesham Heath, revealed the Seagull was prone to weathercock and therefore it was advisable to take off and land into wind. As with many amphibians the track was narrow, the line of thrust high and a considerable keel surface was presented so control on land needed work. On a hard surface the tail wheel was incredibly noisy – described by one former Seagull pilot as sounding 'like a million tin cans being bashed together'. In January 1934 N-2 passed to the RAE at Farnborough for catapult trials, successfully carried out at the end of the month. Little modification was required following the assessment: the undercarriage and catapult attachments were reinforced, the wing-float planing-bottoms were slightly revised, and the cabin windows were enlarged and received splash deflectors.

The Royal Navy then trialled N-2 on behalf of the Australians using the battlecruiser *Repulse*, the crew being Lieutenant Commanders Caspar John and W.T. Couchman, both of whom later became admirals. Visits to the battleship *Valiant* off the Kyles of Bute tested the Seagull in waves of up to 6 feet combined with 30-knot winds but no significant problems were experienced. N-2 also flew from the carriers *Courageous* and *Ark Royal*.

Around August 1934 the RAAF placed an order for 24 Seagull Vs (A2-1–A2-24) to Specification 6/34, drawn up by the Air Ministry, as the standard catapult spotter-

The moment of truth: the Supermarine Seagull V prototype, as N-2, poised on the RAE Farnborough catapult. The aircraft is carrying practice bombs. The shipboard catapults would have a terminal velocity of around 57mph, being driven either by multiplying pulleys or a cordite charge. (*Author's Collection*)

Supermarine Seagull Vs A2-2 (nearer) and A2-12 of the Royal Australian Air Force in formation. The Seagull V's first flights were between June 1935 (A2-1) and April 1937 (A2-24). Two, A2-3 and A2-4, survived to become civil-registered as VH-BGP and VH-ALB respectively: the latter is now with the RAF Museum. *(Author's Collection)*

reconnaissance aircraft for the Australian Leander and County Class cruisers and also for operation by HMAS *Albatross*. The first example, A2-1, was flown by Supermarine test pilot George Pickering on 25 June 1935 and delivered to HMAS *Australia* at Spithead on 9 September. The second arrived at Lee-on-Solent on 18 October and then embarked in HMAS *Sydney*. Seagull Vs also flew with No. 1 Seaplane Training Flight at Point Cook, and later with 101 Flight RAAF based at Richmond, New South Wales. Meanwhile N-2 passed to the Air Ministry as K4797. It was later transported to Gibraltar where it collided with an anti-submarine boom; though the crew were rescued, sadly the aircraft sank.

Singapore, London and Stranraer

During the late 1930s three designs emerged that would mark the end of the large military biplane flying-boat in RAF service though at the time of their introduction they were state-of-the-art in terms of operational types; each proved durable and long-lived. Shorts had received an order for four Short S.19 Singapore IIIs to Specification R.3/33D during August 1933; the first, K3592, flew on 15 June 1934 piloted by John Parker and acceptance trials at Felixstowe were completed by 16 July. The principal changes from the Singapore II were a deeper hull with a revised step slope and position, amended internal layout and a greater number of portholes, blunter wing-tips, larger wing-tip floats, revised fuel tankage and increase of the cockpit width. The three subsequent aircraft (K3593, K3594 and K3595) had all flown by mid-November 1934, the batch being regarded as pre-production prior to the issue of Specification R.12/34 and an order for the mature version with an all-up weight of 31,500lb, powered by four 675hp Kestrels. Production totalled thirty-three: K4577–K4585 delivered between March 1934 and August 1935, together with K6907–K6922, K8565–K8568 and K8856–K8859, all delivered between December 1935 and June 1937.

The pre-production examples were attached to various squadrons for operational training, and the initial production aircraft, K4577, remained at Felixstowe for armament and equipment trials. In January 1935 210 Squadron took on charge four Singapore IIIs for a delivery flight from Pembroke Dock to Seletar and 205 Squadron. Sadly the journey was dogged by engine troubles and K3595 was tragically lost, crashing near Mount Etna in thick fog. The crew of eight were killed. Shortly afterwards the episode was compounded when the sweethearts of the officers aboard, two American sisters, committed suicide by jumping from Hillman Airways' Dragon G-ACEV.

The type also joined 230 Squadron which had re-formed at Pembroke Dock, the first arriving in April 1935. During September 203 Squadron began trading their Rangoons for Singapore IIIs also at Pembroke Dock, before returning to Basra. In October 230 Squadron departed for Alexandria. The following year 209 Squadron swapped their Perths for Singapore IIIs while 228 Squadron employed the type between April and September 1937; 240 Squadron flew Singapores between November 1938 and July 1939. The early accident apart, the aircraft generally performed reliable if undramatic patrol work with very few incidents or technical problems. During May 1936 a 205 Squadron Singapore III surveyed an Empire Air Mail route between Singapore and Sydney, taking along Herbert Brackley as a passenger.

By the time the Singapore III was operational two new biplane flying-boats and one monoplane had appeared to Specification R.24/31, a requirement seeking a twin-engined general purpose and coastal patrol type, reflecting the Ministry's progress from the idea of the three-engined configuration – as the Scapa had also shown. High speed was made secondary to durability and low maintenance; also emphasised were load-carrying, range (1,000 miles) and the ability to maintain level flight on one engine at 60 per cent of fuel load. A crew of five was specified. Saunders-Roe, Supermarine and Shorts entered the competition and each won a contract for a single prototype.

Short Singapore III K4577, the first production example, seen at Felixstowe. The main beaching chassis members embody buoyancy aids and were designed to float clear once the aircraft had been launched. K4577 was of great longevity. Following armament and equipment trials at MAEE it joined 209 Squadron and later served with 203 Squadron. It was holed and beached at Um Rasas during April 1938 but survived to participate as one of the decoys moored out at Aden during June 1940.
(Via Bryan Ribbans)

Singapore III K6919/Y in reduced circumstances under 209 Squadron ownership. Despite its down-and-out appearance the aircraft was subsequently allocated to 240 Squadron, before being sold and scrapped in July 1939. *(Via Bryan Ribbans)*

Singapore III Z of 209 Squadron photographed air-to-air. In the background is a Saunders-Roe London. The squadron began the change-over from Londons to Singapore IIIs early in 1936 and retained the latter until they were replaced by the Stranraer. *(Via Bryan Ribbans)*

Saunders-Roe's offering was Henry Knowler's A.27 London. With a sesquiplane wing of fabric-covered duralumin and stainless steel construction, the A.27 prototype sported two 820hp Bristol Pegasus IIIMS radials, the nacelles attached to the underside of the 80ft-span upper wing. The wings were built in sections to simplify replacement in the event of damage. Ailerons were fitted on the upper wing only, and the four 137-gallon fuel tanks were located in the centre-section. The tail consisted of twin fins and rudders strut-braced to a tailplane equipped with horn-balanced elevators.

The London's two-step duralumin and Alclad hull again employed straight-line frames combined with external longitudinal corrugations, the final Saro type to do so. The hull was reinforced around the planing bottom, the chine forward of the main step and the main step itself, while the planing bottom dispensed with the horizontal planking just inboard of the chines that Knowler had substituted for a curved planing bottom on most of his previous 'corrugated' flying-boats. Aft of the bow mooring/gunnery position, a raised side-by-side dual-control enclosed cockpit gave way to a wardroom equipped with two bunks, and the navigation position. Aft again was the crew cabin which also housed the engineer's panel and the wireless post, and then the dorsal defensive position. Aft of that was a substantial storage area for a spare two-bladed propeller, dinghy, maintenance platforms and domestic items, and a narrow gangway led to the tail gunner's position, all defensive posts

Saunders-Roe's A.27 London prototype, K3560, at Felixstowe in October 1934. Originally the rudders were equipped with prominent servos, but these were removed early in the life of the aircraft and production examples also dispensed with that arrangement. Nine-sided engine cowlings were fitted to the prototype though all subsequent Londons employed the usual circular type. *(Author's Collection)*

K5257, the first of the London Is, at the mouth of the Columbine hangar at East Cowes, 1936. After attending an exhibition at Stockholm, in April 1936 the aircraft joined 201 Squadron, being converted to Mk II standard in May 1938. Via a spell with 204 Squadron it served with 240 Squadron, 202 Squadron and 4(C)OTU, before eventually returning to Saro in November 1942, where it was scrapped. *(Author's Collection)*

being armed with a single Scarff-mounted Lewis gun. The open dorsal and tail positions were protected from the slipstream by folding perambulator-style hoods.

The prototype London, K3560, emerged in March 1934 and visited MAEE for trials. Unlike the A.7 the London was rugged; its hull was sturdy and its construction was praised. No difficulties were reported either in taking off or landing, while flying characteristics were described as pleasant and easy, the controls being light and effective across the speed range with little need for trim changes. At a weight of 18,280lb, K3560 achieved 133mph at 5,000ft. It was not able to maintain height on one engine as required by R.24/31 but none the less the company concluded a contract for seven London Is (K5257–K5263) in March 1935, the first being tested at Felixstowe between June 1936 and February 1937. These aircraft differed only slightly from the prototype; stepped wing-floats were adopted, together with circular cowlings and four-bladed propellers. Boulton Paul Aircraft Ltd carried out nearly all London wing production under sub-contract.

At Supermarine the Scapa was unable to meet the load requirements of R.24/31 so Mitchell developed it further. His proposal came second to the London but he continued to refine it and eventually a contract was secured for a single prototype. At first the new aircraft was named the Southampton V. It was larger than the Scapa with a loaded weight of 19,000lb, a span of 85ft and wing area of 1,457sq ft. Its two Bristol Pegasus IIIMS engines were installed in long chord Townend rings in a similar position to the Scapa's Kestrels, with fuel tanks disposed in the upper centre-section. While the rudders were of the same area as the Scapa's, the trim tabs and elevators were enlarged. The new hull was longer and broader than the Scapa's though generally similar, and accommodated a crew of six. Construction was of duralumin and Alclad, with detail fittings once again of stainless steel, while anodic treatment was widely applied to help counter corrosion. The items and crew comforts sometimes carried as extras during long cruises – servicing derricks, sea anchors, sun awnings and so on – were incorporated as standard in the Southampton V. The aircraft could also transport loads on its flat dorsal decking, as could the London – either a spare engine, a torpedo or overload fuel tanks.

The first flight of the prototype, K3973, took place from Woolston on 27 July 1934 in the hands of Mutt Summers. In August the aircraft was renamed the Stranraer, passing to Felixstowe in October where successful trials confirmed it could fly level with one engine stopped. In the meantime during August Supermarine had secured an order for seventeen Stranraers (K7287–K7303) against Specification 17/35. The production aircraft employed 920hp Bristol Pegasus X engines; the first example was delivered on 16 April 1937. The Stranraer achieved 165mph at 6,000ft, climbed at 1,000 feet per minute to 10,000ft, and had a service ceiling of 18,500ft, a performance unmatched by any other flying-boat at the time of its appearance. It served with 209, 210, 228 and 240 Squadrons as well as B Flight, Flying-Boat Training Squadron (from March 1941, 4 (Coastal) Operational Training Unit). Five aircraft of 228 Squadron carried out a 4,000-mile cruise to Lisbon, Gibraltar and Malta in September 1938, while the squadron travelled to its planned war station at Invergordon during the Munich Crisis.

On 11 June 1937 R.J. Mitchell CBE died, aged 42. He had seen his Spitfire fly, and during just seventeen years had designed an extraordinary, unmatched portfolio of flying-boats, floatplanes and landplanes. Many tributes were made

Stranraers in formation, pre-war. K7293, furthest away, flew with both 228 Squadron and 209 Squadron with the same individual identity, S. In June 1940 surprisingly it joined the strength of BOAC before arriving for service with 240 Squadron in December, assuming the code BN-Z. The following February it sank in a gale, ironically while moored at Stranraer, and was declared damaged beyond repair by Scottish Aviation. The other examples in the photograph (including the camera aircraft) are not identifiable. *(Short Brothers via Bryan Ribbans)*

both to his genius and to his courage and humility; he had borne his illness with great fortitude and was universally admired across the aviation industry and the customer community.

The Knuckleduster

Shorts' response to R.24/31 was referred to by either the sobriquet 'Knuckleduster', or the specification itself, or the company's designation S.18, there being no official name, and represented another major move forward for Rochester. Like Blackburn's Sydney the Knuckleduster was a monoplane; its cantilever, sharply cranked 90ft-span wing was of great benefit in reducing drag though it was of considerable structural complexity. Arthur Gouge employed a thick section around a trussed box spar, a deep rectangular girder created by four stainless steel tubular booms with tubular lift and drag struts, which together provided the primary structure. The wing ribs were of duralumin tube and the wing was fabric covered. Frise ailerons were employed and the wing contained the four fuel tanks. At the wing cranks, or 'knuckles' from which the aircraft

Stranraers of 228 Squadron seen over Calshot spit on Empire Day, 1939. Nearest is K7300, accompanied by K and P. On the ground are a London (left) and Singapore IIIs. *(Jim Halley)*

gained its nickname, were experimental 600hp Rolls-Royce Goshawk IIS steam-cooled engines in faired nacelles, driving large-diameter two-bladed propellers. Above the engines were faired steam condensers and hot-wells, each sporting a stumpy radio aerial. Wing-floats were mounted on pairs of struts, while under-wing bomb-racks were fitted together with a point below the starboard root for carrying (but not launching) a torpedo.

The 63ft 3in hull embodied considerable departures from earlier Short flying-boats. Though its planing bottom was derived from the Sarafand and Singapore III, and employed a similar rearward-pointing step, it was slimmer, a product of modifying the chine to give a clean performance without the traditional flare. The hull sides were almost flat, employing longitudinal stiffening corrugations similar to contemporary Saro designs, together with straight line frames, and braced by diagonal frames at the wing roots; construction was of Alclad with stainless steel fittings. Accommodation comprised a bow mooring position with provision for armament, an enclosed side-by-side cockpit for pilot and navigator with optional dual controls, the navigation, engineer and radio positions set between the spar frames together with two bunks, and a living area comprising three bunks, a galley and washing facilities. The dorsal gunner's position followed, while aft was a toilet and finally the rear gunner's post. The adjustable tailplane was strut-braced, with twin fins and rudders.

Serialled K3574, the Knuckleduster first flew on 30 November 1933 in the hands of John Parker. The narrow beam hull performed cleanly on the water with no porpoising tendency. Air handling was found to be generally stable, but the aircraft could not be trimmed to fly straight and level with one engine stopped and modifications were quickly introduced to counter the flexing of the fin and

Short's R.24/31 Knuckleduster at Felixstowe. The hull layout was kept relatively shallow, despite the adoption of a monoplane, thanks to the acute gull-wing form. *(Gordon Kinsey)*

The Knuckleduster following modifications to the tail and rear fuselage. The aircraft is seen taking off at Rochester. It spent most of its life on experimental work, usually at Felixstowe though service trials were carried out with 209 Squadron during April 1935. The Goshawk engines proved unreliable but the aircraft soldiered on until October 1938 when it became Instructional Airframe 1154M. *(Short Brothers via Bryan Ribbans)*

tailplane attachments. In January 1934 the rudder area was increased; this was found to be effective against a stopped engine, but too heavy to hold over continuously. At that time too the wing-floats were remounted on struts employing diagonal oleo dampers to isolate the wing against shock loads and vibration from the floats when on the water.

The aircraft underwent further modifications over the first year or so of its life. The tail surfaces continued to give problems. Rudder balances were increased and the fin leading-edges toed in slightly, while the rear gunner's fairing was revised following the collapse of the original. John Parker was uneasy about the tail design and Shorts' testing crew wore parachutes while he explored the characteristics of the aircraft during March. Tests included diving from 6,000ft at speeds of up to 200mph. K3574 then underwent further revisions to the tail, the stern frames and the tail gunner's position.

After more test-flying, marred only by engine failures resulting from worn valve springs, during which a level speed of 150mph was reached at 4,500ft, the Knuckleduster travelled to Felixstowe. By October it had returned to Rochester for repairs to damage caused by a collision on the water, and further modifications to the wing-float struts. Via Calshot for further assessment it temporarily joined 209 Squadron in April 1935 while their Perths were out of commission. The Knuckleduster spent most of its subsequent life at Felixstowe undergoing more trials, and in 1938 became Instructional Airframe 1154M. Shorts did not expect it to secure a production contract – it was too experimental. However, the R.24/31 provided invaluable data in support of both monoplane flying-boat development and the characteristics of the slimmer hull form; a beamy hull might be attractive in terms of interior space but the corollary was the effect on performance.

Flying-Boats for the Empire

During the spring of 1935 Imperial Airways ordered a new large passenger and mail-carrying flying-boat. Following its formation in March 1924, Imperial had initially faced only moderate competition, being generally left to develop its European routes and later its far-flung services to India and the Cape. By the early 1930s, however, the airline was being fiercely challenged by rivals from America, France and Germany, and by KLM's Amsterdam–Batavia route, which together seriously affected its long-term commercial prospects. The competing airlines established larger aircraft fleets than Imperial's, and flew more passengers as a result. Moreover, numbers of Imperial's airfields, particularly along the Cape route, were small and often suffered from climatic extremes, which adversely affected services. At that time too, relations between the governments of Persia and Britain were strained, leading Imperial to develop the North Arabian Persian Gulf route passing through the southern side of the Gulf via Bahrain and Sharjah (Oman) and avoiding Persia, for which the strong preference was the flying-boat type. These factors led Imperial to open discussions with Shorts, who by then were working on a very advanced four-engined military monoplane flying-boat to Specification R.2/33.

The flying-boat was the natural choice for linking the British Empire and operating in locations where aerodromes were few. It needed no runway and – depending on the route flown – offered a greater chance of safety in the event of a forced landing because the seas were unencumbered and limitless compared with airports. As the 1930s unfolded the commercial flying-boat reached its heyday, making a contribution of fundamental importance to the progress of international air travel. Imperial's planning was influenced by the success of RAF flying-boat squadrons' overseas tours and by the pioneering flying-boat flights of Alan Cobham and others, together with its own experiences with the Calcutta and Kent. During late 1934 the national carrier decided to re-equip with flying-boats for all trunk routes and in December Parliament approved Imperial's proposed Empire Air Mail Scheme, whereby the company would carry all first-class mail at a flat rate across the British Empire, excluding Canada and the West Indies. This would be very lucrative – 2,000 tons transported per year would yield nearly £1,000,000 from the Post Office. The scheme was scheduled to commence in June 1937.

Imperial's far-sighted general manager (technical), Major Robert H. Mayo, invited Shorts' proposals for a thoroughly updated Kent-type flying-boat, to carry twenty-four passengers and 1½ tons of mail at an economical cruising speed of 150mph over 800 miles, figures calculated after dissection of traffic statistics across the Imperial network. The resultant aircraft was designated the S.23 and was popularly dubbed the Empire Boat, though it was referred to by its operator as the C-class and was later named the Imperial Flying Boat. The Empire Boat became one of the most successful and well-known inter-war commercial flying-boats.

Arthur Gouge chose a monoplane layout, in line with his concurrent project to R.2/33. To offset the increased wing loading (proposed as 27lb/sq.ft – the loading of the Sarafand had been 21lb/sq.ft), improve take-off performance and reduce landing speed of the Empire he developed retractable trailing-edge flaps patented in his own name which increased the lift coefficient by around 30 per cent; the flap technology was tested on Shorts' Scion twin-engined high-wing monoplane, M-3/G-ADDR. The Empire's 114ft-span cantilever wing, also high-mounted, was of all-metal construction with fabric-covered Frise-type ailerons, while the floats employed watertight partitions, bilge pump connections and springing to absorb shock from heavy waters, thereby protecting the wing spar. Four 920hp Bristol Pegasus XC engines were adopted, driving three-bladed de Havilland variable-pitch propellers and attached to monocoque nacelles built into the leading-edge; two fuel tanks each of 326 gallons were situated between the nacelles. The tailplane and fin were again of all-metal structure, though with fabric covering the control surfaces and the areas between the spar booms.

The all-metal 88ft-long two-step hull was radically new, a two-tier configuration with a depth of some 17ft, this partly to simplify the necessarily high wing attachment, while data from the Knuckleduster programme was combined with extensive tank testing to allow the adoption of a comparatively narrow planing bottom. The hull sides were vertical without flare at the chine, to maximise interior room and reduce drag. The main deck ran from the bow to the main passenger door situated on the port side mid-way between the steps, while the upper deck extended to the aft step. The hull was Alclad-plated and flush-riveted to minimise drag, again with little double-curvature. The upper portion housed a roomy flight-deck, rather than a cockpit with separate positions for other crew members, equipped with side-by-side dual controls and a radio position just aft; an engineer was carried on long trips. The remainder of the upper deck consisted of stowage for up to 3,000lb of mail and freight, a purser's position and a passenger bedding store.

Below in the bow was the marine compartment containing the anchor, boat-hook, drogues and lights, aft of which was a seven-seat smoking lounge, with lightweight tables for meals. Aft again were the forward cabin entrance and two toilet compartments to port, with a galley to starboard and a central passage to a mid-ships cabin with three seats convertible to bunks, and a permanent bunk. A promenade cabin seated eight in four rows, convertible to four more bunks, and included a port-side open area for in-flight leg-stretching, with a rail for leaning while looking through the windows. Behind the aft entry door was a further cabin with six seats, and then a second luggage and mail area. The cabins were roomy and well furnished, with reclining, well-padded seats, fitted carpets and plentiful sound-proofing.

Shorts' proposals passed to Imperial in June 1934 and an Instruction To Proceed was placed in January 1935. An order for fourteen examples from the drawing-board followed during May, boldly dispensing with a prototype; in September the figure was increased to twenty-eight. The first Empire Boat, G-ADHL *Canopus*, flew from Rochester on 4 July 1936 in the hands of John Parker, a streamlined and graceful aircraft far distanced from its biplane forebears. Testing led to only minor adjustments and after acquiring its Certificate of Airworthiness on 20 October 1936, Herbert Brackley flew *Canopus* on a route-proving trip to Rome, via Caudebec, Bordeaux and Marseilles, and also visited Alexandria. G-ADHL entered service over the Mediterranean ten days later, the culmination of a programme of well under two

The first Empire Boat: S.23 G-ADHL *Canopus* on the water. In the background is Rochester Castle. The Imperial Airways title is applied in small lettering below the name. The aircraft entered service in October 1936 and survived the war, but was scrapped at Hythe in 1947. *(Author's Collection)*

years. Performance was outstanding: a cruising speed of 165mph, top speed of 200mph and a range of over 700 miles (admittedly not the 800 miles specified at first), while all-up weight was 40,500lb.

The second example, G-ADHM *Caledonia*, was delivered at the end of the year for use in surveying the North Atlantic route. It was unfurnished but had much increased fuel capacity in additional wing tanks. A batch of twelve (G-ADUT–G-ADVE) followed, of which the third example, G-ADUV *Cambria*, was configured similarly to *Caledonia*. The fourteen commenced immediately after consisted of G-AETV–G-AEUI, while QANTAS Empire Airways (formed by Imperial and Australia's QANTAS airline in January 1934) ordered three, allocated G-AFBJ–G-AFBL but subsequently becoming VH-ABA, VH-ABB and VH-ABF. Deliveries ran at just under two Empires per month, produced by a labour force that was largely unused to aviation work, for by that time skilled personnel were being gobbled up in military aircraft programmes. On 4 January 1937 Imperial commenced the Hythe–Marseilles–Alexandria service via Rome, Brindisi and Athens, using G-ADUW *Castor*. On 18 February *Caledonia* flew 2,222 miles to Alexandria non-stop in thirteen hours; on 5 March the new Imperial Airways flying-boat terminal was formally opened at Hythe, while some of Supermarine's buildings were acquired for use as a maintenance base. In the air, high-quality in-flight service and the comfortable surroundings created an elegance previously unseen.

In May *Cambria* commenced a 20,000-mile survey of African routes. During the following month *Cambria* and *Caledonia* travelled from Foynes at the mouth of Ireland's majestic River Shannon to the United States via Botwood, a sheltered harbour in the central region of Newfoundland, and Montreal. It was intended to fly a transatlantic service in cooperation with the Sikorsky S-42 flying-boats of Pan

S.23 G-ADHM *Caledonia* at Felixstowe for its Certificate of Airworthiness trials during the autumn of 1936. At that early stage in its life the aircraft was not equipped with passenger accommodation and few cabin windows are in evidence. *(Author's Collection)*

Challenger, S.23 G-ADVD, revealing its hydrodynamic arrangements. The slim hull bottom terminates in a transverse step. *Challenger* entered service with Imperial during May 1937 but two years later was lost in a fatal accident caused by pilot error, crashing at Mozambique with loss of life. *(Author's Collection)*

Cassiopeia, G-ADUX, together with a pontoon arrangement typical of those adopted for loading and unloading passengers and freight. On 29 December 1941 *Cassiopeia* was lost while taking off from Sabang, Sumatra. *(Author's Collection)*

S.23s G-AEUA *Calypso* and VH-ABD *Corio* berthed side-by-side, the latter serving with QANTAS. The shore berthing arrangements did not change markedly for many years and a similar arrangement was sometimes used post-war to house Sunderland adaptations and derivatives. *(Bryan Ribbans)*

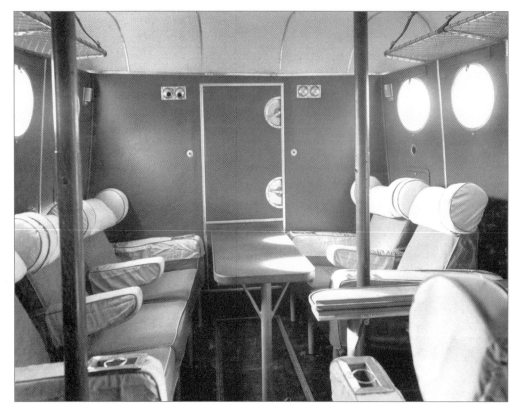

S.23 interior
showing cabin
seating. The larger
windows had
curtains. The degree
of comfort and
privacy provided by
the Empires was
unmatched at that
time, with in-flight
catering to go with
the surroundings.
*(Short Brothers via
Bryan Ribbans)*

American Airways. The southerly route via the Azores was also surveyed that summer. A New York–Bermuda service commenced during June using G-ADUU *Cavalier* and the American flying-boats. That October, G-AEUA *Calypso* began a service between Alexandria and Karachi via Habbaniyah (Iraq) and Sharjah, while on 15 November G-AEUD *Cordelia* left Karachi to survey the route to Singapore. On 3 December *Centaurus* commenced the first ever civil flying-boat survey of the entire route to Australia and New Zealand, arriving at Auckland on the 27th of that month.

By the end of 1937 twenty-two Empire flying-boats had been delivered, while VH-ABA *Carpentaria* and VH-ABB *Coolangatta* were ready for collection by QEA. Sadly though, that year saw three crashes, with loss of life: G-ADVA *Capricornus* owing to navigational error, G-ADVC *Courtier* which flew into a flat sea and G-ADUZ *Cygnus*, which porpoised to destruction when the pilot attempted to take off on a flat calm with flaps down. Subsequently Shorts enlarged the roof emergency exits of the Empire fleet (the dimensions of which had been specified by Imperial) and fitted additional push-out windows. During the first half of 1938 the remaining six S.23s for QEA were delivered and that year only G-AETW *Calpurnia* was lost, crashing into Lake Habbaniyah during a nocturnal sandstorm.

-oOo-

Since 1932 Robert Mayo had contemplated extending Imperial's mail service to North America but the S.23 could only fly between Ireland and Newfoundland if much of its load-carrying capability was made over to additional fuel. At that time, in-flight refuelling was still under development, while a catapult launching scheme based in the Azores was considered but had many disadvantages. Mayo's radical proposition designed to increase range was to fly a heavily laden mailplane pick-a-back aboard a host aircraft and then separate the mail component in mid-air. With no need to carry fuel to make its own take-off, the payload of the mailplane would be proportionately greater. The Air Ministry supported Mayo and agreed with his view that both aircraft should be waterborne. Specification 13/33 for the design of a Mayo Composite was duly issued to Shorts.

The resultant host was the S.21 *Maia* G-ADHK, which resembled the S.23 though its hull employed flared chines with tumble-home sides for a greater beam and increased lateral stability necessitated by the higher centre of gravity than the Empire. The aft portion of the hull was swept up to raise the tailplane in relation to the wing, so as to optimise the position for both the composite and solo configurations in flight. Eighteen passengers could be seated if required and square cabin windows were provided similar to those of the Kent. The wing roots were closer together than those of the S.23, and the engines were positioned further outboard, to allow the location of the upper component. Of equal span to the S.23, G-ADHK had a broader chord providing 250 sq. ft greater wing area, together with an enlarged empennage. John

The sole Mayo Composite: *Maia* G-ADHK and *Mercury* G-ADHJ. The pick-a-back experiment was a great success and a number of commercial flights were undertaken following the understandably thorough trials. Here a crane lowers *Mercury* on to its mountings while *Maia* reveals its flared chine lines and beamy planing bottom. In the background is *Cambria*. (Dave Etheridge, Fawley Historians)

Maia's flight-deck, with throttle mixture and pitch controls at centre. Dual flight instruments are installed. A reminder plate mounted centrally reads: 'Are all boats clear? Are all hatches closed?' *(Short Brothers via Bryan Ribbans)*

Parker first flew *Maia* on 27 July 1937, following which a pylon structure was attached to accommodate the upper aircraft, S.20 *Mercury* G-ADHJ.

Mercury was a carefully streamlined twin-float cantilever monoplane. Of tandem two-seat configuration, it employed four 340hp Napier Rapier V engines (later Rapier VIs) and was flown from Rochester by Parker on 5 September 1937. Tare weight was 10,000lb and normal all-up 15,500lb, but for air launches the latter increased to 20,500lb; 1,000lb of mail could be carried. In coupled flight, apart from the trim tabs *Mercury's* controls were locked until separation, and the combined machine was piloted from *Maia*.

Both aircraft continued test-flying separately until January 1938 when Parker began taxying with the Composite configuration at Rochester. On 20 January a first flight was made with Parker in *Maia* and Harold Piper in *Mercury*. Though all went well it was 6 February before the first in-flight separation took place, at a height of 700ft and a speed of 110 knots; the Composite then passed to Felixstowe for assessment. Tests were continued by Imperial pilots and on 21 July a first transatlantic flight was made when the Composite separated over Foynes, *Mercury* piloted by Captain (later Air Vice-Marshal) D.C.T. Bennett. Flying non-stop, the aircraft arrived at Montreal 20 hours and 20 minutes later, having covered some 2,930 miles. During the return journey *Mercury* flew from New York to the Azores in 7 hours 33 minutes, and arrived at Hythe on 27 July. Again piloted by Bennett, G-ADHJ established a new seaplane distance record on 6 October when separation took place over Dundee and the aircraft travelled non-stop to the mouth of the Orange River, South Africa, some 6,045 miles in 42 hours. The

Short S.30 G-AFCU *Cabot* participated in in-flight refuelling trials and is seen here over Southampton Water, in company with tanker aircraft Handley Page Harrow G-AFRL, converted by Alan Cobham's company Flight Refuelling Ltd. The V-shape protruding from the underside of the hull is fuel jettison piping. *(FR Aviation Ltd)*

final commercial separations were made on 29 November and 12 January 1939 when Bennett flew air mail 2,200 miles non-stop from Southampton to Alexandria.

With this success Imperial sought to maintain segregation of mail from passenger transport but the Ministry did not support that aspiration and plans for a landplane version of *Mercury*, borne by a converted Armstrong Whitworth Ensign, evaporated. In any event by the summer of 1939 the war was about to intervene in all areas of civil

S.30 ZK-AMA *Aotearoa* undergoing maintenance. The operator's name is applied to the hull: Tasman Empire Airways Ltd, Wellington. *Aotearoa* survived until November 1947 when it was withdrawn from use at Auckland. It was removed from the water and displayed at the Walsh Brothers' Flying School until the 1950s. *(Dave Etheridge, Fawley Historians)*

flying. As for the Composite, in the summer of 1940 *Mercury* joined 320 (Netherlands) Squadron as a trainer, working alongside Fokker T-8-W floatplanes and based at Pembroke Dock. It was broken up at Rochester during the autumn of 1941. *Maia* was destroyed by enemy bombing on 11 May 1941 while moored in Poole Harbour.

A larger Empire Boat, the S.30, first flew from Rochester with John Parker on 28 September 1938 as G-AFCT *Champion*. Of similar configuration to the S.23, the S.30 was reinforced to allow a maximum weight of 48,000lb and was powered by four 890hp Bristol Perseus XIIC engines, less powerful than the Pegasus but creating less drag and so improving fuel consumption; the range of the new aircraft was 1,500 miles, the eventual air-to-air refuelled gross weight 53,000lb. *Champion* was used mostly for trials; nine S.30s were eventually delivered. G-AFCU *Cabot*, G-AFCV *Caribou*, G-AFCW *Connemara* and G-AFCX *Clyde* were intended for trans-atlantic flight and were equipped with in-flight refuelling equipment. Three were ordered by QANTAS (G-AFCY *Captain Cook*, G-AFCZ *Canterbury* and G-AFDA *Cumberland*) but became earmarked for Tasman Empire Airways Ltd (TEAL), formed jointly by the governments of Britain, Australia and New Zealand to extend the air mail service to New Zealand. The aircraft were renamed *Australia*, *Aotearoa* ('Long White Cloud', the Maori name for New Zealand) and *Awarua* ('Two Rivers'), but their identities were revised a number of times (see Appendix 4). The overseas examples did not include air-to-air refuelling capability. A ninth example, G-AFKZ *Cathay*, was delivered to Imperial in April 1940, to replace *Connemara*, burned out in a refuelling accident during the previous June.

Walrus and London

In May 1935 the Ministry placed an exploratory order with Supermarine for twelve Seagull Vs (K5772–K5783) to Specification 2/35; the first flew on 18 March 1936 from Woolston, piloted by George Pickering. Under Corrigendum no. 1 to the contract the type was renamed Walrus. There were few differences between the Seagull V and the British version, and though the initial aircraft were powered by the Pegasus Mk IIM2 the main production build employed the Pegasus VI giving an additional 125hp. Via further contracts for eight and twenty-eight examples, on 10 July 1936 the Ministry ordered 168 Walruses to Specification 37/36; while this vindicated Supermarine's earlier investment, production difficulties immediately arose. Only the previous month the company had contracted to supply 310 Spitfires and resources were very stretched. In 1939, with Spitfire production at full tilt, it was agreed that Walrus manufacture would be sub-contracted to Saunders-Roe.

The Royal Navy's County Class cruisers were modified to operate Walruses for spotting and reconnaissance while a new class, the Towns, of which eight had been ordered in 1935, were prepared for the type from their inception. The cruiser-based Walruses were launched from a catapult set athwartships, consisting of a rail along which the aircraft was propelled by a trolley. A successful launch largely depended on the launching officer, who had to order the catapulting of the aircraft at a point when the cruiser itself was at a favourable attitude. On return, a landing would usually be made alongside the ship. However, if the sea was rough the cruiser would describe an arc, creating an area of calmer water aft upon which the aircraft could alight ready for hoisting aboard.

Walrus I L2271/34 is hoisted aboard HMS *Southampton*, in which it was embarked between July 1938 and March 1939 flown by 712 Squadron. It then joined 765 Squadron at Lee-on-Solent where it remained until December of that year. It subsequently served with 276, 277 and 278 Squadrons RAF but on 6 March 1945 hit the sea off Flamborough Head, Yorkshire, while on an ASR search, and sank. *(Fleet Air Arm Museum)*

In addition a number of overseas sales of the Walrus were made. Five or six were delivered to Turkey during 1938. Three were purchased by Eire, two by Argentina and five by Portugal. The Royal Canadian Air Force acquired eight, four from the Royal Canadian Navy, and the Royal New Zealand Air Force was also a customer.

Meanwhile the initial batch of London Is had arrived for service with 201 Squadron at Calshot in April 1936, replacing Southamptons. An updated Specification, R.3/35, gave rise to the London II which sported Pegasus X engines of 1,000hp driving four-bladed (later three-bladed) propellers. The prototype, K3560, was modified to trial the upgrade and six aircraft (K5908–K5913) initially resulted. A subsequent batch of eleven Mk IIs, K6927–K6932 and K9682–K9686, were built to Specification 27/36, incorporating further refinements and delivered between June and December 1937. A further six (L7038–L7043) were delivered between January and May 1938 while the London Is were modified to Mark II specification by Saunders-Roe.

During October 1936 204 Squadron at Mount Batten commenced receipt of Londons, replacing its Scapas; three months later five aircraft began a cruise to New South Wales that lasted until the following July and formed the RAF representation honouring the 150th Anniversary of Sydney University, some 30,000 miles being covered. For the cruise the Londons carried dorsal overload fuel tanks which increased their range to 2,600 miles. 202 Squadron at Malta also received the type that year, which again replaced Scapas. In July 1939 240 Squadron received

A fine study of Walrus I L2278. This aircraft first flew on 8 September 1938, joining 718 Squadron, 8th Cruiser Squadron, embarked in HMS *Berwick* until October 1939, during which period it underwent repairs in Bermuda. *(Author's Collection)*

Londons as their Singapores were withdrawn. The A.27 acquired a reputation for strength and reliability, continuing operations until 1941.

Fulcrum: R.2/33

In November 1933 the Ministry had issued the landmark Specification R.2/33 against Operational Requirement OR.8, seeking a four-engined long-range monoplane flying-boat to replace the biplane types then in production and service. The Specification stipulated a range of 1,600 miles and a ceiling of 15,000ft, while top speed was to be 200mph and cruising speed 170 mph. Four defensive positions were required, together with provision for a 2,000lb bomb-load. The response to R.2/33 marked a major milestone in the history of the British flying-boat. Blackburn, Fairey and (possibly) Supermarine submitted proposals that were not taken up, while Saunders-Roe and Shorts each secured a contract for one prototype.

Saro's design, the unnamed A.33, was a fundamental departure from Henry Knowler's previous offerings. The aircraft dispensed with the corrugated hull form for a much more streamlined and comparatively shallow hull, as with Blackburn's Sydney and Shorts' Knuckleduster. Two steps were utilised and construction was all-metal; the length was 75ft. The enclosed cockpit was high-mounted with an excellent field of view, a layout similar to the London, while an innovation was the defensive machine-gun turret occupying the bow, which could be retracted to make way for mooring activities. Aft of the cockpit were the radio position, sleeping area and cooking facilities. The R.2/33 had provision for two beam defensive positions in a dorsal hump, and a tail gunner's position. Accommodation was for seven: pilot, co-pilot, engineer, radio operator and three gunners.

The shallow hull was combined with a high-mounted 95ft-span parasol wing supported by very large N struts, accomplished in conjunction with General Aircraft Ltd. Of monospar form and metal construction with fabric covering, the wing must have been one of the largest of its type ever built and was tested in scale form by Cloud K2681 during the A.33 development phase. Bending loads were taken through the spar itself, and torsion by a pyramidal system of wires from the top and bottom booms ahead and aft of the spar. Four 830hp Bristol Perseus XII engines were set equidistantly along the leading-edge, driving three-bladed variable-pitch propellers. Aerodynamic sponsons were employed rather than the usual wing-floats, again trialled by the Cloud in scale form, and these bore the wing struts. The tail was of conventional form, a tapered tailplane and a prominent single fin and rudder.

Because of its unusual layout and the extensive aero- and hydrodynamic testing involved, the programme took a considerable time and the prototype A.33, K4773, did not appear until September 1938, a year later than its competitor from Shorts. Taxying trials began at Cowes on 10 October but revealed tendencies to bore through the water at low speeds and to porpoise at high speeds. However, a first flight was made on 14 October from Cowes by Frank Courtney, who had previously tested Saunders' Valkyrie. A slight tail shudder was reported while the water performance was dirty even at a weight of 31,000lb, 10,500lb below the intended maximum.

Before: Saunders-Roe A.33 K4773 on the Cowes slipway. It was a profound departure from previous designs by the company. The aircraft rests on an unusual four-point swivelling beaching chassis. Armament is not fitted. The parasol wing is mounted on thick N struts while the sponsons are raked sharply. The four Perseus engines are positioned in line with one another while the outer wing leading-edge is swept. *(Author's Collection)*

After: K4773 back on dry land at Cowes following the accident on 25 October 1938. The starboard wing has twisted forward and a hefty support takes the weight at the point of the starboard outer engine. The gash in the hull side where the starboard inner propeller penetrated is just visible. The A.33 programme was discontinued following the episode. *(Author's Collection)*

On 25 October, during its fifth take-off run from the Solent, the fast-moving aircraft hit the wake of a nearby Southampton ferry-boat and at once began to porpoise severely, making a great leap from which it at once stalled. On striking the water, the wing failed in torsion and the starboard portion twisted forward about the single spar while the starboard inner propeller penetrated the hull. Fortunately no injuries were sustained and all damage was above the waterline so the aircraft was recovered. However, work was then halted and an initial production contract for eleven A.33s (L2147–L2157), placed in March 1936 to Specification 21/36, was cancelled. Redesign was felt uneconomic: MAEE had not yet received K4773 for testing and might have identified further problems, hydrodynamic characteristics were not of the best, and Shorts' rival programme was going very well. In any case Saro had secured an order for a new twin-engined monoplane flying-boat which at the time probably provided some consolation for the disappointment. Of course, at that point no-one had any idea how enduring the R.2/33 winner would prove to be.

At Rochester Shorts were successfully flying their response to R.2/33, having drawn on their unrivalled experience to produce one of the finest flying-boats ever – the S.25 Sunderland. The Sunderland stayed in production throughout the Second World War, served with the RAF for over twenty years, and with overseas forces into the 1960s, acquiring a peerless reputation for offensive power, defensive capability, reliability and durability.

Few amendments had been made by the Ministry to Arthur Gouge's proposals, apart from revisions to the armament requested during the summer of 1936. The nose-mounted 37mm Vickers cannon was replaced by a machine-gun, while the rear position was revised to include four machine-guns rather than the original singleton. This caused the centre of gravity to move aft; 4.5 degrees of sweep was given to the wing form in all aircraft following the prototype (and retrospectively to the prototype itself), while the planing bottom was also modified.

As the design progressed, in March 1936 an initial production contract was awarded for eleven Sunderland Is (L2158–L2168) to Specification 22/36. The prototype, K4774, was launched on 14 October 1937 employing four temporary 950hp Bristol Pegasus X engines, and first flew two days later piloted by John Parker. By the end of the month three further flights had been made and K4774 returned to the shop where the wing modification was carried out, the step repositioned and 1,010hp Pegasus XXII engines installed. The prototype travelled to MAEE for appraisal in April 1938; L2159 followed during May.

Felixstowe confirmed the aircraft was an excellent performer with no serious problems. Flight characteristics were good and K4774 was found to be very manoeuvrable though the rudder became markedly heavier at high speeds. The controls were reasonably well harmonised and the elevator and ailerons light and responsive over the entire speed range. Control as the stall was approached was good, though as speed decreased the aircraft would suddenly drop rapidly and without warning, though still under control. K4774 could be taken off, flown and landed with the elevator trim tabs at normal without passing any undue load to the controls, while there was little change of trim between engines-on and -off, or between flaps up and flaps down. The cockpit layout was particularly praised in

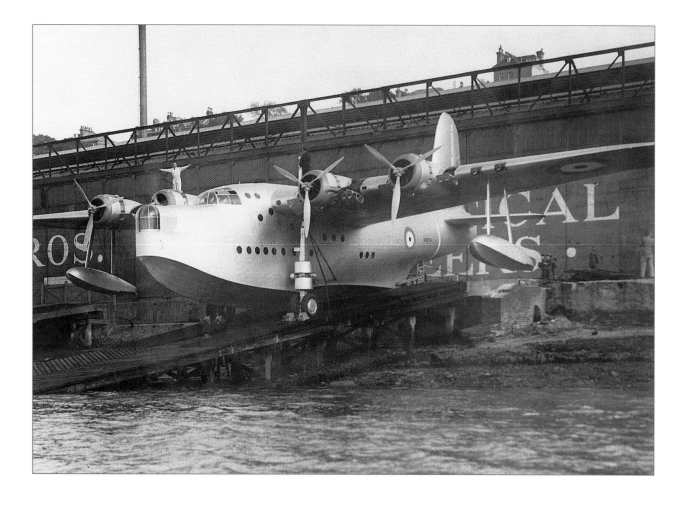

terms of positioning of controls and instruments, soundproofing and view forward and to beam, though for observation aft the crew had to be relied upon to report to the pilot. Structurally the aircraft stood up well to the trials with only minor modifications necessary. The first production Sunderland, L2158, flew on 21 April, again in the hands of John Parker, and the last of that batch on 10 August. L2159 departed for Singapore on 9 June manned by a 210 Squadron crew, arriving on 22 June. It was handed to 230 Squadron in exchange for a Singapore III. By the end of September 230 Squadron had re-equipped, employing eight examples, and a second batch (L5798–L5807) had been ordered.

Trials continued until June 1939, employing L2158 and N9021 (from the third batch), during which MAEE recorded a take-off in 60 seconds at a maximum take-off weight of 56,000lb. Maximum landing weight was 52,000lb; usual all-up weight was around 45,700lb. On the water it was found that as weight approached the maximum the wing-floats were pushed down, increasing resistance and throwing spray on to the outer propellers and damaging them. In addition spray from the hull was found to strike the inboard propellers in a choppy sea. However, by commencing the take-off run using only the outer engines, and carefully bringing in the inboard engines once the bow wave had formed aft of the nacelles, the spray problem was mitigated.

Queen Mother: Sunderland prototype K4774 on the Rochester slipway, minus armament. The aircraft was delivered to MAEE during April 1938 and in fact remained at Felixstowe for much of the war for experimental purposes. It was finally struck off during 1944. Here the starboard inner engine has been started, while the beaching chassis is chocked. (*Short Brothers*)

The hull of the Sunderland I was similar in general form to the S.23, being divided into two decks, but the rear step tapered to a knife-edge to reduce aerodynamic drag, an improvement over the transverse step of the Empire Boat. Construction was based around a series of vertical box frames, sectioned by several watertight bulkheads to retain buoyancy in case of perforation. Once again there was little double curvature in the riveted and anodised skin. At the bow was a power-operated FN.11 turret, manually retractable to allow mooring – the Sunderland was the first British flying-boat to incorporate such a weapon. A bomb-aiming position was situated below the turret behind a hinged window. Aft of the turret was a store containing mooring equipment, and stairs to the upper deck, together with a toilet and a gangway to the officers' wardroom. Aft again was a fully equipped galley, the bomb compartment, the crew's quarters and bunks, and two upper beam defensive positions, each mounting a single Vickers K gun. To the rear were a workshop and marine stowage areas and finally the tail gunner's FN.13 turret mounting four machine-guns. The flight-deck housed pilot, co-pilot, radio operator, navigator and engineer, and was equipped with auto-pilot. Two entry doors were situated one at the port bow and the other to starboard just ahead of the aft step. 2,000lb of bombs could be carried internally on racks that were movable to an underwing position inboard of the inner engines in readiness for dropping.

The shoulder-mounted 112ft 9in span wing was a fully cantilever all-metal two-spar arrangement, metal-skinned except for the Frise ailerons. As with the Empire Boat, Gouge flaps were employed to enlarge the wing and thereby provide up to around 30 per cent increase in lift coefficient. The fuel tanks were located within the wings, with a total capacity of 2,025 gallons. Pegasus XXII engines were adopted, driving three-bladed propellers. The wing-floats were similar to those of the Empire Boat, while the tail and fin were of metal construction, though the

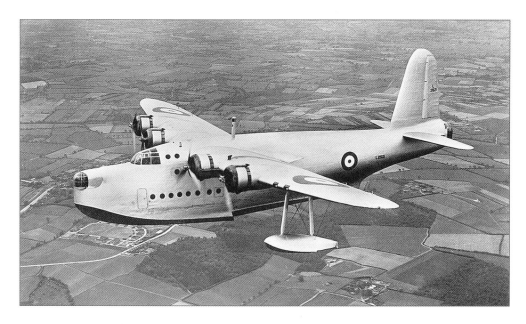

Sunderland I L2160 shows off its graceful lines for the pre-war camera. One of the first production batch, the aircraft flew with 230 Squadron and 4(C)OTU, subsequently becoming Instructional Airframe 3372M (later 4005M). *(Author's Collection)*

Sunderland N9025 of 228 Squadron seen at the Imperial Airways slipway at Alexandria in the summer of 1939. This aircraft later participated in the rescue of the crew of the merchantman *Kensington Court*, but on 4 August 1940, having returned to the Mediterranean, it was shot down by an Italian Fiat CR.42.
(Group Captain David Bevan-John via John Evans)

elevators and rudder were fabric-covered aft of their leading-edges. By the outbreak of war three further squadrons had re-equipped with the Sunderland I, eighty-nine examples of which were eventually built: 210 (June 1938) at Pembroke Dock, 228 (November 1938) also at Pembroke Dock and 204 (June 1939) at Mount Batten.

More Empire Boats

Shorts added to their Empire Boats with the S.33, three examples being ordered by Imperial Airways during 1938 to replace lost S.23s. The new type had a strengthened hull and was initially powered by 920hp Pegasus XC engines, restricting the take-off weight to 40,500lb, but Pegasus XXIIs were later installed which allowed an increase to 53,000lb. The registrations allotted were G-AFPZ *Clifton*, G-AFRA *Cleopatra* and G-AFRB. *Clifton* and *Cleopatra* were eventually launched in April 1940 but on the instructions of Lord Beaverbrook, the Minister of Aircraft Production, work on the third example ceased during May.

By that time a new Shorts presence was well established in Northern Ireland, after it had become apparent that Rochester would not be large enough for the increase in aircraft manufacture necessitated by rearmament. Following discussions between the British and Northern Irish governments, it was agreed the Air Ministry would build a new production site at Belfast which would be owned jointly by Short Brothers and Harland & Wolff Ltd, and managed by a new company, Short & Harland Ltd, formed in 1936. By the end of 1937 over 6,000 men were employed there.

During 1938 in-flight refuelling experiments in support of the Foynes–Botwood Empire service proceeded, Imperial working with Alan Cobham's company Flight

Refuelling Ltd. On 20 January Armstrong Whitworth AW.23 G-AFRX, converted by Flight Refuelling to the role of tanker, had refuelled *Cambria* over Southampton Water for the first time. All-weather trials followed successfully. During the spring of 1939 three Handley Page Harrows were converted to tankers, two (G-AFRG and G-AFRH) travelling to Hattie's Camp, Newfoundland (later Gander), while G-AFRL moved to Rineanna (later Shannon Airport) to support the Imperial route. On 5 August the first weekly scheduled transatlantic service began between Southampton, Foynes, Botwood, Montreal and New York, using S.30s *Cabot* and *Caribou* and refuelling between Foynes and Botwood; some 800 gallons could be transferred in eight minutes. Sixteen crossings were made until the service ended on 30 September. *Cabot's* westbound flight of 23–4 September from Foynes to Botwood was completed in the record time of 13 hours; both aircraft were impressed by the RAF during October.

During March 1939 *Corsair* ran short of fuel after wandering off course during a flight from Port Bell to Juba and force-landed on the River Dangu, 150 miles southwest of Juba in the depths of the Belgian Congo. The aircraft sank in shallow water, fortunately without fatalities. In horrible conditions a joint recovery team from Imperial and Shorts worked tirelessly to effect repairs. In June an attempted take-off from the unsuitably narrow river sustained further damage. Local labour, some provided by prison inmates paid a wage of 2*d* (0.8p) per day, was used to recover the aircraft once again, and to dam the river so that a lake would form during the next rains. A settlement was built for the workers and a track created to bring in spares from Juba. Finally, on 6 January 1940 Captain Kelly Rogers lifted the lightened *Corsair* from the lake, refuelling at Juba before flying to Alexandria for a well-deserved overhaul – and leaving behind the new village of Corsairville!

Meanwhile *Capella* had been wrecked at Batavia in March 1939. During June *Centurion* was capsized by a powerful wind at Karachi. Negotiations between Shorts and TEAL over the TEAL-bound S.30s had not been concluded and they

Short S.26 G-AFCI *Golden Hind* starts an early test flight. In the background crowds have gathered. This aircraft did not operate commercially before the war. It was impressed as X8275, receiving defensive and offensive armament as well as radar, and operating with 119 Squadron. The aircraft later transferred to BOAC and survived to serve briefly in the post-war world. *(Author's Collection)*

were therefore retained pro-tem by Imperial. They served on the Southampton–Karachi route which opened during July, the intention being to ensure their arrival at Sydney during September and commence Tasman operations during October. However, *Aotearoa* and *Awarua* eventually arrived at Sydney during March 1940.

June 1939 had witnessed the launching of the first Short S.26 G Class flying-boat, developed from the Empire Boat and resembling it though it was much larger. Imperial's intention was to use these aircraft for transporting up to 2 tons of mail over distances of up to 2,500 miles but they were also to be able to carry passengers. The initial role contemplated was a non-stop mail service between Foynes and Botwood with a crew of five. At the same time as the order for the second batch of S.23s was placed, three S.26s were contracted: G-AFCI *Golden Hind*, G-AFCJ *Grenadier* (later renamed *Golden Fleece*) and G-AFCK *Grenville* (subsequently *Golden Horn*). At the time of its appearance the S.26 was the largest Short Brothers flying-boat built, with a span of 134ft 4in, a length of 101ft 4in, empty weight of 37,705lb and all-up weight of 74,500lb; power was provided by four 1,380hp Bristol Hercules IV engines, cruising speed was 180mph and maximum range with standard tankage 3,200 miles.

Like the Sunderland the G Class featured an aerodynamic drag-reducing knife-edge rear step, together with a number of detail modifications in common with the military flying-boat. The S.26 also included an enlarged flight-deck rather than a mere cockpit. Flight testing of G-AFCI progressed well over the summer of 1939 and on 24 September *Golden Hind* passed to Imperial for crew training. However, within a short time all three examples had been impressed for RAF service.

A New Spotter

In February 1936, even before the first production Walrus had flown, Supermarine and the Ministry began to consider its successor, contemplating a more powerful engine, increased weight, carrier-borne capability, longer range and (somewhat surprisingly) a dive-bombing capability, all around a wingspan of not greater than 46ft. In April the company received contractual cover to Specification 5/36 for the design, development and construction of two prototype aircraft serialled K8854 and K8855.

In a departure from the Walrus the new design adopted a tractor configuration for its Perseus XI engine. The airframe was somewhat cleaner with greater cockpit glazing, but otherwise the layout was generally similar to that of the Walrus, and again employed folding wings. The prototypes progressed slowly as the company concentrated on production of Spitfires and Walruses, but K8854 first flew on 29 September 1938 in the hands of George Pickering, at which time it was known as the Stingray. The choice of propeller presented a dilemma, for the restrictions imposed by the clearance between engine and hull, and by the height of cruiser hangars from which the aircraft might operate, precluded a large diameter. A two-bladed propeller was tried but hump speed was not achieved while a three-bladed propeller returned only mediocre performance. Experiments using a four-bladed propeller with its two sets of blades set at 35 degrees in a scissors-type configuration were successful but eventually a three-bladed Rotol constant speed propeller was fitted as standard.

The erstwhistle Walrus replacement; Supermarine's Sea Otter prototype, K8854. Initially the aircraft flew in a natural finish but subsequently acquired a degree of camouflage and a large, unconventional fin flash, by when its bow area had been reworked into a sharper profile. Here it is in original configuration sporting the scissors-type propeller that was soon replaced by a more conventional type. In the background, the company buildings. *(Author's Collection)*

Following company testing in February 1939 K8854 passed to Felixstowe where recovery trials were carried out using HMS *Pegasus*. In March its bows were modified slightly to reduce spray and during May the aircraft travelled to RAE Farnborough for land catapult trials. In July *Pegasus* hosted further catapult trials while during September Southampton Water was used for seaworthiness appraisal. In the following January Supermarine was informed that the new type, by then renamed Sea Otter, would be put into production.

Blackburn and Saro: R.1/36

In March 1936 the Ministry had issued Specification R.1/36, to which Blackburn, Fairey, Saunders-Roe, Shorts and Supermarine had responded. R.1/36 sought a high-performance but robust general purpose flying-boat of up to 25,000lb all-up weight with a maximum cruising speed of 230mph. A range of 1,500 miles was specified as well as the ability to maintain height at full load on one engine, while a crew of five or six was stipulated. Armament was to comprise a bow twin machine-gun turret, a dorsal twin gun turret and a tail quad gun turret, together with a bomb-load of 2,000lb.

Supermarine's proposal, the favourite, was not taken up as the company was fully committed to Spitfire production (and was about to receive the Walrus contract for 168 examples), while the Fairey and Short offerings were also put aside. During the summer of 1936 an order was placed for one example of Blackburn's submission, the B-20, its singularity reflecting its novelty. The design represented the culmination of J.D. Rennie's work on one of the fundamental difficulties associated with the monoplane flying-boat – keeping the engines clear of the water while avoiding an excessively deep hull. Rennie's approach physically separated the lower, hydrodynamic hull portion from the main upper hull through the use of movable hydraulically powered struts. The lower part was extended when the aircraft was waterborne, to achieve the necessary clearance, and retracted up to the main portion after take-off to form a comparatively shallow overall profile.

The B-20 was an all-metal cantilever 82ft-span monoplane powered by two 1,720hp Rolls-Royce Vulture X engines. Its wing employed three spars, and Frise ailerons and camber-changing flaps were fitted. In a further effort to improve performance the wing-floats were made retractable, forming the wing-tips when not in use. Provision was made for the carriage of four 500lb bombs. The floats were mounted on faired box girder struts that in the raised position lay flush with the underside of the wings. A conventional tail arrangement was adopted.

The upper hull was of the usual transverse frames and longitudinal stringers over which the Alclad plating was flush-riveted. Accommodation consisted of a side-by-side cockpit, with navigator, engineer and observer just aft, while a wardroom, bunks, a galley and toilet were also provided. A tail turret was planned though the prototype was not armed, and further defensive posts were envisaged in the nose and amidships. On the water, a folding ladder connected the extended hydrodynamic hull portion with a hatch in the floor of the bomb-aiming compartment in the nose. The lower hull was of similar construction to the main part but employed countersunk rivets; it was arranged in five watertight sections and contained four fuel tanks together with marine equipment. However, as Blackburn became heavily committed to production of other aircraft the B-20 programme languished; the prototype, V8914, finally appeared in the spring of 1940.

In the meantime Saunders-Roe's proposal to R.1/36 had entered production as the S.36 Lerwick, ordered off the drawing-board without the benefit of a prototype during Britain's belated pre-war rearmament programme. A contract for ten examples was placed after the original submission had been revised by Knowler from a shallow gull-winged form to a deep-hulled layout. The deliverable quantity of the Lerwick was amended a number of times but in June 1937 was set at twenty-one examples, serialled L7248–L7268. The first to be completed, L7248, flew from Cowes in the hands of Frank Courtney during late October 1938.

The Lerwick was a cantilever monoplane, with a span of just over 80ft and an all-up weight of 28,400lb. Initially two 1,375hp Bristol Hercules HE.1M radials were employed, driving three-bladed propellers, but later aircraft adopted later marks of engine. Structure was all-metal with fabric-covered control surfaces. The single-stepped hull was very deep and the planing bottom ended in a knife-edge beneath the fin; the hull sides were vertical with no flare at the chine and a good number of portholes were provided. Entry was via a door on the port side towards the tail. A retractable FN.7 turret armed with a Vickers K gun was situated in the nose, together with the bomb-aiming position. The tandem dual-control cockpit was generously glazed while just aft and to starboard was the engineer's position. Aft again were sleeping and cooking facilities and a toilet together with a marine storage area. A twin Browning-armed dorsal FN.8 turret and a quad Browning installation in the tail

FN.4A turret completed the heavy defensive armament. The initial crew complement was nine, like the weight well in excess of that stipulated by the specification.

The high-mounted wing was of parallel chord across the engine-bearing centre-section, with tapering outer wings mounting the cantilever wing-floats on shock-absorbing V struts. Main fuel tanks, in two groups of three, were positioned in the wings, with three overload tanks in the hull. The offensive load of 2,000lb of either bombs or depth-charges was carried in the streamlined engine nacelles. Tail surfaces were of conventional layout, with a cantilever tailplane and a single fin and rudder, all control surfaces employing trim tabs.

Company trials with L7248 unfortunately revealed the Lerwick was a problem child. Despite prior test-tank and wind-tunnel tests with models, the real thing suffered with severe hydrodynamic instability as well as overbalance of the elevators and instability in roll and yaw; hands-off flight was impossible. By January 1939 the second example, L7249, had also begun trials while L7248 passed to MAEE during mid-March, where the difficulties were confirmed. L7248 returned to Cowes, receiving two auxiliary fins and an extended chord rudder, but no real improvement resulted. After numerous combinations of enlarged and auxiliary tail surfaces had been tested, as well as a twin fin and rudder configuration, the modification finally adopted consisted of an enlarged fin built out from the leading-edge together with a rudder increased in chord and height, which marginally

Saunders-Roe Lerwick L7250 shows its lofty hull profile at Cowes. The aircraft was criticised from the outset and had been ordered off the drawing-board, though the first three Lerwicks acted as development examples. L7250 wears its pre-war finish and reveals the hydrodynamic portion of its hull that gave such trouble. The fin has been modified from its original profile while the rudder has been given an extension at its upper point. *(Author's Collection)*

improved flight control; water performance continued to be investigated until 1941. Saro Project S/36C appeared during 1939, a civil Lerwick for possible operation by Imperial Airways, but was not pursued – though in fairness the impending hostilities would have precluded such a move.

During MAEE trials it was found that take-off runs were unduly long, which strained the engines, while the top speed was only around 214mph. Efforts were made to shed weight but with limited success, though the crew complement became six. During the summer of 1939 four Lerwicks joined 240 Squadron at Invergordon and others travelled to Calshot while the situation was considered. In October the re-equipment of 240 Squadron was abandoned and the unit retained its Londons instead – older and slower but not tormented by unpleasant or dangerous characteristics. On 24 October the Lerwick programme was cancelled, but was reinstated on 1 November on the understanding that it would not interfere with Saunders-Roe's Walrus work. On 16 December Air Vice-Marshal Sholto Douglas of the Air Staff wrote to Air Chief Marshal Sir Wilfred Freeman suggesting that the Lerwick be scrapped and Saunders-Roe be put to building Sunderlands. However, Sunderland production start-up at Cowes would have taken many months and by that critical time in her history Britain was very short indeed of flying-boats with which to meet her assailant; even the Lerwick was pressed.

Lerwicks at East Cowes in the summer of 1939: left to right, L7250, L7249 and L7248. The latter sports auxiliary fins in an effort to improve control. All the aircraft feature rudder extensions. L7248 sports a maintenance platform attached to its port engine nacelle, while the dorsal turret is retracted and the rear turret aperture has been blanked off. *(Author's Collection)*

5 THE SECOND WORLD WAR

The Big Biplanes Bow Out

By September 1939 the RAF still operated three large biplane maritime patrol flying-boats in small numbers: the Singapore III, the London and the Stranraer. These types' continuing employment served to underline the shortage of flying-boats in the RAF at that time, for by then they were obsolescent.

The Singapore III was the most venerable but the longest-lived. Nineteen examples remained in service in the autumn of 1939, mostly with 203 Squadron which moved to Aden at the outbreak. The aircraft were hurriedly repainted in sand and spinach camouflage, and 203 patrolled the Persian Gulf and Aden until re-equipped with Blenheims in the summer of 1940; the Singapores were then moored out at Aden in an attempt to dissuade incursions from Somaliland. In Scotland the Flying-Boat Training Squadron/4(C)OTU retained their examples until June 1941. No. 205 Squadron at Seletar kept theirs until 1941 but by October four (K6912, K6916, K6917 and K6918) had travelled to Fiji, forming the mainstay of 5 Squadron Royal New Zealand Air Force until 1945 when Catalinas finally arrived.

Three London Squadrons existed when war broke out: 202, based on Malta, and 201 (Sullom Voe) and 240 (Invergordon) patrolling home waters around Scotland

Not made in Britain but a Canadian Vickers Stranraer built at St Hubert, Montreal, under licence from the parent company. These aircraft were flown by the Royal Canadian Air Force from both eastern and western coastlines, serving until January 1946. No fewer than fourteen found their way on to the Canadian post-war civil register. One (920, later CF-BXO) is now exhibited at the RAF Museum. *(Royal Canadian Air Force archives via Bryan Ribbans)*

and the Isles, and east to Norway. 202 Squadron moved to Gibraltar soon after war was declared; the unit lost several aircraft in accidents and bad weather but continued operations. During mid-December 1939 240 Squadron's K5911 encountered nine Heinkel He 111s of KG26 over the Shetlands off Lerwick. Attacked, the London damaged one of its aggressors though the pilot was killed in the exchange. The co-pilot landed in heavy seas and eventually managed to return to base, an episode of great credit to a resolute crew and their rugged aircraft. The surviving Londons were withdrawn from front-line duties over 1940 and 1941, numbers passing to the Flying-Boat Training School/4(C)OTU, before the residue were reduced to produce.

Stranraers had equipped 209 Squadron based at Invergordon and Oban in the autumn of 1939, but were withdrawn from December as 209 received Lerwicks. However, during the following June 240 Squadron acquired Stranraers at the expense of their Londons, before Catalinas arrived in March 1941; the biplanes had gone by April. The Stranraer too ended its days with 4(C)OTU, finally being withdrawn during October 1942.

In addition to the Supermarine-built examples forty Stranraers were manufactured under licence by Canadian Vickers at Montreal. Deliveries to the Royal Canadian Air Force had commenced during November 1937 and the type served with 4, 5, 6, 7, 9, 117 and 120 Bomber Reconnaissance Squadrons during its long tenure, which lasted until January 1946. From 1943 it flew alongside Catalinas and the Canadian-built version, the Canso, but was considered more seaworthy and resilient than the monoplane. No fewer than fourteen Stranraers joined the Canadian civil register following their withdrawal from service use, the final example (920/CF-BXO)

Singapore III K8565/Q seen serving with 4(C)OTU in its latter days. It had also flown with the Flying-Boat Training School and prior to that with 210 and 209 Squadrons. It was finally struck off charge in June 1941. *(Jim Halley)*

passing to Pacific Western Airlines as late as 1963 – this aircraft is now preserved at the RAF Museum at Hendon.

Walrus: On Sea and Land

The operational career of the Walrus began as the initial production batch joined their ships, of which the first were *Nelson, Shropshire, Norfolk, Cumberland* and *Achilles*. These were followed by *Sussex, Exeter, York* and *Devonshire*, and by September 1939 the monitor *Terror*, as well as the seaplane carrier *Albatross*, taken by the Royal Navy in part-exchange for the Leanders of the Royal Australian Navy (RAN). An early engagement took place during February 1940: *Dorsetshire's* aircraft spotted the German merchantman *Waikama* out of Rio which when intercepted was scuttled. However, the task of action observation, foreseen as a major activity, was not widely undertaken. During the important actions against the Axis, the Walrus was only launched during the battles of Cape Spartivento (*Renown* and *Manchester*, 27 November 1940) and Cape Matapan (*Gloucester*, 28 March 1941). None the less, during the early part of the war the Walrus played a vital role in protecting Allied convoys, tirelessly spotting for enemy surface raiders, submarines and their supply ships and carrying out anti-submarine patrols when the Navy was at sea, which released carrier-borne aircraft for other duties.

Over May and June 1940, during the Norwegian campaign, where shore-based airfields were few but sheltered waters abundant, 701 Squadron travelled to

Warpaint: Saro London II K5910 BN-L of 240 Squadron over the North Sea, May 1940. It subsequently served with 4(C)OTU after a short interlude on the books of BOAC, and was finally dismantled at Felixstowe in August 1942. Here, the aircraft shows its ability to mount an overload fuel tank on the dorsal decking. *(Peter H.T. Green Collection)*

Walrus I L2217 departs its catapult. This aircraft was on charge to 712 Squadron 2nd Cruiser Squadron in HMS *Glasgow* between September 1938 and April 1939 but is seen flying from HMS *Sheffield* during 1942 while with 700 Squadron. It was transferred to the RAF in February 1944, joining 293 Squadron for ASR work as ZE-P, and was finally struck off in March 1946. *(Fleet Air Arm Museum)*

Harstad equipped with six Walruses supplemented by others from *Glasgow*, *Southampton* and *Effingham*. The aircraft carried out reconnaissance and anti-submarine patrols during the attempt to capture Narvik, and ferried personnel. On one occasion five strafed an enemy-occupied village, returning without loss. However, *Devonshire*'s aircraft was destroyed by a Heinkel He 111, the first Walrus to be shot down by an enemy aircraft.

By that summer too, *Hobart*, *Leander* and *Dorsetshire* were escorting convoys between Port Suez and Aden. Their Walruses were used as light bombers against the Italians in Somaliland. Rather than the very modest bomb-load contemplated by Supermarine, 250lb bombs were dropped on targets at Zeila, including the airfield occupied by the Regia Aeronautica, and a beached submarine, which was missed.

Meanwhile the first prototype wooden-hulled Walrus, X1045, had been built by Saunders-Roe. The wooden hull was heavier than the metal variety but was easier to repair, and the use of precious light alloys was avoided to a great extent. Supermarine retained design authority, but Saro replaced the metal tailwheel with a pneumatic type which much reduced the noise generated when moving on hard surfaces. Saro eventually manufactured 461 Walruses under licence, of which 191 were Mk IIs. The Walrus II was used widely for training aircrew.

During the summer and autumn Walruses helped to shadow the Vichy French fleet. The battleship *Richelieu* was observed by aircraft from *Albatross* and *Dorsetshire* prior to the air attack at Dakar Roads (Senegal) on 10 July and during September, in a subsequent attack involving the bombardment of Dakar, Walruses from the battleship *Barham* and three County Class cruisers were present, those from *Australia* and *Devonshire* carrying out anti-submarine and spotting patrols. *Australia's* L2247 was shot down by Vichy French Curtiss Hawk 75As while the battleship *Resolution* was torpedoed by the submarine *Beveziers*; Walruses joined in the subsequent counter-attack but the submarine slunk away despite reports at the time that it had been destroyed.

In the Mediterranean two Royal Navy commands had been established. To the east the Mediterranean Fleet (responsible for the Taranto strike on 11 November 1940 through its Fleet Air Arm Swordfish) was equipped with fourteen embarked Walruses flying anti-submarine patrols and spotting for artillery bombardments. Following the Italian invasion of Greece from Albania in October 1940 the aircraft patrolled from Crete. During that period *Glasgow's* Walrus saw off a Regia Aeronautica Fiat CR.42 fighter with the assistance of anti-aircraft fire from a trawler.

Camouflaged Walrus I W2766 was built by Saunders-Roe. It served with the Royal Navy and later with 277 and 278 Squadrons RAF in an ASR role. Here it wears a combination of Royal Navy marks just above the serial number, but the MY code indicates service with 278 Squadron. *(Author's Collection)*

The prototype Walrus II, X1045, seen at Saunders-Roe's East Cowes premises. In the background Lerwick L7248 is going through its twin-tailed phase. The wooden hull was a successful adaptation and Saunders-Roe went on to produce 191 Walrus Mk IIs. X1045 first flew on 2 May 1940 in the hands of Leslie Ash. *(L.S. Ash)*

However, during 1941 the Mediterranean Fleet suffered severe losses and by December their Walruses had all but gone.

In the western Mediterranean the smaller Force H had been established during June 1940, consisting typically of one carrier, a capital ship, two cruisers and various destroyers. Force H was responsible for the disabling of the Vichy French Oran flotilla at Mers-el-Kebir (Algeria) in July to prevent it falling into German hands under Operation Catapult. *Renown* and *Sheffield* were based at Gibraltar for long periods, and also operated in the Atlantic. On 9 February 1941 Genoa was bombarded, with *Sheffield's* aircraft in a spotting role, while others supported the amphibious operation against Vichy Diego Suarez (Madagascar) in May 1942. In November seventeen Walruses flew during Operation Torch, the Allied landings in North Africa, spotting around Oran and Algiers and carrying out anti-submarine and communications work.

Following the German invasion of Russia during the summer of 1941, the Walrus was carried by the escorts of the North Russian convoys, including the notorious PQ17 from Reykjavik to Archangel during June and July 1942. At least two examples operated briefly from Murmansk while their ship, *Trinidad*, was undergoing repairs. A third flew from Archangel, where eventually it fell victim to the harsh Russian climate.

Prior to the end of 1941 the Royal Australian Navy was heavily committed in Atlantic and Mediterranean operations, while in the East Indies and South West Pacific two armed merchantmen were each allocated a Seagull V to help provide local protection. However, following the entry into the war of Japan during December many of the Australian ships returned to Australasia with their aircraft.

Perth was lost at the Battle of the Java Sea during March 1942 while in August *Canberra* was sunk at the Battle of the Solomon Islands. As Seagulls were lost, replacement Walruses were acquired. *Australia* and *Hobart* took part in the Battle of the Coral Sea but by the middle of 1943 only *Australia* retained her flight.

By 1943 advances in radar had much reduced the need for spotting at sea while more effective defences had made spotting on shore-based targets the job of high-performance aircraft. The surviving catapult Walruses were phased out – the last to go were those aboard the battleships *Duke of York* and *Rodney*, and the cruiser *Belfast*. Amphibious Boat Reconnaissance training ceased in April 1943. However, several examples were retained by carriers, notably *Fencer* and *Victorious*, mostly for air-sea rescue and general communications work. The Light Fleet carriers *Glory* and *Venerable* operated their detachments, mostly in South East Asia, until the close of 1945. The Walrus had no flaps or arrester hook; generally a deck landing involved a steep approach and easing down on the throttle to the landing speed of 50 knots. Taking into consideration the movement of the carrier and any headwind, the relative speed of the aircraft to the ship would often have been very slow!

The Royal Navy also employed the Walrus from shore bases. By April 1940 700 Squadron at Hatston was flying anti-submarine patrols around the Orkneys. On returning from Norway, 701 Squadron travelled to Iceland for similar duties aboard

W2706, a Saro-built Walrus I, served with 700 and 701 Squadrons Fleet Air Arm, flying from Aboukir and later Beirut, before joining 294 Squadron RAF. This unit provided Air-Sea Rescue detachments across the Eastern Mediterranean, with aircraft based in Libya, Cyprus, Palestine and later Greece, before moving to Basra. W2706 survived until September 1945 when it was struck off. *(Jim Halley)*

the carrier *Argus* until relieved by 98 Squadron RAF, after which they operated from Donibristle and later Stornaway, flying as convoy escorts in addition to their anti-submarine work. By June 1941 700 Squadron Walruses were operating from the unfortunately named RNAS Twatt, continuing patrols around the Orkneys until March 1944. Home-based 754, 764 and 765 Squadrons were engaged in training, while target-towing was also carried out by Fleet Requirements Units.

During the autumn of 1939 two Walruses had been experimentally equipped with Air to Surface Vessel (ASV) radar and were trialled from Lee-on-Solent. Testing continued for the rest of the year and by March 1941 the first ASV-equipped Walrus entered service, L2336 embarking in the battleship *King George V*. By the summer of 1942 many front-line Walruses were so equipped.

Overseas, several aircraft joined Aboukir-based 201 (Naval Cooperation) Group, patrolling off Alexandria and providing escort cover, while several covert flights were made into Tobruk to evacuate casualties. No. 700 (Levant) Squadron operated six aircraft from various harbours around the Turkish and Egyptian borders, again on anti-submarine and escort duties, until the summer of 1943. The unit also assisted in the destruction or capture of a number of Italian submarines. Meanwhile, at the former Vichy French base at Arzeu (Algeria), 700 (Algiers) Squadron formed in November 1942, participating in several successful submarine strikes. Escort duties were continued but the majority of the unit's Walruses passed to the RAF for Air Sea Rescue (ASR) duties between February and August 1943 – the balance went to the Free French Navy's Flottille 40. Other overseas operators were the Royal Canadian NAS, Yarmouth, Nova Scotia (TAG training) and RNAS Piarco, Trinidad (Observer Training) which also provided anti-submarine patrols and regularly observed the Vichy fleet laid up at Martinique.

As the role of ship-board reconnaissance faded the vital work of shore-based ASR grew, using Walrus-equipped RAF squadrons; their crews braved enemy fighters, anti-aircraft fire and even sea mines during their vital activities. It is not clear how many downed airmen were rescued by Walruses overseas, but around the British Isles the total was over one thousand. 276 Squadron formed at Harrowbeer during October 1941 to patrol the western waters of the English Channel and the Bristol Channel. The squadron flew Spitfires and Defiants for spotting, and Ansons for dropping dinghies and supplies; the Walruses would then pluck the airmen from the water. The squadron later moved to Cherbourg, subsequently serving in Belgium and later Norway.

275 Squadron formed that October at Valley and by the end of the year had on charge several Walrus Is and IIs for operation over the Irish Sea, again in cooperation with Spitfires, Defiants and Ansons. The squadron subsequently flew from Warmwell and later Exeter. In December 277 Squadron formed at Stapleford Tawney, patrolling between the south-east of England and the north of France with Walruses until February 1945 when the unit disbanded. The East Anglian coast was covered by 278 Squadron established at Matlask during December 1941, its aircraft serving until October 1945, by which time the unit was operating over the Channel. 281 Squadron, formed at Ouston in March 1942, received Walruses during the following February and moved frequently; by August 1945 it was based

The Walrus served with the Irish Air Corps, three flying as N-18, N-19 and N-20, these marks being hangovers from the B Conditions identities first allocated by Supermarine. They were delivered to the Coastal Patrol Squadron during March 1939 in the usual pre-war overall silver finish but were subsequently camouflaged. N-20, seen here unarmed and sporting tricolour markings, flew until September 1942 when it crashed. The identities were truncated at some time prior to September 1940, to 18, 19 and 20. *(Author's Collection)*

at Ballykelly, disbanding in October of that year. Meanwhile, the seas off the north of Scotland were covered by 282 Squadron, stationed at Castletown from January 1943. Again an Anson/Walrus team was established, the amphibians serving until July 1945 by which time the squadron had relocated to St Eval via Davidstowe Moor.

ASR duties were also carried out overseas. 283 Squadron formed at Algiers during April 1943, acquiring six Walruses and operating off the North African coast before moving to Sicily in August. Detachments travelled to Italy and Sardinia as the war progressed and the squadron headquarters moved to Corsica, from where cover was provided off southern France and northern Italy. During April 1944 the Walruses transferred to 293 Squadron for ASR duties off the Italian coasts, until disbanding in April 1946. The seas around Malta were served by 284 Squadron which arrived during July and August 1943 and remained until November; detachments also flew from various locations in southern France, Sardinia, Italy and Tunisia. Warwicks started to equip the squadron in March 1944 and the Walruses were phased out by the following September, also passing to 293 Squadron.

On 1 February 1944 292 Squadron formed at Jessore for ASR work over the Bay of Bengal, flying Walruses and later Warwicks in parallel though the latter were later replaced by Liberators. The Walruses remained until June 1945, being supplemented by Sea Otters. Between September 1943 and April 1946 the type also served with 294 Squadron at Berka (Libya) and later Basra where detachments moved to the Persian Gulf and Arabian Sea areas until the squadron was disbanded in April 1946. During December 1944 624 Squadron reformed at Grottaglie (Italy), employing Walruses for mine-spotting duties around the Italian coast and in Greek waters until disbanding during November 1945.

Luckless Lerwick

If the Walrus enjoyed an outstanding wartime career, Saunders-Roe's Lerwick experienced a dismal contrast. In February 1940 it was confirmed that the twenty-one examples originally contemplated would be built. During April L7254 was assessed by MAEE; in September of the previous year the establishment had relocated from Felixstowe to Helensburgh, near Rhu in Strathclyde, an area far less vulnerable to enemy attack. L7254 introduced increased wing incidence, subsequently embodied retrospectively in other examples, which somewhat shortened take-off time, improved flight characteristics and reduced roll and yaw. Even so, power-off stalling characteristics were severe, though no spin was encountered, and with power on and flaps lowered the aircraft was uncontrollable. Throughout its life the Lerwick remained unstable in all three planes and the pilot had to be prepared to re-trim at any time, but particularly during the approach and landing. None the less, with the wing modification the type entered operational

Saro Lerwick L7265 operated with 209 Squadron at Oban as WQ-Q. It arrived with the unit in January 1941 but transferred to 4(C)OTU the following July. It crashed while landing at Invergordon in December, after suffering wing distortion – during heavy alighting practice – and was struck off on New Year's Eve. *(L.S. Ash)*

service. 209 Squadron at Oban began receiving Lerwicks in December 1939, trading in their Stranraers; L7255 made its first operational patrol on Christmas Day though only two neutral ships were sighted.

Unfortunately complaints persisted. On 5 February 1940 all examples were grounded for modification following a throttle lever collapse. Deflectors were installed to prevent a marked pitch-down movement when the rear turret was turned from aft to beam. On one engine, the Lerwick could not maintain height or direction against the torque of the remaining engine at increased power. The centre of gravity was usually at the aft end of the range, which made load distribution complicated. Bomb-doors would droop open in an unplanned way owing to hydraulic failures. The engine nacelles suffered excessive vibration, particularly during take-off and landing, which led to modification of the engine mountings. The wing-floats were given an additional 15 per cent buoyancy to increase nose incidence, which improved water handling somewhat. Corrosion was excessive around the rear turret area, owing to ingestion of take-off spray down the discharge chutes and the openings between the rotating ring and the cupola frame. Wing compression failures were experienced with L7248, caused by an upward deflection probably after a particularly heavy landing or during slide-slip or falling leaf tests.

209 Squadron experienced several crew losses unrelated to enemy action. Returning from its first operational patrol on 20 February L7253 stalled and hit the water hard, collapsing the starboard wing-float and turning turtle with the loss of four personnel. A shortcoming of the flying-boat type generally is the relatively insubstantial means of lateral stability provided by wing-floats vulnerable to abnormal stresses – the Lerwick seems to have suffered more than most. On 29 June L7261 was lost following a similar collapse, fortunately with no casualties.

Saro Lerwick L7257 as TA-S of 4(C)OTU in the summer of 1941. This aircraft had also flown with 209 Squadron. On 11 November 1941 it sank during a gale at Invergordon. Unlike the Singapore III illustrated on p.176, the Lerwick wears its unit code as well as the individual aircraft letter. *(Author's Collection)*

For a short period, as Saunders-Roe desperately sought to improve the characteristics of the Lerwick, the first example was equipped with twin fins and rudders of a form derived from the A.37 Shrimp. However, this configuration was not taken up and L7248 later reverted to its standard single fin and rudder layout. The rear turret is not fitted. *(Jim Halley)*

That summer the squadron moved to Pembroke Dock to join the Battle of the Atlantic and patrol the Irish Sea but the Lerwick was grounded for modifications over most of the period, and 209 commenced a return north to Stranraer from November. On the 21st of that month L7251 sank at its moorings on Loch Ryan after the front turret had been left unsecured. On 6 December L7255, also on Loch Ryan, sank during a gale, the probable cause a collapse of the starboard float which was ascribed to poor workmanship. On 7 January 1941 L7262 was holed during an inordinately long take-off run and sank in two minutes with the loss of two crew, while on 22 February L7263 disappeared in fine weather and was never seen again.

By the end of 1940 extensive tank tests had been carried out at RAE Farnborough, while Short Brothers had been invited to render help. The tests involved movements of the hull step fore and aft, deepening the step, reshaping the planing bottom and fitting a scale Sunderland-type after body. Eventually an arrangement was reached that reduced the porpoising somewhat: a deeper step placed aft of the original together with a slightly lowered planing bottom. The (limited) efficacy of these measures was confirmed using L7248 and L7250.

On operations, meanwhile, strikes against the enemy were rare but on 25 March 1940 L7256 released a bomb at a submerged submarine though without discernible effect. On 20 June L7260 bombed the head of a submarine trail, but again with no apparent success. By April 1941 Catalinas were beginning to arrive with 209 Squadron. The surviving Lerwicks were transferred mostly to 4(C)OTU at Stranraer; two more accidents occurred, one killing nine of twelve in overloaded L7268. Surprisingly, during the summer of 1942 the aircraft briefly re-entered operational service, joining 422 Squadron Royal Canadian Air Force at Lough Erne until Sunderlands became available during October. During that time L7267 was lost. On 21 October the first Lerwick, L7248, flew into a hill near Dumbarton while on calibration tests and the seven crew were killed. From that month the remaining examples were retired via Scottish Aviation and struck off.

Experiments and Policy

In 1937 Blackburn had established a factory at Dumbarton on Clydeside in cooperation with the shipbuilding firm William Denny & Bros Ltd. The factory enabled the transfer of Blackburn's flying-boat interest away from Brough to a region safer in times of conflict. The Blackburn B-20, V8914, was built at Dumbarton in conditions of great secrecy and was launched in early 1940, by which time it was surrounded by sub-contracted Sunderlands. A first flight was made in late March or early April in the hands of the company's chief test pilot, Flight Lieutenant Harry Bailey, but the B-20 was soon damaged by a bird strike.

Following repairs, on 7 April 1940 engine tests were carried out with the lower hull portion both deployed and retracted. The pontoon was slower to retract in flight than on the ground and appeared to move in a jerky fashion. During a test at maximum speed with the pontoon retracted the aircraft began to shudder, probably as a result of aileron flutter, and though the throttles were rapidly closed the

Blackburn's B-20 V8914 at the company's premises in Dumbarton, in the spring of 1940. The crew boarding ladder is at the forward end of the upper hull. The wing-float struts retracted into the wing underside, and the floats formed the wing-tips when retracted. The wing root appears to have undergone some rework, while armament was never fitted. *(Author's Collection)*

vibration became much worse. The B-20 crashed into the water but three of the five crew managed to bale out. Flight Lieutenant Bailey was killed; having attempted to hold V8914 steady to allow the others to escape, he left the aircraft too late for his parachute to fully deploy. Dumbarton continued with Sunderlands but the B-20 programme ended.

-oOo-

Saunders-Roe had also drafted a design with a retracting hull bottom, the four-engined S.39A, but in terms of hardware a more modest type appeared: the dainty A.37. Henry Knowler's aircraft was in fact a flying scale model, built to assess the characteristics of his S.38 project, Cowes' response to Specification R.5/39 issued in April 1939. This sought an eventual replacement for the Sunderland and called for a four-engined flying-boat for worldwide use, weighing around 45,000lb with a range of 1,500 miles and a cruising speed of 235mph. Defensive armament was to comprise four 20mm cannon in a large dorsal turret and one such cannon on a pillar mounting in the tail, while a 4,000lb bomb-load was stipulated. R.5/39 was renumbered from a previous Specification, R.3/38, to which Blackburn, Saro, Shorts and Supermarine had submitted proposals – all rejected because of a perceived general weakness in defensive armament. The four big flying-boat firms also proffered designs to R.5/39, together with Fairey. Perhaps with recent experiences in mind Cowes elected to build a half-scale model of their offering as a private venture, to evaluate S.38 more fully than would ever be possible using models in test-tanks and wind tunnels. Just one A.37 was built, unofficially dubbed the Shrimp and registered G-AFZS; it first flew in September 1939 piloted by Saro test pilot Leslie Ash.

Saro A.37 Shrimp G-AFZS in original configuration. Although a four-engined aircraft, its true size can be appreciated by the scale of the figures in the tandem cockpit. Though the Shrimp has had a hasty coat of camouflage applied it is still civil-registered, but that was to change – as so much of the aircraft did. The lower area of the hull is actually natural metal or perhaps yellow; the darker appearance is caused by use of orthochromatic camera film.
(Author's Collection)

The Shrimp employed four 95hp Pobjoy Niagara III engines, around half the diameter of the high-performance Bristol Hercules contemplated for the S.38. Its cantilever 50ft-span wing was of wood with plywood skinning and fabric-covered control surfaces, and mounted fixed wing-floats. The tail configuration consisted of twin fins and rudders placed at the extremities of the high-mounted tailplane. The single-step hull was all-metal, with a two-seat tandem cockpit and a bow mooring hatch.

During September 1939 R.5/39 was cancelled, partly because the long time-scales of the tendered designs caused the Air Staff anxiety, and so Saro's S.38 never materialised. In any case by then the Air Staff at least felt a replacement for the Sunderland was not needed for the war effort and the best way forward would be to update the aircraft to meet future requirements (particularly in terms of greater range) and to increase production. However, Coastal Command believed long-term needs would include an aircraft with a greater range than the Sunderland could provide whether modified or not.

The life of the Shrimp was linked with two of the many schemes for future flying-boat procurement explored by the Air Staff, the Directorate of Research and Development, the Directorate of Technical Development (DTD), the Director of Operational Requirements (DOR), the Director of Naval Operations (DNO) and Coastal Command from the drafting of R.3/38 onwards; the dialogue spawning R.5/39 continued following its cancellation. Subsequent options considered included a modest general purpose flying-boat to a new Specification, R.13/40 (a replacement for R.1/36), sponsored by DNO; a new 84,000lb aircraft powered by 1,600hp engines favoured by Coastal Command; an improved Sunderland with Pratt & Whitney engines and additional tankage supported by DNO, the Air Staff and also of interest to Coastal Command; a design favoured by the Air Ministry powered by six small engines; and a huge 160,000lb flying-boat to be adaptable for use in the post-war commercial arena, sponsored by the DTD and also supported by DNO. The latter option, advocated particularly by W.S. Farren, by then the Director of Technical Development, could be taken as the starting point of the line of thinking that culminated in Saunders-Roe's Princess. The number of players involved, and the time taken to generate and evaluate the options – let alone decide the way forward – is in hindsight at least remarkable, for once again U-boats were about to exercise their fundamental influence on the progress of the war. On top of that, decisions made were frequently overturned or amended.

Purchase of the American Consolidated PB2Y was contemplated (and a small number were acquired) but it was acknowledged such a move would very seriously undermine the British flying-boat industry. At the time no new flying-boat design was being supported by the government and if that continued, it was conceded that competition with the American manufacturers would be exceedingly difficult in the post-war market. R.5/39 was reinstated in February 1940. Coastal Command's desire for a smaller flying-boat was temporarily accommodated by the idea of a Blackburn B-20 development until that programme ended in April; in contrast DTD continued to favour a very large flying-boat.

In the summer of 1940 the Shrimp moved to Saro's wartime site at Beaumaris, Anglesey. It was assessed by MAEE at Helensburgh during early 1941, by which time it had acquired the serial TK580; praise was fulsome. Water handling was found clean and without porpoising while the flying qualities were described as very good, with light, responsive and well-harmonised controls. The aircraft then returned to Beaumaris, continuing company trials.

-oOo-

A further experimental episode centred on the Slingsby company's T.1 Falcon 1 BGA.266 (ABN) c/n 237, which was reworked to become a breed almost unheard of – a glider flying-boat. The purpose of the scheme was to investigate the possibility of such an aircraft for use when airfields, or areas of open land, were in short supply. It was felt that the type might be used by the newly formed Air Training Corps for air experience flights, and the Director of the ATC, W.W. Wakefield, arranged for the Falcon to travel to Windermere. There the aircraft was redesigned by Thomas Cooper Pattinson, who in a previous exploit had been first pilot of F.2A N4291 when Zeppelin L56 was shot down. Its fuselage was deepened into a 16ft hull with tumble-home sides, to which a planing bottom was grafted incorporating two steps; two small floats were attached to the wing. G.H. Pattinson (Builders) Ltd of Windermere converted the all-wooden airframe, which was launched from the Short Brothers'

The unique modified Slingsby Falcon 1 BGA.266 pictured in early 1943, with T.C. Pattinson to the left. The fuselage of the Waterglider was amended to include a two-step planing bottom while a small beaching assembly was employed. Wing-floats too were added, while the towing mechanism was modified so as to be suitable for use in conjunction with a motor-boat. *(Windermere Nautical Trust, Mrs Diane Matthews)*

manufacturing premises established as a wartime expedient at Calgarth on the east bank of Lake Windermere. The Falcon became known as the Waterglider.

The aircraft first flew on 3 February 1943, launched by speed-boat tow at a speed of around 20mph and piloted by Pattinson. No markings were carried, and all communication between boat and glider was by hand signalling. As it took off, the drag of the tow-line threatened to nose-dive the aircraft into the water but Pattinson managed to release it. The Waterglider soared to around 1,000ft, returning safely, and a handful of subsequent flights were made by Wakefield. Consideration was given to a larger version accommodating twenty passengers, for use in troop landings, but the idea was not pursued. The Falcon, however, had a remarkable longevity, spending many years in Pattinson's store following its trials.

The Waterglider airborne for the first time with T.C. Pattinson at the controls, 3 February 1943. The towing cable has yet to be released. The steps of the aircraft were substantial, and the existing tail skid was left in situ. *(Windermere Nautical Trust, Mrs Diane Matthews)*

Empires at War

During October 1939 the acute shortage of maritime patrol flying-boats led to S.30s *Cabot* and *Caribou* being impressed as V3137 and V3138, joining G Flight at Bowmore on Islay. They participated in ASV trials and, fitted with seven defensive Vickers K guns, in patrols off the north of Scotland. They were used as transports during the Norwegian campaign but at Bodø both were bombed and destroyed; fortunately the crews escaped and were evacuated. During June S.23s *Clio* and *Cordelia* received ASV, two four-gun turrets – one dorsal, the other in the tail – and

provision for carrying depth-charges, before becoming AX659 and AX660 respectively. This work was performed at Queen's Island, Belfast, and *Clio* was relaunched on 12 March 1941; *Cordelia* followed on 16 April. Both joined 119 Squadron, reformed out of G Flight, patrolling between Islay and Iceland and around the Shetlands, Orkneys and Hebrides. *Clio* was lost after an engine failure but *Cordelia* returned to civil use in December.

In September 1939 Imperial's Empire Boats had evacuated from Hythe to a hurriedly prepared terminal at Poole in Dorset. From 1 April 1940 they had belonged to a new owner – the British Overseas Airways Corporation (BOAC), formed from the amalgamation of Imperial Airways and British Airways Limited. They were converted to provide austerity seating for 29, plus maximum cargo capacity. As their Pegasus XCs wore out more powerful Pegasus XXIIs were fitted, in the case of the S.23 allowing all-up weight to increase to 52,500lb.

During that summer two S.30s transported prominent personnel. In June *Cathay*, piloted by Captain D.C.T. Bennett, carried the Polish General Sikorski to Biscarosse, near Bordeaux, to airlift out members of the Polish general staff who were surrounded by German forces. The aircraft was hidden on a beach all day and all night before taking off the following dawn, flying through the smoke from burning oil tanks to escape enemy aircraft. On 5 August *Clyde*, flown by Captain A.C. Loraine,

S.23 G-AETY *Clio* became AX659 and is seen being relaunched on 12 March 1941 following its conversion. ASV aerials proliferate while the defensive armament is in place though under covers. The aircraft crashed into high ground near Bowmore, Loch Indaal, on 22 August 1941 while in the hands of 119 Squadron. *(Short Brothers)*

transported Free French staff officers from Poole to Lagos, via Lisbon, Bathurst (now Banjul, Gambia) and Freetown, but on arrival was diverted to Leopoldville (now Kinshasa). The aircraft became a floating conference room and the talks held on board convinced Colonel Carretier at Brazzaville (Congo) to join the Free French.

On civil duties the Empires flew BOAC's Horseshoe Route between Durban and Sydney, with a maintenance facility at Durban to link the African and Eastern routes. After France fell a route was established between Poole and Lisbon. In September 1940 three Empires, *Corinthian*, *Cassiopeia* and *Cooee*, surveyed the Congo River to Stanleyville (now Kisangani) and Lake Victoria, then joined the Horseshoe route. From October until February 1941 *Clyde* flew the Poole–Lisbon–Lagos route, but on 15 February was sunk in a storm. Services were also maintained across the Atlantic to New York, and between Malta and Alexandria. During the evacuation of Greece, in late April S.23s *Coorong* and *Cambria* rescued 469 Allied troops in thirteen often seriously overloaded flights using Suda Bay, working with their Sunderland cousins. During July a route commenced between Lagos and Libreville, while between October and February 1942 a weekly service began linking Lisbon, Gibraltar, Malta and Cairo using *Clare*, *Champion* and *Cathay*, but this terminated during the German retreat from Libya, though the connection was subsequently maintained by landplanes.

Following Japan's entry into the war, the Horseshoe Route came under threat in the Far East. The route was cut when Singapore fell, being modified to include a stop firstly at Rangoon but then at Calcutta as the Japanese advance continued.

S.30 G-AFCX *Clyde* acquired a wide red, white and blue flash on the hull beneath its civil registration, while camouflage was applied, but a portion of the hull still appears to carry the usual silver. finish. *Clyde* was lost during a hurricane while moored on the River Tagus at Lisbon on 15 February 1941. *(Author's Collection)*

During that time *Corio* was downed by seven Mitsubishi Zero fighters; although wounded, Captain Koch managed to land his aircraft on its two remaining engines and survived, together with five passengers.

From early 1942 a link was flown between Broome in North-Western Australia and Tjilatjap in Java by *Circe*, *Coriolanus* and *Corinthian* but this too was dangerous work; on 28 February *Circe* was shot down. *Coogee*, impressed as A18-12 by the Royal Australian Air Force, crashed at Townsville, North Queensland; *Corinthian* was lost in an accident at Darwin during March. On 3 March Broome was bombed and both *Corinna* and *Centaurus* were destroyed, the latter by then employed as A18-10. That year, the QANTAS flying-boats *Carpentaria*, *Coorong* and *Cooee*, all in India when the Horseshoe Route was cut, were swapped with BOAC's Australian-based *Coriolanus*, *Camilla* and *Clifton*. On 14 September *Clare* was lost en route to Bathurst from Lagos, while *Ceres* exploded at her Durban moorings during December. Though they were supplemented in the latter stages of the war by civilianised Sunderlands, the remaining Empire Boats continued services between Durban and Calcutta, and surveys of new routes. In December 1942, meanwhile, *Coriolanus* and *Camilla* commenced a link between Townsville, Port Moresby and Milne Bay at the south-east of New Guinea Island, but *Camilla* was destroyed in a storm off Port Moresby on 22 April 1943. The pilot was again Captain Koch, who was among the eighteen survivors. *Clifton* crashed in Sydney Harbour during January 1944, as did *Camilla*'s replacement *Coolangatta* in October but *Coriolanus* continued, and on 8 October 1945 became the first QANTAS aircraft to enter liberated Singapore.

-oOo-

The Short S.26s were also impressed, becoming X8275 (*Golden Hind*), X8274 (*Golden Fleece*) and X8273 (*Golden Horn*), still without cabin furnishings. They were fitted with two dorsal turrets each mounting four machine-guns, a tail turret aft of the rudder also with four machine-guns, underwing racks for eight 500lb bombs, radar, and armour plate for the crew area and inner fuel tanks. *Golden Horn* flew in its new form during May 1940 and *Golden Fleece* in July, both from Rochester. *Golden Hind* followed in September, adapted at Dumbarton by Blackburn who also installed radar in all three examples. By April 1941 the aircraft had joined 119 Squadron for long-range reconnaissance duties but by May all were making unscheduled flights to Gibraltar and the Middle East, temporarily attached to 10 Squadron RAAF at Mount Batten.

X8273 and X8275 were overhauled but at the end of the year returned to BOAC. Both were re-civilianised with forty-nine austerity seats and received their first civil Certificates of Airworthiness though they continued to wear camouflage as well as broad red, white and blue bar markings below their registrations. In June 1942 they commenced a route linking Poole, Foynes, Lisbon, Bathurst, Freetown, Accra (Gold Coast, now Ghana) and Lagos, carrying mostly VIPs. On 9 January 1943 *Golden Horn* crashed at Lisbon following an engine failure during a test-flight after a change of engine, and only the radio officer survived. From May *Golden Hind* worked the

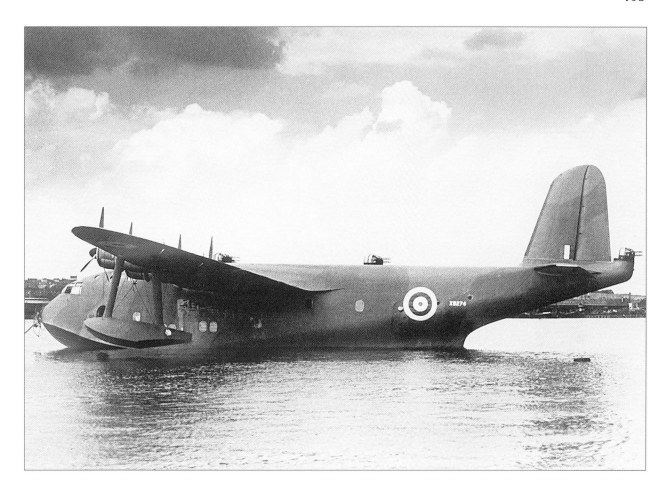

service between Poole and Foynes and, following a refit to more opulent seating for thirty-eight fare-paying passengers, moved to Durban in September, commencing a route between Kisumu, Mombasa, Pamanzi (Comoro Islands), Madagascar and the Seychelles that grew to take in the Maldives and Ceylon. This lasted until 30 August 1945, when the QANTAS direct service from Australia to Ceylon resumed. *Golden Hind* then travelled to Belfast for a major overhaul, and replacement of its Hercules IVs by Hercules XIVs.

Sunderland – Queen of Flying-Boats

Despite the very urgent need for more Sunderlands following the completion of the Mk I build, only twenty examples were delivered during 1940 and thirty-two in 1941. Forty-three Mark IIs were produced, employing Pegasus XVIIIs and later equipped with a dorsal turret mounting two machine-guns which replaced the previous open K-gun positions. The Sunderland II also generally incorporated ASV Mk II radar, the very visible signs being eight transmitter aerials on each side of the hull, four dorsal dipole receiving masts, and central and underwing Yagi homing aerial arrays. All-up weight increased to 56,000lb. The first Sunderland II, T9083 (a converted Mk I) flew in April 1942. Short & Harland commenced flying-boat production with a batch of fifteen Mark IIs.

S.26 X8274 had started life as G-AFCJ *Golden Fleece*. Heavy defensive armament has been installed. The aircraft was lost on 11 June 1941 off Cape Finisterre while detached to 10 Squadron Royal Australian Air Force after alighting with two engines ablaze and breaching the hull. The photograph was taken at Queen's Island, Belfast, before the aircraft arrived with its first operator, 119 Squadron. *(Short Brothers)*

Various hull profiles for proposed later marks of the Sunderland were tested in scale form by Scion Senior L9786, in order to acquire a more accurate assessment of their characteristics than tank testing alone would yield. A single large central float was employed to simulate the hull layouts and the first flight of the modified aircraft took place on 18 October 1939. L9786 was trialled until 1944; its work supported the design of the faired step adopted by the Sunderland III, the most numerous version, 463 of which were produced including the prototype T9042, again a converted Mk I. This first flew on 28 June 1941 in the hands of John Parker; the first true Mk III was W3999 which took to the air on 15 December. The faired step reduced drag without markedly affecting hydrodynamic characteristics, though later Sunderlands were somewhat dirtier in the water than their predecessors. Like the Mk II, the Sunderland III was powered by the Pegasus XVIII. In early 1943 the type was fitted with ASV Mk III. The last of the Sunderland IIIs featured the much improved ASV IVc, the Yagi aerials being replaced by underwing split scanners in protective radomes, and were known as the Mk IIIA.

The Sunderland IV to Specification R.8/42 incorporated much more powerful 1,700hp Bristol Hercules XIX engines driving four-bladed propellers, two prototypes (MZ269 and MZ271) and forty production examples (NJ200–NJ239) being ordered. Length and beam were slightly increased while the planing bottom was modified with a deeper step and the tailplane given pronounced dihedral to clear spray.

MZ269 first flew from Rochester on 30 August 1944, subsequently receiving an enlarged fin, rudder and tailplane to overcome yaw and potential rudder-locking. The Sunderland IV was intended to operate in the Pacific theatre and was later renamed the S.45 Seaford GR Mk I. It was somewhat faster than the Sunderland

Short Seaford, prototype MZ269, displays its mighty fin and rudder for the camera; the standard fin and rudder were not able to control the yaw with two engines stopped on one side. A new tailplane of around 20 per cent greater area was also fitted, while a forward dorsal extension to the fin leading-edge was added. MZ269 was tested extensively by MAEE before being scrapped in July 1947. *(Author's Collection)*

although maximum weight rose to 75,000lb. However, the improvement in performance was not dramatic and with the ending of the Pacific war the planned build was cut back to eight (NJ200–NJ207). Only brief trials with 201 Squadron in April and May 1946 were performed, during which the aircraft was found generally seaworthy but prone to skipping after alighting at high incidence.

The final Sunderland was the Mk V employing 1,200hp Pratt & Whitney Twin Wasps, affording a greater reserve of power than the Pegasus XVIII, which as the aircraft evolved and became heavier had to be run almost continuously at higher ratings with consequent deterioration in reliability. Early in 1944 Mk IIIs ML765 at Rochester and ML839 of 10 Squadron RAAF at Mount Batten were both fitted experimentally with Twin Wasps, acting as prototypes and flying in March and May respectively. The change was a great success; the Mk V could fly under control with both propellers feathered on one side, a feat not previously possible for the Sunderland. A total of 154 Mk Vs were manufactured from new and a further 88 converted from Mk IIIs. The first Mk Vs joined 228 and 461 Squadrons during February 1945. In all, 749 Sunderlands were built: 331 at Rochester, 250 at Blackburn's Dumbarton factory, 133 by Short & Harland and 35 at the Windermere factory.

-oOo-

The Sunderland carried out the first air-sea rescue of the war following the torpedoing of the SS *Kensington Court* off the Isles of Scilly on 18 September 1939. Two aircraft, one from 228 Squadron, the other from 204 Squadron, picked up

twenty-one and thirteen crewmen respectively and returned safely to Mount Batten. This practice was later officially forbidden but continued throughout the war.

In April 1940 the type's defensive qualities were emphasised when N9046 of 204 Squadron shot down one and damaged another of six attacking Junkers Ju 88s off Norway. During the Norwegian campaign aircraft from 204, 210 and 228 Squadrons were detached to Sullom Voe and Invergordon for reconnaissance and transport duties; when Norway fell, they also took part in evacuation flights. However, the Sunderland is probably best remembered for its work in helping protect Allied shipping convoys from U-boat attacks during the Battle of the Atlantic, flying very long escort missions – typically ten to twelve hours – and dogged search patterns over the featureless seas. The first success came on 30 January 1940 when U-55, already damaged by depth-charges from surface vessels, was scuttled following an attack by a Sunderland of 228 Squadron. After the collapse of France the U-boat war embraced the Bay of Biscay while aerial opposition quickly appeared from Ju 88s and Bf 109s stationed along the coastline.

Mount Batten's 10 Squadron RAAF had gone operational on Sunderlands in December 1939, patrolling the Western Approaches, followed by 201 Squadron in April 1940. In June the Australians flew General Lord Gort and the Minister of

Sunderland I L2163 DA-G of 210 Squadron, 1940. At that time the unit flew from Invergordon, Sullom Voe and Oban. The aircraft shows heavy weathering along its leading-edges and at the hull waterline and below. The dorsal machine-gun apertures are open. L2163 subsequently served with 240 Squadron, 10 Squadron RAAF and 228 Squadron, but sank in a gale at Stranraer on 15 January 1942. Recovered, it became 4891M. *(Author's Collection)*

Information Alfred Duff Cooper from Mount Batten to Rabat (Morocco), to discuss cooperation in North Africa with representatives of the Free French government aboard the vessel *Massilia*; however, the meeting was prevented by Marshal Petain. On 1 July the squadron's P9603 helped sink U-26, destroyed by a combination of air- and surface-launched depth-charges. 10 Squadron repeated their success that summer but such triumphs were rather the exception until experience was gained, improved radar evolved and tactics developed. Newly developed 450lb depth-charges lent extra force to the Sunderland's offensive load, replacing the ineffective and unreliable 250lb anti-submarine bombs. The aircraft were sorely needed; as the principal German surface ships became either bottled up or were sunk, Admiral Dönitz rapidly enlarged his U-boat fleet and Allied shipping and crew losses spiralled.

RAF Middle East Command was responsible for the air protection of the sea routes through the Mediterranean, the Suez Canal and the Red Sea, as well as the British bases in the region. By September 1940 228 Squadron's Sunderlands had arrived at Kalafrana from Pembroke Dock, while 230 Squadron had operated from Alexandria since May. During the long patrols some Italian submarines were encountered, notably the *Argonauta* and *Rubino*, both sunk during June 1940 by L5804 of 230 Squadron. On 17 September a 228 Squadron Sunderland attacked and shot down a Regia Aeronautica Cant Z.501 Gabbiano (Seagull) flying-boat. Several 228 Squadron aircraft accompanied Hurricanes flown from carriers to Malta to support its defence. In March 1941 a Malta-based Sunderland located Italian naval forces which led to the Battle of Cape Matapan and a decisive victory for the Royal Navy. Several 230 Squadron aircraft were briefly detached to Greece to provide anti-shipping patrols and transport capability.

Sunderland II W3985 RB-T of 10 Squadron Royal Australian Air Force at Mount Batten sporting prominent ASV MkII arrays. In the foreground is a main beaching chassis member from another example. W3985 failed to return from an anti-submarine patrol over the Bay of Biscay on 18 August 1943 after being attacked by enemy aircraft. *(John Evans)*

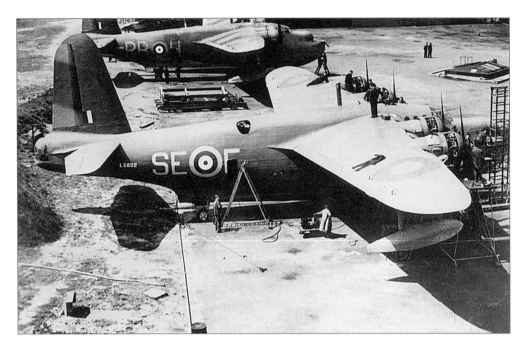

Seen at Pembroke
Dock during May
1941 are
Sunderlands L5802
SE-F of 95 Squadron
and P9603 RB-H of
10 Squadron RAAF.
L5802 has its
cowlings removed
for maintenance.
(Jim Halley)

That spring saw Mediterranean-based Sunderlands airlifting young King Petar II
and his court out of war-torn Yugoslavia, and working alongside Empire Boats in
evacuating personnel from Greece, including King George II and the royal family, as
the Germans advanced. Many of the Greek flights were severely overloaded; on
25 April T9048 left Kalamata carrying no fewer than seventy-two passengers and 10
crew, though with only a low fuel load and no bombs – it was noted that the take-off
run was not excessively long. As Crete was overrun during May and June the
evacuations continued – on one occasion T9050 flew out with seventy-four
passengers. The year 1941 was very lean in terms of available Sunderlands and only
two new units emerged, 95 Squadron (at first a detachment of 210 Squadron) which
travelled to Bathurst and 202 Squadron at Gibraltar. In September 201 Squadron
moved to Lough Erne, which extended cover further into the Atlantic though of
course the Sunderland could not patrol the total transatlantic distance to the United
States. Even after America entered the war a mid-Atlantic 'Air Gap' was left in the
Allied patrol network, eventually plugged by the very long-range Liberator. In 1942
Sunderland output rose and five new squadrons were created: 461 (RAAF, formed at
Mount Batten in April), 423 (Royal Canadian Air Force, Oban, May), 246 (August,
Bowmore), 119 (formed at Bowmore in March 1941 but taking on charge
Sunderlands at Pembroke Dock from September) and 422, also Royal Canadian Air
Force, which received the type at Oban from November. Every possible endeavour
was needed, for in June 1942 alone Allied shipping losses were an appalling 834,000
tons (173 ships together with the majority of their crews), 673,000 tons of which
were sunk in the North Atlantic theatre; by July Dönitz was receiving thirty new
operational U-boats a month. The submarines were elusive for a time because the
Germans had developed a detector of ASV II transmissions. During 1942 not one U-
boat was sunk by UK-based Sunderlands though some were damaged.

The important Allied shipping routes around the West African coast received increasing attention from U-boats toward the end of 1940. At first, Sunderlands were moved to Freetown and Bathurst. 95 and 204 Squadrons, and later 270 Squadron, 343 Free French Squadron and 490 Squadron Royal New Zealand Air Force operated in that theatre, aircraft being also stationed at Apapa (Nigeria), Dakar, and Jui (Sierra Leone). Accommodation and facilities were often very rudimentary, while climate and disease caused further difficulties. In September 1941 Vichy French Mohawk fighters from Senegal appeared, but two of four encountered were shot down on the 29th by 204 Squadron's Sunderland N9044. By the end of that year shipping losses in the region had declined; numbers of the submarines' supply vessels had been sunk and many of the U-boats had returned north.

The year 1943 saw the installation of the improved ASV III, which negated the U-boats' counters to ASV II. That February 330 (Norwegian) Squadron in Iceland went operational on the Sunderland. Engagements in the Bay of Biscay became more frequent and during May the type destroyed five U-boats; at that time Allied merchant losses declined. Realising that countermeasures to ASV III could not be developed quickly Dönitz had his submarines fitted with increased deck armament, ordering his captains to fight it out on the surface with enemy aircraft. German

204 Squadron's Sunderland T9072 KG-F undergoing maintenance at Bathurst during early 1942. The starboard inner engine has been removed and the aircraft shows marked indications of heavy use. The squadron arrived at Bathurst from Gibraltar in August 1941. *(Jim Halley)*

shore-based air cover increased, particularly over the Bay. On 2 June, in an extraordinary action, Sunderland EJ134 of 461 Squadron shot down three of eight attacking Ju 88s and was badly damaged but returned to the British coastline on two engines, beaching at Praa Sands in Cornwall with three injured and the engineer dying. The U-boats began to travel in convoys of their own, trusting to their deck weaponry for protection while surfaced, but the improved cooperation between Allied naval and air forces resulted in many losses, the turning point being May 1943 when forty-one submarines were sunk and thirty-seven damaged. On 30 July all three U-boats forming such a convoy were destroyed, U-461 by Sunderland W6077 of (coincidentally) 461 Squadron. Late in 1943 the armament of the Sunderland III was increased by fitting four fixed nose-mounted machine-guns with which to strafe the U-boats' decks. By then the Sunderland was equipped with the Torpex-filled depth-charge, around 30 per cent more efficient than the Amatol type it replaced.

The sharply increased U-boat casualties led to a period during the latter part of 1943 when encounters reduced almost to nothing, but in the following year the submarines returned, equipped with Schnorkel breathing tubes that improved their capability to travel underwater – even so, two were soon destroyed by Sunderlands. During June Coastal Command's primary task was to protect the D-Day invasion fleet under Operation Cork, and on the night of 6–7 June two more submarines were lost

Some of the West African bases used by Sunderland units were primitive in the extreme. This is Jui, with two aircraft on shore and a third at anchor. Facilities seem almost non-existent while rough ground and rubbish feature strongly. *(Wing Commander Vince Furlong via John Evans)*

to the type. As the western front advanced the U-boats were driven to operate more from Norwegian ports; in 1945 the campaign moved to the north of Britain. Improved ASV IVc radar was installed in the Sunderland Vs of 228 and 461 Squadrons during February 1945. In all, over thirty enemy submarines, of which twenty-seven were U-boats, were destroyed by the type or during attacks in which it participated; Sunderlands flew the first and last of Coastal Command's operational sorties of the war.

In the Far East, after the fall of Singapore 230 Squadron had left Seletar for Alexandria; later 230 flew from Ceylon and Burma, the only fully operational Sunderland squadron based in either location during the war. During February 1944 two aircraft at Koggala (Ceylon) were detached to Assam while in May two Sunderlands (nicknamed Gert and Daisy by their passengers) airlifted casualties of General Wingate's Chindit forces from behind enemy lines in Burma and flew them to Dacca in Bengal (now Dhaka, Bangladesh); 537 troops were brought out in an operation lasting thirty-two days using Lake Indawgyi at the Burma end, without discovery by the Japanese. In early 1945 the unit took up a ferrying role in support of the Burma campaign, a total of around 400,000lb of supplies being transported from Calcutta to Shwegyin on the Chindwin River. Operations against Japanese shipping generally consisted of strikes against small surface vessels; no submarines were ever found. Six aircraft joined 40 Squadron RAAF when it formed in Queensland during March 1944; the unit moved to Port Moresby in July and engaged in transport duties. With the end of the war in the Far East, aircraft from 205, 209, 230 and 240 Squadrons and 40 Squadron RAAF were used to bring home Allied former prisoners of war and civilian internees. 230 Squadron returned to Singapore in December 1945.

BOAC acquired Sunderlands during the war years, civilianised by Shorts. Military items were removed, turret apertures faired over and bench-and-mattress austerity

Sunderland PP107/W, a Mk V built by Rochester and flown by 230 Squadron, pictured at Koggala, Ceylon. Its hull-displayed serial number is repeated on the fin. This aircraft remained in the Far East after the war, serving with 209 and 205 Squadrons, but was tragically lost on 28 January 1951 when it flew into Mount Morrison, Taiwan. *(Bryan Ribbans)*

seating fitted while all examples received civil identities. In December 1942 six Sunderland IIIs, JM660–JM665 (G-AGER–G-AGEW) were so adapted, followed by six more, JM722 (G-AGHV) and ML725–ML729 (G-AGHW, G-AGWX, G-AGWZ, G-AGIA and G-AGIB) over the summer of 1943; another twelve, ML751–ML756 (G-AGJJ–G-AGJO) and ML786–ML791 (G-AGKV–G-AGLA), appeared during 1944. RAF Transport Command formed in March 1943 but the Sunderlands continued under the BOAC flag, flying to West Africa with priority passengers and mail until that October when they moved to the London–Cairo–Karachi route. This took the aircraft through the Egyptian militarised zone so temporary military identities were allocated in the Transport Command range OQZA–OQZZ. During May 1944 the route was extended to include Calcutta, and a specially fitted-out Sunderland flew Lord Wavell to India to take up his appointment as Viceroy; Lord Linlithgow, his predecessor, returned home by the same means. During the war only two civil Sunderlands were lost.

Sea Otter: Limited Action

Always in the shadow of the illustrious Walrus, during the Sea Otter's trials some doubt was expressed over whether it was needed at all. However, it had a longer range and greater load capacity than its forebear, and while naval spotting was in decline the vital Air Sea Rescue role had emerged. Supermarine, flooded with work, could not undertake manufacture; the task was offered to Blackburn who were also too busy. Finally in January 1942 an order was placed with Saunders-Roe by which time several changes had been embodied. The Perseus installation, which suffered from cooling problems, had been discarded for the 855hp Bristol Mercury XXX, already tested in the prototype in Mk XX form during May 1941. Flaps were introduced to reduce landing speed while the bow position was fitted with a Vickers K gun mount and the cockpit given greater headroom.

The first Saro-built Sea Otter, JM738, was test-flown from Cowes on or around 7 January 1943, the pilot being Jeffrey Quill. After trials from Worthy Down and Southampton Water, in the spring the aircraft travelled to Helensburgh while the second example visited Farnborough and then HMS *Pegasus* for catapult trials. Further amendments were incorporated: a larger water rudder – later made retractable – and an improved rear view through introducing blisters to the canopy.

Saunders-Roe built Sea Otters at its Cowes and Weybridge sites, alongside the Walrus. Initially these were designated ABR (Amphibian Boat Reconnaissance) Mk I, intended for naval reconnaissance but from JN249 of the eighth batch the nomenclature ASR Mk II was adopted, conversion being effected by simply removing the armament and some of the other service items. Though 592 Sea Otters were ordered Saro manufactured a total of only 292, the balance being cancelled following the war's end. A total of 241 were earmarked for the RAF, the balance for the Fleet Air Arm. Of the final batch the first example, RD869, was delivered in September 1945 and the last, RD922, during July 1946.

The Sea Otter entered service with the Navy late in the war, joining 1700 Squadron at Lee-on-Solent during November 1944, followed by 1701 Squadron during February 1945 and 1702 Squadron during June, both units also based at Lee.

1700 and 1701 Squadrons sailed for the Far East, 1700 to Koggala though detachments flew from HMS *Stalker* and HMS *Hunter* on anti-shipping sweeps, and with HMS *Ameer* and HMS *Emperor* on mine-sweeping operations off Phuket Island; ASR missions were also carried out. 1701 Squadron joined Mobile Naval Air Bases for ASR work, A Flight at Maryborough in Australia and B Flight at Ponam on the Admiralty Islands, while mine-sweeping operations were also undertaken, but 1702's planned departure east was cancelled with the advent of peace. 1703 Squadron was formed in August intended for service in the Pacific but remained at Lee until it disbanded a month later. By VJ-Day the majority of 1700 Squadron's aircraft were shore-based at Trincomalee. Wartime RAF use consisted of service with 277 Squadron (November 1943–April 1944), 278 (May–October 1945), 279 (July–September 1945), 281 (April 1944–October 1945), 282 (March–July 1945) and 292 (November 1944–June 1945), all of which except 279 Squadron also operated the Walrus.

Biggest to Date – the Shetland

The debate regarding the Sunderland's replacement had continued through 1940. The DTD, supported by the DNO, maintained their preference for a very large flying-boat, continuing to contemplate possibilities in the post-war commercial market. They were joined by the Director of Research and Development, which lent

A Royal Navy Sea Otter ASR.II makes a pass for the camera. Cleaner of line than its Walrus forebear, the Sea Otter experienced a protracted period of development as well as the redefinition of its role. Comparatively few entered service during the war and production was rigorously cropped back following the end of hostilities. *(Author's Collection)* weight to the future direction it (DTD) saw as best for the RAF and industry, and to a significant extent this body of opinion got its way. The specification for the DTD-sponsored flying-boat, R.14/40, was issued by the Air Ministry to Saunders-Roe and Shorts during November. R.14/40 sought a four-engined reconnaissance aircraft of around 100,000lb maximum weight (undeniably very large of course but by no means the 160,000lb originally contemplated by the DTD), a range of 2,000 miles and – optimistically – a speed comparable with contemporary shipboard fighters.

Saunders-Roe submitted their S.39 (revised) proposal mounting a four-cannon dorsal turret and employing reverse-flow radial engine cooling, while Shorts proffered their S.35 design. R.14/40 became superseded by R.14/40 Issue II, in which cruising speed was set at not less than 180 knots at 5,000ft while carrying a 4,000lb bomb-load, and normal range required was 3,000 nautical miles. A maximum 3,500 nautical miles at economical cruising speed was stipulated, and maximum weight was increased to 120,000lb. The Bristol Centaurus engine and heavy defensive armament were both specified, together with a crew of eleven. Saro put forward their S.41 design with an all-up weight of around 110,000lb but Shorts' amended S.35 was preferred.

However, contemplating Shorts' very pressing Sunderland and Stirling programmes, together with the magnitude of R.14/40, the Ministry proposed that the two companies should cooperate to design and build the new aircraft together, assisted by the National Physical Laboratory and RAE as needed. Saro performed detail design and manufacture of the wing and engine installations but despite their other commitments Shorts were much the senior partner, managing the overall design, manufacture and purchase of all other parts, subsystem integration and the entire final assembly, as well as water and air trials, under the leadership of Arthur Gouge. Two prototype S.35s (DX166 and DX171) were contracted, with the name Shetland. The build programme proceeded throughout 1942 and 1943, in a brand new shop at Rochester.

At the time of its appearance the Shetland was the largest British flying-boat ever built, with a span of 150ft 4in and a top speed of 263mph; power came from four 2,500hp Bristol Centaurus VII engines. The wing form was Modified Göttingen 436, with Handley-Page slotted flaps rather than the usual Gouge flaps. Pronounced leading-edge sweepback was embodied at the design stage in order, if necessary, to be able to vary the weight distribution by moving the engines and fuel tanks (though extending the nacelles was a further option) and so avoid relocation of the main step should its position not prove optimum in trials. Four main fuel tanks with a combined capacity of 1,464 gallons were situated in each wing, while two overload fuel tanks totalling 2,681 gallons were placed across the top of the hull over the centre of gravity. It was planned to store bombs, mines or Torpex depth-charges in inner wing bays while installation of ASV Mk 6c was also envisaged.

In calculating the Shetland's ideal hydrodynamic form, beside extensive tank and wind tunnel testing, Saro's Shrimp TK580 played an important part. From early 1944 until the following autumn the Shrimp was employed at Helensburgh in trials with scaled-down assemblies, particularly various planing bottom and step arrangements to 4/11 scale, in forms as near as possible to those contemplated for the Shetland. The optimised planing bottom/step combination was determined in miniature and

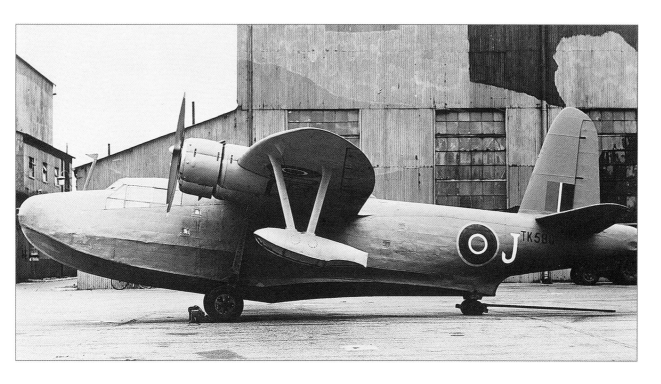

augured well for the full-size aircraft though close comparisons were not possible due to variations in wing sections and tail settings. A scale Shetland tail with single fin and rudder and Shetland-style floats and ailerons were also added. TK580 remained with MAEE after the war, travelling back to Felixstowe in August 1945.

The Shetland's hull, 110ft long, was 20ft high at the main step and too tall to be constructed upright so it was built in ten modules. A faired step was chosen, which would not provide such clean water performance as a sharp step but would significantly reduce drag, while the planing bottom tapered to a knife-edge beneath the fin leading-edge. A raised cockpit canopy reminiscent of the Stirling was provided, while the flight-deck accommodated five; side-by-side seating for pilot and co-pilot with the navigating, radio, radar and engineering positions just aft. Not surprisingly a twin-deck layout was adopted, including an officers' mess, sleeping area, galley, toilet, workshop and marine storage area. A total of eleven crew was planned, together with a very heavy defensive armament: a bow FN.66 turret, a dorsal FN.36 and a tail-mounted FN.59, all powered and equipped with two .50in machine-guns, as well as two single .50in beam guns. A 110-volt AC electrical system was installed, powered by two Rotol 60hp petrol-driven generators. The tail configuration consisted of a single fin and rudder and a tailplane featuring marked dihedral to avoid spray.

However, by mid-1943, with the Sunderland continuing to perform very well and without unanimous support for the Shetland as its successor, the new design was being considered for use as a military or even a civil transport; it seems the momentum supporting the very large patrol flying-boat option dipped at that point. Unfortunately, drawbacks came to light as the time and expense of the adaptations into the transport role were calculated, while the practicality of establishing a production programme started to flake as a shortage of capacity became apparent.

Saro's Shrimp in Shetland configuration, by which time it had acquired the identity TK580. Much of the aircraft has been altered. The planing bottom features a faired step rather than the original knife-edge. The floats have been replaced with Shetland-style types, while the original twin fins and rudders have been superseded by the Shetland-type layout. *(Author's Collection)*

The first Shetland, DX166, rears up on its beaching chassis. The aircraft has its turrets faired over and its nacelle fairings have been removed. The main beaching members are double-wheeled, while a four-wheeled unit supports the rear hull. Various 'port-holes' are open, while cabling is visible running from the windows to the ground. *(Short Brothers via Bryan Ribbans)*

Shetland DX166 on the hump. Felixstowe's reports on both its air and water handling were very favourable but unfortunately the aircraft burned out at its moorings on 28 January 1946 after one of the on-board generators was left running with its cooling shutters closed, and caught fire. *(Short Brothers)*

The whole-life cost of operating and supporting the Shetland in any form would be considerable, while its maximum payload of 15,000lb from a gross weight – up on the original specification – of 130,000lb, would be uncompetitive compared with those of the latest and planned landplane transports. Moreover, the Shetland was piston-engined at a time when the turbo-prop was emerging.

None the less, by the summer a military transport role had been confirmed and DX166 therefore received no armament, its turret apertures being faired over. It was launched on 26 October 1944 and flew in the hands of John Parker and Geoffrey Tyson on 14 December. Transport Command duly considered the acquisition of six Shetlands for long-range freight flights, but in July 1945 the RAF announced it had no use for the type, concluding it would be too expensive to purchase and operate even in penny-packet quantities without financial support from the Ministry of Aircraft Production (MAP). By then too, in the post-war climate the wider question was once again coalescing as to whether any new flying-boats at all were needed for the RAF; Sunderlands would continue to serve for the time being. Notwithstanding such doubts, trials continued during 1945 with Tyson as chief test pilot following Parker's retirement from that post, and in January 1946 DX166 passed to Felixstowe with an overall silver scheme worn until its demise in January 1946.

Civil Shetland G-AGVD reveals the modified nose area that removed any vestige of a defensive position, while the aft portion of the hull has also been remodelled as part of the civilianising conversion. Considered at one stage for use as a Napier Nomad testbed, the idea petered out and the aircraft remained unsold until its demise at the hands of the scrappers. *(Author's Collection)*

BOAC briefly considered the Shetland but also felt that financial support would be required in order to operate it. However, no aid from MAP was forthcoming. For some time the airline earmarked it for possible use on a development programme to explore very long-range transportation using the Napier Nomad, a compound engine combining a two-stroke diesel with an axial compressor and twin turbine to give economic fuel consumption; however, that project faded away. The second Shetland (design index S.40), DX171, was none the less completed as a civil variant, becoming the sole Shetland II G-AGVD and embodying various modifications: new nose and tail sections, no hull fuel tanks but wing tankage of 6,112 gallons, and accommodation for forty passengers – a very modest capacity for such a large machine. With no buyers in sight its construction dawdled on but it finally flew from Rochester on 17 September 1947 piloted by Harold Piper (Tyson's successor following the latter's departure to Saunders-Roe in 1946) and Tom Brooke-Smith. In 1951 G-AGVD was scrapped at Queen's Island without ever having been sold. Meanwhile, the Shrimp had continued to test scale Shetland hull bottoms together with a faired step, and gleaned further data even after interest in the programme had waned; it was eventually dismantled at Felixstowe early during 1949. Ironically the tiny aircraft was used to more purpose than the giants it supported. The Shetland was the only new flying-boat design built in Britain during the war years, a reflection on the Sunderland's capability and the difficulties encountered in agreeing on its successor, if any.

Sunset industry: the sole Short S.40 Shetland G-AGVD heads into the history books. 'VD featured additional windows in the upper mid- and rear hull areas but no fare-paying passengers ever took advantage of the improved view and Short Brothers scaled down their involvement with the flying-boat sector over the next few years. *(Short Brothers via Bryan Ribbans)*

6 CREST OF A TROUGH

In March 1943 Arthur Gouge left Short Brothers following the company's takeover by the government under the Emergency Powers Act 1939 and the assignment of its share capital to the Treasury Solicitor under Defence Regulation 78. Gouge joined Saunders-Roe, his association with Henry Knowler placing formidable flying-boat expertise in the hands of one company. He was convinced of the long-term future of the very large long-range flying-boat but he did not foresee the radical changes in the post-war aviation world – admittedly much easier to contemplate with the benefit of hindsight.

After the war the British flying-boat's days were numbered. The government's wartime Brabazon Committees to determine and recommend the types of commercial aeroplane for service in the post-war world had generated a variety of requirements, but none for a new flying-boat. The failure of the S.40 Shetland to secure funding from MAP in pursuance of operation by BOAC was consistent with the Committees' outputs (though its comparative shortcomings as a commercial type also counted against it). Notably, among the categories considered favourably by the Committee was the large long-range landplane transport, development of which at that time was led by America through Douglas and Lockheed.

In any case, well before the war Blackburn, Saunders-Roe and Supermarine had dropped away from the commercial flying-boat market, at least in terms of cutting metal. Though each continued to design civil flying-boats, by the mid-1930s Shorts had become pre-eminent among the British manufacturers in that field and met the required demand. At the outbreak of hostilities civil business ended; the companies of course remained with the military side. In terms of long-range capability though, by mid-1943 the American Liberator landplane, invaluable in closing the so-called mid-Atlantic 'air gap', was patrolling over open seas at distances where no other aircraft – including the Sunderland – could work. The threat to the future of the flying-boat was therefore not confined to its commercial roles. By 1946 Avro were planning their Shackleton long-range maritime patrol landplane as a replacement for Coastal Command's Lend-Lease Liberators and Fortresses.

After the war some airlines including BOAC continued to employ flying-boats for a time; from the British point of view these were invariably adaptations or derivatives of the Sunderland. In the early post-war years the national carrier had a major rationalisation job on its hands in terms of aircraft types employed, but the Shorts continued until 1950. However, though flying-boats might have been cheaper to operate than some of the interim post-war commercial land-based types, they were uneconomic compared with the big new American long-range transport landplanes. The obdurate pre-war British government policy of allowing the purchase of only indigenous aircraft for its state airlines evaporated; BOAC acquired Constellations, Stratocruisers and Argonauts and the remaining flying-boats were dispensed with. In 1950 BOAC closed their flying-boat operations at Hythe. As time went by the operators of the remaining Short flying-boats, such as Aquila Airways in Britain, faced inevitable problems of support caused by the manufacturer having ceased production.

Of course, the landplanes were able to exploit the wartime proliferation of runways around the world, facilities added to by the building programmes that continued post-war for strategic reasons. Since many of the world's cities are landlocked, the use of flying-boats on commercial routes was sometimes impractical, or involved long additional journeys to the centres from the nearest stretch of water suitable from which to operate, which could set them at a significant disadvantage in terms of service and cost. Also, though not predicted during the immediate post-war period, the flying-boat could not have assimilated developments in low visibility and automatic landing aids.

Blackburn's last flying-boat built remained the B-20 though subsequent studies were undertaken including that to Specification R.13/40 for a general-purpose military flying-boat. This yielded the B-40, a reworked B-20 cancelled in early 1942 following problems with weight and single-engined performance estimates. The company's huge post-war civil Clydesman flying-boat also remained a paper project; other interests had assumed precedence, notably the Firebrand, as well as a large land-based transport and a carrier-borne anti-submarine type. After the war Supermarine too retained only a relatively minor involvement with the breed and were busy moving into the age of the jet fighter. That said, the issue of Specification R.2/48 in 1948 for a new military flying-boat stimulated proposals from all four big 'traditional' players – though this was probably in part a reflection of the general dearth of military business opportunities at the time.

Shorts' post-war flying-boat designs – other than the Sandringham and Solent extrapolated from the Sunderland, and one new type – remained confined to theory. The commercial projects considered but not built included the 82ft span fifteen-passenger SA.7 intended to employ two Armstrong Siddeley Cougar engines, and featuring an optional transport fit; a twin-Hercules-powered twenty passenger design; the four-engined Napier Nomad-powered SA.8 of 160ft span with a double-bubble pressurised hull; and the huge 1946 Long Stage Empire Boat reminiscent of the S.26 in general layout but accommodating one hundred and six passengers and powered by eight engines, with a span of 232ft and a length of 152ft. Shorts' final military designs were the PD.2 to Specification R.2/48; the PD.3, a Solent conversion for anti-submarine use; and the PD.5, a water-based jet fighter to Specification N.114T.

Rochester closed in July 1948, marking the end of a tremendous tradition in maritime aircraft but an end none the less. During 1949 Shorts publicly concluded the large passenger-carrying commercial flying-boat could only achieve parity with the landplane in terms of performance and price above the huge weight of 500,000lb – and at that time a suitable engine to power such an aircraft did not exist. Work transferred to Queen's Island and following its Sealand programme the company continued exclusively with landplanes.

At Saunders-Roe, however, the largest British flying-boat ever to be built emerged in 1952. It tipped the scales at 345,000lb, and it employed no fewer than ten engines.

7 POST-WAR: CIVIL AND COMMERCIAL

Walrus and Sea Otter

With the ending of hostilities some forty Walruses passed either to civil operators or back to Supermarine. United Whalers purchased six for their 1946/7 Antarctic season and three, G-AHFL *Boojum*, G-AHFM *Moby Dick* and G-AHFO *Snark*, flew from the factory ship *Balaena*, mostly without undercarriages which, combined with slow speed and the low regional barometric pressure, improved endurance. Two were embarked in the Dutch whaler *Wilhelm Barendsz* but were not used. During 1947 the RAAF sold two Seagull Vs and two Walrus Is to Amphibious Airways of Rabaul, one each of these serving until 1954 and used for ASR, air ambulance and charter work with licences to carry no fewer than ten passengers in addition to the two crew! L2301 travelled to Aer Lingus, taking up EI-ACC and later becoming G-AIZG, while P5664 became VH-BLD and Z1781 was registered as CF-GKA in

Boojum, Saro-built metal-hulled Walrus I G-AHFL, ex-L2246. The aircraft wore an overall yellow colour scheme for maximum visibility against the snow and ice of the Antarctic. The United Whalers title is just visible beneath the ladder, while the aircraft sits on a former naval catapult. The Walruses were used only briefly by United, and G-AHFL became LN-TAK in July 1948. *(Author's Collection)*

1948. Yellow HD874 *Snow Goose* served very briefly with the Australian National Antarctic Research Expedition in December 1947 but was wrecked in a gale.

Numbers of Sea Otters were also civilianised. One became G-AIDM, a company demonstrator converted to a four-passenger configuration as part of an attempt to resell unwanted RAF examples to either the British civil or overseas markets. Six joined the French Customs Administration in Indo-China as N-82–N-87. VH-AJN and VH-AJO passed to QANTAS at the end of the decade while another, VR-SOL, joined Shell Petroleum, travelling to North Borneo. Well over twenty others became British-registered, including eight transiting for service with the Dutch Naval Air Arm.

Hythe, Sandringham and Solent

The thirteen BOAC Empire flying-boats remaining in the summer of 1945 were scrapped or withdrawn between November 1946 and December 1947. Tasmans' *Awarua* was withdrawn in June 1947 and *Aotearoa* in October, having kept up the Sydney–Auckland route since 1940. The last example still flying, *Coriolanus*, retired in December. Following its overhaul and refit at Queen's Island, S.26 *Golden Hind* commenced the Poole–Augusta–Cairo service on 30 September 1946, taking over from the S.23s. After that route ended the aircraft was eventually purchased in the spring of 1948 by Buchan Marine Services, intended for charter flights to South America and Australia. Instead it remained at Rochester for five years, carefully maintained, before being sold to Australian pilot F.C. Bettison. It was towed to

S.26 G-AFCT *Golden Hind* moored out at Hythe together with two Hythe Class flying-boats, the nearer being G-AHEO *Halstead*. G-AFCT served on BOAC's Poole–Augusta–Cairo route between September 1946 and September 1947. It wears the extended tail cone installed as part of its post-war refit at Belfast, this having been adapted from the rear turret base. *(Dave Etheridge, Fawley Historians)*

Sheerness but was damaged, and following a move to the Swale at Harty Ferry was eventually scrapped in May 1954 after suffering further injuries in a gale.

The surviving civilianised Sunderland 3s were retained by BOAC after the war while Shorts developed lower-drag nose and tail fairings for further versions. The company refitted the Sunderlands more comfortably and the Hythe Class was created by the national carrier, from which G-AGJM took its name – the other examples were also christened. Sixteen passengers were accommodated on a single deck (the H.1 configuration), subsequently expanded by adding a promenade (H.2) or eight additional seats (H.3). The original civil Sunderland nose and tail fairings were retained on the Hythe Class to put them into service quickly. The Hythes flew the Poole–Sydney route, starting on 12 May 1946 with G-AGJN *Hudson* as far as Singapore and G-AGJL *Hobart* on to Australia, the service being shared with QANTAS. It was a 5½ day journey – though the contemporary Lancastrian landplanes operated by BOAC and QANTAS on the Kangaroo route between London Airport and Sydney covered the distance in around 63 hours. On 24 August the Dragon service to Hong Kong commenced via Karachi, Calcutta, Rangoon and Bangkok, the first journey employing G-AGIA *Haslemere* to Karachi and G-AGLA *Hunter* thereafter, the return to Poole being undertaken by G-AGKZ *Harwich*. Also that month *Harwich* commenced a Singapore–Hong Kong route, linking with 88 Squadron's Sunderlands on a courier route serving the occupation forces in Japan. Hythes stayed with BOAC until 1949.

Wait for it! An intrepid passenger seems on the point of prematurely leaving Sunderland 3 *Australis*, Trans-Oceanic Airways' VH-AKO, formerly ML733 and RAAF A26-4. The aircraft has not been radically modified for its peaceful role; the bow turret is still in place, though at least it is empty of machine-guns! *(Dave Etheridge, Fawley Historians)*

Sunderland 3 G-AGIA was ex-ML728 and had also worn OQZA, but became *Haslemere* when BOAC's Hythe Class was formed. Here it still sports a camouflage finish, together with the red, white and blue underlining of its registration. It left for Aquila Airways in July 1948 and was finally cannibalised for spares in July 1952. *(Fleet Air Arm Museum)*

Short S.25 Hythe Class G-AGKW *Hotspur* at the Itchen mooring location that later gave way to Berth 50 at Southampton Docks. This aircraft was civilianised at Belfast and served with BOAC until May 1951. *(Fawley Historians)*

Shorts' Sandringham programme was also based around the conversion of Sunderlands to commercial configuration, but using the improved fairings and with more attractive passenger accommodation. BOAC's G-AGKX, ex-ML788 and OQZF, was converted at Rochester and re-emerged in November 1945 as the Sandringham I with reworked nose and tail areas, twin decks, accommodation for twenty-four day or sixteen night passengers, a dining area and cocktail bar. After trials with Transport Command it returned to BOAC in June 1946, later being christened *Himalaya*. Five Sandringhams were sold to Compañía Argentina de Aeronavegacíon (CAA) of Buenos Aires, also known as Dodero (after its owner), for services along the Río de la Plata. The first, Sandringham 2 G-AGPZ *Argentina* (later LV-AAO), was launched at Belfast on 17 November 1945, the second, G-AGPT *Uruguay* (LV-AAP), on 5 December. These carried twenty-eight passengers on the lower deck and seventeen above, and were used for local flights. The third and fourth, Sandringham 3s G-AGPY *Brazil* (LV-AAR) and G-AGTZ *Inglaterra* (LV-AAQ), appeared in early 1946, operating along the Paraguay River to Asunción and the Paraná to Iguazú Falls, with seating for twenty-

Hythe G-AGJM shows its paces for the camera. This aircraft also joined Aquila, arriving in February 1949 and serving until January 1952 when it was scrapped at Hamble. *(Author's Collection)*

Sunderland ML788 OQZF became Hythe Class G-AGKX and was converted to the sole Sandringham I, *Himalaya*, at Rochester, acquiring its Certificate of Airworthiness on 2 January 1946. The forward hull area was reworked to delete the turret and produce a more streamlined profile. G-AGKX passed from BOAC to Aquila in May 1949 and stayed in service until March 1953, being scrapped at Hamble in August of that year. *(Author's Collection)*

Sandringham 3 G-AGPY *Brazil* became LV-AAR. Seen here in the snow at Belfast it soon left for a warmer climate, and service with Compañía Argentina de Aeronavegacíon (CAA). *(Author's Collection)*

Sandringham 2 LV-ACT had started life as Sunderland ML843 but emerged from Belfast during December 1946 in civil guise and named *Paraguay*. Here, in Aerolineas Argentinas markings, the aircraft certainly looks the worse for wear, with a grubby and battered appearance and minus at least two engines. An area of new skin has been applied to the hull at the waterline just aft of the cockpit. *(Philip Jarrett)*

one below and a dining area and bar above. Civilianised Sunderland 3s G-AGWW (CX-AFA) and G-AGWX (CX-AKF) joined Compañía Aeronáutica Uruguayana SA (CAUSA), a subsidiary of CAA based on the River Plate, while a further Sandringham 2, G-AHRE *Paraguay* (LV-ACT), travelled to CAA following its launch in November 1946. Sunderland 5 CX-AKR served with CAUSA, and two more, LV-AHG and LV-AHH, joined Aerolineas Argentinas in 1947, that airline having absorbed CAA. In 1962 Aerolineas Argentinas ceased flying-boat operations but in 1966 the surviving aircraft (LV-AAO, LV-AAQ, LV-AAR, LV-ACT, LV-AHG and LV-AHM, the latter acquired from Norway) were leased by Co-operativa Argentina de Aeronavegantes, intended for use as freighters. However, after a few flights they were scrapped in January 1967. LV-AAO had been built as DV964 in 1942.

TEAL ordered four Sandringham 4s with accommodation for thirty day passengers, a galley and a bar, as the Dominion Class (later the Tasman Class). TEAL was encouraged to acquire flying-boats through political pressure; given a free hand the company would have selected DC-4s. The first, ZK-AMB *Tasman*, was delivered in July 1946; ZK-AMD *Australia*, ZK-AME *New Zealand* and ZK-AMH *Auckland* followed. New Zealand National Airways acquired four Sunderland 3s (ZK-AMF, ZK-AMG, ZK-AMJ and ZK-AMK), linking Auckland, Suva and Labasa, while Trans-Oceanic Airways Ltd operated Sunderland 3s VH-BKQ *Pacific Star*, VH-AKO *Australis* and VH-AKP *Antilles* between Sydney and Lord Howe Island until July 1952. By December 1949, meanwhile, following engine overheating troubles the TEAL Sandringhams had been withdrawn. Barrier Reef Airways acquired ZK-AME and ZK-AMH as VH-BRD *Princess of Cairns* and VH-BRC *Beachcomber* respectively, *Beachcomber* being stored and *Princess of Cairns* flying between Brisbane and Townsville before being written off in a Brisbane storm during September 1952. During 1953 Ansett Airways of Sydney

ZK-AMD *Australia*, a Sandringham 4 operated by Tasman Empire Airways Ltd, seen at Belfast prior to delivery. This aircraft was later acquired by QANTAS, becoming VH-EBX, and subsequently served with Barrier Reef Airways and Ansett as VH-BRE. It was eventually damaged beyond repair during July 1963. *(Philip Jarrett)*

Sandringham 5 G-AHZA *Penzance*, seen at Felixstowe. The aircraft entered service with BOAC in April 1947 and though the national carrier ceased flying-boat operations in November 1950 it survived until 1959, being scrapped at Hamworthy in March of that year. *(Gordon Kinsey)*

Sandringham 7 G-AKCO *Frigate Bird III* at East Cowes in October 1954. This aircraft had started its revamped life as BOAC's *St George* and was purchased by Captain Sir Gordon Taylor in October 1954 as VH-APG; Saunders-Roe carried out an overhaul at that time. It travelled to Tahiti in May 1958 as F-OBIP and was operated by Réseau Aérien Interinsulaire before finding a safe haven at the Musée de l'Air. (*Author's Collection*)

bought Barrier Reef and *Beachcomber* was converted to a 41-seater, taking over the Sydney–Lord Howe Island route. Ansett also acquired VH-BRE, the ex-ZK-AMD, and VH-EBX.

BOAC took three more Hythes, G-AHEO *Halstead*, G-AHEP *Hanbury* and G-AHER *Helmsdale,* while awaiting delivery of Tudor and Hermes landplanes, and Sunderland 5 G-AHJR was loaned between 1946 and 1948. In May 1947 the Sandringham 5 Plymouth Class entered service, furnished on one deck only with accommodation for twenty-two day or sixteen night passengers and also a pantry, and powered by Twin Wasp R-1830-90D engines. Nine were delivered, G-AHYY to G-AHZG, respectively named *Portsmouth, Perth, Penzance, Portland, Pembroke, Portmarnock, Portsea, Poole* and *Pevensey*; a second *Perth*, G-AJMZ, was commissioned after the first was gutted at Queen's Island prior to entering service. The Sandringham 5s relieved the Hythes on the Poole to Bahrain, Hong Kong and Sydney routes and between Singapore and Sydney. Later, Hong Kong was linked with the former Japanese Naval Training School at Iwakuni, near Hiroshima in southern Japan. The Corporation also acquired three Sandringham 7s accommodating thirty passengers, known as the Bermuda Class: G-AKCO *St George*, G-AKCP *Saint David* and G-AKCR *Saint Andrew*. These flew on the Far East service from 1947 until 1950, two subsequently passing to CAUSA, the third acquired for charter cruises around New Guinea as VH-APG.

The Norwegian carrier Det Norske Luftfartsselskap (DNL) employed Sandringham 6s between Oslo and Tromsø. LN-IAU *Bamse Brakar*, LN-IAV *Kvitbjørn* and LN-IAW *Bukken Bruse* were equipped for thirty-seven day passengers on two decks. Due to winter sea ice and several weeks of continuous darkness at Tromsø the link was not operable all year round, and as a navigation aid the aircraft retained the ASV 6c as installed in the Sunderland 5. In fact conditions were frequently very severe and by 1950 all three aircraft had been lost in accidents; two replacements, LN-LAI *Jutulen* and LN-LMK *Polarbjørn*

Sandringham 6 LN-IAV of Norwegian Airlines (DNL) on the water. It was lost in a crash at Tjeldsund on 28 August 1947, a victim of the difficult operating conditions experienced in flying in and out of the northern fjords. The ASV radome is visible beneath the starboard outer wing. *(Philip Jarrett)*

arrived, but in February 1951 DNL became a non-operating holding company within the Scandinavian Airlines System and their Sandringhams were sold off.

-oOo-

In 1946 BOAC had evaluated the second production Short Seaford, NJ201 OZZA, which became G-AGWU, for possible use as a passenger type. Shorts proposed a version named the S.45 Solent 1 with three cabins on the lower deck together with a promenade and two cabins on the upper deck, providing accommodation for either thirty day or twenty night passengers. The Ministry of Civil Aviation ordered twelve examples, G-AHIL–G-AHIY, which were built at Rochester using the jigs vacated by the cancellation of Seaford production, equipped to carry only day passengers and known as the Solent 2; respectively *Salisbury, Scarborough, Southampton, Somerset, Sark, Scapa, Severn, Solway, Salcombe, Stornoway, Sussex* and *Southsea.* The aircraft was powered by four 1,690hp Bristol Hercules 637 engines and accommodation was revised to seat 34, with a dining room and cocktail bar as well as the promenade, and a crew of seven. All-up weight was 78,000lb, a little heavier than the Seaford. *Salisbury* first flew from Rochester in November 1946 in the hands of Geoffrey Tyson. Water and air trials followed and the final example, *Southsea,* was launched on 8 April 1948. As it turned out, it was the last aircraft to be built at Rochester. BOAC's new terminal at Southampton Docks' Berth 50 was opened in April 1948, where passengers could embark from the dockside rather than by launch and where maintenance was easier, and the Solent 2 entered service on the Johannesburg route in the following month, the service inaugurated by *Severn.*

The type was withdrawn temporarily, undergoing modifications to the wing-floats and struts to increase clearance while taxiing at maximum weight, but returned to service in October by which time BOAC was also in the process of taking Seafords NJ202–NJ207, declared redundant with the RAF. Modified at Queen's Island for thirty-nine passengers on two decks, these became the Solent 3, registered G-AKNO, G-AKNP and G-AKNR–G-AKNU and named *City of London*, *City of Cardiff*, *City of Belfast*, *City of Liverpool*, *Singapore* and *Sydney*. In May 1949 the Solents commenced operations on the Karachi service, replacing the Sandringhams. However, on 10 November 1950 BOAC ceased flying-boat operations and their flying-boats went into storage.

Meanwhile, the independent operator Aquila Airways had been formed in May 1948 by Barry Aikman, acquiring numbers of Hythes withdrawn by BOAC. From July 1948 to October 1949 Aquila secured thirteen Hythes: *Hadfield*, *Hampshire*, *Hawkesbury*, *Haslemere*, *Henley*, *Howard*, *Hobart*, *Hythe*, *Hudson*, *Hungerford*, *Hunter*, *Halstead* and *Helmsdale*. In May 1949 the Sandringham 1 *Himalaya* arrived at the company's Hamble base; maintenance there was provided by Air Service Training. Aquila participated in the Berlin Airlift from August 1949 using the Havel See until it began to freeze over, and that year also commenced a holiday service

Solent 2 G-AHIO *Somerset* about to leave Southampton at the end of October 1950. The aircraft is receiving a rather staged send-off from the hat-raisers considering it is still moored! This aircraft later joined Trans-Oceanic Airways, becoming VH-TOD. *(Author's Collection)*

Aquila Airways' Solent 3 G-ANAJ *City of Funchal* seen at Southampton during May 1954, shortly after joining the company. It was withdrawn from use in September 1956 after being wrecked in a gale and driven ashore at Santa Margherita, Italy. *(Author's Collection)*

between Falmouth and the Isles of Scilly. Sunderland 5 G-ANAK (ex-PP162) arrived but was wrecked by bad weather in November 1954 prior to civil conversion. Seaford NJ201 was modified to Solent 3 standard, becoming G-ANAJ *City of Funchal.* In June 1949 a service commenced to Lisbon and Funchal, Madeira, continuing over the three following summer seasons though in an eventful passage *Haslemere* and *Hawkesbury* had to be cannibalised for spares while in one week during January 1953 *Hudson* was lost in a collision at Funchal and *Hungerford* sank at Calshot.

To replace its Sandringhams TEAL acquired a single Solent 3, ZK-AMQ *Aparima* (ex-*City of Belfast* with BOAC) in November 1951, and ordered four Solent 4s, a heavier version derived from experiments at MAEE and overseas with Solent 3 *City of Liverpool.* This aircraft had temporarily become WM759, being used for rough weather water trials at weights of up to 84,000lb and contributing to the RAF's assessment of its future flying-boat needs being carried out at that time. The first Solent 4, ZK-AML *Aotearoa II,* was launched at Belfast in May 1949; ZK-AMM *Ararangi,* ZK-AMN *Awatere* and ZK-AMO *Aranui* completed the fleet. The Solent 4 carried forty-four passengers at a maximum weight of 81,000lb. More powerful 2,040hp Hercules 733 engines were mounted parallel to the airframe centre-line, rather than being toed out as previously; its range was 3,000 miles, not far off 50 per cent more than the Solent 3. The aircraft took over the Wellington–Sydney route in October 1950 and also the Coral Route to Suva, the Cook Islands, Tahiti and later Samoa and Tonga, frequency of the latter varying between once and twice monthly and concentrating on mail, though the small number of passengers were carried in very comfortable conditions. However, by the summer of 1954 TEAL had replaced their flying-boats on all routes except the Fiji–Tonga service, DC-6Bs coming into use. *Aranui* served until September 1960 and was later preserved.

Four ex-BOAC Solents (G-AKNO, G-AKNP, G-AHIV and G-AHIO) were sold to Trans-Oceanic Airways during early 1951, becoming VH-TOA, VH-TOB, VH-TOC and VH-TOD respectively, intended for use between Sydney and Hobart. VH-TOA

Solent 4 ZK-AML *Aotearoa* II was the first of its type and joined TEAL in November 1949. The Solent 4 employed more powerful engines than its predecessors, while the propellers sometimes mounted prominent spinners. ZK-AML joined Aquila in May 1955 as G-AOBL but was sold to Portugal in October 1958, being eventually abandoned in the Tagus estuary. *(Author's Collection)*

Ex-TEAL Solent 4 ZK-AMN was also acquired by Aquila, becoming G-ANYI. It continued to carry the name *Awatere*, and like G-AOBL it was later sold to Portugal where it decayed and was eventually scrapped. *(Author's Collection)*

was wrecked at Malta during delivery and the service never developed as planned, though VH-TOC ran a weekly flight linking Sydney and New Guinea; the other examples passed to South Pacific Airlines at Oakland, California, as N9945F and N9946F, joining G-AKNT which had become N9947F. Unfortunately the licence for South Pacific's intended Honolulu–Tahiti–Fiji service was refused.

In December 1951 Aquila had acquired Solent 3 G-AKNU and during 1955 the airline took two Solent 4s from TEAL, ZK-AML and ZK-AMN, which became respectively G-AOBL and G-ANYI. These received Solent 3 cabins and served on routes to the Canary Islands, Madeira and Montreux along with G-ANAJ and G-AKNU. However, on 15 November 1957 G-AKNU was tragically lost, crashing at Shalcombe on the Isle of Wight with the loss of thirty-five lives. On 30 November 1958 Aquila's Madeira service ended. The growing popularity of speedy, reasonably priced tourist charter flights, the cost of maintaining the ageing flying-boats and the lack of any replacement aircraft had brought the business to a close. Aquila's decline marked the end of British commercial flying-boat operations. Numbers of Sandringhams were scrapped at Hamworthy during 1959. Solents G-AHIN, G-AOBL and G-ANYI passed to Artop of Portugal but that company failed and the aircraft were abandoned on a beach in the Tagus estuary near Lisbon, being broken up in 1971.

Meanwhile, in July 1963 Ansett's Sandringham 4 VH-BRE had been lost in a cyclone at Lord Howe Island, leaving only VH-BRC *Beachcomber* available. However, Sunderland NZ4108 was released by the Royal New Zealand Air Force to help maintain the route, being civilianised by Ansett at their Rose Bay base in Sydney, to carry forty-three passengers, and launched as the so-called 'near-Sandringham' VH-BRF *Islander* in October 1964, with a more prominent bow than the Short-converted examples.

Rochester's Last Flying-Boat

During the immediate post-war years, C.P.T. Lipscomb, Shorts' Chief Designer following Arthur Gouge, considered at least five possible future flying-boat projects. However, it was concluded neither the Long Stage Empire Boat nor the Nomad-powered SA.8 would be able to compete economically with the new commercial landplanes. The SA.7 was set aside partly because its intended Cougar powerplant failed to mature while the Hercules-powered twenty-passenger project was also dispensed with. The smallest of the group did materialise, born of the belief in a need for a modest civil type for use particularly in undeveloped parts of the world. This was the SA.6 Sealand.

The Sealand was an all-metal twin-engined amphibian, the prototype (G-AIVX) powered by two 345hp de Havilland Gipsy Queen 70-2 engines. Rochester undertook the single step hull, which featured side-by-side seating for pilot and navigator and accommodation for five or seven passengers. The cabin included six large oval windows on each side while the passenger door was to port. Mooring was facilitated through movable panels below the cockpit glazing, and a bow hatch. The hull form was similar to that of the Solent, while the retractable undercarriage tucked flush into the hull sides; the tail wheel was also retractable. The 59ft-span wing, designed and manufactured at Queen's Island, was high-mounted and bore scaled-down Shetland-derived floats on cantilever struts. The engines drove reversible-pitch propellers, which assisted water handling and shortened the landing run on terra firma. The prototype flew from Belfast on 22 January 1948 initially as a flying-boat, in the hands of Harold Piper. With the undercarriage installed, trials continued from nearby Sydenham airfield with Tom Brooke-Smith after Piper returned to his native New Zealand. A Certificate of Airworthiness followed on 28 July 1949. A second prototype, employing Alvis Leonides engines, was considered but not pursued.

Four pre-production examples emerged (G-AKLM–G-AKLP). The first entered the 1949 King's Cup Air Race on 1 August but was not placed, before travelling to Scandinavia in October. Sadly it crashed in fog at Lindesnes in Norway on 15 October with loss of life. G-AKLN was retained by Shorts as a development aircraft while G-AKLO became the European demonstrator. G-AKLP travelled to the West Indies for use by British West Indian Airways, becoming VP-TBA RMA *St Vincent,* and was seen as the first of three such purchases. However, BWIA intended to operate from the open sea rather than the sheltered waters for which the Sealand had been designed, and the scheme faltered. VP-TBA returned to Belfast and reverted to G-AKLP before being renamed *Festival of Britain* in 1951 and embarking on an extensive sales tour of North and South America. However, the only aircraft sold as a result of those labours was G-AKLT, to the Christian & Missionary Alliance of New York. Arriving in Indonesia on 31 December 1950, the aircraft became PK-CMA, the first British post-war commercial aircraft sold to the United States.

Modifications were found necessary to reduce take-off and landing speeds, mitigate skipping and a tendency to swing and roll to starboard during take-off from calm waters. These consisted of an increased wing span, an increase in rudder chord, reinforcement of the hull, a small asymmetric fin introduced to the planing bottom just forward of the tail wheel and a weight reduction exercise that yielded 330lb. In 1951 G-AKLU passed in flying-boat form to Vestlandske Luftfartsselskap

Short Sealand prototype G-AIVX flew twice as a flying-boat but then received amphibian undercarriage. Early tests revealed high interference drag, low-speed throttle sensitivity and engine overheating. Accordingly the engine position was lowered, smaller-diameter three-bladed propellers fitted and the oil collers relocated from the top of the engine nacelles to the wing leading-edges. *(Short Brothers via Brian Ribbans)*

(VLS) of Bergen, operating a passenger service linking Bergen, Ålesund and Trondheim as LN-SUH; following the modification programme sales improved. G-AKLN became LN-SUF, joining LN-SUH, both Norwegian examples being operated as pure flying-boats, while in September 1951 G-AKLR and G-AKLS joined Jugoslovenski Aerotransport (JAT) as YU-CFJ and YU-CFK on a coastal service around the Adriatic though both were subsequently flown by the Yugoslav Air Force. G-AKLW became SU-AHY *Nadia* in 1951, used privately as an air yacht equipped with dual controls, additional fuel tanks and a luxury cabin for six. The civil production aircraft employed 340hp Gipsy Queen 70-3s.

G-AKLX and G-AKLY travelled to Bengal during late 1952, becoming AP-AGB and AP-AGC and joining the East Bengal Transport Commission. G-AKLO passed to the Shell Petroleum Company in December 1952, based at Balik Papaan in Borneo as VR-SDS (subsequently, VR-UDS); it was joined two years later by G-AKLP, which assumed VR-UDV. Shell subsequently took delivery of a third example, YV-P-AEG, stationed on Lake Maracaibo in Venezuela. In November 1953 the Christian & Missionary Alliance acquired JZ-PTA which became based at Hollandia, New Guinea; JZ-PTA replaced PK-CMA, ironically damaged by act of God – a thunderstorm in Java earlier that year. However, that aircraft was also lost with all aboard, on 10 May 1955, when it crashed into a mountain. The last of the civil Sealands was AP-AFM *Pegasus*, ex-G-AKLV, which joined Ralli Brothers at Dacca during June 1952, employed on East Pakistan's jute plantations. The aircraft returned to Shorts in crates during October 1957 and was scrapped soon afterwards.

8 POST-WAR: MILITARY

Walrus and Sea Otter

The Walrus began to part company with the Royal Navy and RAF soon after the war but eight travelled to Argentina in 1947, employed by the Argentine Antarctic survey of Deception Island and Discovery Bay; two seem to have operated from the cruiser *Argentina* until at least 1958. The French Aeronavale acquired several for use by Flottille 53.S in training flying-boat pilots at Hourtin.

Though orders for Sea Otters were much reduced at the end of hostilities, the type continued ASR service with 18 and 19 Groups RAF and with the Royal Navy. By April 1949 30 examples were recorded at Service stations, seven at sea and another 48 in store or undergoing repair, as well as others serving overseas. Sea Otters were also exported, eight joining the Royal Danish Air Force: 801–806, an intended 807 damaged beyond repair before acquiring that identity, plus a spares ship. The aircraft served until 1952 on search and rescue, as well as training. Eight more went to the Dutch Naval Air Arm during 1949–50 as 18-1–18-8 (later 12-1–12-8) for similar duties.

March 1949: RNAS Culdrose Station Flight Sea Otter ASR.2 JN201 903/CW is pushed away from the incoming tide at Poldhu Cove on the Lizard in Cornwall. The aircraft developed engine trouble while rescuing the pilot of a ditched Sea Fury and stayed at its temporary home for a week until the seas abated sufficiently for a take-off to be made. JN201 was one of six Station Flight Sea Otters employed by Culdrose between 1949 and 1953. *(Keith Lee)*

Final Seagull

Air Ministry Specification S.12/40 had called for a reconnaissance and spotter amphibian for catapult operation with the eventual replacement of the Sea Otter in mind. The new aircraft would employ a Rolls-Royce Merlin XXX engine driving contra-rotating propellers, and have a four-gun powered turret. Maximum range would be 1,000 miles and a maximum all-up weight of 12,000lb was specified. S.12/40 was issued to Fairey and Supermarine and initial responses were made in October 1940. Fairey's offering did not proceed but Supermarine's eventually emerged following a development period made very lengthy because of the company's preoccupation with more pressing programmes, and the innovation involved. The initial proposal, produced by Joseph Smith, R.J. Mitchell's successor, described both a biplane and a monoplane but indicated a clear preference for the latter as the better performer. The Ministry agreed and eventually in April 1943 the company received an order for three prototypes, serialled PA143, PA147 and PA152.

The Seagull featured a pylon-mounted variable-incidence 52ft 6in wing developed from earlier high-lift research using Supermarine's S.24/37 Dumbo landplane. Wind-tunnel tests were carried out between 1942 and 1944 in co-operation with RAE Farnborough to determine stability characteristics with various wing positions and the effects of moving the wing on the performance of the tail. The wing form finally adopted included full-span slotted flaps with inset ailerons and full-span leading-edge slats. The front spar root joints were allowed to pivot, while two incidence-varying screw jacks were placed on the movable auxiliary rear spar, powered by a 1½hp electric motor. Such a wing permitted a smaller area than was otherwise necessary – most useful in terms of ship-board accommodation – as well as improving the lift coefficient and reducing stalling speed. Light alloy cantilever wing-floats were attached to the front spar. Various tail configurations were tested including assorted dihedrals, a butterfly and a T-tail. The chosen arrangement initially comprised a tailplane employing a dramatic 20 degree dihedral and endplate fins and rudders positioned at 90 degrees to the tailplane

The hull consisted of two longerons and the chines, light alloy frames and a flush-riveted Alclad skin, with a sharp-edged single step and at the knife-edge a water rudder-cum-tailwheel. A crew of three was envisaged, accommodated in the side-by-side cockpit and aft; an aperture led into the pylon where observation windows were positioned. The main undercarriage members retracted neatly into hull recesses. Both the Merlin 30 and Bristol Taurus were considered but after the Admiralty withdrew the requirement for the aircraft to be storable below decks (and thereby lifted the accompanying restrictions on dimensions and weight) the 1,815hp Rolls-Royce Griffon 29 was selected. Radiators were housed in the pylon, through the leading-edge of which the cooling air entered. November 1944 saw a Specification change as S.14/44 (later S.14/44/2) was issued defining an air-sea rescue function, the age of the spotter aircraft having passed. The requirement for the four-gun turret was deleted when the Specification was amended, and the type received the nomenclature ASR.I.

Seagull PA143 first flew on 14 July 1948 from Southampton Water in the hands of Supermarine test-pilot Lieutenant Commander Mike Lithgow, more than five years after the order had been placed. The aircraft went to Chilbolton soon afterwards and appeared at Farnborough's SBAC Show in September. A buffeting trait was corrected by sealing the wing-to-fuselage joins with rubber strips and fitting louvres over the radiator flaps and duct exits to improve airflow, while a tendency to yaw was mitigated by adding a small central fin and rudder. Flight tests over 1949 confirmed these steps were effective. The second Seagull, PA147, was flown on 2 September 1949 by Mike Lithgow and later that month appeared at the SBAC Show.

With the war's end any chance of securing a production order had evaporated. None the less testing continued, PA147 undergoing deck arrester trials at RAE Farnborough in September 1949 followed by deck landing trials aboard HMS *Illustrious* during October, in various wind speeds and employing wing angles of incidence of between 5 degrees and 8.5 degrees. These went satisfactorily and the high-lift wing twice underlined its worth when two abortive landings by A&AEE pilots resulted in overshoots. An evaluation of PA143 at Felixstowe during December 1949 resulted in further modifications to the fins and rudders, and to the water-rudder.

Mike Lithgow could fly the Seagull at only 35mph, but Leslie Colquhoun, who had joined Supermarine from the RAF, gained the World Air Speed Record for amphibians over 100km in PA147 during the Air League Cup Race at Sherburn-in-

Supermarine's first Seagull to S.14/44/2, PA143, shows its lines for the Vickers-Armstrongs camera at Woolston. The aircraft is simply poles apart from its Walrus ancestor, the Griffon 29 driving a contra-rotating (and torque-eliminating) Rotol propeller and its hull presenting a sleek planing bottom. The original tail arrangement is seen, while the pylon exhibits a small window at its aft extremity. *(Vickers-Armstrong Ltd)*

Elmet on 22 July 1950, at 241.9mph – quite a contrast! Experiments continued for a time and included rocket-assisted take-offs but in 1952 the two Seagulls were scrapped, along with the partly completed PA152. The era of helicopter search and rescue was dawning – the Navy's 705 Squadron had re-formed in May 1947 as a Helicopter Fleet Requirement Unit with Hoverflies and by early 1950 the Dragonfly 1 was being trialled. In April 1953 275 Squadron RAF re-formed at Linton-on-Ouse; previously equipped with the Walrus, the Squadron now adopted Sycamores and became the RAF's first dedicated helicopter SAR unit.

Saro's Unique Fighter

At Cowes as far back as the summer of 1943 Henry Knowler had contemplated a flying-boat fighter powered by the newly developed jet engine, which Saunders-Roe felt could be a valuable asset in the Pacific theatre. While the Japanese continued to rely on piston-engined types, the traditional advantage of the land-based fighter over its water-based equivalent would be cancelled out. The absence of a propeller would dispense with the necessity for a high thrust-line and deep hull, thereby reducing weight and drag. Following discussions with MAEE and Metropolitan-Vickers' Gas Turbine Department, in December Saro submitted plans to MAP for a twin jet-powered flying-boat fighter operable from sheltered coastal waters. In May 1944 a contract with a limit of liability of £305,000 was placed for three examples to the experimental Specification E.6/44, as a DTD venture. The aircraft was

Seagull PA147, with the addition of a vertical tail fin and rudder, which was subsequently enlarged and which in conjunction with water rudder modifications improved air and on-water manoeuvra-bility. The propeller configuration is experimental, a scissors-type arrangement reminiscent of that trialled by the prototype Sea Otter, and put forward because of consider-ations of storage space. The float struts have been length-ened to prevent a tendency to roll on the water. *(Author's Collection)*

designated SR.A/1 and soon received the sobriquet 'Squirt'. Design commenced at Beaumaris but following the war's end was completed at Cowes and the aircraft (TG263, TG267 and TG271) were constructed there. The company initially contemplated a very slender planing bottom to help minimise drag but this was incompatible with a side-by-side engine installation (the favoured configuration) while model tests suggested inadequate stability, so the idea was dropped. Models of the revised design showed an inclination to porpoise at overload weight, eliminated by moving the step slightly aft.

The SR.A/1 was powered by two Metropolitan-Vickers F.2/4 Beryl axial-flow turbojets, sufficiently small to permit a side-by-side layout without a markedly beamy hull and leaving adequate space within the mid-hull section to allow inspection and maintenance in situ. The single nose air intake was bifurcated internally to feed both engines and was equipped with an extendible external snout intended to prevent spray ingestion, which could be linked to the retractable wing-floats and deployed when the floats were lowered. However, only the third aircraft had the linkage connected, and trials revealed the snout was unnecessary; at low taxying speeds the SR.A/1 was designed to sit tail-down while at high surface speeds it lifted partially out of the water in the usual way of flying-boats. Engine exhausts were situated just aft of the wing-roots, toed out 5 degrees to clear efflux from the hull.

The hull bottom employed a faired V-form single step tapering to a knife-edge at the water-rudder, the latter an essential inclusion since the engines could not be used for steering because of their location. The hull structure consisted of main keel members, closely spaced frames and light stringers beneath a riveted and filled skin. The high-perched pressurised single-seat cockpit was protected with armour plate and equipped with a Martin Baker ejector seat, the first delivered to an aircraft manufacturer from that company's factory. Wing form was of high-speed Goldstein section, with a single main spar and a subordinate spar to the rear. Dive-brakes and dive recovery flaps were fitted, while the wings contained the fuel tanks. A fine titanine finish was applied over the exterior, preserving laminar flow far back over the wing. The wing-floats rotated through 180 degrees during the retraction sequence, leaving only the more streamlined portions exposed. The tail assembly was high-mounted to avoid spray and efflux. Armament consisted of four nose-mounted 20mm Hispano Mk 5 cannon together with various disposable underwing loads.

In January 1946 the Ministry of Supply (MoS) considered reducing the order to one SR.A/1 but all three were eventually completed, progress being slowed by the company's concentration on the giant Princess project. Geoffrey Tyson first flew TG263 on 16 July 1947, from Cowes. The aircraft handled generally well on the water and in the air, but a slight snaking tendency was eliminated during August by the addition of an acorn fairing at the junction of the tailplane and fin. An inclination to roll, also discovered, was removed by reducing the rudder horn balance and adding metal strips to the rudder trailing-edge, while premature tip stall was countered by increasing the nose radii of the wing outer sections. At an all-up weight of around 16,000lb the aircraft was somewhat bigger than its land-based equivalent but by waterborne standards the SR.A/1 was in a class of its

July 1947: Saro SR.A/1 TG263, the first of three prototypes, gets away at Cowes in the hands of Geoffrey Tyson, who has already retracted the wing-floats. The aircraft has yet to receive its acorn fairing at the junction of fin and tailplane. Trials of the SR.A/1 at Cowes and later MAEE were very favourable. *(British Hovercraft Corporation)*

Post-May 1948: TG263 with the addition of the acorn fairing, and a rather ugly metal cockpit canopy. The following year the aircraft was put into store, but that was not quite the end of the project, for it re-emerged for the 1951 Festival of Britain. *(British Hovercraft Corporation)*

The third SR.A/1, TG271, at rest off East Cowes. The intake snout designed to prevent ingestion of water is extended. Built with an acorn tail fairing, later in its life TG271 received a modification to the hull area around the engine exhausts to provide protection against efflux, the only example to do so. In the background is a Sunderland, possibly RN297 used for trials of the Princess power control system. (J.C. Hamon)

own. TG263 visited the 1947 SBAC Show before passing to MAEE for trials that confirmed it was an impressive performer.

By 1948 all three examples were airborne, TG267 flying on 30 April and TG271 on 17 August, the latter appearing at that year's SBAC Show. The first SR.A/1 had employed Beryls of 3,230lb st., but TG267 had uprated versions of 3,500lb st. and TG271 fully rated examples of 3,850lb st. The performance of TG271 at Farnborough during September was memorable, Geoffrey Tyson providing a superb aerobatic display including a low inverted pass along the runway. TG271 became generally based at Cowes for aero- and hydrodynamic testing while TG267 was evaluated by MAEE over the summer of 1949. By then, TG263 had been stored while the programme's future was considered. It was wearing its final modification: a metal canopy to replace the transparent hood which had become detached during a test-flight in May 1948.

During 1949 both TG267 and TG271 were lost. In August TG271 was flown by Lieutenant Commander E.M. Brown and on alighting at Cowes struck a half-submerged obstacle that holed the hull. The aircraft lost its starboard float and turned turtle; Brown escaped but TG271 sank and was never recovered. During September TG267, piloted by Squadron Leader Peter Major, who was rehearsing an aerobatic display for a Battle of Britain Day, crashed off Felixstowe; it seems the aircraft suffered loss of control in roll and dived into the sea.

By then a serious problem had emerged regarding the supply of Beryls. Metropolitan-Vickers had transferred custody of the Beryl to Armstrong Siddeley who chose not to continue its production. In the meantime only eleven more engines had been built. Consideration was given under Project P.103 to substituting just one Armstrong Siddeley Sapphire (swept wings were also mooted at that time) but the SR.A/1 airframe redesign and modification would have been extensive. With no official or company funding available the idea was a non-starter.

G-12-1, the former TG263, displaying the beaching arrangements adopted for the SR.A/1. Following its appearance at the 1951 Festival of Britain the aircraft was presented to the College of Aeronautics at Cranfield before passing in 1966 to the Skyfame Museum at Staverton. During 1978 it arrived at Duxford and is now in the custody of the Southampton Hall of Aviation. *(Author's Collection)*

The cockpit of TG263. Throttle and trim controls are to the port side, single-exposure camera-gun controls in the centre, fuel controls to the right. The button indicated by the X is marked PORT IGN. Just above the X is the water-rudder toggle, a unique accoutrement in a jet fighter cockpit. *(Aeronautical Quality Assurance Directorate)*

Nevertheless, in November 1950 TG263 was taken out of store. The Korean War briefly resuscitated the notion of a flying-boat fighter able to operate from remote areas and by that time the United States had been passed technical details of the programme. However, the re-engining problem remained and though it was in a class of its own as a flying-boat the SR.A/1 had lost parity with leading-edge land-based opposition even before its first flight. In Korea the MiG 15 would have made short work of the Squirt.

The last public flying appearance of the SR.A/1 took place in June 1951. Geoffrey Tyson took the first example to London for display on the Thames at the Festival of Britain, by that time wearing Saro B conditions identity G-12-1. The aircraft later passed to the College of Aeronautics at Cranfield; the starboard Beryl was removed and used to power Donald Campbell's *Bluebird*.

Sealand Export

The Sealand had been evaluated by MAEE during the autumn of 1950 for possible use in an ASR role, but the idea was not pursued. This was partly due to its water-handling at that time, which needed marked improvement, and partly because the helicopter was becoming an increasingly strong contender for such activities. However, the Sealand did enter military service with the Indian Navy. A contract for the supply of ten aircraft designated the Sealand 1L was concluded during 1952. A number of modifications were carried out to provide a suitable aircraft: 340hp

Indian Navy Sealand INS-105 shows its paces on a pre-delivery flight from Belfast. The asymmetric skeg is visible at the rear of the hull bottom. The Cochin base was taken over by the Indian Navy during 1953 following its decommissioning by the RAF in 1946, and the Sealands flew with the Fleet Requirements Unit. The FRU subsequently shifted to Dabolim. *(Short Brothers via Bryan Ribbans)*

Gipsy Queen 70-4s were installed, the fuel tankage was increased to provide 6 hours' endurance rather than the 3.5 hours of the civil version, while dual-control and constant-speed propellers were fitted. The Sealands were serialled INS-101–INS-110, deliveries commencing in January 1953. The first and second were ex-G-AKLZ and ex-G-AKMA, and the final example arrived in Cochin during November of that year. The Sealand remained with the Indian Navy until at least 1959, serving with the Fleet Requirement Unit (later INAS 550).

9 WINDING SHEET

The Princess

At Saunders-Roe, stemming from work on Specifications R.5/39 and R.14/40, a study had been completed by 1943 for a six-Centaurus-powered 187,000lb long-range flying-boat transport with a maximum speed of 250mph at 25,000ft, intended for a London–New York service. A second project covered an eight-engined (coupled Centaurus) 250,000lb flying-boat with a predicted speed of 331mph at 14,000ft and a range of 3,600 miles. A subsequent design featured six Rolls-Royce Eagles and an all-up weight of 260,000lb. By the end of the year Gouge and Knowler had adopted the new gas turbine and included a pressurised hull. The development of the gas-turbine, offering higher power/weight ratios than were hitherto available, supported the company's aspirations towards ever larger flying-boats.

By mid-1945 the study known as SR.45 was underway. Initially it was a 220ft-span 266,000lb aircraft employing six Rolls-Royce Clyde turbines, subsequently amended to Armstrong Siddeley Cobras. The wing-form was of very thick section inboard but the engines were situated in conventional nacelles rather than in a buried installation. The twin-deck hull, 146ft long, was of 'figure eight cross-section' as described by Knowler but became known as a 'double-bubble' section, and was pressurised to 8psi. Range would be 3,300 miles and ideal operating height 39,000ft. The company tabled its proposals for SR.45 to the Ministry of Supply (MOS): the minister, George Strauss, received the submission enthusiastically and concluded that the design was suitable for use by BOAC, who in turn indicated a degree of interest to both the MoS and the Ministry of Civil Aviation (MCA).

On 7 May 1946 an Instruction To Proceed for £2.8 million was placed with Saunders-Roe for three SR.45s to MoS Specification C.10/46, against a draft technical baseline; in other words a virtually uncapped licence to spend big money. It seems astonishing even with hindsight that the minister set aside the absence of such a type from the conclusions of the Brabazon Reports, and authorised a huge and ground-breaking programme, without firstly securing any unequivocal commitment from the airlines to purchase the resulting aircraft. The parties on both sides of the ITP appear to have simply assumed BOAC would choose to operate the SR.45. However, the national carrier is thought never to have given an absolute undertaking in that regard. Meanwhile, C.10/46 remained uncompleted and Saro prepared its own specification, P.136/7.

By January 1947 the Rolls-Royce Tweed had replaced the Cobra as choice of engine though Armstrong Siddeley's Python had also been considered. Wing design was well advanced when it was learned that the Tweed would not enter production. Finally, early in 1948, Bristol's Proteus 2 was selected, rated on paper at 3,200shp/800lb thrust, ten engines to be installed as four coupled pairs with two singletons outboard. The choice of the Proteus, a reverse-flow engine, necessitated considerable wing redesign; large inlets and ducts were inserted ahead of the front spar. Other revisions revealed in 1948 included a larger fin and a higher mounted tailplane than hitherto while the cockpit was extended slightly forward to improve the view. The floats were repositioned and by then formed the wing-tips when retracted.

SR.45 featured hull pressurisation, air-conditioning and power-operated irreversible flying controls – very advanced features for the time. Pressurisation and air-conditioning were provided by a two-stage centrifugal compressor driven by each inboard power installation, utilising a labyrinth of piping and valves. Power control, the greatest of the innovations, was considered essential for an aircraft as large as SR.45, and the flight-deck dual controls were linked to three power units, two in the stern managing the rudder and elevators and one in the top hull centre-section for the ailerons. Each employed two torque-converters driving a differential

The second Princess, G-ALUO, under construction in Saunders-Roe's Columbine hangar at East Cowes, during 1949. The hull and main gunwale member were laid down first and the flight surfaces are being added. *(Author's Collection)*

gearbox so that failure of either converter merely reduced output speed. The converters were geared down to hydraulic variable-delivery pump/motor units. The motors ran at all times but mostly the pump action was zero, the hydraulic aspect remaining dormant until a manoeuvre was called for. The pump then came into operation, driving the hydraulic motor at a speed proportional to the handling of the controls. The output shafts drove rotating shafts via change-speed gearboxes, right-angle boxes and universal joints, along to the surfaces. The surfaces were split; three parts to the rudder, two to each elevator and four to each aileron. Each split section was separately driven by its own screw-jack from the main drive, and an added safeguard was the provision of hand-wheels enabling the surfaces to be placed in the trail position.

The power control system was tested firstly on a rig and from 1949 on Sunderland 5 RN297, converted at Cowes and featuring a slightly enlarged fin. It was flown by Geoffrey Tyson, and the results were good. A hydraulic-feel generator was inserted in the SR.45 flight-deck, while consideration was also given to the development of an artificial q-feel arrangement, reduction of the power unit size and weight through the use of aerodynamically balanced surfaces, and relocation of the units adjacent to their respective surfaces. Even a form of fly-by-wire was contemplated.

Delays were inevitable on such a complex programme. In January 1948 the first flight date was put at late 1949; that year the aircraft acquired the name Princess. During March 1949 the company described progress as on schedule but gave a completion date of late 1950. That October, owing to a revised delivery date for the engines, it was announced that flight trials would commence in the summer of 1951. In February 1951 the date was changed again, to some unspecified time in 1952. In the meantime a half-scale wing (and later hull) was evaluated at RAE Farnborough while the mechanical, electrical and hydraulic systems were constructed and tested at Cowes, and full hull sections were mocked-up.

Construction took a great deal of planning – there was very little physical room to spare at Cowes. On 30 October 1951 the first airframe, minus engines, outer wings and fin tip, was moved on to the apron because there was insufficient space to complete it within the main hangar. By then a coupled Proteus and two single units had been delivered but the coupled unit was not installed until after the move; the single units could not be fitted until the outer wings were in place.

The Princess was a true giant and a magnificent technical achievement. Its 148ft long double-bubble hull provided the rigid structure necessary for cabin pressurisation, the waist forming the division between the two decks. A chined planing bottom was attached, unpressurised and with many individual watertight compartments, and employing a single tiny step of $\frac{5}{16}$in; the planing bottom tapered to a knife-edge under the fin leading-edge. A section of the upper hull was cut out to receive the high-mounted wing, and edged with an extruded-channel gunwale member to which the wing attached. On the flight-deck, captain and first officer positions were situated in the extreme bow while aft and to starboard were the two flight engineers; navigator and radio operator positions were to port. A crew rest-room and forward galley were aft of the flight-deck while below were mooring

facilities; an automatic mooring arrangement was also installed. Two cargo holds with a total capacity of 18,000lb were situated in the lower deck. Various passenger layouts were considered, some together with BOAC, among them a version accommodating one hundred and five passengers in tourist and first-class cabins and including a cocktail bar, powder rooms and toilets, bunks, and two spiral staircases connecting the decks. A further galley was planned adjacent to a spacious dining-room.

The wing, a two-spar arrangement, was basically a five-piece Saro-developed Goldstein section optimised for low cruising drag. The centre-section bridged the hull and extended to the inboard nacelle, inner wings mounted the engines and outer wings extended to the tip floats. Centre-section and inner wing spars ran parallel, at a chord-wise spacing of 12ft, but in the outer panels converged to 5ft 4in at the float support rib. The centre-section was of parallel chord but the inner wings were slightly tapered and the leading-edges of the outer wings were swept. Span was 209ft 6in; with the floats retracted this increased to 219ft 6in. Four integral fuel tanks were situated within the inner wing, providing a total capacity of 14,000 gallons. The wing leading-edges were complex because of the various intakes and nacelle fairings that had to be accommodated. The single-slotted flaps were divided into three per wing, and the aileron sections employed servo-tabs. The wing-tip floats were actuated by a Dowty hydraulic system, while the wing de-icing mechanism used hot air from the tail-pipe cooling shrouds.

30 October 1951: the huge airframe of Princess G-ALUN is moved out on to the Columbine apron. The outer wings have yet to be added and scaffolding is visible around the unfinished fin. The route of the aircraft from the hangar to the outside world was marked on the apron – there wasn't much room to spare. Water ballast in tanks at the rear of the hull was used to tilt the aircraft so as to clear the hangar doors. *(Author's Collection)*

The huge tail was of conventional overall configuration though the tailplane featured a marked 12-degree dihedral to keep it relatively free of spray. The rudder incorporated a servo-tab within its lowest section while the split elevators were also fitted with tabs. At the dorsal fin fillet, a ram orifice fed the tail de-icing heaters. In the top of the fin and on the inner edges of the elevators were housed three plate aerials.

Power was supplied by ten Bristol Proteus 2s which actually each produced 2,500shp and 820lb jet thrust, driving specially developed 16ft 6in diameter de Havilland four-blade propellers; singletons were fitted to the outboard engines, contra-rotating pairs to the coupled units and all incorporated electric de-icing. The outer propellers had a 12-degree pitch range to assist on-water manoeuvring. Parts of the engine nacelles could be opened out to provide maintenance platforms, while engine changes could be effected without external help, using purpose-built hoists erected on the upper wing surface.

Drive from the coupled engines was via unifying and reduction gearboxes powering the propellers on co-axial shafts, arranged such that if one engine failed, the remaining unit would continue to drive its propeller. The ten intakes were each split vertically, feeding air to the engines, the jet-pipe heat-exchangers, the generators, and the engine and gearbox oil coolers. The engine tailpipes emerged near the trailing-edge and the flaps were tailored around them.

Air-conditioning was provided by the compound units housed in the wing-root leading-edges; air serving the cabin heater was taken from the tailpipe shrouds, while the cooler feed was ducted from the main intakes. Cabin conditions were regulated by a Normalair pressure system and a Teddington Controls humidity and

The day before the first launch of G-ALUN, carried out shortly after midnight on 20 August because of the tidal conditions; the aircraft was then moored in the Medina. Taxying trials began two days later but after 28 minutes of that exercise Tyson felt sufficiently confident to take off, carrying out a 35-minute flight around the Isle of Wight. (Author's Collection)

G-ALUN: the pilot's view of the bridge. To the left are the flight instruments; top centre elevator, aileron and rudder displays; middle centre ten engine failure warning indicators and below, elevator, aileron and rudder trim indicators. The aircraft operating limits are recorded by the engine throttles. The flight engineer's panels were placed aft and to starboard. *(Aeronautical Quality Assurance Directorate)*

temperature system. The total generating capacity of the SR.45 electrical system was a huge 4x39kW at 120V and 2x6kW at 24V; the generator busbars fed a pair of distributor busbars from which services were taken.

The Proteus 3 would prove lighter and more powerful than the Proteus 2 but it was not available in 1952 and to keep the project moving along the Princess had to be fitted with the earlier Mark, which unfortunately was down on estimated output and not suitable for commercial use. On the other hand expenditure had soared; by

March 1951 the price of the airframes had risen to £10.8 million while the engine programme had increased from £407,000 in 1946 to £4.9 million. Bristol was challenged regarding the cost increase of the latter, but did not explain why the numbers had risen so much.

The Princesses were registered to the MoS as G-ALUN, G-ALUO and G-ALUP. By August 1952 the first, G-ALUN, was complete. On 22 August, following brief engine runs and taxying trials, it flew for the first time, piloted by Geoffrey Tyson with John Booth as co-pilot, and a fastest speed of 280mph was recorded. The flight was a great occasion attended by many spectators both on shore and afloat. Tyson reported trouble-free air and water handling. G-ALUN made its public debut at the 1952 SBAC Show at Farnborough on 2 September, where it is fair to say that the aircraft created a – literally – huge impression. On its return to Cowes, inspection and resonance tests were commenced which lasted until October.

When it emerged, the Princess was the heaviest all-metal passenger transport ever built, the biggest ever metal flying-boat and the largest aircraft powered by gas-turbines. Its commercial future, however, was never certain. In October 1950 BOAC had created a Princess Unit under Captain H.W.C. Alger, an experienced

G-ALUN on an early test-flight over the Solent, in natural finish. An aircraft of undoubted beauty, its simplicity of line belied the considerable technical complexity of the project. Trials found the lift to drag ratio of the Princess was 18.9, compared with the 15.7 of Short's Shetland. *(British Hovercraft Corporation)*

flying-boat pilot, to study the preparations needed for the introduction into service of flying-boats in the 105-seater class. However, during the following month the Corporation ceased flying-boat operations, a move presumably planned for some time. Conflicting possibilities began to circulate. In February 1951 it was unofficially announced that the third example would be scrapped and that this would save £1 million. It was then rumoured that British South American Airways might operate the aircraft but in March the suggestion was made that all three would go to the RAF. This was repeated in October, the proposed accommodation being for 200 troops (in reduced comfort) rather than 105 civilians. During December 1951 a new company named Princess Air Transport Co. Ltd was formed by Saro in cooperation with Airwork to 'study the factors affecting the operation of the Princess flying-boats and to be in a position to tender for their operation should the opportunity arise'.

   BOAC seconded Captain Alger to Princess Air Transport as general manager and in September 1952 offered to establish a marine development flight for the Princess, but the proposal was withdrawn after it became clear that there was no immediate prospect of the aircraft entering commercial service. Later that year Sir Miles Thomas, Chairman of BOAC, stated that in his opinion the Princess was out of date technically, although having watched G-ALUN's maiden flight he had claimed the Corporation was 'tremendously interested' in the aircraft. Thomas suggested the new Bristol BE.25 propeller-turbine (later named the Orion) might prove the saviour of the programme.

The first Princess eventually acquired a pseudo-commercial colour scheme. However, it never entered operational service despite the various plans that came and went through the years. The aircraft is making a low pass at Farnborough during September 1953, its wing-floats deployed. *(Author's Collection)*

However, the Orion would not be available for a considerable time, perhaps not until 1957, while the rework involved in its substitution would have been extensive; other engines were considered including Ghost and Avon turbojets, and the Eland turbo-prop but Saunders-Roe decided to wait for the later Proteus. In any case the Princess could not have begun commercial operations before 1956 because comprehensive water and flight trials were necessary, while the question of additional funding for modifications might have proved a rather delicate one given the enormous overspends already incurred. And there were still no buyers in sight.

Meanwhile, in March 1952 the MoS had halted work on G-ALUO and G-ALUP; they were cocooned in polyvinyl plastic and bitumen, and towed across the Solent to Calshot Spit where they were stored in the open, each loaded with eight tons of silica gel. During September 1953 G-ALUN visited the SBAC Show wearing a blue, yellow and white colour scheme, in what turned out to be its final public appearance. The following month the MoS invited independent operators to submit bids for the aircraft. Eoin C. Mekie, Chairman of Aquila Airways, proposed the purchase of all three at a price of well over £1 million each but his offer was not accepted by the Minister, Duncan Sandys – a terrible mistake, though the howls from the watchdogs of the public purse would have been awful. Between August 1952 and June 1954, when the programme effectively stopped, G-ALUN accumulated a paltry 96 hours 50 minutes flying time over forty-seven flights. Following its trials G-ALUN was cocooned too, its engines removed, but was kept at Cowes; none of the proposed passenger layouts was ever installed.

MAEE at least was enthusiastic about the Princess. Aero- and hydrodynamic performance was described as satisfactory and on the water the aircraft was adequately stable during take-off and alighting, while spray characteristics were considered good overall. In the air, the only real criticism concerned the simulated

G-ALUN late in its short life before cocooning took place, seen moored at the mouth of the Medina and dwarfing the boats nearby. In the background is Cowes. *(Author's Collection)*

feel characteristics and control to surface ratios which needed modification to improve the feel of positive stability. Even under asymmetric power, the Princess was adequately controllable, right down to the stall. Stall behaviour itself was good with good stall warning.

Schemes continued to emerge through the 1950s and even into the 1960s concerning possible operators, while from time to time Saunders-Roe worked with the government and even BOAC to examine operational requirements associated with the aircraft. The continuing participation of the Corporation is a puzzle; by 1952 BOAC was operating American commercial landplanes and was bringing the Comet into service – real life had moved on. None the less, the three parties cooperated in making searches for suitable flying-boat bases, while docking procedures, maintenance facilities and passenger transfer were all studied. Even route planning was examined, such destinations as Cape Town, Hong Kong, Sydney, Wellington, Vancouver, San Francisco, New York and Jamaica being mooted.

During 1955 rumours grew over a possible purchase of the aircraft by the United States Navy for use as flying test-beds for atomic reactors but nothing came of the talks. By that time too, consideration had been given to employing the RB.109 engine, while a military study with an extended hull mounted two Saro SR.53-type mixed-power (turbojet and rocket) interceptors underwing (P.173), and was also equipped with early warning radar. The following year a scheme was drawn up for a

The Princess G-ALUO airframe in cocooned state at Calshot, parked by the unique tower. Cocooning was successful and preserved the airframes well, and the two aircraft spent twelve years at Calshot waiting patiently for a buyer. In 1965 both were moved to the yard of a Southampton breaker and scrapped. *(Author's Collection)*

more conventional AEW version (Project P.193) mounting an APS 20E radar employing nose-, dorsal- and tail-mounted antennae. During the latter stages of 1957 the company considered converting the Princess into a Rolls-Royce Tyne-powered landplane (by then the Tyne was about to receive Treasury funding at the expense of the Orion), believing the aircraft (P.199/1) might make a troop transport of interest to the RAF; it was envisaged that the converted type would be floated from Cowes and flown from Thorney Island. Unfortunately, once again no enthusiasm was forthcoming. In terms of operational resources and dependencies, training, maintenance, repairs, spares holdings and enhancements it must be very hard to portray a mere three aircraft as attractive, be they landplane or flying-boat; such disadvantages were (and are) as relevant to military operators as civil.

For all that, in 1958 a new potential buyer emerged. Air Vice-Marshal D.C.T. Bennett, of earlier Imperial Airways association, together with Southampton businessman B.G. Halpin made an offer for all three airframes, intending to install six Tyne 11s in each. They were kept waiting over a year for a decision and dropped the idea in March 1960. However, in November a new company named British Princess Flying-Boats Ltd was registered by Halpin, who remained interested in the aircraft provided the government would guarantee operating rights on at least one high-density route; he was keen to commence a service between Southampton, Baltimore, Chicago and Detroit. Again, Tynes were to be installed

Death of G-ALUN. Over the summer of 1967 the airframe was broken up but the upper component of the double-bubble hull was utilised by the scrapyard to provide temporary office and workshop accommodation. Through the cocoon material, the cheat-line of the later finish can be distinguished at the nose. *(Author's Collection)*

and it was hoped to begin services in late 1962. The government would not provide a route guarantee, however, and that idea too was shelved.

In May 1962 the Ministry of Aviation (MoA) announced the sale of G-ALUN for an undisclosed five-figure sum to the Winder Corporation based in Florida. That deal too evaporated, and during November 1963 the War Office, acting for the MoA, requested tenders from any interested parties by 12 December. In January 1964 the sale was announced of all three aircraft to Eoin Mekie, who had previously bought them for Aquila, for a trifling £30,000. Mekie intended to supply them to the American company Aero Spacelines, which had carried out a study for NASA to determine the possibility of the Princess transporting Saturn V components. The study had considered a twinned flying-boat with a new wing centre-section. In July 1965 G-ALUO and G-ALUP were de-cocooned but sadly were found to be corroded. Though cocooning had worked and the airframes had remained in good condition for twelve years, the contract between Westland (who by then had taken over Saunders-Roe) and the MoA covering their inspection and maintenance had not been renewed following its expiry in the summer of 1964, and a year later the aircraft had begun to deteriorate. Neither aircraft left Calshot except for their final journey to a Southampton scrapyard later in 1965.

In May 1966 G-ALUN too was de-cocooned ready for Aero Spacelines but again was found to have seen better days. On 12 April 1967 it was towed across the Solent to a Southampton breaker. Though the wings and tail were scrapped, part of the hull became an extension to the breaker's premises, the upper deck serving as an office and the lower as a workshop – particularly ignominious employment. When the breaker further expanded his premises the hull was broken up. By then the Cowes site had moved into a very different line of business – the hovercraft.

Blackburn Clydesman model: the real thing was never built. With 160 passengers and 30,400lb of freight, range was calculated at 2,500 miles, but with 72 passengers and 2,980lb of freight the range grew to 4,375 miles. The model is in the safe custody of the Yorkshire Air Museum at Elvington. *(Photo: Charles McKenzie; Artwork: Bryan Ribbans)*

Saunders-Roe's Duchess Project P.131, in this artist's impression powered by six Rolls-Royce Avons. A previous version had featured a V-tail, while a subsequent iteration employed a fuselage-mounted under-carriage combined with underwing stabilisers. Saro claimed the Duchess was the most economical medium-range aircraft in the world at the time of its appearance, and also emphasised the simplicity of its construction, but sadly it remained a paper project. *(Saunders-Roe via Bob Wealthy)*

Stillborn Civil Projects

After the war, Blackburn continued to consider further flying-boats but the company's activities remained confined to studies. The B-49 Clydesman project was commenced by J.D. Rennie in 1945, a huge six-engined flying-boat of 138 tons with a high-mounted 202ft-span wing and a 148ft-long hull. The aircraft was intended to cruise at 270mph at 15,000ft. The hull was planned to contain twin pressurised decks with sleeping accommodation, toilets and galley. Maximum speed was calculated at 307mph, and ceiling 20,000ft.

Saunders-Roe's 1950–51 P.131 Duchess project was a medium-stage commercial flying-boat powered by either six Rolls-Royce Avons placed three in each wing root, or four Napier Nomads in tractor-pusher pairs driving contra-props; a version employing six de Havilland Ghost turbojets (P.135) was also contemplated. Span varied between 141 and 145ft; the wings, sharply swept, were mounted on a prominent shoulder 'hump' to keep water from entering the engines and featured slotted flaps designed to droop with the ailerons. Wing-tip floats were proposed, retractable in the same way as those of the Princess. The tailplane was also swept, and high-mounted to avoid water and jet efflux. All flight controls except the flaps were to be power-operated using the system developed for the Princess.

The hull of the Duchess was unusual in that length-to-beam ratio was rather less than had become the norm, though the fore-body surface loading remained low; an elliptical faired step was employed together with a long after-body terminating at a knife-edge. The engines were not well positioned to assist on-water manoeuvres so a split water rudder/drogue was provided, while the wing-floats were of adjustable pitch. Seating for seventy-four passengers in two interconnected cabins was planned, along with a 3,500lb freight hold and 600cu. ft for passenger baggage. A crew of four was contemplated, while the aircraft was to weigh in at 150,000lb all-up (130,000 in the case of P.135) and have a cruising speed of 468mph. However, with the commercial future of the Princess unclear at the time the Duchess was drawn up, it was never built.

Neither was the company's truly extraordinary P.192 of 1956. This project was for a 1,000 passenger, 1,500,000lb flying-boat employing twenty-four 18,500lb thrust Rolls-Royce Conways, for possible use by the P&O Shipping Line on a route between Britain and Australia, flying stage lengths of around 2,000 miles. Six passenger cabins and four decks were envisaged together with a flight crew of seven and a cabin crew of forty. Wing span was 313ft and hull length 318ft while a huge butterfly tail was adopted and the aircraft would have had a cruising speed of 454mph at 40,000ft. Needless to say, P.192 remained a study.

Military End Game

In August 1945, as the war ended, the Air Staff proposed a new flying-boat programme that later appeared briefly as Specification R.36/46, for a type around the size of the Shetland in which range would be extended through in-flight refuelling. The Air Staff at least felt that the development of R.36/46 might be funded jointly with commercial operators; however, the idea was soon shelved and debate continued regarding future needs. Fifteen months later draft Operational Requirement 231 appeared, covering a reconnaissance and anti-submarine flying-boat for use in the Indian and Pacific Oceans. This led to consideration of a giant in the 200,000–240,000lb class employing six or eight Centaurus engines, then to a 175,000lb six-Nomad-powered type. However, it was concluded that these schemes would be too expensive to purchase and operate in any numbers and thus would be of limited efficacy in anti-submarine patrol work.

The idea emerged of a re-engined (or possibly further developed) Sunderland as a stopgap, because the output from OR.231 was expected to take six years or more. Meanwhile OR.231 was amended to include a requirement to serve in Arctic waters as well as tropical, and the ability to be lifted by crane on and off depot ships. Other key requirements were maximum range and patrol capability, plentiful anti-submarine ordnance and simple maintenance to support remote operation. A crew of nine was envisaged. ASP20 ASV radar would be installed together with defensive armament of two 20mm cannon in a dorsal turret, and two further such weapons nose-mounted for surface attacks. Engines contemplated were exhaust-driven Turbo-Griffons or Nomads. The quantity required became eighty, many more than would have been the case with the 200,000lb-plus flying-boat in combination with a seriously finite post-war budget. Accordingly in November 1948 Specification R.2/48 was issued, the last to call for a British military flying-boat. The required bomb- or depth-charge load for the new aircraft was 8,000lb, while carriage of air-to-surface rockets was to be optional. In-flight refuelling was retained while a spare engine and beaching gear were to be carried. Range and endurance were to be 1,000 nautical miles for 4 hours, or 100 nautical miles for 12 hours. A loiter speed of 130 knots, maximum speed of 350 knots and a ceiling of 20,000ft were specified.

Blackburn submitted their B-78 design, Saunders-Roe the P.162 and Shorts the Type PD.2, while Supermarine proffered its Proteus-powered Type 524. The Air Staff selected the P.162, having given the other contenders a lukewarm reception. Various forms of P.162 were generated. Power either from four Taurus, Nomads or BE.25s was considered and use of supplementary Avons evaluated, while all-up weight varied between 135,000lb and 155,000lb (the crane requirement having been abandoned), span between 137ft and 157ft, and length between 120ft and 126ft 6in. The final version contemplated used RB.109 turboprops. The wing included a marked anhedral outboard of the engines while single- and twin-fin arrangements were mooted and optional hydroskis introduced to allow surface skimming. Equipment fit included a retractable ASV scanner and active sonar lowered through doors aft of the step. Various turret configurations were drawn up employing 20mm and 30mm cannon while the crew complement was typically fourteen. However, in 1952 all work was halted; finally it had been decided once and for all that future long-range maritime patrol by the RAF would be undertaken by landplanes and the Avro Shackleton took up the mantle.

Following an examination into a 70,000lb twin-turboprop design for the Royal New Zealand Air Force (RNZAF), the P.176, Saunders-Roe's final military flying-

P.162 model undergoing test-tank trials at Cowes. This model sports the single fin and rudder configuration but other variants utilised a twin-fin and rudder layout. *(British Hovercraft Corporation)*

boat project was drawn up as the result of a 1958 NATO requirement. The company responded with the 73,000lb P.208 powered by two Tynes, with a cruising speed of 300 knots at 39,000ft and a radius of action of 1,000 miles or an 8-hour endurance. Length was 92ft while the high aspect-ratio wing spanned 150ft. Once again a hydroski was adopted. However, the project never came to fruition, and that proved the end of the line for new British military flying-boats.

Sunderland Round-Out

Meanwhile, Sunderlands continued to serve reliably around the globe, and the type was never replaced despite all the years of planning and expense to that end. The RNZAF flew Sunderlands from 1944 until 1967. The RAAF took several while the South African Air Force employed sixteen, of which all but one served until 1955, the singleton lasting until 1957. 343 Free French Squadron RAF transferred to the Aeronavale in November 1945, becoming Flottille 7FE (later 7F, then 27F) and retaining its Sunderlands while a further batch was subsequently purchased, flying with Escadrilles 12S, 50S and 53S. With two exceptions the French examples were decommissioned in 1960, the survivors soldiering on until 1962.

Faithful servant: Royal New Zealand Air Force Sunderland 5 NZ4107/D. The RNZAF operated the type from 1944 until 1967, the country's geography being particularly suitable for such aircraft. *(Author's Collection)*

The Sunderland flew in the post-war RAF in GR.5 and MR.5 guises though by September 1946 only 201 and 230 Squadrons at Calshot, 88 Squadron at Kai Tak (Hong Kong), 205 (Koggala) and 209 (Seletar) continued, along with training under 4(C)OTU. From July 1948 201 and 230 Squadrons participated in the Berlin Airlift, flying from Hamburg to the Havel See together with their Hythe stablemates; both squadrons then transferred to Pembroke Dock.

Far East action was seen from June 1948 when a state of emergency was declared in Malaya after the Malayan Races Liberation Army rose up, British-trained to harry the wartime Japanese occupiers but of communist persuasion. Operation Firedog commenced under which the RAF undertook strike actions against the terrorists. The Sunderlands of 205 and 209 Squadrons bombed Communist forces, being hurriedly adapted to carry anti-personnel bombs, and continued maritime patrols and ASR work over a four-year period.

In April 1949 88 Squadron suspended its courier duties between various Far East bases, instead participating in the support of HMS *Amethyst*, damaged on the Yangtse near Chinkiang in an attack by communist Chinese forces, and later helped in the evacuation of Shanghai; it also participated in Firedog. During the Korean War 88, 205 and 209 Squadrons carried out ASR duties and maritime patrols against enemy shipping in cooperation with the US 7th Fleet. The main patrol areas were over the Yellow Sea and along the Korean coastline. Transport activities and weather reconnaissance were also undertaken. The aircraft flew from the RAAF base at Iwakuni, sometimes in very poor weather; generally, five would be on detachment at any one time, moored out on trots. Routine maintenance was carried out locally, major overhauls at Seletar. Anti-piracy patrols were also flown.

In July 1957 the last Sunderland unit based in Britain, 230 Squadron, disbanded at Pembroke Dock. However, the so-called 'Kipper Fleet' was retained at Seletar, 205 Squadron absorbing 209 Squadron's examples in January 1955 because of aircraft shortages. However, by May 1959 205 Squadron had fully converted to Shackletons; its last Sunderland flight took place on 20 May, after which the aircraft

230 Squadron was the final RAF unit stationed in the United Kingdom to operate the Sunderland. Here, SZ567 230-Z is caught at Gibraltar during December 1956. *(John Hirst/Squadron Leader Bill Holloway via John Evans)*

were stored and later scrapped at Seletar. By then, Shorts' finest flying-boat had been in RAF service for twenty-one years.

Conclusion

Eight Sunderland-type flying-boats survive today. NZ4115 (ex-SZ854/G-AHJR) is at the Museum of Transport and Technology at Auckland, New Zealand, and ML824, ex-Aeronavale, is with the RAF Museum at Hendon. ML796, also previously flown by the French, was acquired by the Imperial War Museum at Duxford in 1976. Beautifully restored Sandringham 4 VH-BRC *Beachcomber* is at Southampton's Hall of Aviation wearing Ansett colours while the ex-RAI Sandringham 7 F-OBIP survives at Le Bourget. Solent 3 *City of Cardiff* (later N9946F) resides at the Western Aerospace Museum, California, painted as NJ203, while TEAL's Solent 4 ZK-AMO is undergoing a thorough restoration, also at Auckland. The sole flying example is the unique 'near-Sandringham' VH-BRF *Islander* operated by Ansett from 1964 before moving to Antilles Air Boats in 1974 as N158J. In 1979 it was purchased by Edward Hulton and refitted, becoming G-BJHS *Juliet*. A short association with Ryan Air followed during the late 1980s but the aircraft is currently based at the Fantasy of Flight Museum at Polk City, Florida, in the hands of Kermit Weeks, as N814ML.

A Walrus resides with the Fleet Air Arm Museum at Yeovilton, a composite the hull of which is from L2301, while Seagull V A2-4/VH-ALB is in the custody of the Royal Air Force Museum. W2718 is being restored, a Saro-built Mk I for which the civil registration G-RNLI has been reserved, for it is intended that the completed example will fly; a Pegasus VI has been located in the United States. In 1980 HD874 was

The sole so-called 'Near-Sandringham' as G-BJHS seen on the Thames during 1982. At that time the aircraft was owned by Edward Hulton and had returned to Britain from the Virgin Islands during March 1981. This is the sole flying S.25 and in 1993 was acquired by Kermit Weeks for his Fantasy of Flight centre at Florida. *(John Evans)*

recovered from Heard Island, Antarctica, and is currently being restored at the RAAF Museum, Point Cook; final assembly is now (March 2002) complete. The nose section of Sea Otter JN200 is preserved at the Australian Naval Aviation Museum.

As for other types, Sealands survive at Dabolim's Naval Air Museum in Goa, where INS-106 is preserved minus floats and with its undercarriage secured in the extended position; at the Ulster Folk and Transport Museum (G-AKLW); and at the Belgrade Aeronautical Museum (0662). Saunders-Roe SR.A/1 TG263 is still at Southampton's Hall of Aviation while Canadian-Vickers Stranraer c/n CV209 coded 920 resides at the RAF Museum, Hendon, the nearest to the British-built Stranraer that it is now possible to see. The sole Slingsby Waterglider, BGA.266, is kept at the Windermere Steamboat Centre, re-assembled from parts retained for many years at Pattinson's joinery shop though its wings are not the originals. The spectacular wooden hull of Supermarine Southampton N9899 is at the RAF Museum and is well worth careful study, while at the Southampton Hall of Aviation a safe haven is provided for the forward hull of a Seagull II. A propeller formerly employed by Shorts' Cockle was preserved by an ex-Felixstowe airman.

The Norfolk and Suffolk Aviation Museum is custodian of a Felixstowe F.5 nose section which is currently under restoration. Parts of a specially built cutaway F.5L, A-3882, are held by the Smithsonian Institution: A-3882 is a genuine US Navy serial number but the 'aircraft' was never intended to fly, being constructed as an exhibition piece by the Naval Aircraft Factory in Philadelphia during 1919. The surviving

The hull of Sea Eagle G-EBGR (wrongly bearing G-EBGS), at Hythe alongside Short Solent 3 G-AKNS *City of Liverpool*. At the time the oldest surviving major assembly of a British transport aircraft, the hull was presented to BOAC by Vickers (Aviation) during 1949 and was moved to Heston. On 13 February 1954, as mainte-nance and storage problems grew, it was burned – a great loss to the history of the British flying-boat. *(Author's Collection)*

elements are the hull, a wing float, one propeller and a bomb – and while this is not a British flying-boat, being in effect a replica of a type built under licence, it is as close as you can get to viewing a substantial reminder of the British F.5. An F.3 propeller is kept at Malta's Aviation Museum. Parts of other aircraft still with us include six Princess portholes incorporated in a yacht based at Cowes, a Cloud float at the Southampton Hall of Aviation and a Cloud propeller at Ronaldsway while amazingly, a propeller from the pre-First World War Perry Beadle B3 also survives.

The British flying-boat existed for just over fifty years. Its contribution to the development and growth of civil and commercial aviation, and to Britain's military security during two world wars, was fundamental. In fact, if all goes well a rebirth will soon occur, for Warrior (Aeromarine) Ltd of Salisbury currently has exciting plans to build a new type, the Centaur (see Appendix 13). Web-foot enthusiasts everywhere will wish them well.

APPENDICES

1. British Flying-Boat Specifications

Not surprisingly in view of the passage of time, during the compilation of this Appendix it was found the surviving records can be inconsistent. Firstly there is a degree of conflicting information. Secondly, the data available is sometimes expressed in different

Type	Powerplant	Span	Length	Height	Wing Area sq ft
			Dimensions		
A D Flying Boat	One 150 hp Sunbeam	50 ft 4 in	30 ft 7 in	13 ft 1 in	479
	One 150 hp Hispano-Suiza				
	One 200 hp Hispano-Suiza				
	One 200 hp Wolseley Python				
	One 200 hp Sunbeam Arab				
Beardmore BeRo 2 Inverness	Two 450 hp Napier Lion V	94 ft 0 in	56 ft 11 in	16 ft 3 in	760.7
Blackburn N.1B	One 200 hp Hispano-Suiza	34 ft 10 in	28 ft 3.5 in	11 ft 0 in	314
Blackburn Pellet	One 450 hp Napier Lion	34 ft 0 in	28 ft 7 in	10 ft 8 in	306
Blackburn R.B.1 Iris	(Iris I) Three 650 hp Rolls-Royce Condor III	95 ft 6 in	66 ft 6 in	24 ft 6.5 in	2,461
	(Iris II) Three 675 hp Rolls-Royce Condor IIIA	95 ft 6 in	66 ft 6 in	24 ft 6.5 in	2,461
	(Iris III) Three 675 Rolls-Royce Condor IIIB	97 ft 0 in	67 ft 4.5 in	25 ft 6 in	2,229
	(Iris IV) Three 800 hp Armstrong Siddeley Leopard	95 ft 6 in	66 ft 6 in	24 ft 6.5 in	2,461
	(Iris V) Three 825 hp Rolls-Royce Buzzard IIMS	97 ft 0 in	67 ft 4.5 in	25 ft 6 in	2,229
	(Iris V) Three 720 hp Napier Culverin Series I				
Blackburn R.B.2 Sydney	Three 525 hp Rolls-Royce FXIIMS	100 ft 0 in	65 ft 7 in	20 ft 4 in	1,500
Blackburn R.B.3A Perth	Three 825 hp Rolls-Royce Buzzard IIMS	97 ft 0 in	70 ft 0 in	26 ft 5.5 in	2,511
Blackburn B-20	Two 1,720 hp Rolls-Royce Vulture X	82 ft 2 in (floats up) 76ft 0in (floats down)	69 ft 7.5 in	26 ft 7.5 in (float down) 11ft 8in (hull depth, float up)	1,066
English Electric P.5 Kingston	Two 450 hp Napier Lion IIB	85 ft 6 in	Prototype and Mk I: 52 ft 9 in Mk II: 54 ft 4.5 in Mk III: 57 ft 1.5 in	Prototype and Mk I: 20 ft 11 in Mk II: 21 ft 10.5 in Mk III: 21 ft 6.5 in	All: 1,282.5
English Electric M.3 Ayr	Two 450 hp Napier lion IIB	46 ft 0 in	40 ft 8 in	13 ft 8 in	466
Fairey N.4 Class	Four 650 hp Rolls-Royce Condor IA (Atalanta)	139 ft 0 in	66 ft 0 in		2,900
	Four 650 hp Rolls-Royce Condor III (Titania)				
Felixstowe F.1	Two 100 hp Anzani	72 ft 0 in	39 ft 2 in		842 (?)
	Two 150 hp Hispano-Suiza				
Felixstowe F.2A	Two 360 hp Rolls-Royce Eagle VIII	95 ft 7.5 in	46 ft 3 in	17 ft 6 in	1,133
Felixstowe F.2C	Two 360 hp Rolls-Royce Eagle VIII (N64)	95 ft 0 in	46 ft 0 in	17 ft 6 in	1,136
	Two 322 hp Rolls-Royce Eagle VI (N65)				
	Two 250 hp Sunbeam (N65)				
Felixstowe F.3	N64 (revised): two 320 hp Sunbeam Cossack	102 ft 0 in	49 ft 2 in	18 ft 8 in	1,432
	Two 360 hp Rolls-Royce Eagle VIII				
Felixstowe F.5	Two 325 hp Rolls-Royce Eagle VII	103 ft 8 in	49 ft 3 in	18 ft 9 in	1,409
	Two 360 hp Rolls-Royce Eagle VIII				
	Two 400 hp Liberty 12 (Canadian-built and F-5L)				
Felixstowe F.4 Fury	Five 325 hp Rolls-Royce Eagle VII	123 ft 0 in	63 ft 2 in	27 ft 6 in	3,108
	Five 345 hp Rolls-Royce Eagle VIII				
Humphreys Biplane	One 35 hp JAP	45 ft 0 in	38 ft 0 in		c 650
Norman Thompson NT.4 and NT.4A	Two 100 hp Green (8338, initially)	77 ft 10 in (NT.4) 78 ft 7 in (NT.4A)	40 ft 9 in 41 ft 6 in	14 ft 7 in 14 ft 10 in	1,014 998
	Two 150 hp Hispano-Suiza				
	Two 200 hp Hispano-Suiza				
Norman Thompson NT.2B	One 120 hp or 160 hp Beardmore Austro-Daimler	48 ft 5 in	27 ft 4.5 in	10 ft 8 in	453
	One 200 hp Sunbeam Arab				
	One 150 hp Hispano-Suiza				
	One 200 hp Hispano-Suiza				
Norman Thompson NT.5	One 100 hp Gnôme Monosoupape	44 ft 0 in	28 ft 8 in	9 ft 9 in	358
	One 130 hp Clerget				
Norman Thompson N.1B	One 150 hp Hispano-Suiza 8A	34 ft 3 in	26 ft 5 in	9 ft 7 in	357
	One 200 hp Hispano-Suiza 8B				
Norman Thompson N.2C	Two 200 hp Sunbeam Arab	78 ft 7 in	42 ft 2 in	14 ft 7 in	936
Parnall P.1 Prawn	One 65 hp Ricardo-Burt	28 ft 0 in	c 18 ft 0 in	7 ft 0 in (on beaching chassis)	

ways, so that information on one type will set out some characteristics, and on another, others. This Appendix is an amalgam of available information that hopes to give a rounded view.

Weights		Max Speed mph	Cruising Speed mph	Performance		Range Miles	Ceiling ft	Armament
Empty lbs	Normal All-Up lbs			Initial Climb ft/min	Endurance			
2,400	3,327	91		c 330	5 hr		7,500	One .303 in Lewis gun
2,508	3,567	100		c 660	4 hr 30 min		11,000	
2,360	3,388	87.5		c 670	3 hr 30 min		8,800	
(N183) 9,597	(N183) 12,500	110		550	4 hr 30 min (est)		8,750	Provision for .303 in machine-guns in nose and dorsal
(N184) 10,580	(N184) 13,160							gunners' positions
1,721	2,390	114 (est)		c 720	3 hr	340	16,000	Provision for one, possibly two .303 in Lewis guns
c 2,105	c 2,800	160 (est)						n/a
18,930	27,608	115	86	602	c 5 hr	560	11,850	Up to four .303 in Lewis guns; 1,040 lb bomb load
18,930	27,538	111	92	450	c 7 hr	805	13,100	(Iris I, II, IV)
19,048	29,489	118	97	630	4 hr 50 min	800	12,800	Three .303 in Lewis guns; 1,040 lb bomb load
17,500	35,000	130	100	665	c 6 hr	505	10,350	(Iris III, V)
21,510	32,300	129	103	660	c 8 hr	985	12,000	One 30 mm COW quick-firing cannon (S1593)
17,065	23,350	123	100	390	7 hr 30 min		16,500	Three .303 in Lewis guns; 1,100 bomb load or two Mk VIII or Whitehead torpedoes
20,927	32,500 (normal)	132	109	800		780 (normal)	11,500	One 37 mm recoilless quick-firing cannon; up to four
	38,000 (maximum)					1,500 (max)		.303 in Lewis guns; 2,000 lb bomb load
	35,000	306 (est)	200 (est)		8 hr (est)	1,500 (est)		None in prototype. Planned in production: two .303 in machine-guns in nose, two in dorsal turret, four in tail turret, plus 2,000 bomb load
Mk I: 9,130	Mk I: 14,508	Mk I: 104.8			I: 8 – 9 hr		I: 9,060	I, II and III: three .303 in Lewis guns; two 520 lb bombs
Mk II: 9,663	Mk II: 14,961	Mk II: 103.5			II: 8 – 9 hr		II: 8,310	
Mk III: 9,868	Mk III: 14,981	Mk III: 104.8			III: 8 – 9 hr		III: 9,180	
4,406 (est)	6,846 (est)	127 (est)					14,500 (est)	Two .303 in Lewis guns
	30,500	115			7 – 9 hr		14,100	Provision for up to six .303 in Lewis guns and 1,000 lb bomb load (both)
	31,612							None thought to have been fitted
7,549	10,978	95.5	c 78	c 520	6 hr – 9 hr 30 min		9,600	Four to nine .303 in Lewis guns; two 230 lb bombs
6,768	10,240	95	c 78	c420	c 6 hr		10,300	Two .303 in Lewis guns; four 230 lb bombs
7,958	12,235	91	c 74	c 360	6 hr – 9 hr 30 min		8,000	Four or five .303 in Lewis guns; four 230 lb bombs
		88.5						
9,100	12,682	88	c 70	c 305	c 7 hr		6,800	Four .303 in Lewis guns; four 230 lb bombs
(F-5L 8,250)	(F-5L 13,000)	(F-5L 87)			(F-5L 10 hr)			
18,563	24,000	97.5	78	c 550	8 – 13 hr (initial)		12,000	Provision for four .303 in Lewis guns plus bomb load
	c 1,750							n/a
		96	c 70	c 500	6 hr		14,500	One .303 in Lewis gun; two 230 lb bombs.
4,572	6,469	95		c 520	6 hr		14,000	Experimental: one two-pounder Davis non-recoil gun (8338)
2,321 lb	3,169 lb	85		c 490			11,400	None
1,231	1,950	60			4 hr			One .303 in Lewis gun; light bomb load
1,895	2,673	93		c 580	3 hr 30 min		12,600	Provision for one, possibly two .303 in Lewis guns
	6,194							(Intended) one .303 in Lewis gun; two 230 lb bombs
		c 100						n/a

Type	Powerplant	Span	Length	Height	Wing Area sq ft
				Dimensions	
Pemberton Billing PB.1	One 50 hp Gnôme	30 ft 0 in			293
Perry Beadle B.3	One 60 hp ENV F Type	35 ft 0 in	26 ft 0 in	9 ft 0 in	290
Phoenix P.5 Cork	Two 360 hp Rolls-Royce Eagle VIII	85 ft 6 in	49 ft 2 in	21 ft 2 in	1,273
Porte Baby	Prototype: three 250 hp Rolls-Royce	124 ft 0 in	63 ft 0 in	25 ft 0 in	2,364
	Two 250 hp Rolls-Royce + one 260 hp Green				
	Three 325 hp Rolls-Royce Eagle VII				
	Three 360 hp Rolls-Royce Eagle VIII				
Radley-England Waterplane 1	Three 50 hp Gnôme	45 ft 4 in	29 ft 3 in		505
Radley-England Waterplane 2	One 150 hp Sunbeam	51 ft 7.5 in	29 ft 9 in		560
Royal Aircraft Factory CE.1	One 230 hp RAF 3a	46 ft 0 in	36 ft 3 in	13 ft 4 in	609
	One 260 hp Sunbeam Maori	46 ft 0 in	36 ft 3 in	13 ft 4 in	609
Saunders Kittiwake	Two 200 hp ABC Wasp II	68 ft 3 in	43 ft 8 in	14 ft 10.5 in	864
Saunders A.3 Valkyrie	Three 675 hp Rolls-Royce Condor IIIA	97 ft 0 in	65 ft 6 in	18 ft 5.5 in	1,967.50
Saunders A.4 Medina	Two 450 hp Bristol Jupiter VI	52 ft 0 in	49 ft 0 in	16 ft 0 in	1,007
Saunders A.7 Severn	Three 490 hp Bristol Jupiter XIFP	88 ft 0 in	64 ft 6 in	19 ft 3 in	1,567
Saunders A.14	Two 500 hp Napier Lion VA	75 ft 0 in	48 ft 8 in	18 ft 7 in	1,448
Saunders-Roe A.17 Cutty Sark	Two 105 hp ADC Cirrus Hermes I	45 ft 0 in	34 ft 4 in	11 ft 2 in	320
	Two 120 hp de Havilland Gipsy II	45 ft 0 in	34 ft 4 in	11 ft 2 in	320
	Two 130 hp de Havilland Gipsy III	45 ft 0 in	34 ft 4 in	11 ft 2 in	320
	Two 140 hp Armstrong Siddeley Genet Major I	45 ft 0 in	34 ft 4 in	11 ft 2 in	320
	One 240 hp Armstrong Siddeley Lynx IVC	45 ft 0 in	34 ft 4 in	11 ft 2 in	320
Saunders-Roe A.19 and A.29 Cloud	Two 300 hp Wright Whirlwind J-6 (A.19)	64 ft 0 in	47 ft 9 in	13 ft 2 in	650
	Three 240 hp Armstrong Siddeley Lynx IVC (A.19)	64 ft 0 in	47 ft 9 in	13 ft 2 in	650
	Two 425 hp Pratt & Whitney Wasp C (A.19)	64 ft 0 in	47 ft 9 in	13 ft 2 in	650
	Two 340 hp Napier Rapier IV (A.19)	64 ft 0 in	48 ft 8 in	13 ft 2 in	650
	Two 300 hp Walter Pollux (A.19)	64 ft 0 in	48 ft 8 in	13 ft 2 in	650
	Two 340 hp Armstrong Siddeley Double Mongoose II (A.19 K2681)	64 ft 0 in	47 ft 9 in/48 ft 8 in	13 ft 2 in	650
	Two 340 Armstrong Siddeley Serval I and III (A.29)	64 ft 0 in	47 ft 9 in/49 ft 9 in	13 ft 2 in	650
Saunders-Roe A.21 Windhover	Three 120 hp de Havilland Gipsy II	54 ft 4 in	41 ft 4 in	12 ft 6 in (as amphibian)	450 + 72
Saunders-Roe A.27 London I and II	Two 820/875 hp Bristol Pegasus IIIM3 (London I)	80 ft 0 in	57 ft 0 in	20 ft 3 in	1,427
	Two 915/1,055 hp Bristol Pegasus X (London II)	80 ft 0 in	57 ft 0 in	20 ft 3 in	1,427
Saunders-Roe A.33	Four 830 hp Bristol Perseus XII	95 ft 0 in	75 ft 0 in	22 ft 8.5 in	1,194
Saunders-Roe S.36 Lerwick	Two 1,375 Bristol Hercules HE.1M/ Hercules II/ Hercules IV	80 ft 10 in	63 ft 7.5 in	20 ft 0 in	845
Saunders-Roe A.37 (original configuration)	Four 95 hp Pobjoy Niagara III	50 ft 0 in	42 ft 3.25 in	12 ft 8.75 in	340
Saunders-Roe SR.A/1 'Squirt'	Two 3,230/3,500/3,850 lb st Metropolitan-Vickers F.2/4 Beryl	46 ft 0 in	50 ft 0 in	16 ft 9 in	415
Saunders-Roe SR.45 Princess	See Appendix 8				
Short N.3 Cromarty	Two 650 hp Rolls-Royce Condor IA	113 ft 6 in	59 ft 0 in		2,243
Short S.1 Cockle	Two 32 hp Bristol Cherub II	36 ft 0 in	24 ft 8 in		210
	Two 16 hp Blackburne				
Short S.5 Singapore I	Two 650 hp Rolls-Royce Condor III; later, 675 hp IIIA	93 ft 0 in	64 ft 0 in		1,723
	Two 825 hp Rolls-Royce H.10 (Buzzard I)				
Short S.8 Calcutta	Three 525 hp Bristol Jupiter XIF	93 ft 0 in	66 ft 0 in	23 ft 9 in	1,825
	Three 840 hp Armstrong Siddeley Tiger VI				
	Three 520 hp Gnôme-Rhône Jupiter 9Akx				
Short S.8/8 Rangoon	Three 525 hp Bristol Jupiter XIF	93 ft 0 in	66 ft 9.5 in	23 ft 9 in	1,828
Short S.12 Singapore II	Four 480 hp Rolls-Royce pre-production FXII (initial);	90 ft 0 in	63 ft 9 in		1,750
	Two 550 hp Rolls-Royce Kestrel II (tractor) plus				
	Two 600 hp Rolls-Royce Kestrel IIMS (pusher)				
Short S.14 Sarafand	Six 825 hp Rolls-Royce Buzzard II	120 ft 0 in	89 ft 6 in		3,640
Short S.15 K.F.1	Three 820 hp Rolls-Royce Buzzard	101 ft 10 in	74 ft 5 in		2,300
Short S.17 Kent	Four 555 hp Bristol Jupiter XFBM	113 ft 0 in	78 ft 5 in	28 ft 0 in	2,640
Short S.18 Knuckleduster	Two 600 hp Rolls-Royce Goshawk IIS	90 ft 0 in	63 ft 3 in		1,147
Short S.19 Singapore III	Four 675 hp Rolls-Royce Kestrel IX (DR)	90 ft 0 in	64 ft 2 in	23 ft 7 in	1,834

Weights		Max Speed mph	Cruising Speed mph	Performance		Range Miles	Ceiling ft	Armament
Empty lbs	Normal All-Up lbs			Initial Climb ft/min	Endurance			
750	970	est 50						n/a
1,100	1,600	est 72			est 3 hr 30 min			
7,437	11,600	106			8 hr		13,000	Five to seven .303 in Lewis guns; up to 1,040 lb bomb load
14,700	18,600	P'type: 78	62	c 375	c 7 hr		8,000	Up to three .303 in Lewis guns. Experimental: one
		Prod'n: 92	72	c 425	c 8 hr		c 8,400	six-pounder Davis non-recoil gun carried by prototype.
1,400	1,800	60			1 hr 30 min			n/a
	2,500	60			c 1 hr 30 min			n/a
3,241	4,912	88.5			4 hr 30 min		9,000	Provision for three .303 in Lewis guns. Small bomb load
3,342	4,994	92.5			3 hr 45 min		10,000	
3,840	6,200	110	92		4 hr	c 340		n/a
17,851	26,000	125	95		9 hr 20 min		15,000	Three .303 in Lewis guns; 1,100 lb bomb load
8,060	11,560	115	90		4 hr	360		n/a
14,800	22,000	126	96	590	6 hr		8,930	Three .303 in Lewis guns; 1,840 lb bomb load
8,870	14,000	97	87		6 hr 30 min	600	8,400	Three .303 in Lewis guns; 1,900 lb bomb load
2,375	3,500	105	85	600		340	9,500	n/a except for L5: one machine-gun, small bomb load
2,670	3,850	103	85	550		300	9,000	
2,430	3,700	104	92	540		c 300	9,200	
2,725	3,900	107	90	550		315		
2,400	3,700	102	85	550			10,000	
5,500	8,100	120	95	520	c 4 hr			n/a
6,075	9,000	120	95	c 520	5 hr 25 min			n/a
5,687	10,000	125	98	c 520	c 4 hr			n/a
6,450	9,700	121	102	c 520	c 4 hr			n/a
6,500	9,500	120	95	520	c 4 hr			n/a
6,845/6,970	9,530/10,090	118	95	455	c 4 hr		7,630	Provision for two .303 in Lewis guns; 200 lb bomb load
6,875/6,990	9,380/10,030	120	98	480	4 hr		10,000	Provision for two .303 in Lewis guns; 200 lb bomb load
3,650 f/b	5,500 f/b	110 f/b	90 f/b	600 f/b	4 hr		10,020 f/b	n/a
4,180 amph	5,700 amph	108 amph	87 amph	510 amph	4hr		9,680 amph	
12,285	19,000	145	99	758	8 – 13 hr	Up to 2,600	14,050	Three .303 in Lewis guns; 2,000 bomb load
12,800	19,300	155	106	850	8 – 13 hr	Up to 2,600	18,000	
31,500 (test-flying weight)	41,500	200	174		12 hr		14,280	Provision for single or multiple .303 in machine guns in bow and tail turrets; two Vickers K guns in beam positions; 2,000 lb bomb load
	28,400	214	166	880		1,540	14,000	One .303 in Vickers K gun (nose); two .303 in machine guns (dorsal); four .303 in machine guns (tail); 2,000 bomb or depth charge load
4,362	5,700	152	114	635	3 hr		8,000	n/a
11,262	16,000	512			1 hr 48 min		43,000	Four 20 mm Hispano Mk 5 cannon; provision for two 250 lb, 500 lb or 1,000 lb bombs, or rocket projectiles
12,220	18,000	95			6 hrs (normal) 11 hrs (max)	900		Provision for one 37 mm anti-submarine gun, and dorsal .303 in Lewis gun; 2,000 lb bomb load
Ch: 880	Ch: 1,205	Ch: 73						n/a
Bl: 814	Bl: 1,062	Bl: 68						
Co: 12,875	Co: 19,560	Co: 128				900	15,500	Military version: provision for three .303 in Lewis guns
H.10: 12,955	H.10: 20,000	H.10: 132						
13,845	22,500	118	97	750		650	13,500	n/a
14,000	22,500	115	92	550	Up to 7 hrs	650	12,000	Three .303 in Lewis guns; 1,000 lb bomb load
17,940	31,500	140	c 112	625		1,000	14,000	Three .303 in Lewis guns; 2,000 lb bomb load
44,750	70,000	153			Up to 11 hours	1,450	12,000	Four .303 in Lewis guns; provision for installation of 1.5 pounder shell-firing gun in bow
22,100	39,000	124			11 hours (normal)	2,000		Three .303 in Lewis guns; provision for bomb load
20,460	32,000	c 123	99	840		450	17,500	n/a
11,720	18,500	150			6 hr 30 min	1,040	15,500	Provision for three .303 in Lewis guns
20,364	31,500	145	105	700	6 hrs 15 min	1,000	15,000	Three .303 in Lewis guns; 2,000 lb bomb load

Type	Powerplant	Span	Length	Height	Wing Area sq ft
		\<span colspan>Dimensions\			
Short S.23 Empire	Four 920 hp Bristol Pegasus XC Four 1,010 hp Bristol Pegasus XXII	114 ft 0 in	88 ft 0 in	31 ft 9.75 in	1,500
Short S.30 Empire	Four 890 hp Bristol Perseus XIIC	114 ft 0 in	88 ft 0 in	31 ft 9.75 in	1,500
Short S.33 Empire	Four 920 hp Bristol Pegasus XC Four 1,010 hp Bristol Pegasus XXII	114 ft 0 in	88 ft 0 in	31 ft 9.75 in	1,500
Short S.21 Maia	Four 910 hp Bristol Pegasus XC	114 ft 0 in	84 ft 11 in		1,750
Short S.25 Sunderland I	Four 1,010 hp Bristol Pegasus XXII	112 ft 9 in	85 ft 4 in	32 ft 10.5 in	1,488 (one-third flaps)
Short S.25 Sunderland V	Four 1,200 hp Pratt & Whitney Twin Wasp	112 ft 9.5 in	85 ft 4 in	32 ft 10.5 in	1,488 (one-third flaps)
Short S.26	Four 1,380 hp Bristol Hercules IV Four 1,380 hp Bristol Hercules XIV	134 ft 4 in	101 ft 4 in	37 ft 7 in	2,160
Short S.45 Seaford I	Four 1,800 hp Bristol Hercules 130	112 ft 9.5 in	88 ft 7 in	34 ft 3.25 in	1,687
Short S.35 Shetland	Four 2,500 hp Bristol Centaurus VII (S.40: Four 2,500 hp Bristol Centaurus 660)	150 ft 4 in	110 ft 0 in (S.35) 107 ft 0 in (S.40)	c 37 ft 0 in	2,624
Short S.25 Hythe Class	Four 1,030 hp Bristol Pegasus XVIII, 38 or 48	112 ft 9.5 in	88 ft 6.75 in	22 ft 10.5 in	1,687
Short S.25 Sandringham 1	Four 1,030 hp Bristol Pegasus 38	112 ft 9.5 in	85 ft 4 in	22 ft 10.5 in	1,687
Short S.25 Sandringham 2	four 1,200 hp Pratt & Whitney Twin Wasp	112 ft 9.5 in	86 ft 3 in	22 ft 10.5 in	1,687
Short S.25 Sandringham 3	four 1,200 hp Pratt & Whitney Twin Wasp	112 ft 9.5 in	86 ft 3 in	22 ft 10.5 in	1,687
Short S.25 Sandringham 4	four 1,200 hp Pratt & Whitney Twin Wasp	112 ft 9.5 in	86 ft 3 in	22 ft 10.5 in	1,687
Short S.25 Sandringham 5	four 1,200 hp Pratt & Whitney Twin Wasp	112 ft 9.5 in	86 ft 3 in	22 ft 10.5 in	1,687
Short S.25 Sandringham 6	four 1,200 hp Pratt & Whitney Twin Wasp	112 ft 9.5 in	86 ft 3 in	22 ft 10.5 in	1,687
Short S.25 Sandringham 7	four 1,200 hp Pratt & Whitney Twin Wasp	112 ft 9.5 in	86 ft 3 in	22 ft 10.5 in	1,687
Short S.45 Solent 2	Four 1,690 hp Bristol Hercules 637	112 ft 9.5 in	87 ft 8 in	34 ft 3.25 in	1,687
Short S.45 Solent 3	Four 1,690 hp Bristol Hercules 637	112 ft 9.5 in	87 ft 8 in	34 ft 3.25 in	1,687
Short S.45 Solent 4	Four 2,040 hp Bristol Hercules 733	112 ft 9.5 in	87 ft 8 in	34 ft 3.25 in	1,687
Short SA.6 Sealand	Two 340 hp de Havilland Gipsy Queen 70-2 (prototype) Two 340 hp de Havilland Gipsy Queen 70-3 (civil) Two 340 hp de Havilland Gipsy Queen 70-4 (Indian AF)	59 ft 0 in (later 61 ft 6 in)	42 ft 2 in	15 ft 0 in	353 (later 358.6)
Sopwith Bat Boat Type 1	One 90 hp Austro-Daimler One 100 hp Green	41 ft 0 in	30 ft 4 in (later 32 ft 0 in)	11 ft 6 in	400
Sopwith Bat Boat Type 2	One 200 hp Salmson (Canton Unne)	54 ft 0 in	36 ft 6 in	10 ft 0 in	600
Sopwith Bat Boat Type 2 (Circuit of Britain)	One 225 hp Sunbeam Mohawk	55 ft 0 in	36 ft 6 in	11 ft 0 in	
Supermarine N.1B	One 200 hp Hispano Suiza One 200 hp Sunbeam Arab	30 ft 6 in	26 ft 3.5 in	10 ft 7 in	309
Supermarine Channel I	One 160 hp Beardmore (Channel II: one 240 hp Siddeley Puma)	50 ft 5 in	30 ft 0 in	13 ft 0 in	453
Supermarine Sea King I	One 160 hp Beardmore One 240 hp Siddeley Puma	35 ft 6 in	27 ft 4 in	11 ft 7 in	339
Supermarine Sea King II	One 300 hp Hispano-Suiza	32 ft 0 in	26 ft 9 in	11 ft 7 in	
Supermarine Sea Lion I	One 450 hp Napier Lion IA	35 ft 0 in	26 ft 4 in	c 12 ft 3 in	380
Supermarine Sea Lion II	One 450 hp Napier Lion II	32 ft 0 in	24 ft 9 in	c 12 ft 0 in	384
Supermarine Sea Lion III	One 525 hp Napier Lion III	28 ft 0 in	28 ft 0 in	c 12 ft 0 in	360
Supermarine Commercial Amphibian	One 350 hp Rolls-Royce Eagle VIII	50 ft 0 in	32 ft 6 in	14 ft 6 in	600
Supermarine Sea Eagle	One 360 hp Rolls-Royce Eagle IX	46 ft 0 in	37 ft 4 in	15 ft 11 in	620
Supermarine Seal II	One 450 hp Napier Lion IB One 480 hp Napier lion II	46 ft 0 in	32 ft 10 in	14 ft 10 in	620

Weights		Performance				Range Miles	Ceiling ft	Armament
Empty lbs	Normal All-Up lbs	Max Speed mph	Cruising Speed mph	Initial Climb ft/min	Endurance			
23,500	40,500 (later, 43,500, then 52,500)	200	165	950	4 hrs 30 min	660 – 703	20,000	Impressed examples only: eight .303 in machine-guns
27,180	48,000 (air – air refuelled 53,000)	200	165	950		1,500		Impressed examples only: seven .303 in machine-guns
27,180	40,500 (later 53,000)	200	165	950		760		n/a
24,745	38,000 (Maia launch max as composite: 27,000)	200	165			850	20,000	n/a
28,920	50,100	206	142		13 hr 30 min	1,850	14,800	One or two .303 in machine guns (nose turret); four .303 in machine guns (tail turret); two .303 in machine guns (beam); 2,000 lb bomb or depth charge load
37,000	65,000	229	142		15–21 hr	Up to 3,100	22,600	Up to fourteen .303 in and (optional) up to four .5 in machine guns 2,000 lb bomb or depth charge load
37,705	74,500	209	180			3,200		Impressed aircraft only: twelve .303 in machine-guns, 4,000 lb bomb load
45,000	75,000	245	163			3,100	15,000	Planned: four .303 in machine-guns in forward body; two .5 in machine-guns (nose turret); two .5 in machine-guns (tail turret); two .5 in machine-guns (dorsal turret); two .5 in machine-guns (beam positions); 1,680 lb depth charges.
75,860	125,000 (S.35) 130,000 (S.40)	263	183	900	25 hr 50 min	4,000 (S.35) 3,000 (S.40)		S.35, planned: two .5 in machine-guns in each of nose, dorsal and tail turrets, plus two .5 in machine-guns in beam positions, plus 4,000 lb bomb/depth charge load; actual, none. S.40: n/a
35,862	50,000	178	165	720		2,350	16,000	n/a
34,150	56,000	216	184	720		2,550	16,150	n/a
41,370	56,000	238	221	1,000		2,410	21,300	n/a
41,370	56,000	238	221	1,000		2,410	21,300	n/a
41,000	56,000	238	221	1,000		2,400	21,300	n/a
39,498	60,000	206	176	840		2,440	17,900	n/a
41,000	56,000	238	221	1,000		2,410	21,300	n/a
39,498	60,000	206	176	840		2,440	17,900	n/a
47,760	78,000	273	244	925		1,800	17,000	n/a
48,210	78,600	267	236	830		2,190	15,500	n/a
49,145	81,000	282	251	925		3,000	17,100	n/a
7,397 (later 7,065)	9,100	189 (later 185)	175 (later 169)	880 (later 780)	3 hr 30 (civil) 6 hr (Indian Navy)	525 (later 660)	20,600 (later 21,000)	n/a
1,200	1,650	60 – 65	c 50		2 hr			n/a
2,300	3,120	70	c 55	500	4 hr 30 min			n/a
	3,180	75	c 58		5 hr			n/a
1,699	2,326	116			3 hr			Provision for one, possibly two .303 in Lewis guns
1,902	2,508			c 430	3 hr		10,700	
2,356	3,400	80	71		3 hr		7,500	n/a except for Swedish and Chilean examples: one .303 in Lewis gun
	2,500	110.5						Provision for one .303 in Lewis gun
	2,646	121						
2,115	2,850	125			2 hr			Provision for one .303 in Lewis gun
2,000	2,900	147			2 hr 30 min			n/a
2,115	2,850	160			3 hr			n/a
2,400	3,275	175			3 hr			n/a
3,996	5,700	94.4	80			312	8,000	n/a
3,950	6,050	93	84			230	8,000	n/a
4,100	5,600	112	95		4 hr			Provision for two .303 in Lewis guns

Type	Powerplant	Dimensions			
		Span	Length	Height	Wing Area sq ft
Supermarine Seagull I	One 480 hp Napier Lion II	45 ft 11 in	34 ft 6 in	13 ft 6 in	605
Supermarine Seagull II and III	One 492 hp Napier Lion IIB (Seagull II)	46 ft 0 in	37 ft 9 in	14 ft 0 in	593
	One 492 hp Napier Lion V (Seagull III)				
Supermarine Scarab	One 360 hp Rolls-Royce Eagle IX	46 ft 0 in	37 ft 0 in	c 16 ft 2 in	610
Supermarine Sheldrake	One 450 hp Napier Lion V	46 ft 0 in	37 ft 4.5 in	16 ft 2.5 in	593
Supermarine Swan	Two 360 hp Rolls-Royce Eagle IX	68 ft 8 in	48 ft 6 in	18 ft 3.75 in	1,264.80
	Two 450 Napier Lion IIB				
Supermarine Southampton II	Two 500 hp Napier Lion VA	75 ft 0 in	49 ft 8.5 in	20 ft 5 in	1,448
	Two 450 hp Bristol Jupiter IX (N218)				
	Two 570 hp Bristol Jupiter XFBM (N218)				
	Two 550 hp Rolls-Royce Kestrel IIMS; later, Kestrel IV (N253)				
	Two 450 hp Lorraine 12E				
	Two 600 hp Hispano-Suiza 12 Nbr				
	Two 430 hp Armstrong Siddeley Jaguar IV				
Supermarine Seamew	Two 230 hp Armstrong Siddeley Lynx IV	46 ft 0 in	36 ft 5.5 in	15 ft 1 in	610
Supermarine Nanok	Three 430 hp Armstrong Siddeley Jaguar IV	75 ft 0 in	50 ft 6 in	19 ft 6 in	1,571.80
Supermarine Solent	Three 400 hp Armstrong Siddeley Jaguar IVA	75 ft 0 in	50 ft 2 in	19 ft 0 in	1,576
Supermarine Southampton X	Two 430 hp Armstrong Siddeley Jaguar IV	79 ft 0 in	55 ft 6 in	21 ft 0 in	1,235
	Two 525 hp Armstrong Siddeley Panther IIA				
	Three 570 hp Bristol Jupiter XFBM				
Supermarine Seagull V	One 625 hp Bristol Pegasus IIM2	46 ft 0 in	38 ft 0 in	15 ft 0 in (on undercarriage)	610
Supermarine Air Yacht	Three 490 hp Armstrong Siddeley Jaguar VI	92 ft 0 in	66 ft 6 in	19 ft 0 in	1,472
	Three 525 hp Armstrong Siddeley Panther IIA				
Supermarine Scapa	Two 525 hp Rolls-Royce Kestrel IIIMS	75 ft 0 in	53 ft 0 in	c 19 ft 0 in	1,300
Supermarine Stranraer	Two 820 hp Bristol Pegasus IIIM (prototype)	85 ft 0 in	54 ft 10 in	c 19 ft 9 in	1,457
	Two 920 hp Bristol Pegasus X				
Supermarine Walrus II	One 750 hp Bristol Pegasus VI	45 ft 10 in	37 ft 7 in	15 ft 3 in (on undercarriage)	610
Supermarine Sea Otter II	One 965 hp Bristol Mercury XXX	46 ft 0 in	39 ft 5 in	16 ft 2 in	610
Supermarine Seagull ASR.I	One 1,815 hp Rolls-Royce Griffon 29	52 ft 6 in	44 ft 1.5 in	15 ft 10.5 in	432
Vickers-Saunders Valentia BS.1	Two 650 hp Rolls-Royce Condor IA	112 ft 0 in	58 ft 0 in		
Vickers Viking I	One 275 hp Rolls-Royce Falcon III	37 ft 0 in	30 ft 0 in	13 ft 0 in	368
Vickers Viking III	One 450 hp Napier Lion	46 ft 0 in	32 ft 0 in	13 ft 0 in	585
Vickers Viking IV	One 450 hp Napier Lion	50 ft 0 in	34 ft 2 in	14 ft 0 in	635
	One 360 hp Rolls-Royce Eagle IX	50 ft 0 in	34 ft 0 in	14 ft 2 in	635
Vickers Viking V	(As for Viking IV with minor revisions for use by RAF in Iraq)				
Vickers Viking VI – Vulture	Vulture I: one 450 hp Napier Lion	49 ft 0 in	38 ft 2 in	14 ft 6 in	828
	Vulture II: one 360 hp Rolls-Royce Eagle IX, later one 450 hp Napier Lion				
Vickers Viking VII – Vanellus	One 450 hp Napier Lion	46 ft 0 in	34 ft 0 in	14 ft 2 in	635
White and Thompson No 1	Two 90 hp Curtiss OX	52 ft 0 in	32 ft 3 in	c 10 ft 6 in	500
White and Thompson No 2	One 120 hp Beardmore Austro-Daimler	45 ft 0 in	27 ft 6 in	c 11 ft 6 in	400
White and Thompson No 3 (NT.2 and NT.2A)	One 120 hp Beardmore Austro-Daimler (NT.2, NT.2A 3807) One 150 hp Hispano-Suiza (NT.2A 3808)	45 ft 0 in	27 ft 6 in	10 ft 5 in	400

Weights		Performance						Armament
Empty lbs	Normal All-Up lbs	Max Speed mph	Cruising Speed mph	Initial Climb ft/min	Endurance	Range Miles	Ceiling ft	
3,691	5,462	80	74		3 hr 30 min		9,000	One .303 in Lewis gun
3,820	5,691	90 (Seagull II) 85 (Seagull III)	86		4 hr 30 min		9,150	One .303 in Lewis gun
3,975	5,750	93	80			250 (estimated)		One .303 in Lewis gun; 1,000 lb bomb load
4,125	6,100	103	85			250		One .303 in Lewis gun; one .303 in Vickers K gun; 1,000 lb bomb load
7,800	11,900	92	83				10,200	n/a
9,170	13,710	108.5	87					
9,696	15,200	95	86	368	6 hr 20 min	540	8,100	Three .303 in Lewis guns; 1,000 lb bomb load
4,675	5,800	95	86				10,950	Two .303 in Lewis guns
10,619	16,311	113.5	80	607		240	10,920	Two .303 in Lewis guns; two torpedoes
9,840	16,500	111	80				11,000	n/a
13,427	21,117	130		500		1,000	6,400	Three .303 in Lewis guns; 1,000 bomb load
4,640	6,847	125		900		634	15,500	Two .303 in Vickers K Guns or Lewis guns; up to 660 lb bomb load, or two 380 lb depth charges
16,808	23,348	117	96	380	c 5 hr 20 min		6,500	n/a
10,030	16,040	141		625		1,100	15,480	Three .303 in Lewis guns; 1,000 lb bomb load
11,250	19,000	165	105	1,350	9 hr 30 min	1,000	18,500	Three .303 in Lewis guns; 1,000 lb bomb load
4,900	7,200	135	95	1,050		600	18,500	Two .303 in Vickers K guns; 760 lb bomb or depth charge load
6,805	10,000	163	100			690	17,000	Opt: three .303 in machine guns
10,510	14,500	260	131	1,430		875	23,700	None
10,000	21,300	105	78		4 hrs 30 min			Provision for two .303 in machine-guns. N126 trialled with COW recoilless gun
2,030	3,600	104	85			340		n/a
2,740	4,545	110	90		c 3 hr	420		n/a
4,040	5,790	113	91		4 hrs 45 min	Lion:		Military version: provision for one .303in Lewis gun
4,020	5,650	100	84			up to 925 (long range tanks)		
4,530	6,500	98	85			c 450		Provision for two .303 in Lewis machine guns
4,020	5,650	100	86			c 450		Provision for two .303 in Lewis machine guns
c 2,000	c 3,000	78			6 hr			n/a
c 1,600	c 2,400	70			6 hr			n/a
1,850	2,803	70 (prototype) 85		c 250	6 hr			One .303 in Lewis gun; 150 lb bomb load

2. British Flying-Boat Serial Numbers and Registrations

This Appendix lists generally the first identity of each type or production run, though a few aircraft never received identities particularly during the early days. A few civil types also received military serials and these are also set out. Where parts of batches were built and the balance cancelled these are noted.

A D Flying Boat	1412–1413, N1290 (possibly), N1520–N1529, N1710–N1719, N2450–2455
Beardmore WB.IX	G-EAQI (not completed)
Beardmore BeRo 2 Inverness	N183, N184
Blackburn N.1B	N56, (not built) N57, N58
Blackburn Pellet	G-EBHF
Blackburn Iris	N185 (Iris I, later II, later IV), N238, S1263, S1264, S1593 (Iris III), S1263, S1264, S1593 (Iris V)
Blackburn Sydney	N241
Blackburn Perth	K3580, K3581, K3582, K4011
Blackburn B-20	V8914
English Electric P.5 Kingston	N168 (Kingston I), N9709– N9712 (of which N9712 converted from Kingston I to Kingston II), N9713 (Kingston III)
English Electric M.3 Ayr	N148, (not built) N149
Fairey N.4 Class	N118 (not completed), N119 (Atalanta), N129 (Titania)
Felixstowe F.1	3580
Felixstowe F.2	8650
Felixstowe F.2A	N1160–N1174 (delivered as H.16s N4060–N4074), N1890–N1949 (cancelled), N1950–N1959 (cancelled), N2530–N2554 (renumbered N4510–N4554), N4080–N4099, N4280–N4309, N4430–N4479 (some delivered as F.5s), N4480–N4504 (21 built), N4510–N4519, N4520–N4529 (cancelled), N4530–N4554, N4555–N4559 (cancelled), N4560–N4579 (13 built), N4890–N4999 (60 built)
Felixstowe F.2C	N64, N65
Felixstowe F.3	N64, N4000–N4049 (some delivered as F.5s), N4100–N4159, N4160–N4179, N4180–N4229 (some delivered as F.5s), N4230–N4279, N4310–N4321, N4360–N4373, N4378, N4379, N4386–N4388, N4400–N4429
Felixstowe F.5	N90, N4000–N4049 (some originally ordered as F.3s), N4080–N4099 (some originally ordered as F.2As), N4180–N4229 (some originally ordered as F.3s), N4430–N4479 (some originally ordered as F.2As), N4480–N4504 (some originally ordered as F.2As), N4580–N4589 (but no evidence of delivery), N4630–N4679 (of which N4630, N4632, N4634, N4635, N4636, N4637, N4639 confirmed built), N4830–N4879 (of which N4830–N4839 built)
Felixstowe Fury	N123
Handley Page Type T/400	N62, N63 (both cancelled)
Norman Thompson NT.4 and NT.4A	8338–8343, 9061–9064 (NT.4), N2140–N2159 (NT.4A, of which 16 completed), N2740–N2759 (cancelled)
Norman Thompson NT.2A Tractor Biplane	N26

Norman Thompson NT.2B	N1180–N1189, N2260–N2359 (35 completed), N2400–N2429, N2500–N2523 (15 completed), N2555–N2579, N2760–N2789 (25 completed), N3300–N3374 (15 completed)
Norman Thompson NT.5	N1040–N1059, 3201, 3206, 9607, 9608
Norman Thompson Cruiser	N18, N19 (both cancelled)
Norman Thompson N.1B	N37
Norman Thompson N.2C	N82, (not built) N83
Parnall P.1 Prawn	S1576
Phoenix P.5 Cork	N86, N87
Porte Baby	9800–9820 (9800–9810 completed, balance hulls only)
Royal Aircraft Factory CE.1	N97, N98
Saunders Kittiwake	G-EAUD
Saunders A.3 Valkyrie	N186
Saunders A.4 Medina	G-EBMG/N214
Saunders A.14	N251
Saunders A.7 Severn	N240, (not built) N245
Saunders-Roe A.17 Cutty Sark	G-AAIP, VH-UNV, L3, G-AAVX, G-ABBC, S1575, VR-HAY, L5/G-AETI, G-ABVF, G-ACDP, G-ACDR, G-ADAF
Saunders-Roe A.19 Cloud	G-ABCJ, G-ABHG, G-ABXW, G-ACGO, K2681
Saunders-Roe A.29 Cloud	K2894–K2898, K3722–K3729, K4300–K4302
Saunders-Roe A.21 Windhover	ZK-ABW/VH-UPB, G-ABJP
Saunders-Roe A.27 London	K3560, K5257–K5263, K5908–K5913, K6927–K6932, K9682–K9686, L7038–L7043
Saunders-Roe A.33	K4773
Saunders-Roe S.36 Lerwick	L7248–L7268
Saunders-Roe A.37	G-AFZS/TK580
Saunders-Roe SR.A/1	TG263, TG267, TG271
Saunders-Roe SR.45 Princess	G-ALUN, G-ALUO, G-ALUP
Short N.3 Cromarty	N120, (not built) N121, N122
Short S.1 Cockle	G-EBKA/N193
Short S.2	N177
Short S.5 Singapore I	N179/G-EBUP
Short S.8 Calcutta	G-EBVG, G-EBVH, G-AADN, G-AASJ, F-AJDB, unmarked example (S.762) for French Navy, G-AATZ
Short S.8/8 Rangoon	S1433 (later G-AEIM), S1434, S1435, K2134, K2809, K3678, four further examples manufactured by Breguet under licence
Short S.12 Singapore II	N246
Short S.14 Sarafand	S1589
Short S.15	M-2

Short S.17 Kent	G-ABFA, G-ABFB, G-ABFC
Short S.18 Knuckleduster	K3574
Short S.19 Singapore III	K3592–K3595, K4577–K4585, K6907–K6922, K8565–K8568, K8856–K8859
Short S.23 Empire	See Appendix 4
Short S.30 Empire	See Appendix 4
Short S.33 Empire	See Appendix 4
Short S.20 Maia	See Appendix 4
Short S.25 Sunderland	See Appendix 6
Short S.26	See Appendix 4
Short S.45 Seaford	See Appendix 6
Short S.35 Shetland	DX166, DX171 (later S.40 G-AGVD)
Short S.25 Hythe Class	See Appendix 7
Short S.25 Sandringham	See Appendix 7
Short S.45 Solent	See Appendix 7
Short SA.6 Sealand	G-AIVX, G-AKLM–G-AKLP, G-AKLR–G-AKMA, Indian Navy INS-103–INS-110 (INS-101 ex-G-AKLZ, INS-102 ex-G-AKMA)
Sopwith Bat Boat Type 1	38, 118
Sopwith Bat Boat Type 2	127, 879, plus 44 for German Naval Air Arm
Supermarine N.1B	N59, N60, (not built) N61
Supermarine Channel I and II	G-EAED–G-EAEM; F-38, F-40, F-42, F-44 to Norwegian Navy; three to Japanese Navy; 46 to Royal Swedish Navy; G-NZAI to New Zealand; G-EAWC to Venezuela; G-EAWP to Chile as 8; another to Venezuela
Supermarine Sea King I	One example, no identity
Supermarine Sea King II	One example, no identity. To Sea Lion II
Supermarine Sea Lion I	G-EALP
Supermarine Sea Lion II	G-EBAH/N170
Supermarine Sea Lion III	G-EBAH/N170
Supermarine Commercial Amphibian	G-EAVE
Supermarine Sea Eagle	G-EBFK, G-EBGR, G-EBGS
Supermarine Scylla	N174
Supermarine Seal I	Name believed to have been allocated to the Commercial Amphibian.
Supermarine Seal II	N146; re-named Seagull I. One to Japanese Navy
Supermarine Seagull I, II and III	N146 converted from Seal II; N158–N159; N9562–N9566; N9603–N9607; N9642–N9654. Seagull III to RAAF: six supplied though seven serials allocated: A9–1, A9–2, A9–4, A9–6, A9–7, A9–8, A9–9. One Mk II to Japanese Navy

Supermarine Scarab	M-NSAA–M-NSAL
Supermarine Sheldrake	N180
Supermarine Swan	N175/G-EBJY
Supermarine Southampton	N9896–N9901; S1036–S1045; S1058–S1059; S1121–S1128; S1149– S1152; S1158– S1162; S1228–S1236; S1248–S1249; S1298–S1302; S1419–S1423; S1464; S1643– S1647; K2888(ex N253)–K2889; K2964–K2965; N218, N251, N252, N253 (experimental); J-BAID *Kirin* to Japan; A11-1 and A11-2 to RAAF (probably ex RAF Mk Is); HB-1–HB-8 to Argentina though five known to have carried 1-E-61–1-E-64 and E-151, while three others wore P-156, P-157 and P-158; N3–N8 to Turkey; S1235 to G-AAFH (incorrect allocation), then G-AASH; S1648 ordered as Improved Southampton, built as Southampton IV but re-named Scapa
Supermarine Seamew	N212, N213
Supermarine Nanok/Solent	99/G-AAAB
Supermarine Air Yacht	G-AASE
Supermarine Seagull V	See Appendix 5
Supermarine Scapa	S1648 ex-Southampton IV; K4192–4200; K7304–K7306
Supermarine Stranraer	K3973; K7287–K7303; Canadian-built for RCAF: 907–916; 918–923; 927–938; 946–957
Supermarine Walrus	See Appendix 5
Supermarine Sea Otter	K8854–K8855; JM738–JM773; JM796–JM837; JM861–JM885; JM905–JM922; JM943– JM989; JN104–JN142; JN179–JN205; JN242–JN257; RD869–RD922. Of these, main exports were eight, serialled 801–807 plus one unserialled, to Royal Danish Air Force; eight, serialled 18–1–18–8, to Dutch Naval Air Arm; six, serialled N–82–N–87, to French Customs Administration, Indo-China; two, registered VH-AJN and VH-AJO, to QANTAS
Supermarine Seagull ASR.1	PA143, PA147, (not built) PA152
Vickers-Saunders Valentia BS.1	N124– N126
Vickers Viking I	G-EAOV
Vickers Viking II	G-EASC
Vickers Viking III	G-EAUK
Vickers Viking IV	F-ADBL; V201-V210 to Royal Netherlands Indies Air Arm; two to Japanese Navy; one to United States Government; G-EBBZ, G-EBED; one to Russian Trade Delegation; one to Lawrentide Air Services, Canada; two for River Plate Aviation Company; R3-R6 to Argentine Navy; G-CYES, G-CYET to Royal Canadian Air Force; six built under licence in Canada by Canadian Vickers Ltd as G-CYEU–G-CYEZ
Vickers Viking V	N156, N157
Vickers Viking VI - Vulture	G-EBGO (Vulture I), G-EBHO (Vulture II, later Vulture I)
Vickers Viking VII - Vanellus	N169
White and Thompson No 1	883
White and Thompson No 2	882
White and Thompson No 3	1195–1200, 3807–3808
Wight Triplane	N14
Wight Biplane (also suggested Nieuport As14 seaplane)	N15

3. Experimental RNAS/RAF N Serials

Commencing with No 1, the RNAS allotted numbers in their 'N' serial series to all landplanes, seaplanes and flying-boats ordered on experimental contracts. The first recipient was Porte Victoria PV.2 seaplane N1, which was tested over the summer of 1916. The RAF maintained the system until 1928. Set out below are the flying-boat types allotted such serials.

Serial	Type
N14	Wight Triplane
N15	Wight Biplane (also suggested Nieuport As14 seaplane)
N18, N19	Norman Thompson Cruiser (cancelled)
N26	Norman Thompson Tractor Biplane
N37	Norman Thompson Tandem Seater Fighter
N56, N57, N58	Blackburn N.1B
N59, N60, N61	Supermarine N.1B
N62, N63	Handley Page Type T/400 Biplane (cancelled)
N64, N65	Felixstowe F.2C
N82, N83	Norman Thompson N.2C (cancelled)
N86, N87	Phoenix P.5 Cork
N88, N89	Fairey F.2A (cancelled)
N90	Felixstowe F.5
N97, N98	Royal Aircraft factory CE.1
N107, N108, N109	Norman Thompson School Biplane (cancelled)
N118	Fairey Atalanta I (Gosport-built)
N119	Fairey Atalanta I (hull May, Harden and May-built)
N120, N121, N122	Short Cromarty (N121, N122 cancelled)
N123	Felixstowe Fury
N124, N125, N126	Vickers-Saunders Valentia BS.1
N127	Felixstowe F.5 (cancelled)
N128	Felixstowe F.5L
N129	Fairey Titania
N130	Felixstowe Fury (construction abandoned following crash of N123)
N131, N132	Vickers Vigilant (cancelled)
N146	Supermarine Seal II/Seagull I
N147	Vickers Viking III
N148, N149	English Electric M.3 Ayr (N149 not completed)
N156, N157	Vickers Viking V
N158, N159	Supermarine Seagull II
N168	English Electric P.5 Kingston I
N169	Vickers Viking VII - Vanellus
N170	Supermarine Sea Lion II
N174	Supermarine Scylla
N175	Supermarine Swan
N177	Short S.2
N178	Felixstowe F.5 (Saunders hollow-bottomed hull)
N179	Short Singapore I
N180	Supermarine Sheldrake
N183, N184	Beardmore BeRo.2 Inverness
N185	Blackburn Iris
N186	Saunders A.3 Valkyrie
N193	Short S.1 Cockle
N197	Saunders A.4 Medina (serial not taken up)
N212, N213	Supermarine Seamew
N214, N215	Short S.8 Calcutta (serials not taken up)
N214	Saunders A.4 Medina (presumed testing allocation)
N218	Supermarine Southampton I
N238	Blackburn Iris III
N240	Saunders A.7 Severn
N241	Blackburn Sydney
N243, N244, N245	Supermarine Southampton II (renumbered S1298-S1300 before delivery)
N251	Saunders A.14
N252	Supermarine Southampton X
N253	Supermarine Southampton

4. Short Empire Boats, S.21 and S.26 G Class: Registrations, Names and Serials

S.23

Registration	Name
G-ADHL	Canopus
G-ADHM	Caledonia
G-ADUT	Centaurus (to RAAF as A18-10, 9.39)
G-ADUU	Cavalier
G-ADUV	Cambria
G-ADUW	Castor
G-ADUX	Cassiopeia
G-ADUY	Capella
G-ADUZ	Cygnus
G-ADVA	Capricornus
G-ADVB	Corsair
G-ADVC	Courtier
G-ADVD	Challenger
G-ADVE	Centurion
G-AETV	Coriolanus (to QANTAS as VH-ABG, 9.42)
G-AETW	Calpurnia
G-AETX	Ceres
G-AETY	Clio (to AX659, 7.40)
G-AETZ	Circe
G-AEUA	Calypso (to RAAF as A18-11, 9.39, to QANTAS, 4.42)
G-AEUB	Camilla (to QANTAS as VH-ADU, 7.42)
G-AEUC	Corinna (to QANTAS)
G-AEUD	Cordelia (to AX660, 7.40)
G-AEUE	Cameronian (initially named Cairngorm)
G-AEUF	Corinthian (initially named Cotswold)
G-AEUG	Coogee (initially named Cheviot. To QANTAS as VH-ABC, 7.38, to RAAF as A18-12, 6.40)
G-AEUH	Corio (initially named Coolin. To QANTAS as VH-ABD, 2.38)
G-AEUI	Coorong (Initially named Calpe. To QANTAS as VH-ABE, 3.38, to BOAC as G-AEUI, 11.40)
G-AFBJ	Carpentaria (to QANTAS as VH-ABA, 6.38, to BOAC as G-AFBJ, 6.42)
G-AFBK	Coolangatta (to QANTAS as VH-ABB, 3.38, to RAAF as A18-13, to VH-CRB, 7.43)
G-AFBL	Cooee (to VH-ABF, 3.38, to BOAC, 6.42)

S.33

Registration	Name
G-AFPZ	Clifton (to RAAF as A18-14, 3.42, to QANTAS as VH-ACD, 7.43)
G-AFRA	Cleopatra
G-AFRB	Unnamed (not completed)

S.26

Registration	Name
G-AFCI	Golden Hind (to X8275, 7.40, to BOAC, 12.41)
G-AFCJ	Golden Fleece (to X8274)
G-AFCK	Golden Horn (to X8273, 7.40, to BOAC, 12.41)

S.21

Registration	Name
G-ADHK	Maia

S.30

Registration	Name
G-AFCT	Champion
G-AFCU	Cabot (to V3137, 10.39)
G-AFCV	Caribou (to V3138, 10.39)
G-AFCW	Connemara
G-AFCX	Clyde
G-AFCY	Ordered for QANTAS as Captain Cook: launched as ZK-AMA Aotearoa for TEAL: became G-AFCY Awarua, 4.39
G-AFCZ	Ordered for QANTAS as Canterbury: launched as ZK-AMB Australia for TEAL: rebuilt as G-AFCZ Clare
G-AFDA	Ordered for QANTAS as Cumberland: launched as ZK-AMA Awarua: briefly reverted to G-AFDA: to ZK-AMC: to ZK-AMA Aotearoa

5. Supermarine Seagull V and Walrus: Production and Service

Seagull V Production
A2-1 – A2-24 to Specification 6/34 for RAAF. A2-4 became VH-ALB and is now with the RAF Museum.

Walrus Production
Prototype N-1, later N-2, later K4797.
Mk I:
K5772–K5783 (12) contract 391700/35/C.4(c), K8338–K8345 (8) contract 472708/35 and K8537–K8564 (28) contract 472708/35, all to Specification 2/35.
L2169–L2336 (168) contract 534432/36 to Specification 37/36.
L2301 to L2303 (3) to Eire as N-18–N-20. L2222, L2236 and L2285 to New Zealand as NZ151–NZ153. L2301 joined Aer Lingus as EI-ACC and later became G-AIZG; renovated and displayed at the Fleet Air Arm Museum. L2263–L2267 (5) to Portugal as 97–101.
N-9–N-14 (6) to Turkey between 2.38 and 4.38 (though N-14 thought not to have been delivered).
N-15 and N-16 to Argentina as M-0-9 and M-0-10, delivered 1.39.
P5646–P5670 and P5696–P5720 (50) to Specification I/P3, contract B.974377/39.
R6543–R6557 (15) to contract B.21120/39 (11 only built).
Total Supermarine build: 285.

R6582–R6591 (10) to contract B.43393/39 (Saro).
W2670–W2689, W2700–W2729, W2731–W2760, W2766–W2798, W3005–W3051 and W3062–W3101 (200) to contract B.43393/39 (Saro). W2700, W2707, W2724, W2740 and W3021 to RNZAF as NZ157, NZ154, NZ155, NZ159 and NZ160 respectively.
W3089 to Royal Canadian Navy.
X1045 and X1046 prototype Mk II aircraft – wooden hulls (Saro).
X9460–X9484, X9498–X9532, X9554–X9593 (100) Mk I to X9558, balance Mk II, to contract B.43393/39 (Saro). X9512 and X9567 to RNZAF as NZ158 and NZ156 respectively. X9499, X9518, X9525, X9554, X9557, X9558 and X9560 (7) cancelled.
Z1755–Z1784, Z1804–Z1823 (50) all Mk II to contract B.119490/40 (Saro). Z1768, Z1771, Z1775, Z1781 and Z1814 to Royal Canadian Navy.
HD804–HD837, HD851–HD878, HD899–HD936 (100), 70 as Mk I (Saro). HD878, HD902–HD908, HD910, HD912, HD914–HD915, HD917–HD918, HD920–HD923 and HD925–HD936 as Mk II to contract B.119490/40 (Saro). HD909 to Royal Canadian Navy.
N-33 to N-40, later variously coded M-0-1, 2-0-24, M-0-4, 1-0-2, 2-0-1, 2-0-2 to 2-0-10, 2-0-29 and 2-0-30 (8) to Argentina 1947 (five possibly ex X9564, X9571, X9573, Z1758 and HD823).
Total Saunders-Roe build: 461 including 191 Mk IIs.

Royal Navy Walrus: Principal Squadrons/Flights, Dates and Bases
700: Hatston, Twatt, Algiers, Levant; 701: 1940–43, shore-based; 702: 1935–40, HMS *Nelson*; 710: 1939–43 Lee-on-Solent, HMS *Albatross*, South Atlantic and Indian Ocean; 711: 1936–40, Mediterranean Fleet cruisers; 712: 1938–40, Home Fleet cruisers; 714: 1938–40, East Indies Fleet cruisers; 715: 1937–40, China Station; 716: 1939, Lee-on-Solent/Simonstown, Catapult Flight; 718: 1936–40, America and West Indies cruisers; 720: 1937–40, New Zealand Division; 722: 1944, Tambaram/Juhu, FRU; 728: 1945–46, Italy (various), FRU; 730: 1944, Abbotsinch, communications; 733, 1946, China Bay, ASR; 737: 1943, ABR training, Dunino; 740: 1943, Arbroath, Observer training; 742: 1944, Far East links, communications; 743: 1943–45, TAG training, Yarmouth NS; 747: 1943–44, Inskip/Fearn, Naval OTU; 749: 1941–45, Observer training, Piarco; 751: 1939–44, Scotland (various), Observer training; 754: 1940–44, training, Lee-on-Solent and Arbroath; 757: 1943–45 Puttalam, Naval OTU; 763: 1942–44, *Pegasus*, Seaplane training; 764: 1940–43, training, Lee-on-Solent and Lawrenny Ferry; 765: 1940–43, training, Lee-on-Solent and Sandbanks; 771: 1939–40, UK (various), FRU; 772: 1942–44, Machrihanish, ASR; 773: 1940–44, FRU Bermuda; 777: 1941–44, FRU Freetown; 778: 1939–43, UK (various), service trials; 779: 1941–45, Gibraltar and Taranto; 781: 1940–42, Lee-on-Solent, communications; 783: 1942–44, Arbroath, ASV training; 787: 1942, Duxford, communications; 788: 1942–45, East Africa (various), FRU; 789: 1942–45, FRU Cape Town; 796: 1943–44, Tanga, OTU; 810: 1939–40, *Ark Royal*; 820: 1940, *Ark Royal*, Norway; 836: 1943, Maydown, communications; 1700: 1945, ASR East Indies; 1701: 1945, ASR Manus and Hong Kong.

Ships operating the Walrus included
HMS/HMNZS *Achilles*, HMS *Ajax*, HMAS/HMS *Albatross*, HMS *Anson*, HMS *Ark Royal (1) (Pegasus)*, HMAS *Australia* (Seagull V and Walrus), HMS *Barham* (Seagull V and Walrus), HMS *Belfast*, HMS *Bermuda*, HMS *Berwick*, HMS *Birmingham*, HMAS *Canberra* (Seagull V and Walrus), HMS *Ceylon*, HMS *Cornwall*, HMS *Cumberland*, HMS *Devonshire*, HMS *Dorsetshire*, HMS *Duke of York*, HMS *Edinburgh*, HMS *Effingham*,

HMS *Exeter*, HMS *Fencer*, HMS *Fiji*, HMS *Gambia*, HMS *Glasgow*, HMS *Glory*, HMS *Gloucester*, HMAS *Hobart*, HMS *Howe*, HMS *Jamaica*, HMS *Kent*, HMS *Kenya*, HMS *King George V*, HMNZS *Leander*, HMS *Liverpool*, HMS *London*, HMS *Malaya*, HMS *Manchester*, HMS *Mauritius*, HMS *Nelson*, HMS *Neptune*, HMS *Newcastle*, HMS *Newfoundland*, HMS *Nigeria*, HMS *Norfolk*, HMS *Pegasus (2)*, HMAS *Perth*, HMS *Prince of Wales*, HMS *Queen Elizabeth*, HMS *Ramillies*, HMS *Renown* (Seagull V and Walrus), HMS *Rodney*, HMS *Sheffield*, HMS *Shropshire*, HMS *Southampton*, HMS *Suffolk*, HMS *Sussex*, HMAS *Sydney* (Seagull V and Walrus), HMS *Terror*, HMS *Trinidad*, HMS *Uganda*, HMS *Valiant* (Seagull V and Walrus), HMS *Venerable*, HMS *Victorious*, HMS *Warspite*, HMAS *Westralia*, HMS *York*.

RAF Walrus: Principal Squadrons, Detachments and Bases
Home ASR: 269 (Davidstowe Moor, Lagens); 275 (Valley, Warmwell, Bolt Head, Exeter); 276 (Harrowbeer and detachments); 277 (Stapleford Tawney, Gravesend, Shoreham); 278 (Matlask, Coltishall, Bradwell Bay and detachments); 281 (Ouston, Ballykelly, Woolsington, Drem); 282 (Castletown, Davidstowe Moor, St Eval).

Overseas ASR: 89 (Singapore); 283 (Algiers and detachments, ASR and anti-submarine patrols); 284 (Southern France, Malta, Sardinia, Southern Italy, Corsica); 292 (India: Jessore, Agartala); 293 (Italy: North African patrols); 294 (Berka and detachments, ASR and anti-submarine patrols); 624 (Italy, ASR and mine-spotting); 1350 Flight (Ceylon).

6. Short S.25 Sunderland: Production, RAF Service and Service with Other Nations

Prototype (1): K4774, built at Rochester

Sunderland l (89): L2158–L2168, L5798–L5807, N6133, N6135, N6138, N9020–N9030, N9044–N9050, P9600–P9606, P9620–P9624, T9040–T9050, T9070–T9078 built at Rochester, T9083–T9090, T9109–T9115 built at Dumbarton

Sunderland ll (1 prototype + 43): T9083 (prototype converted from Mk l), W3976–W3998 Rochester, W6000–W6004 Dumbarton, W6050–W6064 Belfast

Sunderland lll (1 prototype + 462): T9042 (prototype converted from Mk l), W3999–W4004, W4017–W4037 Rochester, W6005–W6016, W6026–W6033 Dumbarton, W6065–W6068, W6075–W6080 Belfast, DD828–DD867 Dumbarton, DP176–DP200 Windermere, DV956–DV980 Rochester, DV985–DV994, DW104–DW113 Belfast, EJ131–EJ145 Rochester, EJ149–EJ158 Windermere, EJ163–EJ172 Belfast, EK572–EK596 Dumbarton, JM659–JM689, JM704–JM722, ML725–ML774, ML777–ML795 Rochester, ML807–ML831 Belfast, ML835–ML884, NJ170–NJ194 Dumbarton, NJ253–NJ258 Belfast, PP135–PP144 Dumbarton

Sunderland IV (Seaford GR1) (10): MZ269, MZ271 (prototypes), NJ200–NJ207 Rochester (NJ208–NJ219 not built though jigs used for Solent production; NJ220–NJ239, 160 more all cancelled)

Sunderland V (2 prototypes + 154): ML765, ML839 (prototypes converted from Mk lll), ML796–ML801 Rochester, NJ259–NJ277 Belfast, PP103–PP132 Rochester, PP145–PP164 Dumbarton, RN264–RN273 Rochester, RN277–RN306 Dumbarton, SZ559–SZ584, SZ598–SZ599 Belfast, TX293 Rochester, VB880–VB889 Dumbarton

Sunderland lll converted to V (88): Examples DP198, EJ155, JM717, ML780, ML816, ML866, NJ182, PP414. Cancelled (93): AX936–AX950, AX973–AX997, NE836–NE855, TW774–TW803, TX294–TX296

RAF Squadron Service

Sqn	Mark(s)	Location(s)	Dates of Service
88	GR.5	Kai Tak, Seletar	09.46–10.54
95	I, III	Pembroke Dock, Freetown, Jui, Bathurst	01.41–06.45
119	II, III	Pembroke Dock	09.42–04.43
201	I, II, III, V, GR.5	Invergordon, Sullom Voe, Castle Archdale, Pembroke Dock, Calshot	04.40–02.57
202	I, II, III	Gibraltar	12.41–09.42
204	I, II, III, V	Mount Batten, Sullom Voe, Reykjavik, Gibraltar, Bathurst, Half Die, Jui	06.39–06.45
209	V, GR.5	Kipevu, Koggala, Kai Tak, Seletar, Iwakuni	02.45–12.54
210	I	Pembroke Dock, Tayport, Invergordon, Sullom Voe, Oban	06.38–04.41
228	I, II, III, V, GR.5	Pembroke Dock, Alexandria, Kalafrana, Aboukir, Half Die, Stranraer, Oban, Castle Archdale	11.38–06.45
230	I, II, III, V, GR.5	Seletar, Penang, Trincomalee, Colombo, Koggala, Alexandria, Scaramanga, Aboukir, Kasfareet, Dar es Salaam, Akyab, Rangoon, Redhills Lake, Castle Archdale, Calshot, Pembroke Dock	06.38–02.57

Sqn	Mark(s)	Location(s)	Dates of Service
240	V	Redhills Lake, Koggala	07.45–03.46
246	I, II	Bowmore	10.42–04.43
259	V	Dar es Salaam	03.45–04.45
270	III	Apapa	12.43–06.45
330	III, V	Oban, Sullom Voe, Stavanger	02.43–11.45
422 (RCAF)	III	Oban, Bowmore, Castle Archdale Pembroke Dock	11.42–06.45
423 (RCAF)	II, III	Oban, Lough Erne, Castle Archdale, Pembroke Dock	07.42–09.44
10 (RAAF)	I, II, III, V	Pembroke Dock, Mount Batten, Oban	09.39–06.45
461 (RAAF)	II, III	Mount Batten, Hamworthy, Pembroke Dock, Sullom Voe	04.42–06.45

Other RAF Units: 4 (Coastal) Operational Training Unit; 10 Operational Training Unit; Far East Flying-Boat Wing (Seletar 2.50, controlling and supporting 88, 205 and 209 Squadrons); Air-Sea Warfare Development Unit; 131 Operational Training Unit; Coastal Command Flying Instructors' School, Turnberry; 302 Ferry Training Unit (9.42 Lough Erne, later Stranraer, Oban, Killadeas, Alness); 308 Ferry Training Unit (3.43 Pembroke Dock, absorbed into 302 FTU Oban 1.44); MAEE; Coastal Command Development Unit (11.40 Carew Cheriton, to ASWDU 1.45).

Royal Australian Air Force (ex-RAF serials and RAAF serials shown): A26-1 ex-ML730, A26-2 ex-ML731, A26-3 ex-ML732, A26-4 ex-ML733, A26-5 ex-ML734, A26-6 ex-DP192.

Royal New Zealand Air Force (ex-RAF serials and RNZAF serials shown): Mk lll ML792–ML795 as NZ4101–NZ4104, 12.44; Mk 5 PP110, RN280, VB883, ML814, DP191, PP129, VB880, VB881, PP124, SZ561, SZ584, EJ167, RN286, RN306, PP143 and RN291 as NZ4105–NZ4120, 1952

South African Air Force (ex-RAF and SAAF serials shown): Mk V NJ262, PP125, PP109, RN279, RN296, RN305, NJ258, NJ263, ML798, RN281, NJ266, PP156, NJ259, RN295, PP104 as 1701–1715, 1945, plus PP153 not allocated new serial

French Aeronavale (ex-RAF serials shown): 343 (Free French) Squadron Mk lll aircraft, to French ownership 11.45 including DP187, EJ135, EJ163, EJ168, EK587, JM689, ML835, ML841, ML851, ML854, ML871 and ML874. Later Mk llls and 5s transferred: ML750 and NJ172, 1947; ML757, ML764, ML778, ML779, ML781, ML796, ML799, ML816, ML819, ML820, ML821, ML824, ML866, ML872 and NJ170, 1951; ML739, ML877, NJ182 and NJ190, 1952; ML800, RN284, SZ571, SZ576 ,1957

Portugal: P9623 acquired by Portuguese Navy following forced landing off Portugal 14.02.41 and allocated 136. Used on transport duties to the Azores.

7. Short S.25 and S.45 Civil Flying-Boats: S.25 Sunderland 3 Civilian Conversion and Hythe Class, S.25 Sunderland 3 Civilian Conversion, S.25 Sunderland 5, S.25 Sandringham, S.45 Seaford and S.45 Solent

S.25 Sunderland 3 Civilian Conversion

Origin	Civil Identity	Initial Operator and Name	Remarks
EJ156	G-AGWW	CAUSA as CX-AFA	
ML876	G-AGWX	CAUSA as CX-AKF	
ML731/RAAF A26-2	VH-BKQ	Trans-Oceanic Airways 10.50 as *Pacific Star*	Scrapped .51
ML733/RAAF A26-4	VH-AKO	Trans-Oceanic Airways as *Australis*	Later *Australia Star*, then *Samoa Star*. Scrapped .52
ML734/RAAF A26-5	VH-AKP	Trans-Oceanic Airways as *Antilles*	Later *Tahiti Star*. Chartered by Barrier Reef Airways. To Ansett 22.5.53
ML792/RNZAF NZ4101	ZK-AMF	NZ National Airways	ex-RNZAF Flying-Boat Transport Flt. Wdn 6.50
ML793/RNZAF NZ4102	ZK-AMG	Mataatua NZ National Airways	ex-RNZAF Flying-Boat Transport Flt. Wdn 6.50
ML794/RNZAF NZ4103	ZK-AMJ	NZ National Airways	ex-RNZAF Flying-Boat Transport Flt. Wdn 6.50
ML795/RNZAF NZ4104	ZK-AMK	Takitimu NZ National Airways	ex-RNZAF Flying-Boat Transport Flt. Wdn 6.50
ML814/RNZAF NZ4108	VH-BRF	To Ansett Flying-Boat Services 10.64 as 'near-Sandringham' *Islander*	To Antilles Air Boats Virgin Is 9.74 as N158J *Excalibur VIII*, stored San Juan, to Edward Hulton .79 and to G-BJHS *Islander*, also *Juliet*, also *Sir Arthur Gouge*. To Chatham .84 (restoration). Briefly associated with Ryan Air. To N814ML 16.1.93. Currently based Fantasy of Flight, Florida. Sole flying S.25

S.25 Sunderland 3 Hythe Class

JM660/OQZR	G-AGER	BOAC *Hadfield*	To Aquila Airways 12.48, wfu 7.56
JM661/OQZS	G-AGES	BOAC *Unnamed**	Crashed 7.43
JM662/OQZT	G-AGET	BOAC *Unnamed**	Dbr 2.43
JM663/OQZU	G-AGEU	BOAC *Hampshire*	To Aquila Airways 7.48, wfu 3.53
JM664/OQZV	G-AGEV	BOAC *Hailsham*	
JM665/OQZW	G-AGEW	BOAC *Hanwell*	
JM772/OQZB	G-AGHV	BOAC *Hamble*	Sank Rod-el-Faraq 10.3.46
ML725/OQZC	GAGHW	BOAC *Hamilton*	Crashed Isle of Wight 19.11.47
ML726/OQZX	G-AGHX	BOAC *Harlequin*	
ML727/OQZZ	G-AGHZ	BOAC *Hawkesbury*	To Aquila Airways 1.49, wfu 1.49
ML728/OQZA	G-AGIA	BOAC *Haslemere*	To Aquila Airways 7.48, wfu 2.51
ML729	G-AGIB	BOAC *Unnamed**	Crashed Sollum 5/6.11.43
ML751/OQZJ	G-AGJJ	BOAC *Henley*	To Aquila Airways 2.49, wfu 1.51
ML752/OQZK	G-AGJK	BOAC *Howard*	To Aquila Airways 2.49, wfu 1.52
ML753/OQZL	G-AGJL	BOAC *Hobart*	To Aquila Airways 2.49, wfu 1.52
ML754/OQZM	G-AGJM	BOAC *Hythe*	To Aquila Airways 2.49, wfu 1.52
ML755/OQZN	G-AGJN	BOAC *Hudson*	To Aquila Airways 2.49, w/o Funchal Bay 21.1.53
ML756/OQZO	G-AGJO	BOAC *Honduras*	Dbr Hythe 21.2.49

Origin	Civil Identity	Initial Operator and Name	Remarks
ML786/OQZD	G-AGKV	BOAC Huntingdon	Withdrawn 5.51
ML787/OQZE	G-AGKW	BOAC Hotspur	To Sandringham I Himalaya. To Aquila 5.49 - 3.53
ML788/OQZF	G-AGKX	BOAC Unnamed	To Aquila Airways 1.49, dbr Calshot 28.1.53
ML789/OQZG	G-AGKY	BOAC Hungerford	
ML790/OQZH	G-AGKZ	BOAC Harwich	
ML791/OQZI	G-AGLA	BOAC Hunter	To Aquila Airways 1.49, wfu 8.49
JM716	G-AHEO	BOAC Halstead	To Aquila Airways 7.48, wfu 11.49
DD860	G-AHEP	BOAC Hanbury	
PP142	G-AHER	BOAC Helmsdale	Cargo carrier. To Aquila Airways 10.49, wfu 1.52
S.25 Sunderland 5			
SZ584	G-AHJR	BOAC	Loaned from RAF. Later NZ4115
PP162	G-ANAK	Aquila Airways	Destroyed in gale, Hamble, prior to conversion, 27.11.54
DP195	CX-AKR	CAUSA Capitan Bosio Lanza	
EK579	LV-AHG	Aerolineas Argentinas Uruguay	
EJ171	LV-AHH	Aerolineas Argentinas Rio de la Plata	
S.25 Sandringham 1			
ML788/OQZF	G-AGKX	BOAC Himalaya	To Aquila Airways 5.49, wfu 3.53
S.25 Sandringham 2			
DV964	G-AGPZ	CAA/Dodero as LV-AAO Argentina	Later to Aerolineas Argentinas
DD834	G-AGPT	CAA/Dodero as LV-AAP Uruguay	
ML843	G-AHRE	CAA/Dodero as LV-ACT Paraguay	
S.25 Sandringham 3			
DD841	G-AGPY	CAA/Dodero as LV-AAR Brazil	
EJ170	G-AGTZ	CAA/Dodero as LV-AAQ Inglaterra	
S.25 Sandringham 4 Dominion, later Tasman Class			
ML761	ZK-AMB	TEAL Tasman	To QANTAS as VH-EBW Tasman 4.50. Sunk 10.6.51, Vila, New Hebrides
NJ255	ZK-AMD	TEAL Australia	To QANTAS as VH-EBX Pacific Chieftain 4.50, to Barrier Reef Airways 12.54 as VH-BRE, later to Ansett, dbr 3.7.63 in gale.
NJ179	ZK-AME	TEAL New Zealand	To Barrier Reef Airways 4.50 as VH-BRD Capricorn, later Princess of Cairns. Sank 10.9.52 and hull acquired for use as night club, Coolangatta, but sank under tow while relocating

Origin	Civil Identity	Initial Operator and Name	Remarks
JM715	ZK-AMH	TEAL *Auckland*	To Barrier Reef Airways 4.50 as VH-BRC *Coral Clipper*, later *Beachcomber*; to Ansett .53; to Antilles Air Boats 12.74 as N158C *Southern Cross*; to VP-LVE *Southern Cross*. Visits to Lough Derg, Poole .76; Calshot .77. Stored Puerto Rico and deteriorated, but restored to flying condition and to Eire .80 (Capt R. Gillies). UK .82. Stored Lee-on-Solent; to Southampton .83 for restoration to static standard; to Southampton Hall of Aviation 28.8.83 as Ansett VH-BRC *Beachcomber*

S.25 Sandringham 5 Plymouth Class

Origin	Civil Identity	Initial Operator and Name	Remarks
ML838	G-AHYY	BOAC *Portsmouth*	
ML784	G-AHYZ	BOAC *Perth*	Destroyed by fire 18.1.47 prior to delivery
ML783	G-AHZA	BOAC *Penzance*	Scrapped 3.59
NJ171	G-AHZB	BOAC *Portland*	Crashed Bahrain 23.8.47
NJ253	G-AHZC	BOAC *Pembroke*	
NJ257	G-AHZD	BOAC *Portmarnock*	To QANTAS 7.51 as VH-EBV *Pacific Warrior*. Wdn 8.55
ML818	G-AHZE	BOAC *Portsea*	
NJ188	G-AHZF	BOAC *Poole*	To QANTAS 12.51 as VH-EBY *Pacific Voyager*. Wdn 8.55
ML828	G-AHZG	BOAC *Pevensey*	To QANTAS 7.51 as VH-EBZ *Pacific Explorer*. Wdn 8.55
JM681	G-AJMZ	BOAC *Perth*	Replacement for G-AHYZ

All examples in use by BOAC leased from Ministry of Civil Aviation

S.25 Sandringham 6

Origin	Civil Identity	Initial Operator and Name	Remarks
ML809	LN-IAU	DNL *Bamse Brakar*	Crashed Harstad 15.5.50
ML807	LN-IAV	DNL *Kvitbjorn*	Crashed Tjeldsund 28.8.47
JM720	LN-IAW	DNL *Bukken Bruse*	Crashed Hommelvik 2.10.48
W4037	LN-LAI	DNL *Jutulen*	To SAS. Sunk Bangui 15.11.52
JM714	LN-LMK	DNL *Polarbjorn*	To IV-AHM *Almirante Zar* 6.55. Broken up Buenos Aires 1.67

Sandringham 7 Bermuda Class

Origin	Civil Identity	Initial Operator and Name	Remarks
JM719	G-AKCO	BOAC *St George*	Overhauled by Saro at Cowes for Capt Sir G. P. G. Taylor; to VH-APG *Frigate Bird III* 10.54; to Air Polynesie as F-OBIP 23.5.58; to Reseau Aérien Interinsulaire 13.4.63, unofficially named *Bermuda*. Wdn .70 and to Musee de l'Air 7.78
EJ172	G-AKCP	BOAC *St David*	To CAUSA as CX-ANI
ML840	G-AKCR	BOAC *St Andrew*	To CAUSA as CX-ANA

S.45 Seaford 1

Origin	Civil Identity	Initial Operator and Name	Remarks
NJ201/OZZA	G-AGWU	MoS	For BOAC evaluation 12.45 - 2.46 as G-AGWU; reverted to NJ201. To Solent 3 G-ANAJ 4.54 for Aquila ntu
NJ200	G-ALIJ	R L Whyham	

281

Origin	Civil Identity	Initial Operator and Name	Remarks
S.45 Solent 2			
c/n S.1300	G-AHIL	BOAC Salisbury (later City of Salisbury)	To Solent 3. .50
c/n S.1301	G-AHIM	BOAC Scarborough	To Felixstowe .53
c/n S.1302	G-AHIN	BOAC Southampton (later City of Southampton)	To Solent 3. .50. To Aquila .56. To Artop 10.58. scrapped .71
c/n S.1303	G-AHIO	BOAC Somerset	To Trans-Oceanic Airways 11.51 as VH-TOD Star of Australia, to South Pacific Airlines .56 as N9945F, to Howard Hughes .59, scrapped .74
c/n S.1304	G-AHIR	BOAC Sark	To Felixstowe .53
c/n S.1305	G-AHIS	BOAC Scapa	To Solent 3. .50
c/n S.1306	G-AHIT	BOAC Severn	
c/n S.1307	G-AHIU	BOAC Solway	
c/n S.1308	G-AHIV	BOAC Salcombe	To Trans-Oceanic Airways 7.51 as VH-TOC Star of Hobart. W/o 28.10.51
c/n S.1309	G-AHIW	BOAC Stornoway	To Solent 3. .49. Crashed Southampton Water 1.2.50
c/n S.1310	G-AHIX	BOAC Sussex (later City of Edinburgh)	To Solent 3. .50
c/n S.1311	G-AHIY	BOAC Southsea	Last new aircraft built at Rochester
S.45 Solent 3			
NJ202	G-AKNO	BOAC Seaforth (later City of London)	Intended to pass to Trans-Oceanic Airways as VH-TOA but w/o on delivery flight 28.1.51. Malta
NJ203	G-AKNP	BOAC Sutherland (later City of Cardiff)	To Trans-Oceanic Airways 4.51 as VH-TOB Star of Papua; to South Pacific Airlines 6.56 as N9946F Isle of Tahiti; to Howard Hughes .59; preserved as NJ203
NJ204	G-AKNR	BOAC Selkirk (later City of Belfast)	To TEAL .50 as ZK-AMQ Aparima. Scrapped .57 Auckland
NJ205	G-AKNS	BOAC Sheerness (later City of Liverpool)	Loaned to MAEE for overload rough weather trials as WM759. 51
NJ206	G-AKNT	Ministry of Transport and Civil Aviation Singapore	To South Pacific Airlines as N9947F 11.55. To Howard Hughes .59. Scrapped .74
NJ207	G-AKNU	Aquila Airways Sydney	To City of Sydney. To Aquila Airways 12.51, destroyed Shalcombe, Isle of Wight, 15.11.57
NJ201	G-ANAJ	Aquila Airways City of Funchal	Ex- G-AGWU. To Aquila 4.54, wrecked in gale Santa Margherita, Italy, 26.9.56
S.45 Solent 4			
c/n SH.1556	ZK-AML	TEAL Aotearoa II	To Aquila Airways 5.55 as G-AOBL. To Artop 10.58. scrapped .71
c/n SH.1557	ZK-AMM	TEAL Ararangi	Broken up Auckland following fire damage 28.5.54
c/n SH.1558	ZK-AMN	TEAL Awateri	To Aquila Airways 1.55 as G-ANYI. To Artop 10.58. scrapped .71
c/n SH.1559	ZK-AMO	TEAL Aranui	Wdn 14.9.60. To Museum of Transport and Technology, Auckland, for restoration

Note: * Aircraft belonging to the wartime BOAC fleet but which did not survive the war and therefore did not receive refurbishment to Hythe standard.

8. Saunders-Roe SR.45 Princess: Leading Technical Details

Powerplant
Ten Bristol Proteus 2 (later designated Proteus 600 for single units, and Proteus 610 for coupled units). Various power outputs have been quoted for these engines. The following data is taken from Saunders-Roe Report FT/15/0/24 Part 1 dated January 1955, covering trials of Princess G-ALUN at MAEE:
Nominal rating, sea level, static: Maximum 10,000crpm, 2,500shp and 820lb jet thrust, maximum continuous 9,500crpm, 2,050shp and 700lb jet thrust.

Dimensions
Span 209ft 6in floats down, 219ft 6in floats raised; dihedral 0 degrees; root chord 30ft; tip chord (at wing/float junction) 12ft 6in; gross wing area 5,019sq. ft; root thickness/chord ratio 18 per cent; tip (at wing/float junction) thickness/chord ratio 15 per cent; float track 199ft. Airscrew diameter 16ft 6in. Length 148ft; beam 16ft 7in; maximum hull depth 24ft 3in; draught 8ft; length to beam ratio 7.24. Tailplane span 77ft 2in; tailplane dihedral 12 degrees; height of fin 31ft 6in; overall height 55ft 9in. Pressure differential 8psi; maximum during trials 4.25psi.

Weights
Empty weight 190,000lb; normal maximum disposable load 137,000lb; normal maximum weight 330,000lb; design overload weight 345,000lb; normal wing loading 61.3lb/sq. ft.

Performance
Maximum cruising speed at 37,000ft: 380mph; maximum cruising speed at 32,500ft: 360mph; take-off run approximately 2,880ft; rate of climb at 184mph at sea level 1,900ft/min; stalling speed 127mph flaps up, 113mph flaps down; absolute ceiling 39,000ft; range with maximum payload 5,720 miles; maximum endurance 15 hours.

Limitations in force during testing of G-ALUN at MAEE Felixstowe
1 Weight range:
220,000lb–315,000lb; normal alighting weight 250,000lb; emergency alighting weight up to 315,000lb; handling, stability and control tests were usually undertaken within the range of 250,000lb–270,000lb.

2 Level flight and diving speed limitations:

Altitude	Level	Dive
0–10,000ft	301mph	335mph
15,000ft	289mph	not listed
20,000ft	279mph	309mph
25,000ft	262mph	not listed
30,000ft	247mph	274mph

Maximum speed undertaken with floats down 198mph. Maximum speed undertaken while operating floats 169mph. For tests, an astro-hatch was fitted in place of the dorsal escape hatch.

3 Engine operating limitations:

rpm	Compressor	Propeller-turbine	
		Single	Coupled
Maximum for take-off (5 minute limit)	10,000	10,300	10,700
Maximum continuous	9,500	9,250	9,650
Ground idling	3,000/3,250	–	–
Minimum approach idling	6,500	–	–
Maximum for reverse pitch (5 minute limit)	10,000	10,300	n/a
Maximum for reverse pitch (10 minute limit)	9,500	9,250	n/a

9. Air Board and RAF Specifications for Procurement of Flying-Boats, 1917–20

The Air Board was established in May 1916 to improve the procurement processes under which new aircraft were acquired for the Royal Naval Air Service and the Royal Flying Corps. In April 1917 the Air Board began to issue procurement specifications for new types defining the required technical and performance parameters. The specifications issued by the Air Board on behalf of the Admiralty in respect of flying-boats were as follows:

Specification	Date issued	Flying-boat types influenced by Requirements
N.1(b)	April 1917	Blackburn N.1B, Norman Thompson TNT, Supermarine N.1B, Wight Triplane, ?Wight Biplane
N.2(c)	April 1917	Norman Thompson N.2C
N.3(b)	April 1917	F.2A, F.2C, F.3, Fairey F.2A, Phoenix Cork, Short Cromarty
N.4	April 1917	Fairey Atalanta, Fairey Titania

Following the creation of the Royal Air Force in April 1918, the RNAS and RFC procurement specifications were amalgamated and reissued with a revised nomenclature employing Roman numerals. This system stayed in place until 1920. Those specifications reissued in respect of flying-boats were as follows:

RAF Specification	Former Specification	Flying-boat types influenced by Requirements
Type XXX	N3(b)	Short Cromarty, Vickers-Saunders Valentia
Type XXXIII	N.4	Fairey Atalanta, Fairey Titania

10. Air Ministry Specifications for Procurement of Flying-Boats, 1920–48

The Air Ministry nomenclature identifying its specifications inviting industry to tender for its requirements was straightforward, the first number indicating the number of the requirement itself and the number following the oblique indicating the year of issue. Specification 7/20, the first entry shown below, was the seventh specification issued to industry during the year 1920. The system embraced flying-boats and other types of aircraft; for example Specification 8/20 happened to be a requirement for a Fleet Landplane that gave rise to the Westland Walrus (just to add a tiny confusion) but those below are confined to the flying-boat breed.

Specification	Aircraft	Date	Serial(s), Remarks
7/20	Supermarine Seagull I	.20	N146
12/21	English Electric M.3 Ayr	.21	N148, N149 (N149 not built)
14/21	Supermarine Scylla	.21	N174
21/21	Supermarine Seagull II	.21	N9562–N9566
2/22	Vickers Viking V	.22	N156, N157
20/22	English Electric P.5 Cork	.22	Cancelled
21/22	Supermarine Swan	.22	N175
46/22	Vickers Viking VII – Vanellus	.22	N169
9/23	Blackburn RB.1 Iris I	.23	Superseded
13/23	Supermarine Seagull II	.23	N9603–N9607, N9642–N9654
23/23	English Electric P.5 Kingston I	.23	N168
13/24	Short S.5 Singapore I	.24	N179
14/24	Blackburn RB.1 Iris I and II	.24	N185
18/24	Supermarine Southampton I	.24	N9896–N9901, N218
20/24	Beardmore BeRo IV Inverness	.24	N183, N184
21/24	Parnall P.1 Prawn	.24	S1576
22/24	Saunders A.3 Valkyrie	.24	N186
29/24	Supermarine Seamew	.24	N212, N213
31/24	Saunders A.4 Medina	.24	G-EBMG/N214
11/25	Supermarine Southampton I	.25	S1036–S1045, S1058–S1059
14/26	Short S.8 Calcutta	.26	G-EBVG, G-EBVH
25/26	Supermarine Southampton II	.26	S1127, S1149–S1152

Specification	Aircraft	Date	Serial(s), Remarks
R.4/27	Saunders A.7 Severn Supermarine R.4/27 Air Yacht (probable)	.27	N240, N245 (latter not built) G-AASE
R.5/27	Blackburn RB.2 Sydney	.27	N241
R.6/27	Supermarine Southampton X	.27	N252
R.16/27	Supermarine Southampton II	.27	S1228–S1235, S1248–S1249
R.31/27	Blackburn RB.1B Iris III	.27	N238, S1263– S1264
R.32/27	Short S.12 Singapore II	.27	N246
R.6/28	Short S.14 Sarafand, Supermarine Type 179	.28	S1589 (Supermarine proposal declined)
10/28	Supermarine Southampton II	.28	S1298–S1302, S1419–S1423, S1464, S1643–S1647
20/28	Supermarine Type 179 Giant	.28	G-ABLE (not completed)
22/28	Fairey design for commercial amphibian		Contract not placed
R.18/29	Short S.8/8 Rangoon	.29	S1433, S1434–S1435
4/30	Saunders A.14	.30	N251
R.10/30E	Short S.14 Sarafand	.30	Contract not placed
14/31P	Supermarine Southampton II	.31	S1643–S1647
R.19/31D	Short S.8/8 Rangoon	.31	K2134, K2809
R.20/31D	Supermarine Southampton IV	.31	S1648 (renamed Scapa)
R.24/31	Saunders-Roe A.27 London Short S.18 Knuckleduster Supermarine Stranraer I	.31	K3560 K3574 K3973
7/32	Supermarine Southampton II	.32	K2889: magnesium/aluminium alloy hull and floats
15/32D	Saunders-Roe A.29 Cloud	.32	K2894–K2898, K3722–K3729
18/32	Saunders-Roe A.19 Cloud	.32	K2681 with monospar wing and sponsons
20/32	Blackburn RB.3A Perth	.32	K3580–K3582, K4011
R.1/33	Westland Pterodactyl VII	.33	Tail-less flying boat. Outline only
R.2/33	Saunders-Roe A.33 Short S.25 Sunderland	.33	K4773 K4774
3/33D	Short S.19 Singapore III	.33	K3592–K3595
13/33	Short S.20 and S.21	.33	G-ADHK and G-ADHJ (Mayo Composite)
19/33D	Supermarine Scapa	.33	S1648, K4191–K4202, K4565, K7304– K7305
R.28/33E	Supermarine Southampton IV with Jumo engines		Contract not placed
6/34D	Supermarine Seagull V	.34	A2-1–A2-24
14/34D	Short S.19 Singapore III	.34	K4577–K4585, K6907–K6922, K8565–K8568, K8856–K8859
25/34	Saunders-Roe A.29 Cloud	.34	K4300–K4302
33/34D	Blackburn RB.3A Perth	.34	Modification design work on tail
2/35D	Supermarine Walrus I	.35	K5772–K5783, K8338–K8345, K8537–K8564
3/35	Saunders-Roe A.27 London II	.35	K3560, K5908–K5913
R.12/35E	Supermarine 308, 310 Blackburn and Fairey designs		Not proceeded with
17/35D	Supermarine Stranraer I	.35	K7287–K7303
R.1/36	Blackburn B-20 Saunders-Roe S.36 Lerwick	.36	V8914 L7248–L7268
5/36	Supermarine Sea Otter I	.36	K8854, K8855
21/36P	Saunders-Roe A.33	.36	L2147–L2157: cancelled
22/36P	Short S.25 Sunderland I	.36	L2158–L2168
27/36	Saunders-Roe A.27 London II	.36	K3560, K6927–K6932, K9682–K9686, (poss) L7038–L7043
35/36	Short S.27 Civet	.36	Not built
37/36	Supermarine Walrus I	.36	L2169–L2336

Specification	Aircraft	Date	Serial(s), Remarks
4/37P	Saunders-Roe London II	.37	Poss L7038–L7043, or not proceeded with
35/37P	Conversion of London	.37	Conversion of Mk I aircraft to Mk II
R.3/38	Fairey project, Saunders-Roe A.38, Supermarine Type 328	.38	Not proceeded with. Replaced by R.5/39
S.7/38	Supermarine Sea Otter Supermarine Walrus	.38	Both designs rewritten
S.10/38	Fleet Air Arm amphibian	.38	Not proceeded with
B.11/38	Flying-Boat	.38	Not proceeded with
R.5/39	Saunders-Roe S.38 Blackburn B-32 and B-39 Fairey project	.39	Cancelled
S.14/39	Amphibian Reconnaissance aircraft	.39	Specification renumbered S.12/40
R.16/39	Large Flying-Boat	.39	Not proceeded with
S.24/39	Spotter Aircraft for Fleet Air Arm	.39	Not proceeded with
S.12/40	Supermarine Seagull ABR.1	.40	PA143, PA147, PA152; superseded
R.13/40	Blackburn B-40	.40	Cancelled
R.14/40	Saunders-Roe S.39, Short S.35 Shetland	.40	Cancelled
R.14/40/2	Short S.35 Shetland	.40	DX166, DX171
N.2/42	Blackburn B-44, Saunders-Roe project	.42	Not proceeded with
R.8/42	Short S.45 Seaford	.42	MZ269, MZ271, NJ200–NJ239 (initial allocation)
E.6/44	Saunders-Roe SR.A/1	.44	TG263, TG267, TG271
S.14/44	Air-Sea Rescue amphibian	.44	Developed from S.12/40; superseded
S.14/44/2	Supermarine Seagull ASR.1	.44	PA143, PA147, PA152
10/46	Saunders-Roe SR.45 Princess	.46	Superseded by Saro specification
R.36/46	Saunders-Roe P.162	.46	Cancelled
R.2/48	Blackburn B-78, Saunders-Roe P.162, Short PD.2, Supermarine 524	.48	Cancelled

11. Principal United Kingdom Stations Supporting Flying-Boat Operations: First World War

Name	Location	Dates Commissioned and Closed	Main Activities
Calshot	Solent, Hampshire	22.3.13. Continued post-war	Experimental programmes, trials; training; anti-submarine patrols. Became School of Naval Cooperation and Aerial Navigation 23.12.19
Catfirth	Shetland Islands	11.17–.19	Anti-submarine patrols
Cattewater	Plymouth, Devon	3.17–3.22	Anti-submarine patrols. Later, storage to 3.22. Placed on reserve until .25 when land purchased as permanent base.
Dundee/ Stannergate	Forfar	3.14–.19	Anti-submarine patrols
Eastchurch	Isle of Sheppey, Kent	11.11–.19	Naval Flying School, training, trials, test-flying by Shorts. To 204 TDS 1.4.18. Some use by flying-boats
Felixstowe	Suffolk	15.4.13. Continued post-war	Anti-submarine patrols, development of Felixstowe types, trials. To Marine Aircraft Experimental Establishment 1.4.24
Fort George	Inverness-shire	13–7.14	Seaplane and flying-boat sub-station prior to move to Dundee.
Grain (Port Victoria)	Kent	30.12.12 Continued post-war	Trials and experiments; repairs. To Marine Aircraft Experimental Depot 6.18. To Marine Aircraft Experimental Unit 3.20. MAEU to Marine Aircraft Experimental Establishment 1.4.24 and transferred to Felixstowe
Houton Bay	Orkney	7.17–.19	Anti-submarine patrols
Killingholme	Lincolnshire	7.14–.19	Flying-boat and seaplane base. Included Acceptance Park. Anti-submarine patrols. To US Naval Air Station 20.7.18
Lee-on-Solent	Hampshire	7.17–(C&M) 12.19	Training. To Naval Seaplane Training School 30.7.17. To 209 TDS 1.4.18. To RAF Seaplane School 7.19
Scapa Flow	Orkney	11.08.14–.19	To Fleet Aircraft Repair Base and Storage Depot
Stennes Loch	Orkney	05.18–.19	Anti-submarine patrols

Name	Location	Dates Commissioned and Closed	Main Activities
Tresco	Isles of Scilly	02.17–15.05.19	Anti-submarine patrols
Westgate/ St Mildred's Bay	Kent	6.14–.20	Anti-submarine patrols; training
Windermere	Bowness, Cumbria	*c.* 10.15–08.16	Training. Ex-Lakes Flying Co. and Northern Aircraft Co. site
Yarmouth (Great)	Norfolk	15.04.13–01.20	Anti-submarine patrols

The majority of the above stations hosted a mix of flying-boats and seaplanes over their lives. Westgate accommodated landplanes as well as marine aircraft.

12. Principal United Kingdom Stations Supporting Flying-Boat Operations: Second World War

Name	Location	Dates Commissioned and Closed	Summary of Activities
Bowmore	Loch Indaal, Islay, Strathclyde	9.40–7.45	Maritime patrol: 119 Sqn (S.23, S.26), 246 Sqn, 422 Sqn RCAF (Sunderland)
Calshot	Solent, Hampshire	RAF Stn 5.2.22–5.61	FBTS/4(C)OTU training; support (Marine Training School); ASR. 228 Sqn (Sunderland); 240 Sqn (Scapa, Singapore, Lerwick, London); 765 Sqn (incl Walrus) (Post-war, use by 201, 230 Sqns, 4(C)OTU/235 OTU (all Sunderland); to 238 MU)
Castle Archdale (renamed Lough Erne 18.02.41, reverted to Castle Archdale 1.43)	Co.Fermanagh	2.41–13.05.45	Maritime patrol: 209 Sqn (Lerwick), 201 Sqn, 202 Sqn, 228 Sqn, 422 Sqn RCAF, 423 Sqn RCAF (all Sunderland, 422 Lerwick also). (Post-war, use by 230 Sqn (Sunderland) 4–9.46)
Felixstowe	Suffolk	1.4.24 (MAEE)–21.6.62	Marine Aircraft Experimental Establishment from 1.4.24. Relocated to Helensburgh 9.39. Returned to Felixstowe 5.45. (Post-war: Marine Training School, Link Trainer Instrument Blind Flying School 7.45. To 26 Group 4.54. To 22 Group 6.58. MAEE disbanded 31.7.58)
Greenock	Clyde	10.10.40–(C&M) autumn .45	Maintenance, storage, conversion
Hamworthy	Poole, Dorset	Imperial Airways/BOAC use 9.39–31.3.48 RAF Hamworthy 1.8.42–1.5.44	National Air Communications flights by Imperial Airways and BOAC. Maritime patrol: 461 Sqn RAAF (Sunderland)
Helensburgh (Alt: Rhu)	Firth of Clyde	9.39–5.45	Relocated Marine Aircraft Experimental Establishment for duration of Second World War
Invergordon (To RAF Alness 10.2.43)	Ross and	10.38 (first recorded Squadron use) – 8.46 (then only occasional use)	Maritime patrol: 240 Sqn (London); 201 Sqn (London, later Sunderland), 210 Sqn det (Sunderland), 4(C)OTU (Singapore, Stranraer, Lerwick, Sunderland). To RAF Marine Branch, still ext 84, RAFMB disbanded 1.4.86

Name	Location	Dates Commissioned and Closed	Summary of Activities
Killadeas	Co.Fermanagh	RAF Stn 6.42–2.47	Training: 131 OTU (Sunderland), 12(O)FIS (Sunderland), 302 FTU. Storage: 57 MU. To 272 MU
Kirkcolm (to RAF Carsewell 5.42)	Wig Bay, Dumfries and Galloway	5.42 – .45	Instructional airframe Sunderlands used for practice towing, mooring and beaching
Lee-on-Solent	Gosport, Hampshire	Reopened 1.6.20. To HMS *Daedalus* 24.5.39; 17 Group; Closed 3.96	Training and communications. 710 Sqn, 764 Sqn (Walrus), 765 Sqn (incl. Walrus), 1700, 1701, 1702, 1703 Sqns (Sea Otter), 2 Observer School (incl. Walrus)
Mount Batten (ex Cattewater Renamed 1.10.29)	Plymouth, Devon	Returned to operational use 9.28. To C&M 5.11.45.	Maritime patrol: 204 Sqn (Sunderland), 10 Sqn RAAF (Sunderland, S.26), 210 Sqn (Sunderland), 461 Sqn RAAF (Sunderland), 238 MU, 84 MU. (Postwar, hosted occasional Sunderlands until .57. RAF Marine Branch disbanded 1.4.86, station closed .92)
Oban	Argyll, Oban Bay Strathclyde	9.39–(C&M) 28.4.45	Maritime patrol: 209 Sqn (Stranraer, later Lerwick), 210 Sqn, 228 Sqn, 330 Sqn, 422 Sqn RCAF, 423 Sqn RCAF 10 Sqn RAAF (all Sunderland). Training (302 and 308 FTU)
Pembroke Dock	Pembrokeshire	31.3.30–31.3.59	95 Sqn (Sunderland), 119 Sqn (S.23, S.26, Sunderland), 201 Sqn (Sunderland), 209 Sqn (Stranraer, Lerwick), 210 Sqn, 228 Sqn, 422 Sqn RCAF, 461 Sqn RAAF, 10 Sqn RAAF (all Sunderland). (Post-war: 201 Sqn, 230 Sqn, 4(C)OTU (Sunderland))
Stranraer (Wig Bay)	Wigtown, Dumfries and Galloway	7.40–11.09.57	Maritime patrol: 240 Sqn (Stranraer), 209 Sqn (Lerwick), 228 Sqn (Sunderland). Training: FBTS/4(C)OTU, 302 FTU. Maintenance and conversions: 1 FBSU, 11 FBSU, to 15 Group; 57 MU; all to 41 Group 1.2.44. (Post-war: 57 MU disbanded 10.51 and subsequent Sunderland maintenance at Wig Bay carried out by Shorts)

Name	Location	Dates Commissioned and Closed	Summary of Activities
Sullom Voe	Shetland	8.39–(C&M) .46	Maritime patrol: 201 Sqn (Sunderland), 240 Sqn (London), 210 Sqn det (Sunderland), 204 Sqn (Sunderland), 461 Sqn RAAF (Sunderland), 700 Sqn (Walrus), 330 Sqn (Sunderland)

Excluded are stations without any dedicated flying-boat connection but which happened to host amphibians from time to time. For example, 282 Squadron flew the Walrus on ASR duties from RAF Davidstowe Moor between February and September 1944, but at 970ft above sea level, Britain's highest operational wartime airfield was far removed from the water!

13. Warrior (Aero-Marine) Centaur

Warrior (Aero-Marine) Ltd based at Old Sarum near Salisbury is currently developing its Centaur amphibian for business, private utility and recreational use. To be powered by a single tractor engine in the class of the Lycoming IO-540 300BHP, the Warrior design features a high-wing 42ft 3in folding monoplane mounted on a small pylon, supporting the powerplant on a prominent projection. Stub-wings provide lateral stability on the water and act as utility platforms while loading. A single fin and rudder are combined with a mid-mounted tailplane.

The revolutionary low-drag hull features a fine bow with no step or fore-body chines but scalloped sides and is designed to accommodate six. The amphibian undercarriage retracts into the hull and sponsons while a pure flying-boat option is also planned, with an extra seat. Large loading doors are provided, together with generous cabin glazing. A water-rudder is fitted. Options include an 8hp water-jet for engine-out taxying and operation among waterside facilities. Extensive use is made of composites, with carbon and glass fibres, to minimise maintenance and allow a long structural life in salt water. Bow, sponson and tail extremities are detachable for field replacement. The company has concentrated on providing a high-load capacity and payload-range while also emphasising the flexibility of the Centaur in leisure and business use. Exceptional qualities are also anticipated in terms of wave handling capability and utility in accessing waterside facilities with wings folded. Funding for the first part of the Centaur Certification Programme including the construction and testing of the first prototype has recently been secured.

The graceful Warrior (Aeromarine) Centaur amphibian design features a revolutionary stepless hull while the tractor Lycoming powerplant affords a relatively low thrust line and allows a deeper after-body than a pusher configuration. The water rudder is integral with the bottom of the air rudder. *(Warrior (Aeromarine) Ltd)*

Provisional Specification
Engine option:
Lycoming IO-540 300BHP
Lycoming TIO-540 310BHP

Span:	44ft 10in
Overall length:	36ft 7in
Height on land:	12ft 5in
Width folded:	14ft 10in
Equipped weight:	2,426lb
Operating weight:	2,637lb
Payload (amphibian):	1,414lb
Payload (flying-boat):	1,583lb
Maximum take-off weight:	4,000lb
Rec cruise power SL, ISA	119 knots
Max cruise power, 5,000ft ISA	127 knots
Climb to 10,000ft, max cruise power, ISA	13.4 min
Max range ISA	*c.* 1,200 nm

INDEX

Note: bold page numbers indicate photographs.